Thunder and Lament

Thunder and Lament

Lucan on the Beginnings and Ends of Epic

TIMOTHY A. JOSEPH

OXFORD
UNIVERSITY PRESS

Oxford University Press is a department of the University of Oxford. It furthers
the University's objective of excellence in research, scholarship, and education
by publishing worldwide. Oxford is a registered trade mark of Oxford University
Press in the UK and certain other countries.

Published in the United States of America by Oxford University Press
198 Madison Avenue, New York, NY 10016, United States of America.

© Oxford University Press 2022

All rights reserved. No part of this publication may be reproduced, stored in
a retrieval system, or transmitted, in any form or by any means, without the
prior permission in writing of Oxford University Press, or as expressly permitted
by law, by license, or under terms agreed with the appropriate reproduction
rights organization. Inquiries concerning reproduction outside the scope of the
above should be sent to the Rights Department, Oxford University Press, at the
address above.

You must not circulate this work in any other form
and you must impose this same condition on any acquirer.

Library of Congress Cataloging-in-Publication Data
Names: Joseph, Timothy A., author.
Title: Thunder and lament : Lucan on the beginnings and ends of epic / Timothy A. Joseph.
Description: New York : Oxford University Press, 2022. |
Includes bibliographical references and index.
Identifiers: LCCN 2021038640 (print) | LCCN 2021038641 (ebook) |
ISBN 9780197582145 (hardcover) | ISBN 9780197582169 (epub)
Subjects: LCSH: Lucan, 39–65. Pharsalia. |
Rome—History—Civil War, 49–45 B.C.—Literature and the war.
Classification: LCC PA6480 .J67 2022 (print) | LCC PA6480 (ebook) |
DDC 873/.01—dc23
LC record available at https://lccn.loc.gov/2021038640
LC ebook record available at https://lccn.loc.gov/2021038641

DOI: 10.1093/oso/9780197582145.001.0001

1 3 5 7 9 8 6 4 2

Printed by Integrated Books International, United States of America

For my mother and father

Contents

Acknowledgments   ix
Editions and Abbreviations   xi

Introduction: "You Who Will Surpass the Poets of Old"   1

1. Lucan at and against Epic's Beginnings   22
2. Toppling *Topoi*: Epic's Violence Directed against Itself   54
3. The *Pharsalia* and the End of the Ennian Story   95
4. Lucan and the Closing of the Maritime Moment   143
5. The *Pharsalia* and the Loss of *Nostos*   185
6. Epic's Last Lament   224

Conclusion: Lucan and the Living Dead   262

Bibliography   273
Index of Passages Discussed   287
General Index   297

Acknowledgments

My work on the *Pharsalia* and early epic began several years ago (with thoughts of a brief scholarly note!), and over this time I have been fortunate to receive the help, support, and insight of many friends and colleagues. Mary Ebbott, Jackie Elliott, Casey Dué Hackney, Andrew Johnston, Dominic Machado, Aaron Seider, and Richard Thomas generously read and commented on various chapters at various stages. I am thankful to them for their time and thought. For suggestions on any number of matters, timely advice, and support in a variety of ways, I am grateful to Peter Barrios-Lech, Matthew Berry, Louise Chapman, Jeri DeBrohun, Janis DesMarais, Martin Dinter, Lee Fratantuono, Lauren Donovan Ginsberg, Karen Harney, Elizabeth Keitel, Isabel Köster, Justin Lake, John Marincola, Thomas Martin, Antoinette Methe, Andy Miller, Michael Putnam, John Schafer, Neel Smith, James Uden, Tom Van Vuren, Steve Vineberg, Lynne Weissberg, David Wright, Teresa Wu, and Stephanie Yuhl. I thank Massimo Cè, Virginia Closs, Jason Nethercut, and Anja Wolkenhauer for sharing forthcoming or newly published material. For healthy exchanges of ideas, I thank the students in my 2015 course on Lucan and Caesar at the College of the Holy Cross, as well as audiences at Florida State University, Harvard University, and the University of Massachusetts Amherst, and at meetings of the Celtic Conference in Classics, the Classical Association of the Middle West and South, the Classical Association of New England, and the New England Ancient Historians Colloquium. I am also grateful to the Provost's Office at Holy Cross for supporting this work with a 2017 Batchelor Ford summer fellowship and 2018 faculty research fellowship, and to Brown University's Department of Classics for sponsoring my research at Rockefeller Library.

I offer many thanks to Dorothy Bauhoff, Rachel Gilman, Ponneelan Moorthy, Ashita Shah, and Stefan Vranka at Oxford University Press for their careful assistance along the way and to the press's anonymous referees, whose numerous corrections and suggestions improved the book considerably. All errors, oversights, and flights of interpretive fancy are solely my own.

Members of my family have been most important. I am grateful to my brother Paul Joseph for his words of encouragement and to my uncle

Lawrence Joseph for his unfailing advice over these years. The patient and loving support of my wife Kelly Gillespie Joseph has been invaluable, the curiosity and creative thinking of our children Anna and Alex have been inspiring. My final thanks go to the dedicatees of this book, Sarah Granger Joseph and Robert Joseph, lovers of words and ideas, and the best of parents.

Timothy A. Joseph
Pawtucket, Rhode Island

Editions and Abbreviations

Unless otherwise noted, the text used for Lucan is Shackleton Bailey (1988), and standard editions of other ancient authors are cited per the abbreviations in S. Hornblower, A. Spawforth, and E. Eidinow, eds., *The Oxford Classical Dictionary*, 4th edition (Oxford, 2012). Other abbreviations used in the text and Bibliography are as follows.

AJP	*American Journal of Philology*
ANRW	*Aufstieg und Niedergang der römischen Welt*
BICS	*Bulletin of the Institute of Classical Studies*
CA	*Classical Antiquity*
CJ	*Classical Journal*
CP	*Classical Philology*
CQ	*Classical Quarterly*
CW	*Classical World*
HSCP	*Harvard Studies in Classical Philology*
ICS	*Illinois Classical Studies*
JRS	*Journal of Roman Studies*
LSJ	H. Liddell, R. Scott, and H. Jones, eds., *A Greek-English Lexicon*, 9th edition (Oxford, 1996)
MD	*Materiali e discussioni per l'analisi dei testi classici*
OLD	P. Glare, ed., *Oxford Latin Dictionary* (Oxford, 1982)
PCPS	*Proceedings of the Cambridge Philological Society*
TAPA	*Transaction of the American Philological Association*
ZPE	*Zeitschrift für Papyrologie und Epigraphik*

Calliope (second century CE; artist unknown)
from the Museo Pio-Clementino, Vatican Museums.

Introduction

"You Who Will Surpass the Poets of Old"

The occasion was Lucan's birthday, some twenty-five to thirty years after his death in the year 65 CE. His widow Polla called on Statius to write a poem in honor of her husband. The *genethliacon*, as Statius calls it in the prologue to his second book of *Silvae*, appears as the seventh and final poem of that book.[1] At its center (lines 36–106) is a striking conceit: the Muse of epic poetry, Calliope, turns away from lamenting her son Orpheus (39–40) to address the newborn Lucan, foretell his poetic achievements, and proleptically lament his untimely death. The poem and Calliope's speech in particular offer a powerful statement on Lucan's place in the Greek and Roman epic tradition.

The Muse begins her speech by addressing the newborn with the words *puer o dicate Musis | longaeuos cito transiture uates* (2.7.41–2: "Boy, dedicated to the Muses, you who will quickly surpass the poets of old"). Her claim is unambiguous: in just a short time (note *cito*), Lucan will excel all the poets who preceded him. Over the next forty or so lines, Calliope backs up this assertion, in a long expression of praise that includes a catalog of his works (54–74) and, later, a priamel of several of the Roman poets he will best:

> cedet Musa rudis ferocis Enni
> et docti furor arduus Lucreti,
> et qui per freta duxit Argonautas,
> et qui corpora prima transfigurat.
> quid? maius loquar: ipsa te Latinis
> Aeneis uenerabitur canentem.

> The rough Muse of fierce Ennius will give way, as well as the lofty madness of learned Lucretius, the one who led the Argonauts through the straits

---

[1] On *Silv.* 2.7, see Ahl (1976) 334–43; Quint (1993) 131–5; Malamud (1995); Newlands (2011a) and (2011b); and Hardie (2013a) 225–6.

[Varro Atacinus], and he who transforms bodies from their original shapes [Ovid]. What more? I shall make a greater claim: the *Aeneid* itself will venerate you as you sing to the people of Latium. (*Silv.* 2.7.75–80)

The priamel concludes with the image of Virgil's *Aeneid* itself venerating Lucan's poetic greatness. Calliope's climactic claim follows upon two polemical gestures toward Virgil earlier in the poem: an imagined contest between the poets' places of birth (35) and a reminder of how much Lucan accomplished before Virgil's career even began (73–4). The import of this "series of agonistic comparisons"[2] is clear: Lucan's poetic output was greater than Virgil's—and what is more, he completed all of it at a much younger age.

The positioning of Lucan as superior to Virgil is memorable, and readers have had much to say about the dynamic between the two poets that Statius creates in this poem. But Statius's assertions about Lucan's poetic primacy and place in the epic tradition are much stronger and more far-reaching. While the *Aeneid* stands meaningfully at the end of the Muse's list, how Calliope begins the litany of bested poets is also significant: with the very first hexametrical Latin poet, "fierce Ennius," whose "rough Muse will give way" (2.7.75: *cedet Musa rudis ferocis Enni*) to Lucan. In a speech about the precociousness but unmatched maturity of Lucan's corpus, it is fitting that Calliope includes reference to the "rough" or "raw" (*rudis*) poetry of Ennius at the beginning of the Latin epic tradition. If Statius is aiming to show that Lucan's oeuvre exhibits a startling completeness, then the inclusion of Ennius's *Musa rudis* makes for a fitting and indeed crucial foil. This is the only explicit reference to Ennius in *Silvae* 2.7, but references earlier in the poem to the sacredness of Lucan's poetry may work in conjunction with the statement in line 75. Statius's contemporary Quintilian wrote that "we must adore Ennius as we would sacred groves" (*sacros . . . lucos*, 10.1.88); and another, Silius Italicus, includes Ennius as a character in his *Punica*,[3] describing him as "sacred (*sacer*) and accompanied by the great care of the Aonian sisters, and a poet worthy of Apollo" (*Pun.* 12.408–9). When Statius extols Lucan as "the priest of the Roman chorus" (*Romani . . . chori sacerdos*) in line 23, he may well be snatching the mantle of the high priest of Roman epic away from the genre's holy and venerable old master and handing it to Lucan.

The poet's statement in line 23 about Lucan's priestly status is significant, but, again, it is his character Calliope who makes the boldest claims about

---

[2] Quint (1993) 131.
[3] See Casali (2006) on this passage.

Lucan's place in the epic tradition. The first thirteen lines of her speech merit consideration in full:

>   puer o dicate Musis,
> longaeuos cito transiture uates,
> non tu flumina nec greges ferarum
> nec plectro Geticas mouebis ornos,
> sed septem iuga Martiumque Thybrim   45
> et doctos equites et eloquente
> cantu purpureum trahes senatum.
> nocturnas alii Phrygum ruinas
> et tardi reduces uias Ulixis
> et puppem temerariam Mineruae   50
> trita uatibus orbita sequantur:
> tu carus Latio memorque gentis
> carmen fortior exseres togatum.

Boy, dedicated to the Muses, you who will quickly surpass the poets of old, you will not move rivers or flocks of beasts or Getic ash trees with your quill. But the seven hills and Mars's Tiber and the learned knights and the purple-clad senate you will draw out with your eloquent song. Let others take on the nighttime destruction of the Phrygians and the return paths of slow Ulysses and Minerva's brash ship, on a track that has been worn out by poets. You, dear to Latium and mindful of its race, you will be bolder as you put forth your togaed song. (*Silv.* 2.7.41–53)

After addressing Lucan as the one "who will quickly surpass the poets of old," Calliope elaborates on the point with a set of contrasts. Lucan will not charm nature in the ways that Orpheus did (43–4), but he will be the bard of Rome's landscape (45) and Rome's men (46–7). He will not follow a worn-out path (*trita . . . orbita*, 51) and relate Troy's fall, Ulysses's return, or the Argo's journey, but he will produce a "togaed song" (*carmen . . . togatum*, 53). And so Calliope distinguishes Lucan as a composer not of mythological epic, but of epic about Roman history.[4] Of course Rome's epic poets had commonly narrated Roman affairs, from Naevius's *Bellum Punicum* to Ennius's *Annales*, Hostius's *Bellum Histricum*, Cicero's numerous epics, and beyond. The critical

---

[4] A point emphasized by Newlands (2011a) 235–6. Hardie and Moore (2010b) 8 position Lucan's poetic career, with *Sil.* 2.7 as a guide, alongside the career arcs of other Latin poets.

point is that Lucan will do it with eloquence (*eloquente* | *cantu*, 46–7) and do it *better*, stronger, more boldly (*fortior*). Lucan will take the place of any earlier poet with claims to be the narrator of Roman history par excellence. Calliope's identification of Lucan as the definitive singer of a *carmen togatum* comes to bear on our reading of the litany of epic poets at 75–80, and in particular on the inclusion of Ennius in line 75. If Ennius was *fortis* (an epithet Horace uses of him at *Epist.* 2.1.50)[5] and fierce (*ferox*, *Silv.* 2.7.75), Calliope makes it clear that Lucan will outmuscle (*fortior*) and outmatch that poet of old, an image intensified by her description in line 53 of Lucan's poetic process with the forceful verb *exsero*, which is used of unsheathing swords.[6]

At the same time, the comparative *fortior* begins to position Lucan's oeuvre as superior to the entire Greek epic tradition, which Calliope evokes in her references to the tales of Troy, Ulysses, and the Argo. Though these topics were by this point well-worn in Greek and Latin verse,[7] they of course stand at the very beginning of Greco-Roman epic. Calliope's elevation of Lucan to a station above his Greek predecessors becomes more explicit in her catalog of his output, which begins with:

> ac primum teneris adhuc in annis
> ludes Hectora Thessalosque currus
> et supplex Priami potentis aurum,
> et sedes reserabis inferorum;
>
> And at first, when still in your tender years, you will play with Hector and the Thessalian chariot and the suppliant gold of powerful Priam, and you will unlock the dwellings of the dead. (*Silv.* 2.7.54–7)

These lines appear to describe the earliest poetry of Lucan the child prodigy, namely his *Iliacon* and *Catachthonion*, testaments to his great precocity.[8] But at the same time the verb *ludes*, following upon the evocative expression *teneris . . . in annis*, marks the content of that poetry as child's play, juvenile, trifling.[9] The assertion—that in his tender years Lucan was able to take on

---

[5] *Ep.* 2.1.50: *Ennius, et sapiens et fortis et alter Homerus*. Skutsch (1985) 17: "*ferocis* [at *Silv.* 2.7.75] . . . must be much the same as *fortis*, Hor. *ep.* 2.1.50."
[6] So Van Dam (1984) 477 and Newlands (2011a) 235–6. See too Biggs (2019) 978–80 and 988–9 on Statius's use of these terms.
[7] So Newlands (2011a) 235.
[8] Van Dam (1984) 478–9; Newlands (2011a) 236–7. See Fantham (2011) 8–11 on these poems.
[9] Van Dam (1984) 478.

Hector, Achilles's Thessalian chariot, and the supplication of Priam, and to unlock and so disclose the secrets of (*resero*, OLD 4b) the Underworld—is an extraordinary one, a direct provocation of Homer himself.

And all of this from no less than Calliope herself. A commentator on *Silvae* 2 has argued that Statius's "main reason for letting Calliope deliver a speech is compositional: he wants to break the monotony of a long poem by a speech as its longest and most important part."[10] It is true that Statius employs the device of a speech from a deity or mythical figure in several of the *Silvae*.[11] As in other poems, this speech lends variety to what is a fairly long birthday ode. But surely there is more to Statius's use of the Muse of epic poetry as the voice for his claims about Lucan's preeminence. Certainly his choice of Calliope, as opposed to the Parcae, the typical voices of prophecy in birthday poems,[12] underlines the poem's claim of Lucan's superior place in the epic tradition. If Statius wanted to convey that Lucan surpassed all the "poets of old"—not just Virgil, but Ennius and the entire Roman tradition, Homer and the entire Greek tradition—then there could be no more effective strategy than attributing that argument to the divine entity that empowers and animates the tradition, the Muse herself, the unmoved mover of *epos*.

The argument gains additional force when we observe that Statius presents Calliope's speech act as, fundamentally, a lament. At the outset of the speech, she is said to "put aside her lamentation" (39) for Orpheus and turn to address the newborn Lucan. But far from being a retreat from lamentation, the speech builds up to and closes with a lament for Lucan himself (89–104). Here again, Calliope places Lucan at the very apex of achievement ("Oh, long lives are never granted to those at the very top [*summis*]," 90), and again she contextualizes Lucan's life and death through reference to Greek models. When recalling the similarly youthful deaths of Achilles (96–7), and Orpheus (98–9), she once more evokes the very beginnings of epic, and of poetry more broadly, as essential for the appraisal of Lucan's legacy. The lament ends with reference to the suicide (101) that silenced the poet (104). The very last word from Calliope, who wipes away tears as she concludes (105–6), is *tacebis* ("you will go silent"): as Lucan goes silent, so too does the Muse.

Calliope's speech, we see, reveals itself as a powerful expression of lament. And if, as she maintains, Lucan's poetry stood as the apogee of the epic

---

[10] Van Dam (1984) 472.
[11] See *Silv.* 1.1.74–83 (Marcus Curtius); 1.2.162–93 (Venus); 1.4.61–105 (Apollo?); 3.1.91–116 (Hercules); 4.1.17–43 (Janus); 4.3.72–94 (the river Vulturnus); and 4.3.124–61 (the Cumaean Sybil).
[12] Van Dam (1984) 472.

tradition, then it appears she is lamenting more than just this poet's death. If her own silence comes at the same time as Lucan's, is her speech a lament not just for Lucan but for epic as a whole? When Calliope—the genre's aboriginal voice, its *source*—weeps and then abruptly goes silent, is she marking Lucan's output and death as a greater end, an end of epic itself?

* * *

I have begun this study of the *Pharsalia* with a reading of *Silvae* 2.7 because Statius's poem points us to an important way of reading Lucan's epic. Readers of *Silvae* 2.7 have noted how it operates as a work of self-fashioning, how here Statius positions his own epic efforts alongside Lucan's and the poetic tradition as a whole.[13] Whether Statius actually thought that Lucan was unsurpassable, that the genre had reached its apex and end, and that his *Thebaid* and *Achilleid* could only be afterthoughts is less important for my purposes than what *Silvae* 2.7 offers as a reading of Lucan, as an act of reception of the *Pharsalia*. While he certainly had poetic ambitions of his own, from this poem it is clear that Statius *got* it; he got what Lucan was trying to claim with his epic. Statius understood that Lucan was presenting his work as "surpassing the poets of old," as eclipsing the epic genre, as putting an end to it, as—in Statius's conceit—compelling Calliope herself to lament and then fall silent. The fashioning of this reading of the *Pharsalia* is especially valuable and worthy of our attention given Statius's proximity in time to Lucan and his status as an extraordinarily astute and sensitive reader of Lucan's poetry.[14]

In the last fifty years, there has been a burst of scholarship on Lucan. We might say that, after a few centuries of devaluation of the poet, we have entered a new *aetas lucanea*.[15] Readers of the poem have again come to understand the *Pharsalia* for the original, dynamic, terrifying epic masterpiece that it is. The preponderance of recent scholarship on Lucan's engagement with prior epic has focused on the *Pharsalia*'s relationship with the *Aeneid*, which by Lucan's time had established itself as Rome's national epic. Lucan's adaptations of Virgilian language and themes are numerous, indeed pervasive; and scholars have explored at length how he positions his story of

---

[13] Malamud (1995) and Newlands (2011b).
[14] See Keith (2000) 4 on how *Silv.* 2.7 "probably reflects the reading practices current in Flavian Rome more accurately than Quintilian's ideal reading list."
[15] See Maes (2013), Paleit (2013), and Goldschmidt (2019) 85–129 on the *aetas lucanea* of the late sixteenth to early eighteenth centuries.

Roman self-destruction as a reversal or implosion of Virgil's poem of Roman foundation, as well as the ways he builds on tensions and darker strains that are already visible in the *Aeneid*.[16] Many others have drawn special attention to Lucan's involvement of language and imagery from Ovid's *Metamorphoses*, with emphasis on, for example, how Lucan redirects Ovid's language of metamorphosis toward the transformation of Rome and how he integrates references to the frequently violent myths that populate the *Metamorphoses* into his epic of self-destruction.[17] These two epic predecessors were of great importance to Lucan, and any literary study of the *Pharsalia* must take account of their influence. But if Lucan was aiming, as Statius's Calliope puts it, to "surpass the poets of old," then his ambition surely encompassed more than polemics with Virgil and Ovid.[18] If his project was intended to recast and eclipse the genre, then certainly close interaction with epic's beginnings was part of his plan. Put another way, a fuller appreciation of Lucan's poetic accomplishment requires us to follow Calliope's lead in *Silvae* 2.7 and examine Lucan's *aemulatio* with not only more recent epic models such as the *Aeneid* and the *Metamorphoses*, but also the earliest works in the epic tradition: the *Iliad* and *Odyssey*, together with the foundational Latin epics by Livius Andronicus, Naevius, and Ennius. This is the task I will undertake in this book.[19]

To read Lucan's epic with this focus also follows naturally from the poem's contents. There existed an "intimate connection between epic subject matter and epic poetics,"[20] and Lucan's poetics of undoing and closing the epic

---

[16] The scholarship on the *Ph.* and the *Aen.* is vast. On Lucan's poem as an "anti-*Aeneid*" see, e.g., Von Albrecht (1970) 281–92; Ahl (1976) *passim*; Narducci (1979) and (2002) 75–85; Martindale (1993) 48–53; Quint (1993) 131–57; Hardie (1986) 381 and (1993) *passim*; Rossi (2000); Roche (2009) 20–4 and *passim*; Casali (2011); Fratantuono (2012) *passim*; and Roche (2019) 12–15. See Thomas (2001) 83–92 on Lucan as a reader of tensions in the *Aen.*, as well as Leigh (1997) *passim* and Tesoriero (2005) 203 on his capacity to draw upon and oppose Virgil.

[17] See Bruère (1951b); Phillips (1968); Wheeler (2002) (with extensive bibliography at 366–7, n. 16); Tarrant (2002) 356–60; Keith (2011); and Fratantuono (2012) *passim*, esp. 27–8, 120–22, and 386–8.

[18] See Hutchinson (2013) 329 for the assessment that scholarship on Lucan has been slow to look for models beyond Virgil. The study by Boyd (2017) of Ovid's "Homeric inheritance" (7) makes a similar assessment of the "large Virgilian shadow that for so long shaded our reading of Ovid" (4). See Ambühl (2016) and Biggs (2019) on Lucan's engagement with Cat. 64 and Varro Atacinus, respectively.

[19] Scholarship on parallels between Lucan and early Latin epic has been limited to brief discussions of Ennian parallels. See Heitland (1887) cxxviii–cxxix; Conte (1970) (= [1988] 25–32); Von Albrecht (1970) 277–80; Prinzen (1998) 333–6; Asso (2010) 287–8; and Day (2013) 79–82; as well as the cautious remarks of Skutsch (1985) 16–17. The somewhat more substantial work on Lucan and Homer includes Conte (1966) (= [1988] 11–23); Von Albrecht (1970) 272–7; Lausberg (1985); Green (1991); Sklenář (2003) 45–58; and Christophorou (2010) and (2017).

[20] Hardie (1993) 99.

genre, I will argue, stands side by side with the content of the *Pharsalia*.[21] "Here Rome dies" (*hic Roma perit*, 7.634), declares the narrator amid the vast slaughter at the Battle of Pharsalia,[22] and he narrates the death of old Rome / "what Rome was" (7.132) across the poem. The graphic images of self-slaughter in the proem (1.1–7) and, soon after, of the lifeless Italian wasteland resulting from that self-slaughter (1.24–32) make clear from the outset that this is a poem about Rome's death. Lucan will go on to narrate the death of the entities that defined Rome, such as the consulship, the electoral process, and the practice of augury (5.381–402); the passing of the old families who once maintained these institutions (7.356–60; cf. 6.784–90); the collapse of Rome's once ever-widening sway (7.419–36; cf. 1.9–23); and the stunning absence, if not the death, of the gods who had long bolstered Roman success (7.445–59; cf. 2.1–15 and 4.807–9). In short, the poem tells the story of the bloodbath of Rome and of all that had bolstered Rome and kept her going from the beginning.[23] While influential readers of the epic have argued for its "endlessness" and lack of teleology,[24] I shall argue that the poem achieves closure for both its content (the story of Rome) and the literary vehicle for that content (the epic genre).

Moreover, Lucan's impulse toward finality in the *Pharsalia* may be reflective of the thinking about "end times" that seems to have surfaced under the increasingly destructive and chaotic reign of Nero. Rome was witnessing rapid change, and finding the right words to describe the seismic changes was a struggle for Neronian authors.[25] What words and what forms could accurately capture this? The apocalyptic images from Stoic cosmology of a final conflagration (1.72–80) and a sweeping flood (4.48–120) that Lucan includes[26] are explored at length in the writings of his uncle Seneca, and recent scholarship has interpreted the latter's frequent considerations of the end of the world as veiled commentary on Nero's destructiveness.[27]

---

[21] Malamud (1995) 19: "Lucan's poetic accomplishment is a text in stasis representing a world in crisis." See also the suggestions to this effect by Masters (1992) 137–8 and 158.

[22] Latin authors, including Lucan, most often refer to the battle as Pharsalia (not Pharsalus), a practice I follow. See Bruère (1951a) and Heslin (1997).

[23] See Thorne (2011), Dinter (2012), and McClellan (2019) 115–69 on the pervasive images of death in the poem.

[24] See Masters (1992) 258–9 and Quint (1993) 133–5.

[25] Freudenberg (2018) relates the difficulty of articulating the horrors of Nero's time to the difficulty of capturing in words the events of the Trump era in the United States.

[26] See Lapidge (1979) and Masters (1992) 58–65 on Lucan's incorporation of this imagery.

[27] On Seneca's preoccupation with end times and the Neronian context, see Berno (2019) and Closs (2020) 131–8 (amid her broader treatment of apocalyptic thinking under the empire). See Ker (2009) on Seneca's preoccupation with death more generally. On the identification of Nero with an apocalyptic demon or Antichrist in early Christian literature, see Maier (2013) 388–90 and Malik

Suetonius would later cast the *orbis terrarum* as engaged in a fourteen-year conflict with Nero (*Nero* 40.1). And while the world would ultimately, as Suetonius puts it, "shake off" Nero, the damage he did to "old Rome" would be profound. Beyond the escalated humiliation of the Senate and the denigration of old Republican families, there was the Great Fire of 64 CE and the subsequent erection of Nero's Golden House, erasing huge stretches of the old city and indeed "anything worth seeing or memorable that had survived from antiquity" (Suet., *Nero* 38.2).[28] Lucan would be moved enough to narrate the infamous event—and seemingly indict Nero for the crime[29]—in his *De Incendio Urbis*. It seems fair to conclude that thoughts of ends—to the physical appearance and the very idea of Rome, to the greater *orbis terrarum*, and in turn to the means by which humans thought and wrote about these things—were swirling around him as he sat down to pen the *Pharsalia*. With Rome herself and the world itself seemingly in collapse, was it not the case that the genre that took on these most grandiose of topics was due to end too? Did the traditional form of the epic genre no longer fit the material of post-Pharsalian and now Neronian Rome?

It is important to emphasize that for Lucan to sing a "Roman song" (*Romana . . . carmina*, 1.66) was conventional. Epic had long been the textual messenger of the Roman story. Beginning with Naevius's *Bellum Punicum* and then Ennius's *Annales*, the genre had accompanied Roman success and had preserved it in textual form.[30] But as the subject matter—Roman success / *Rome*—perishes, so too must the textual vehicle of that subject matter. Naevius's and especially Ennius's stories of Roman advance, I will argue in this book, are overturned and undone by the *Pharsalia*. At the same time, just as the Roman story had become global—the *urbs* coterminous with the *orbis*—Roman epic had become coterminous with the genre as a whole. And Lucan, I will maintain, sought to close off not just the beginnings of epic at Rome but also the genre's first, foundational stories, the *Odyssey* and the *Iliad*.

(2020). Kimmerle (2015), especially 268–302, considers the limitations of our knowledge of the political conditions under which Lucan wrote.

[28] Gowing (2005) 96–101 discusses Nero's literal and symbolic desecration of the Republican past.

[29] See Ahl (1971) and Closs (2020) 143–4.

[30] See Goldberg (1995); Leigh (2010); Walde (2011) 289; Elliott (2013) 233–94 and (2014); Feeney (2016); and Biggs (2017). Narducci (2002) 27 aligns Lucan's choice of material specifically with the tradition of Naevius and Ennius. Given the problems in any strict division between historical and mythological epic (see Nethercut [2019]), I eschew the term "historical epic." Häußler (1976–78) is an extensive treatment of historical themes in Greek and Roman epic.

I.1. "You will thunder ... and you will lament": Lucan's modes of intertextual closure

How does he do this? Lucan's manner of closing epic is characterized by gestures of violence and destruction and simultaneously by expressions of lament. To these two modes and their correspondence I will turn shortly, but prior to doing so it is necessary to address the types of intertextuality I will consider in this study. I will analyze Lucan's engagement with particular passages and phrases in early epic texts, especially Ennius's *Annales* and the Homeric poems, but more often I will foreground the *Pharsalia*'s involvement of broader constitutive motifs in those texts. In Gian Biagio Conte's formulation, these early texts provide for Lucan instances of "source models" ("modelli-esemplari") along with wide-ranging "code models" ("modelli-codice").[31] Adaptations of specific *loci* and of these predecessors' language and phraseology exist alongside co-options and reversals of major elements or "master tropes" in those texts.[32]

The adaptation of particular Homeric and Ennian phrases is not pervasive in the *Pharsalia* in the way that, for example, Virgilian and Senecan language is frequently reworked in the poem.[33] But there are a number of allusions that operate, to use Joseph Farrell's term, as "anchors."[34] These are conspicuous allusions that seem to anchor the relationship between one text and another, to "ground allusion in the text and in the mind of an intending author."[35] We will observe intertextual anchors of this sort at several points, notably in programmatic passages such as the *Pharsalia*'s proem and the author's statement about poetic fame at the site of Troy in Book 9; and in Lucan's uses of epic *topoi*, where he engages with the epic tradition and its codes in a general

---

[31] Conte (1986 [1974]) 31. Hinds (1998) 41 helpfully translates Conte's "esemplare" as "source" with the gloss "modelling by particular source-passage" (42 n. 46), as opposed to "exemplary," which Segal uses in his translation of Conte. See Conte's further discussion of the terms "code" and "norm" at 141–54, writing that "[s]uch a code is a source or warehouse of interconnected values, vividly displayed in the actions of heroes, on which the community can draw as an organic arrangement of its own cultural foundations" (142). See too Barchiesi (2015 [1984]) 69–93 on the concepts of genre model and exemplary model, as seen in Virgil's engagement with Homer.

[32] "Master trope" is the helpful translation of Conte's "modello-codice" by Seo (2011) 212.

[33] On Lucan's use of Senecan language, see Diels (1886); Narducci (2002), esp. 52–70; Roche (2019) 15–16 and (2020); and D'Alessandro Behr (2020).

[34] See Farrell (2005), with discussion at 104–5 of anchoring allusions as making it "possible to begin discovering the network of intertextuality that does correspond with sufficient accuracy to the author's intentions." For overviews of the study of intertextuality in Latin literature, see Coffee et al. (2012); Baraz and Van den Berg (2013); and Coffee (2018) on the digital tools available to scholars of intertextuality.

[35] Farrell (2005) 108.

way, but at the same time with particular model texts as source models. This means that in many of the book's readings I will consider Lucan's involvement of numerous model texts together, taking what Farrell has called a "synoptic view" of allusion.[36] So, in arguing that Lucan aims to close the entire epic tradition, my focus will fall on his engagement with the genre's earliest model texts, but I will not lose sight of his simultaneous and often complementary interaction with other predecessors.

When proposing his rubric of a "double vision of a literary model," Conte uses the example of Virgil's relationship with Homer, who stands as "the representative of the epic institution that guarantees the ideological and literary functions of poetry itself" and whose "rules and codifications" Virgil "assimilates."[37] But as Conte well understood from his own work on the *Pharsalia*, a modification of that rubric is required for our reading of Lucan's engagement with the epic tradition. Lucan directly takes on the rules, codifications, and master tropes established and developed in the earliest epic poems, but his process is not one of assimilation or even remodeling. The *Pharsalia* asserts radical difference and departure, indeed the ending of the tradition. Readers of the *Pharsalia* have articulated well the poetic mien of Lucan the violent disrupter, assailant, and uprooter of convention. John Henderson captures this aspect of Lucan's poetics:

> His epic defaces his city's walls, unmakes its foundation and its history, implodes its traditions and ideologies along with the documents which bear them; it stains the language of public propriety, twists Latin into self-revulsion, writes the continuing aetiology of its own accursed Fall.[38]

As I noted earlier, scholarship has concentrated on one particular text as an anti-model. "Lucan's negative rewriting of the *Aeneid*," his "violent displacement of the father, who is indispensable and yet hated," has received much valuable treatment,[39] as has his co-option of Ovidian imagery to underscore that poetic disruption. Scholars have also turned profitably to his response to Caesar's *De Bello Civili*, a work that he systematically "deforms" while also embracing the revolutionary and destructive spirit of its

---

[36] Farrell (1991) 24. The discussion by Thomas (1986) 197–8 of "multiple reference" is also informative.
[37] Conte (1986 [1974]) 31.
[38] Henderson (1987) 143.
[39] See n. 16 in this Introduction. The quotations are from Hardie (1993) 118 and Martindale (1993) 48.

author.[40] I will argue that these violent, closural poetics extend just as forcefully and just as importantly toward epic's beginning texts. Lucan's poetic aims are grander: the polemical reach of his pen stretches all the way back to Ennius, Naevius, Livius, and Homer.

Alongside this violent poetics of ending lies a complementary poetics of lament, as Lucan the toppler of the epic tradition at the same time laments the tradition's passing. Here too there is a close correspondence between content and poetics, an overarching metapoetics: this poem that, as we shall see, is full of expressions of lament for the dead, itself laments the genre it aims to end.

That Lucan would foreground lament in the *Pharsalia* should not be surprising. For one, Roman authors had long understood lamentation as a fitting response to the civil wars of the first century BCE: Asinius Pollio writes to Cicero that he "often lamented (*defleui*) the outbreak of civil war" (Cic. *Fam.* 10.31[368].2); Velleius Paterculus concludes that "no one has been able to lament (*deflere*) the fortune of that whole period [of the late Republic] in a sufficiently worthy manner" (2.67.1); and the younger Seneca writes of the historian Cremutius Cordus's "genius with which he lamented (*defleuit*) the civil wars" (*Dial.* 6.26.1 = *FRHist* 71 T 3).[41] For Lucan to lament the cataclysm of the civil wars would be entirely in keeping with the responses advocated by these Roman predecessors. Second, the coexistence of violence and lament is generically conventional, lying at the heart of epic poetry. Their complementarity is a fundamental component of the genre's code as established in Homer's poems, where death in war results inexorably in lament by the dead's kin and companions, which in turn is a principal medium for the *kleos* of the dead warriors.[42] Recent scholarship has highlighted the foundational place of lament in the Homeric poems, with Christos Tsagalis writing that "the theme and diction of lament appear to have shaped the *Iliad*," and Gregory Nagy concluding that the traditions of lament are present in the "nature of Homeric poetry."[43] In a similar and even more expansive way, Casey Dué identifies lament

---

[40] See, e.g., Rambaud (1960); Lounsbury (1975); Masters (1992); Zissos (2013); Joseph (2017a) 130–7; and Roche (2019) 11; *pace* Radicke (2004), esp. 9–43, arguing for Livy as Lucan's sole source. See too Seidman's (2017) argument for a poetic rivalry within the text between Lucan and the character Caesar.

[41] I thank John Marincola for these references.

[42] Murnaghan (1999) 217: "a hero's achievement is measured in the suffering that it causes, in the grief that it inspires." See too Bowra (1952) 10 (on lament communicating both grief and praise); Nagy (1979) 111–13 and (2013) 295; and the book-length study of *gooi* by Tsagalis (2004), building on the seminal work by Alexiou (1974).

[43] Tsagalis (2004) 22 and Nagy (2013) 295. See too Nagy (1979) 94–117 and Flatt (2017) 389–90.

as the mode "around which epic poetry is built and with which epic poetry is infused at every point," while other scholars have understood lament as the *telos* of Homeric epic, the end to which its narrative heads.[44]

Like the *Iliad*, the *Pharsalia* is unmistakably a work of *Todesdichtung*.[45] And just as in Homer's epic, expressions of lament accompany and come to define the violent endings and ends of life in the poem. The traditional vehicle for lament in Homeric and subsequent epic is the *goos*, the mourner's speech over the body of the deceased. These speeches have a number of recurring thematic and stylistic features,[46] which frequently reflect the tensions that come with the process of lament. For one, *gooi* typically offer praise for the deceased, conveyed through features such as laudatory addresses at the beginning and end and the use of superlatives. But they also commonly express reproach for the dead, in, for example, plaintive rhetorical questions and harsh words of critique. Another tension lies in the focus on contrasts (between present and past; place of death and the deceased's homeland; conditions of the mourner and the deceased) as well as commonalities (such as the common fate of the mourner and deceased). The interplay of contrast and commonality is brought out by the juxtaposition of first- and second-person verbs and deictics. *Gooi* in Homeric poetry are also antiphonal: multiple commiserating voices frequently complement and build upon one another. As in other poems that follow in the Homeric tradition, the expressions of lament in the *Pharsalia* commonly employ these hallmarks of the *goos*; and across this study, culminating in my detailed treatment of expressions of lament in Chapter 6, I will trace Lucan's use and transformation of these conventional features into a radically expansive and conclusive statement of lament.

In discussing the place of lament in Homeric epic, Sheila Murnaghan underscores how voices of lament complement but at the same time compete for space with the prevailing voices that celebrate heroic achievements. In Homeric poetry, she writes, lament is "originary yet marginal, indispensable yet subversive."[47] I will argue that a fundamental way in which Lucan rivals

---

[44] Dué (2002) 89. On lament as *telos*, see Greene (1999) 192 ("tears can properly be said to constitute the authentic narrative telos" of Homeric epic) and Flatt (2017).

[45] So Reinhardt (1960) 13; Griffin (1980) 142; and Tsagalis (2004) 1–2 on the *Il*. See Thorne (2011) on the *Ph*. as a monument to the death of Rome; Connolly (2016) on the *Ph*. as a "death work" (291); and McClellan (2020) on the poem's "necropolitics" (229), building on Mbembe (2003).

[46] See Alexiou (1974); Dué (2002); Tsagalis (2004); and Perkell (2008); with my further discussion of these features in Chapter 6.

[47] Murnaghan (1999) 204.

Homer and in a sense completes the epic tradition's long "song of sorrow" is by bringing lamenting voices right to the center of his text—involving a range of characters as well as the narrator and even, in a gesture that both builds upon and convulses his Homeric model, stretching beyond the text to the poem's post-Pharsalian readers. In this light it is important to bear in mind the gendered quality of lament, given that *gooi* in the *Iliad* and later epic are most commonly delivered by female characters, and that "laments incorporated into the larger structures of epic may bear traces of authentic women's voices and offer women's perspectives on actions that are carried out primarily by men and primarily to promote male interests."[48] Lucan in a sense transcends this conventional distinction not only by putting the characteristically female practice of lament on equal footing with the characteristically male practice of violent combat, but also by extending the practice of lament to an infinitely wide range of voices. This act of centering and expanding the expression of lament is crucial to the *Pharsalia*'s assertion of the completion of the Homeric tradition and so to its claims of poetic finality.

In this way, the lamenting voices in the *Pharsalia*, like the language of violence that scholars have read so profitably as reflective of Lucan's poetic aims, offer commentary on his poetic project. And just as the poem's content of violent destruction and the accompanying lamentation have a fundamental synergy, these metapoetic modes do too: if Lucan's poem is to declare an end to epic, then taking on and closing off *both* of these complementary modes introduced in epic's first poems is required. This duality in Lucan's poetic voice was understood well by that most revealing of his early readers, Statius's Calliope. Let us recall that the epic Muse's entire speech in *Silvae* 2.7 is an act of preemptive lament for Lucan, and so points to something fundamental about her poetic medium. In her catalog of the poet's works, Calliope says to the infant Lucan, "You will thunder out (*detonabis*) Philippi, white with Italian bones, and the Pharsalian wars" (2.7.66); and, soon afterward, "You will dutifully lament (*deflebis*) the crime of Palusian Canopus and give Pompey a tomb higher than bloody Pharos" (2.7.70–2). Lucan thunders and he laments.[49] His poetic voice is explosive, violent, and (self-)destructive, wreaking havoc much like his character Caesar, who is compared in the

---

[48] Murnaghan (1999) 204. See too Holst-Warhaft (1992), esp. 1–6 and 108–14, and Perkell (2008) on the place of women's laments in Homer; as well as Nugent (1992), Fantham (1999), Keith (2008), and Westerhold (2011) on women's laments in Latin epic (with my further discussion in Chapter 6).

[49] Malamud (1995) 7–8 notes that this pair of verbs "mirrors with precise economy the conflicting impulses within Lucan's poem of civil war." See too Newlands (2011b) 442.

programmatic simile at 1.151–7 to a roaring thunderbolt that lays waste far and wide—and even, like Caesar at 1.195–6, daring to rival the terrifying boom of Jupiter Tonans.[50] At the same time, that voice is mournful and, as I shall address in Chapter 6, celebratory of the people and the city that it mourns. With these complementary registers of ending—of destruction and grief, of the destroyer and the lamenter, each expanded to a scale surpassing the poets of old—Lucan hails the end of the epic song.[51]

I.2. The place of Homer and "the second Homer"

I turn now to consider in brief the poets who had come to stand as representatives of the beginning of epic, the anti-models on whom this study will focus.

Homer's standing as the progenitor of the genre, and of Greek and Roman culture generally, was axiomatic in the ancient world. The ancient references are countless. I note here that, in the early empire, Velleius Paterculus regarded him as having both begun and perfected the epic genre (1.5.1–2). Lucan's contemporary the elder Pliny goes further in describing him as the "first father (*primus parens*) of learning and of the things of old" (*NH* 25.5.11), and Quintilian considers Homer to have "provided the model and the origin for all areas of eloquence" (10.1.46; see too 10.1.88).[52] These statements are not mere commonplaces: it appears that educated Romans of the imperial period knew their Homer well. Lucan's uncle Seneca remarks that the names of Ulixes, Achilles, and Priam were as well known to Romans as the names of their teachers (*Ep.* 27.5). The poetic output of Lucan's direct contemporaries may provide the best testament, as "the Neronian poets were addicted to Trojan themes."[53] In that period, Attius Labeo translated both the *Iliad* and the *Odyssey* into Latin, Baebius Italicus wrote a short hexametrical *Ilias Latina*, and Homeric references and themes run throughout Petronius's *Satyrica*.[54] Moreover, the emperor himself penned a *Troica*, and the youthful

---

[50] See Nix (2008) on the rivalry between Caesar and Jupiter in the poem.

[51] In this way my argument shares with the influential studies by Masters (1992), Bartsch (1997), and Leigh (1997) sustained attention to a fundamental duality in the poem, but from a critical perspective that foregrounds the constitutive elements of the epic genre.

[52] On Homer's authoritative standing among Latin authors, see Tolkiehn (1991 [1900]); Farrell (2006); Hutchinson (2013) 27; and Boyd (2017) 11–23. On the reception of Homer in antiquity, see the essays in Lamberton and Keaney (1992); Hall (2008) on the *Od.* in particular; Hunter (2018); and Johnston (2019).

[53] Mayer (1981) 3. See too Ambühl (2010) 20–1.

[54] See Cé (2021) on the *Ilias Latina* and Murgatroyd (2013) 244–8 on Homeric themes in the *Satyr.*

Lucan wrote both an *Iliacon* about Trojan themes and a *Catachthonion* about a visit to the Underworld (as Statius commemorates at *Silv.* 2.7.54–7; see earlier discussion). While long established as the *primus parens*, Homer was—perhaps for this very reason—as alive and seemingly well read as ever in Lucan's time.

The matter of the first epic poet in Rome is more complicated. Livius Andronicus's translation of Homer's *Odyssey*, the *Odusia*, is the first known epic in Latin. His act of bringing Homer's poetry into Latin marks the arrival of the genre in Roman culture.[55] Naevius's *Bellum Punicum* is the first known epic on a Roman topic. Only scant fragments of these two works survive, but these and the testimonia provide a solid sense of their themes and scope; and Lucan engages closely with fundamental themes of these poems, as I will explore especially in Chapters 4 and 5. Though written several years after the *Odusia* and the *Bellum Punicum*, Ennius's *Annales* came to stake a strong claim on epic primacy in Rome.[56] It is Rome's first hexametrical epic; and its sheer scale and scope—narrating Rome's expansion across space and time from the fall of Troy to the author's own day—established it as the authoritative telling of the Roman story. Later authors give the *Annales* pride of place in the Roman epic tradition, with several writers holding Ennius up as the Roman equivalent of Homer.[57] Along with Statius's inclusion of Ennius as the first in his list of forerunners to the *Pharsalia* (2.7.75), Lucretius, for example, celebrates Ennius as *primus* at *DRN* 1.116–18, and Ovid lists him first in his recounting of Roman poets at *Amores* 1.15.19–30. The fourth-century grammarian Diomedes describes Ennius as the first to write Latin epic of any worthiness (*epos Latinum primus digne scripsit*).[58] One of our earliest

---

[55] See Mariotti (1952); Goldberg (1995) 46–57 and 64–73; McElduff (2013) 43–55; and Feeney (2016) 53–6 and 62–4; and the linguistic commentary by Livingston (2004).

[56] On this contest for epic primacy among Livius, Naevius, and Ennius, see Elliott (2013) 234–5; Goldschmidt (2013) 18–19; Hutchinson (2013) 35–8; McElduff (2013) 39–60; and Feeney (2016) 165–6. See too Boyd (2017) 11–14 on Livius and Ennius as "conduits of the Greek past to the Roman future" (13); Mariotti (1955); Goldberg (1995) 73–82; and Biggs (2017) on Naevius' pioneering efforts.

[57] Skutsch (1985) 8–46 surveys the testimonia and sources for the *Ann*. See also Prinzen (1998); Goldberg (2006); Consoli (2014) 27–116; and Goldberg and Manuwald (2018) xxvii–xxix. Goldschmidt (2013) 18–35 considers the reception of Ennius by later authors and as a school text and writes that under the early empire "[t]he backlash against Ennius' 'traditional' status and style grew, and the poet was widely rejected during the Neronian period" (33); *pace* Prinzen (1998) 333, who asks of the Neronian period, "War Ennius wirklich so fern?" It is my argument that Lucan did not reject Ennius as unworthy of being read, but rather that he engages with and counters Ennius because he is a crucial, necessary representative of Latin epic. For further recent appraisal of Ennius's literary standing and later reception, see the essays in Damon and Farrell (2020), a collection I learned of after the completion of this manuscript.

[58] Wiseman (2006) 513.

comments on Ennius's place in the tradition is attributed by Varro to a certain Pompilius, who states that Ennius was a student of the Muses themselves.[59] To be sure, Virgil's *Aeneid* came to replace the *Annales* as Rome's most widely read epic,[60] and the earlier poet's style would be the subject of criticism under the empire;[61] however, *pater Ennius* or *noster Ennius*, titles he is frequently given well into later antiquity,[62] would continue to hold an authoritative position at the beginning of the Latin epic tradition. Perhaps the best testament to Ennius's continued hold on a place of primacy among Latin authors—and writers of epic in particular—comes in Silius's depiction of the poet on the battlefield in Sardinia at *Punica* 12.387–413. Silius characterizes Ennius as "engaged in the first fights" (*miscebat primas acies*, 12.394); then, more to the point, he has Apollo himself swoop in to save the poet on the grounds that "this man will be the first (*primus*) to sing of Italian wars in illustrious verse" (12.410).[63] Like his near-contemporary Silius, Lucan too, I will argue, read and engaged with the *Annales* as a crucial literary starting point for the Roman epic story, one that he will conclusively bring to a close. If it was his aim for the *Pharsalia* to have the last word on Rome—to be the *carmen Romanum* for the end times—then taking on the epic that launched that story was necessary.

As we will see, Lucan engages with Homer and Ennius individually but also together. At the opening of the *Annales* Ennius had famously claimed not just to follow Homer but to *be* Homer, to be the Roman Homer.[64] A metempsychosis had taken place—and readers seemed to accept it. Horace writes at *Epist*. 2.1.50–1 that critics regarded Ennius as "another Homer" (*alter Homerus*), and Jerome ascribes this same sentiment to Lucilius.[65] For Lucan, rivaling and closing off Ennius meant closing off the Roman Homer—in a

---

[59] Courtney fr. 1 (= Non. 87 = Varro *Sat. Men.* 356B): *Pacui discipulus dicor, porro is fuit <Enni>* | *Ennius Musarum. Pompilius clueor*.
[60] See esp. Goldschmidt (2013) and Hutchinson (2013) 36–8.
[61] See Ov., *Trist.* 2.424 (*ingenio maximus, arte rudis*) and *Am.* 1.15.7 (*arte carens*); Val. Max. 8.14.1, writing of Scipio Africanus: *uir Homerico quam rudi atque impolito praeconio dignior*; and the quotations of Sen. at Gell. *NA* 12.2.2–11.
[62] *Pater Ennius*: Prop. 3.3.6; Hor., *Epist* 1.19.7; Serenus, *Liber Medicinalis* 36.706. *Noster Ennius*: Lucr. 1.117; Cic. *Arch.* 18 and 22, *De Rep.* 1.25.16, *De Senec.* 10.15, *De. Div.* 2.104.9; Fronto, *Ad M Caesarem* 1.4.5.1.
[63] See Casali (2006); Augoustakis (2009b) 10 n. 29 (with further bibliography); and Tipping (2010) 194–7.
[64] See Porph. ad Hor. *Epist.* 2.1.51; *Commentum Cornuti in Persium* 6.10. On Ennius's claim of fusion with Homer, see Skutsch (1985) 153–7; Goldberg (1995) 88–9; Fisher (2012); and Elliott (2013) 253–5.
[65] Jerome writes in his commentary on Micah (2.7.5): *Homerus alter ut Lucilius de Ennio suspicatur* (before disagreeing with the assessment and granting the analogue to Virgil). See Skutsch (1985) 11. Lucilius (341–7 M) and Varro (*Sat. Men.* 398B) also place Homer and Ennius beside one another.

sense, doubly closing off the beginning. In the coming chapters I will consider several passages in which Lucan seems to adapt and confront Homer and Ennius at the same time, as inextricably joined representatives of epic's beginnings.

* * *

The study begins in Chapter 1 ("Lucan at and against Epic's Beginnings") with close readings of three programmatic passages in which Lucan holds up his polemical engagement with early epic models. First, I address Caesar's visit to Troy in Book 9, a passage including Lucan's most explicit statement about his place in the epic tradition. Here, through a series of evocative allusions to model texts, he places his work alongside and indeed beyond the epics of Ovid, Virgil, Ennius, and Homer—the last two imagined together. I also address the age-old crux of how to refer to the poem. Reading the name "Pharsalia" included at 9.985 as representing a destructive place and time for Rome, I argue that this name speaks in meaningful ways to the poem's relationship with its model texts, especially the *Iliad* (as a toponym and central epic place that is dislocated by Pharsalia) and the *Annales* (as a marker of the progression of Roman time that is ended by the day of Pharsalia). From there I turn back to the bravura opening lines of the poem (1.1–32), with a focus on the passage's crucial anchoring allusions to Homer, Livius Andronicus, and Ennius, and on the themes and master tropes from early epic embraced here. Chapter 1 concludes with a new reading of the poetics in the first episode of the *Pharsalia*'s narrative (1.183–205), where Caesar's spurning of the goddess Roma at the Rubicon also marks the poet's rejection of the spirit of epic continuation that had carried through from Homer to Ennius to Virgil.

Chapter 2 ("Toppling *Topoi*: Epic's Violence Directed against Itself") considers the *Pharsalia*'s inclusion of conventional episodes of violence that go back to epic's foundational texts and Lucan's redirection of the violence in those episodes toward self-destruction. Each of these episodes (the mutilation of Marius Gratidianus at 2.173–93; Caesar's deforestation of a grove at 3.394–452; and the defiant battlefield stand of Scaeva at 6.140–262) contains anchoring allusions to early epic texts; and in each passage Lucan develops, at the lexical and thematic levels, his conception of the genre coming to an end by mutilating, crashing upon, and slaughtering itself. As in the passages considered in Chapter 1, here Ennius and Homer frequently emerge as joint models of epic primacy and joint foils for Lucan's agenda of epic closure.

Chapters 3–6 take a closer look at Lucan's engagement with master tropes in early epic models in more or less reverse chronological order. Chapter 3 concentrates on the chronologically latest epic beginning-point (Ennius's *Annales*), Chapter 4 considers the earliest Latin epicists (Livius, Naevius, and Ennius) together, and Chapters 5 and 6 focus on Homer's *Odyssey* and *Iliad*. This progression is not strict—for example, Homer's place of primacy is ever-present—but it offers a path for tracing back Lucan's program of closing off the genre's beginning-points.

Chapter 3 ("The *Pharsalia* and the End of the Ennian Story") builds upon the anchoring allusions to Ennius discussed in Chapters 1–2 to consider the poem's narrative closure of Ennius's epic on a broader thematic scale. While Nora Goldschmidt has profitably argued that Virgil's *Aeneid* works to "prewrite" and thus push aside the *Annales*,[66] I maintain that Lucan takes a similarly combative approach to Ennius, but rather than asserting priority, he aims to be the first to end the Ennian project, to close the book on the Roman story narrated in the *Annales*. In a broad polemic against the Ennian master trope of Roman spatial and temporal expansion,[67] the *Pharsalia* forcefully and emphatically closes this narrative—figuring Roman movement inward, into and against itself, with Pharsalia as a space and time of collapse and self-destruction for Rome. This chapter focuses on crucial passages on the end of Rome (and the Roman story) in *Pharsalia* 7, read alongside numerous fragments from the *Annales*, while also proposing that Lucan's structuring of the *Pharsalia* takes on the *Annales* as code model and structural foil. The collapse at the end of Book 10 of the poem's essentially annalistic framework, I argue, mirrors and underscores the poem's attention to the collapse of the Ennian master trope of Roman dominance in time and space.

Chapter 4 ("Lucan and the Closing of the Maritime Moment") explores Lucan's closure of a theme that is central to Livius's *Odusia* and Naevius's *Bellum Punicum*, as well as Ennius's epic: Rome's emerging control of the sea. Recent scholarly work has looked closely at the confluence of Rome's "maritime moment" in the third century BCE and its epic moment, that is, the near simultaneous emergence of Roman ascendancy on the sea and Roman epic.[68] I propose that the *Pharsalia*—in its concentration on sinking ships, crashing fleets, and the "un-winning" of the contest with Rome's maritime rival Carthage—narrates the loss of Roman sway over the sea and, with it, the

---

[66] Goldschmidt (2013); see too Casali (2006).
[67] On which see Elliott (2013) and (2014).
[68] See Leigh (2010) and Biggs (2017).

corresponding fall of the genre that captured and monumentalized that sway. Readers of the poem have noted how extraordinary Lucan's attention to the sea is, and have also long mused on his focus on Africa and the Carthaginian threat, points of focus that are, I argue, central to the project of revisiting and closing the epic genre's beginnings on the sea. The progression of Chapter 4 is similar to that of Chapters 3–6 as a whole, proceeding in more or less reverse order, from the issue of Roman primacy on the Mediterranean to the matter of individual Roman ships on the sea. An additional consideration is that these early epics exhibit a keen sense of the precariousness of Rome's launch onto the sea, but ultimately highlight the success of Roman naval expansion—and so, I maintain, they are keyed into the uncertainty but ultimate success of the genre of epic too. Lucan's poem strikes a sharp difference by directing that sense of peril and contingency not toward progress (of Rome on the sea or of the Roman epic story) but toward wholesale destruction and closure.

In Chapter 5 ("The *Pharsalia* and the Loss of *Nostos*") I move from the theme of Rome's conquest and loss of the sea to the related matter of return, or *nostos*, from the sea. My argument builds on the work of Homeric scholarship on *nostos* as a binding master trope in the *Odyssey*, and as an end accomplished by hero (Odysseus) and poet (Homer) alike. While scholars have considered similarities between the wanderings of Lucan's Cato and Caesar and Odysseus,[69] I argue that Lucan crafts the journeys of each of his central characters—Caesar, Cato, and Pompey—as reversals of Odysseus's *nostos*, each in a distinct way, but with none reaching home in the poem, and each conspicuously failing to achieve the spousal reunion that is so central to Odysseus's *nostos*. I go on to examine how each narrative arc is emblematic of the larger story in the *Pharsalia* of Rome's own imperiled journey and ultimate loss of *nostos* and even of the very idea of "home." In this process, epic poetry too is undone, left without the fulfillment and completion of *nostos*—and so here the marker of closure comes in thematic exploration of opening up. Within this chapter, the place of Homer's *Odyssey* as an anti-model is paramount, but I also propose that Livius's *Odusia*—the poem that first carried over and initiated the telling of epic at Rome—stands alongside the Homeric poem as a foil for Lucan, and in this way the unraveling of the epic arc of *nostos* carries a doubly powerful poetic force.

[69] See Lausberg (1985) 1599–1602 on Cato and Odysseus; Matthews (2008), esp. 225–7 and 315–18, and Hutchinson (2013) 330–1 on Caesar and Odysseus.

Throughout this book, I follow Statius's lead and address the many passages where Lucan gives voice to lament—for Rome, the Roman story, the epic story—while also thundering against that story and against his epic models. And while the poetics of reversal, undoing, and violence will receive more attention in Chapters 1–5, Chapter 6 ("Epic's Last Lament") puts the matter of the poem's corresponding expressions of lament front and center. In this way the book's progression in primary focus from violence to lament mirrors epic storytelling's natural progression. In Chapter 6, I show that Lucan follows Homer in his use of the common stylistic and thematic components of the *goos* and in his incorporation of an antiphony of commiserating voices; but that he also forcefully moves the voice of lament from epic's margins to its center, creating an antiphony that includes not only communal voices in the poem, but also the voice of the narrator himself, and even the inclusive "we" of the poem's readers living under the reign of the Caesars. The sweeping nature of Lucan's use of the master trope of lament leads me to read the poem itself as a grand lament and thus a completion of Homeric epic. I conclude the chapter by focusing on the way lament in the *Pharsalia* communicates greatness, and thus has the capacity to sound—and celebrate—the end of epic's song of sorrow.

In the Conclusion, I tie together the variety of ways Lucan seeks to uproot and close off the epic genre before considering what he *does* make survive—that is, where there may be openings in this grand gesture of closure. With the story of Rome dead and now an object of lament, with that story transformed into the story of the place that killed Rome, what lives on is *Pharsalia nostra*. This is the story of a dead thing that lives on; and Lucan's persistent manner of personifying and giving agency to "Pharsalia" throughout the poem reinforces this sense. In this regard, Lucan has it both ways: he puts an end to the epic genre while his own epic lives on, opening itself up to new readers in new times.

1
Lucan at and against Epic's Beginnings

In the Introduction we heard Statius's Calliope celebrate Lucan as besting all of his predecessors, and the *Pharsalia* as surpassing all prior epic. In this chapter I turn to three programmatic passages in which Lucan himself makes precisely such a claim: the proem and opening apostrophe to Roma (1.1–32); the poem's first episode, of Caesar at the Rubicon (1.183–205); and Caesar's visit to the ruins of Troy (9.961–99). In each passage the poet makes it clear, as Statius's Calliope will understand, that he aims to supplant not only more recent predecessors, such as Virgil, but also the genre's formative poems, its first beginnings. The intertextual connections I will consider in these "purple passages" operate as anchoring allusions for Lucan's broader polemical engagement with epic's foundational texts. The episode in Book 9 contains the work's most explicit consideration of its place in the literary tradition (9.980–6), and here Lucan refers to his poem by the evocative toponym *Pharsalia nostra*, a phrase with great significance for our understanding of his closural poetics. To this end, I begin now with that passage in Book 9, on the fraught textual ground of Troy.

1.1. Caesar and Lucan on Trojan ground

The interpretive importance of the authorial statement at 9.980–6 and its Trojan textual surroundings has long been appreciated, with readers highlighting the passage as "[i]n a certain sense ... the climax of the poem as we have it" and as Lucan's "*sphragis*, his seal of poetic authority, on his epic."[1] But the breadth and sweeping totality of Lucan's poetic claims in this episode have not been duly addressed. The entire episode, which Lucan seems

---

[1] Johnson (1987) 121 and Fratantuono (2012) 386. Ahl (1976) 328 refers to the visit to Troy as a whole as "the climactic point in the ten books that Lucan wrote." On the passage, see too Ahl (1976) 214–21; Narducci (1979) 77–9 and (2002) 177–80; Zwierlein (1986); Johnson (1987) 119–21; Ormand (1994) 50–3; Rossi (2001); Wick (2004) 401–21; Tesoriero (2005); Thorne (2011); and McClellan (2019) 153–5.

to have concocted whole cloth, is packed with metapoetic markers, as his polemical diction moves in lockstep with his character Caesar's brash actions. Their joint enterprise in irreverence and upheaval begins immediately upon Caesar's arrival at the site of the city:

> circumit exustae nomen memorabile Troiae
> magnaque Phoebei quaerit uestigia muri.   965
> iam siluae steriles et putres robore trunci
> Assaraci pressere domos et templa deorum
> iam lassa radice tenent, ac tota teguntur
> Pergama dumetis: etiam periere ruinae.

> He goes around the memorable name of burned-out Troy, and he looks for the great traces of Phoebus's wall. Now sterile woods and trunks rotting in their wood have pressed down on the homes of Assaracus and hold on to the temples of the gods with their already worn-out roots, and all of Pergama is covered by bramble. Even the ruins have died. (9.964–9)

A series of metapoetic cues signals Lucan's disregard for Trojan material—and indeed the deadness of the material. Like his character Caesar, Lucan will go around (*circumit*) the name or story of Troy, confronting but choosing to eschew the poetic act of narrating this narratable (*memorabile*; see *memoro OLD* 3) story. After all, at this point a search for traces (*uestigia*)[2] of old stories does not necessarily reveal much. What can be found are lifeless (*steriles*) "woods," *siluae*, a word functioning as a marker of literary output.[3] The literature that told the story of Troy is now "rotting (*putres*) in its wood" (*robore*, another word used of texts)[4] and its very roots or foundations are weary (*lassa radice*). This decaying material now only presses down on (*pressere*) and thus keeps stifled the story of the house of Assaracus, ancestor of Priam and Anchises. When we recall from *Silvae* 2.7.48 and 54–7 that in his "tender years" Lucan had already tackled the tales of Troy's fall and the realm of the Underworld, the lines make even more sense: the stories of Troy told in Homer's foundational texts and then picked up again and again by subsequent epic poets were the stuff of the past—lifeless, now rotting.

---

[2] See my discussion in Chapter 4 of the metapoetic valences of *uestigium*.
[3] As I shall address at length in Chapter 2.
[4] See Masters (1992) 27 and 29, n. 44, and Dinter (2012) 134 on how *robor* "often serves in Lucan as a metaphor for the literary tradition."

Here, while surely marking an end for the most celebrated singers of Troy, the *primus parens* Homer as well as Virgil, Lucan is also taking aim at the very *process* of bringing the Trojan story into Latin—of making the Trojan story constitutive of the Roman story. To do so, he evokes and confronts Ennius, that crucial and self-styled pious (*Ann.* 4; see later in this chapter) carrier of Homer into the Latin epic tradition. This becomes clear in the imagery and diction in 9.964–9, which recall and seemingly counter a passage from Book 10 of the *Annales*. The fragment is preserved by Macrobius, who writes that in his tenth book Ennius said "about Pergama" (*de Pergamis*):

quae neque Dardaniis campis potuere perire
nec cum capta capi nec cum combusta cremari

[Pergama] which could not die in the Dardanian fields, or be captured though it was captured, or be burned down even when consumed by flames. (*Ann.* 344–5 = Macr. 6.1.60)

Since the passage appeared later in Ennius's narrative,[5] its placement together with its content speak to the lastingness of Troy, its inability to stay down or defeated. As Elliott puts it, the passage "assures us that Troy continued to be a relevant and redeployed notion late into the poem."[6] The Troy introduced into epic by Homer, Ennius conveys, is not burned down, does not die in the *Annales*—it lives on in his narrative long past his treatment of Aeneas's departure from the city in Book 1 (see *Ann.* 14–19). The statements in *Ann.* 344–5 are thus representative of the embrace of the Trojan story in the *Annales* as a whole: Troy does not—could not (*neque . . . potuere perire*)—die.

Lucan is clear in his presentation of just the opposite in *Pharsalia* 9. The language he uses to convey Troy's death reads in many ways as a corrective of the Ennian language in *Ann.* 344–5. Whereas Ennius had written that the Trojan citadel Pergama could not "be burned down even when consumed by flames" (*nec cum combusta cremari*), for Lucan the site is introduced as "the memorable name of burned-out Troy" (*exustae nomen memorabile Troiae*, 9.964). The emphatic *exustae* thus gives the lie to the Ennian image of Troy's burning (*combusta*, from the same verb as *exustae*, *uro*) as impermanent.

---

[5] Skutsch (1985) 514, building on Badian (1972) 178–9, writes: "the context can only be . . . the embassy from Lambascus [in the Troad] to Massilia and Rome in 197 or 196."
[6] Elliott (2013) 277.

Then, in a more pointed inversion, Lucan writes that "all of the citadel Pergama is covered by bramble. Even the ruins have died" (*ac tota teguntur | Pergama dumetis: etiam periere ruinae*, 9.968–9). When we recall from Macrobius that Pergama, a transliteration of the Homeric name for the citadel of Troy,[7] is the subject of *potuere* in *Ann.* 344, we see that Lucan appears to be refuting the Ennian statement. While Ennius had brought Homer's *Pergama* over into Latin epic, thwarting its death (*neque . . . potuere perire*), Lucan makes *Pergama* totally (*tota*) covered in weeds. Its ruins have indeed died (*periere ruinae*). The lexical similarities in the key words *Pergama* and then *pereo* bring the two passages together, as does Lucan's conspicuous use of the Greek borrowing *Pergama*. He uses the word only here and at the end of this episode, when Caesar states that "a Roman Pergama will rise" (*Romanaque Pergama surgent*, 9.999), a declaration that, appropriately, will not be proven true.

Here among the ruins of Troy, Lucan presents as dead not just the aboriginal epic tale of Troy, but also the inheritance and perpetuation of that tale in the Latin tradition. This metapoetic picture of the story of Troy as now rotten and ready to be uprooted is followed by the ignorant (*inscius*, 9.974) and careless (*securus*, 9.975) Caesar's trampling on barely visible Trojan sites (9.974–9), a passage reinforcing Lucan's effrontery toward predecessors such as Homer, Ennius, and Virgil. It may be that "no stone lacks a story" (*nullum est sine nomine saxum*, 9.973), but Lucan's Caesar—and Lucan himself—has no interest in turning those stones. Later in the passage the irreverent Caesar takes a different tack when he co-opts the Trojan story as his own, aggressively embracing the gods of "*my* Aeneas" (*Aeneaeque mei*, 9.991) and claiming to be "the most distinguished of the race of Iulus" (9.995).[8] The Trojan story is *my* story, Caesar asserts; all that Trojan epic was nothing but prelude to *my* epic, the poet asserts.[9]

For much of the passage, then, Lucan's claims to surpass and put an end to the epic project of his predecessors operate on a metapoetic level. But right at the heart of the Trojan episode, the narrator turns and makes these assertions explicit:

---

[7] See *Il.* 4.508, 5.446, 5.460, 6.512, 7. 21, and 24.700.
[8] Rossi (2001) argues that Lucan's Caesar transforms Troy into an exclusively Julian Troy. See too Quint (1993) 7 and Ormand (1994) 51 on Caesar's selective reading.
[9] *Pace* Martindale (1993), arguing that Lucan is "displaying a kind of self-loathing" (50) when presenting his epic predecessors' tales as hackneyed.

> o sacer et magnus uatum labor! omnia fato
> eripis et populis donas mortalibus aeuum.
> inuidia sacrae, Caesar, ne tangere famae;
> nam, si quid Latiis fas est promittere Musis,
> quantum Zmyrnaei durabunt uatis honores,
> uenturi me teque legent; Pharsalia nostra   985
> uiuet, et a nullo tenebris damnabimur aeuo.

> O sacred and great work of bards! You rescue everything from fate, and you bestow the gift of eternal life on mortal peoples. Caesar, do not be touched by envy of sacred glory; for, if it is right for the Latin Muses to promise anything, as long as the honors of the Smyrnaean poet will endure, posterity will read me and you; our Pharsalia will live on, and we shall be condemned to darkness by no age.

The apostrophe here to the "sacred and great work of bards" (9.980) is followed by an address to Caesar; and with the statement that "posterity will read me and you" together (9.985), Lucan declares that his telling of the Battle of Pharsalia will be the authoritative one, pushing aside Caesar's own account in his *commentarii*.[10] Caesar will secure the fame he longed for (9.982; cf. *famae mirator* at 9.961), but on Lucan's terms, and on the epic genre's terms, in the form of the "sacred and great work of bards." What we find is that the two addressees in these lines, Caesar and the *uatum labor*, are each objects of Lucan's *aemulatio*. He is taking on Caesar—along with the entirety of the epic tradition.

Lucan's careful and cutting engagement with his epic predecessors indeed fills these seven lines. The climactic statement about the eternal fame of the *Pharsalia* comes at 9.985-6, but it is preceded at 9.983-4 by two qualifications, introduced by *si quid* (983) and then *quantum* (984). This formulation recalls the structure of Virgil's statement about his poetic powers at *Aeneid* 9.446-9,[11] as well as Ovid's declaration about his poetic immortality at the close of the *Metamorphoses* (15.878-9: *ore legar populi, perque omnia saecula fama, | siquid habent ueri uatum praesagia, uiuam*, "I will be

---

[10] Thorne (2011) 366-7, Fratantuono (2012) 387, and Zissos (2013) 140-44, building on O'Higgins (1988) 216, write of Lucan's displacement of Caesar and his *commentarii* in this passage. See too Joseph (2017a) 131-7 and Seidman (2017) 92.

[11] *Aen.* 9.446 (*si quid mea carmina possunt*), a qualification (matched by a second in the *dum* clause at 9.448-9) for the Virgilian narrator's statement about the fame that Nisus and Euryalus will gain from his poetry.

read in the mouths of the people; and in my fame throughout the ages—if the predictions of the poets have anything true to them—I shall live on"). Lucan's words in 9.983 (*si quid Latiis fas est promittere Musis*) thus seem to evoke each of these model passages. But the qualification in 9.983 moves beyond these individual predecessors to take aim at the Latin epic tradition as a whole. This is Lucan's first and only mention of the Muses in the poem, and the equivocation in this clause speaks to the poem's fundamental questioning of divine interaction and in particular divine providence, a matter I will explore in Chapter 3. But at this moment, in his most direct statement about his place in the epic tradition, Lucan is happy to leverage a reference to the Latin Muses to assert that, if it is divinely right (*fas*) for them to pass on any (*quid*) of the "sacred (*sacer*) and great work of bards" (9.980), it is his.

This assertion about his place among the Latin Muses is immediately followed by another parry that extends still further back in the tradition: "as long as the honors of the Smyrnaean poet will endure" (9.984: *quantum Zmyrnaei durabunt uatis honores*). This proviso appears to be an explicit claim of connection with Homer and even of contingency upon his literary success.[12] But a problem arises: we have seen that in the immediately preceding lines, Lucan traces the decay into irrelevance and near nonexistence of Homer's Trojan story. With the *quantum* clause in 9.984, is Lucan implying that, if the Homeric poems fall into oblivion, his epic is headed there too?

We may resolve this interpretive crux by focusing on Lucan's word choice of *honores*. He is asserting that, for his poetic achievement to be rightly appreciated, Homer's place in the epic tradition, his *honores*, must survive. The idea of the Smyrnaean bard as epic's forefather must live on, if only as prelude and to serve as a foil to Lucan's own endeavor. Lucan's epic *does* need the anti-model of Homer and the tradition that follows, as a mark against which to measure and define itself. Central to Lucan's poetic project is its closural claim, its triumphant pronouncement about the end of epic; and any ending-point emerges much more clearly when positioned against a beginning-point. The eristic gesture in 9.984 is enhanced by Lucan's definition of Homer as a *uates*. This is the uniquely Latin term for a prophet or bard. Its use, as opposed to *poeta* (a translation of the Greek *poiētēs*), had been a source of

---

[12] And so it is strange that much scholarship on this passage has tended to concentrate on polemics with Virgil. See, e.g., Hardie (1993) 17; Ormand (1994) 50 ("Caesar goes to Troy, then, *because* of the *Aeneid*"); Leigh (1997) 18 ("Lucan's point of reference here is fundamentally Vergilian"); and Martindale (1993) 49–53, focusing on the passage as a moment of reception of Aeneas's visit to Pallanteum in *Aen.* 8. Narducci (2002) 179–80 emphasizes Homer's importance.

contention among Latin epic poets over the centuries, but it is the term that Lucan uses of himself at 1.63 and 7.553.[13] Here in 9.980–6 he defines the epic enterprise as the *sacer et magnus uatum labor* (9.980) and then attaches the word to Homer (*Zmyrnaei ... uatis*). The gesture of applying this Latin term to Homer serves to place Homer in Lucan's tradition, not the other way around. The implication—reinforced across this passage and the poem as a whole—is that Homeric poetry was a precursor to Lucanian poetry, was leading up to the vatic, Roman project of the *Pharsalia*.[14]

I come now to the central claim, that "posterity will read me and you; our Pharsalia will live on, and we shall be condemned to darkness by no age" (9.985–6: *uenturi me teque legent; Pharsalia nostra | uiuet, et a nullo tenebris damnabimur aeuo*). In addition to the gesture toward Caesar's own *commentarii*, an Ovidian model also seems to be clear, in the appeals to future readers (*legent* and *ore legar populi* at *Met*. 15.878) and the conquest of time (cf. *a nullo ... aeuo* and *perque omnia saecula* at *Met*. 15.878), and also in the clear, potent use of a future form of *uiuo* to characterize the poet's everlasting fame (*uiuet* and *uiuam* at *Met*. 15.879).[15] But intertwined with the emulative gestures toward Caesar, Homer, Virgil, and Ovid in this sequence of lines is Lucan's self-positioning alongside Ennius. This should not be surprising: if he is angling for pride of place among the Latin Muses (9.983), if he is presenting his poem in dialogue with Latin epic as a whole, then he must involve Ennius in his claims. And indeed 9.985–6 recall[16] Ennius's own words of self-presentation in Book 1 of the *Annales*:

> latos <per> populos res atque poemata nostra
> <clara> cluebunt

> Across a wide range of peoples my poetry and its contents will be heard and be distinguished. (*Ann*. 12–13 = *De ult. syll.*, *GL* IV, p. 231.11–18)

Lucan's phrase *Pharsalia nostra* recalls Ennius's *poemata nostra*, in its metrical length, scansion, and position in the verse, as well as in its sense, a self-reference to the work at hand.

---

[13] See O'Higgins (1988) on Lucan's use of the term.
[14] Narducci (2002) 179 argues that here Lucan presents himself as the "third Latin Homer" after Ennius and Virgil, and that, by naming neither of them, he establishes a direct emulative line back to Homer himself.
[15] See Fratantuono (2012) 386–8 and 397 on Lucan's claims vis-à-vis Ovid.
[16] As Zwierlein (1982) 95–6 and Skutsch (1985) 167–8 note.

We can go further by reading the Ennian phrase *res atque poemata* as a sort of intertextual gloss on *Pharsalia*, a word that signifies both the content (*res*) and the form (*poemata*) of Lucan's work.[17] Moreover, both *poemata* and *Pharsalia* are the subjects of future verbs,[18] but with a meaningful difference. While Ennius's poem "will be famous" (*cluebunt*),[19] Lucan makes claims for greater temporal transcendence—his *Pharsalia* "will live on" (*uiuet*). This verb choice may point not only to Ovid's triumphant *uiuam* at *Met.* 15.789, but also to the separate Ennian passage that lies behind Ovid's *sphragis*: the long-famous epigram in which Ennius states that he "flies about, alive on the mouths of men" (*uolito uiuos per ora uirum*, fr. 46 Courtney).[20] Lucan's *uiuet* would thus draw upon one well-known Ennian passage for polemical positioning against another, with an emphatic claim to superior dominance over time, as the following statement in 9.986 hammers home ("we shall be condemned to darkness by no age").

Furthermore, Lucan appears to emulate Ennius's aspirations for not just temporal but also spatial sway. Just above he had written of poetry that "you bestow the gift of eternal life on mortal peoples" (9.981: *populis donas mortalibus aeuum*), phrasing that again recalls not only Ovid's diction at *Met.* 15.878 (*ore legar populi, perque omnia saecula fama*), but also the statement that may have served as a model for Ovid: Ennius's claims for poetic transcendence across space in the phrase *latos <per> populos*.[21] It was Ennius who first boasted of writing a Latin epic whose content and fame would reach far and wide,[22] and Ovid and Lucan alike seem to express their aspirations in his idiom. If we accept Ilberg's addition of the predicate adjective *clara* in *Ann.* 13,[23] then an additional gesture of *aemulatio* is apparent in Lucan's claim. While the *Annales*' story of Rome's advance made claims to be "bright"

---

[17] Skutsch (1985) 168 considers a similar connection between *res atque poemata* and the preceding words in *Ph.* 9.985: "In the Lucan passage quoted above, which may contain an echo of this line, *me* [Lucan] corresponds to *poemata*, *te* [Caesar] to *res*." Gildenhard (2003) 104 discusses how Ennius's phrase *res atque poemata* marks the lastingness of both the deeds he narrates and his poetic achievement.

[18] Zwierlein (1982) 95.

[19] See Skutsch (1985) 168–9 on the necessary emendation to *cluebunt* from the transmitted reading *cluebant*.

[20] Quoted by Cic. at *Tusc.* 1.34 and 1.117; and *Cato* 73; adapted at Virg., *G.* 3.9 and Ov., *Met.* 15.878–9. See Courtney (1993) 42–3 and Goldberg (1995) 16–18.

[21] Skutsch (1985) 167 compares *Ann.* 12–13 with *Met.* 15.871ff., along with Hor., *C.* 3.30.

[22] On this phrase as a signifier of both Rome's expansion and Ennius's fame, see Elliott (2013) 251 and Feeney (2016) 182–3, as well as Dominik (1993) 38–48 on this and other fragments that capture Ennius's self-consciousness as a poet.

[23] See Skutsch (1985) 167–8. Ilberg pointed to the phrase *clara clueret* in the assessment of Ennius's fame at Lucr. 1.117–19.

(*clara*), Lucan's telling of Rome's defeat to Caesarism will manage to avoid darkness (*tenebris*) altogether—a suggestion, perhaps, that his song will reach so many peoples that the sun will never set on the singing of it.

We saw in Lucan's image of Pergama perishing how the poet carefully construes Homer and his Roman receiver Ennius together—only to close them off together too. This dynamic seems to carry into the statement at 9.980–6 as well, if we follow a reading that Elliott proposes for the phrase *res atque poemata nostra* in *Ann.* 12. While *nostra* could represent the first-person plural for singular (thus "my poem(s)"), Elliott notes how our source for the fragment[24] places it in Book 1, and that other passages that editors place just before this one explicitly address the close spiritual association with Homer that Ennius develops so fully and memorably.[25] Thus *nostra* in *res atque poemata nostra* may well be a true plural, referring to the poems of *both* Homer *and* Ennius, as conjoined epic poets—unified progenitors of the Greek and then Latin epic traditions. In the allusion at 9.985–6, then, Lucan's *Pharsalia nostra* would supplant the joint Ennian-Homeric poetic complex.

Lucan's uses of the word *uates* in this passage may also serve to fold Homer and Ennius together. We have seen how the term may contribute to Lucan's polemics against Homer, but it also has a particular potency with respect to Ennius. In the proem to *Annales* 7, Ennius distances himself from Naevius, who had used the Saturnian meter, when writing: *scripsere alii rem uorsibus quos olim Faunei uatesque canebant* ("Others wrote about affairs in verses that the fauns and bards used to sing"; *Ann.* 206–7 = Cic., *Brut.* 76 and 71). Ennius thus makes clear that he is no bumpkin bard, no *uates*.[26] Rather, it was the Greek *poeta* Homer who appeared to him and whose soul passed into him (*Ann.* 3: *uisus Homerus adesse poeta*); it is Homeric-style *poemata* (*Ann.* 12) that he brings to the Roman story. The distinction Ennius makes here became famous: the line is quoted not only by Cicero (who quotes it again at *Div.* 1.114), but by Varro (*LL* 7.36), Quintilian (9.4.115), and Origen (4.4–5). Virgil will bring back the term *uates*, which he uses in evocative ways of himself (*Aen.* 7.41) and other poets (see, e.g., *Ecl.* 9.34); subsequent poets then embrace it.[27] When Lucan begins the statement at 9.980–6 with the exclamation *o sacer et magnus uatum labor*, he calls to mind the term's rich and contentious history. And given how clear his *aemulatio* with Ennius becomes

---

[24] The anonymous author of *De Ultimis Syllabis*; see Elliott (2013) 523.
[25] Elliott (2013) 275, n. 146.
[26] See Skutsch (1985) 369–72; Goldberg (1995) 90; and McElduff (2013) 59–60.
[27] See Newman (1967) and O'Hara (1990) 176–83.

in the surrounding lines, the designation of the genre as a whole as the work of *uates* amounts to a provocative gesture of reclamation toward not only the progenitor he calls the Smyrnaean *uates*, but also the one who so famously rejected this Latin title.

1.2. Ph. 9.980–6 and the importance of the ~~title~~ name *Pharsalia*

The polemical use of *uates* for Homer and all other epic poets also signals that the genre is reaching a specifically Roman end, coming to a close in Lucan's *carmen Romanum*. But while Lucan asserts his own Roman-ness as prevailing *vates*, the Greek toponym he uses of the poem in 9.985, *Pharsalia*, brings with it very different closural dynamics. In the coming pages I will explore how this name both emphasizes the conclusion of the Roman story and signals closure of both Homer's and Ennius's model texts.

But first, a few words on the long-standing crux of 9.985 and what to call the poem are in order. On the strength of the statement *uenturi me teque legent; Pharsalia nostra | uiuet*, occurring in a passage that reflects explicitly on poetic fame, centuries of readers going back to at least Dante understood *Pharsalia* to be the title of the poem.[28] But a reconsideration took hold in 1926 when A. E. Housman glossed the phrase *Pharsalia nostra* with the explanation *proelium a te gestum, a me scriptum* ("the battle waged by you, described by me").[29] This reading, which aligns the phrase with contents of the poem (the Battle of Pharsalia) and nothing more, has been influential with subsequent readers. The text's most recent editor, D. R. Shackleton Bailey, went so far as to begin the preface for his edition by castigating the "blockheads, amateurs, or fools who, deaf to the warnings of Hosius and Housman, continue to force upon it the false title 'Pharsalia.'"[30] The title preferred by Housman, Shackleton Bailey, and most recent editors of individual books is *Bellum Civile* or *De Bello Civili*. But the arguments for these titles

---

[28] See Dante, *De Monarchia* 2.4 and *Convivio* 4.28, noted by Ahl (1976) 331 n. 54. Recent (heterodox) advocates of *Pharsalia* as the title are Ahl (1976) 306–32; Lebek (1976) 13 n. 1; Johnson (1987) 120–1; Leigh (1997) 74 n. 72; Radicke (2004) 64–5; Bexley (2009) 466 and 469; and Fratantuono (2012) 386.

[29] Housman (1926) on 9.985, followed by Tarrant (1983) 215 n. 1, and Shackleton Bailey (1988) iii. Horsfall (1981) 106 concludes similarly.

[30] Shackleton Bailey (1988) iii.

rely on ancient testimonia that are either unclear (Suetonius, *Vita Lucani* 5)[31] or late (Vacca's introduction to the poem, from the fifth or sixth century), and on the inconsistent evidence of the manuscripts, in which the poem is identified as *Bellum Civile, De Bello Civili*, by Lucan's name alone, or by nothing at all.[32] Early manuscripts offer no evidence of *Pharsalia* as the title, though Ahl has considered the possibility that Lucan never did include a *titulus* per se on or in his papyri.[33]

The best evidence for what Lucan called the poem is the internal evidence that we have: this very line that Housman so influentially cast aside. I agree with Matthew Leigh that Housman's reading of *Pharsalia nostra | uiuet* "sets up a bogus opposition" and that 9.985–6 is "obviously metapoetic."[34] Whether we read this statement as evidence for the title per se or just as a reference to the poem's contents, what seems clear is that he uses the phrase *Pharsalia nostra* in 9.985 to characterize the story that he is telling. His story—this poem—is the story of Pharsalia.[35] In his extensive discussion of the issue, Ahl advocates for *Pharsalia* and rightly emphasizes the centrality of the place and time of Pharsalia in the poem.[36] Lucan's poem leads inexorably toward Pharsalia in Books 1–6, narrates its occurrence as the pivotal place and time in Roman history in Book 7, and then keeps it in the reader's mind during the aftermath of Books 8–10.[37] It is fitting that he—and we—call this poem about Pharsalia *Pharsalia*.

---

[31] Suetonius writes: *dein ciuile bellum quod a Pompeio et Caesare gestum est recitauit*. Editors have capitalized *ciuile bellum*, in so doing making the title *Civile Bellum*. But apart from the fact that the order of the two words is reversed, the inclusion of the relative clause seems to suggest that Suetonius is describing the content of Lucan's recitation, not the title: "then he recounted / sang about the civil war that was waged by Pompey and Caesar."

[32] See the descriptions of early manuscripts in Gotoff (1971) 15–17; Ahl (1976) 331 ("it was probably the *lack* of title in early manuscripts that led to the search for a title within the work and the establishment of *Pharsalia* as the canonical title by the time of Dante"); and Werner (1998) 10–11; along with the more extended account of manuscripts by Fleischer (1831) 3.xxxiv–liv.

[33] Ahl (1976) 331, raising the possibility that Nero's death-order prevented Lucan from applying a *titulus*. Tarrant (1983) 215 n. 1 echoes Ahl's assessment. See Horsfall (1981), Ballester (1990), and Fruyt (1997) on Roman practices in using titles; further, Jansen (2014b), building on Genette (1997 [1987]), on titles as paratextual thresholds of interpretation.

[34] Leigh (1997) 74 n. 72, who goes on to write: "If the title *De Bello Civili* appears on many manuscripts, it is surely because that is just the sort of title to which an uninspired editor would resort." See too Fratantuono (2012) 386: "the insufferably flat '*Bellum Civile*' is a pale replacement for the dramatic title Lucan clearly sets forth here."

[35] Just as the similarly toponymic *Ilias* tells the story of Ilium, and the *Thebais* tells the story of Thebes.

[36] Ahl (1976) 331. So too Bexley (2009) 466 n. 35: "*Pharsalia* really is the most ironically appropriate title for this epic, and the central placement and importance of the eponymous battle contribute some justification for this nomenclature."

[37] See Joseph (2017a) and further discussion in Chapter 3. This design and progression are lost on the likes of Duff (1928), whose Loeb edition remains an important entry point for those interested in the poem. At page xii in his preface he writes: "The poem used to be called 'The Pharsalia,' and the

This name also operates as a concise and forceful marker of self-fashioning in the epic tradition, and the inclusion of *Pharsalia* in 9.985 works in conjunction with the provocative pronouncements about Homer and Ennius in the preceding lines. For one, this "story of Pharsalia" positions itself against the similarly toponymic "story of Ilium." As I noted earlier, it is surely significant that Lucan presents this toponym at the very point in his story when Ilium is being trampled upon and buried deeper. Here—over 90% of the way into his poem, well after his narration of the Battle of Pharsalia itself, but once Caesar and his story have taken him to Troy—is where Lucan opts to include his clearest poetic statement and to present the name *Pharsalia*. This location and this textual *locus*—with its layers of Ovidian, Virgilian, Ennian, and Homeric textual tissue—is just the right place for Lucan and his readers to pause and consider what this epic is about, where it stands in the tradition of "the sacred and great work of bards," *what it is*. Put another way, when considering where best to assert the *Pharsalia*'s authority and preeminence, Lucan would understandably be drawn to Caesar's visit to Ilium.[38]

Furthermore, the gesture at 9.980–6 appears to build on a connection between the site of Pharsalia and the *Iliad* that Lucan had made in Book 6. There, with the decisive battle imminent, the poet dwells ominously on the land of Thessaly in a long excursus (6.333–412).[39] He makes Thessaly the birthplace not only of war and its implements (6.395–407), but also of the *story* of war, when he casts the hero of the genre's first epic, Achilles, as a native of Pharsalos:[40]

>   postquam discessit Olympo
> Herculea grauis Ossa manu subitaeque ruinam
> sensit aquae Nereus, melius mansura sub undis
> Emathis aequorei regnum Pharsalos Achillis   350
> eminet.

---

title is convenient. But it is not appropriate, because it applies only to the events of one book, the seventh." Doubling down on his misreading of the poem's design, he goes on to write: "No reasonable judgment can rank Lucan among the world's great epic poets. He does not tell his story well."

[38] Peirano (2013, 2014) explores the use of the poetic seal or *sphragis* as a means of communicating authority to readers.

[39] See Masters (1992) 150–78 on the excursus, and Ambühl (2015) 145–8 and (2016) 302–8 on the range of intertexts in the passage.

[40] Perhaps building on Cat. 64.37, where Cat. places the wedding of Achilles's parents, Peleus and Thetis, not on Mt. Pelion like other sources but at Pharsalus. See Ambühl (2016) 305.

> After heavy Ossa fell from Mt. Olympus by Hercules's hand and Nereus
> felt the rush of sudden water, then Pharsalos, the kingdom of watery
> Achilles, rose up—better if it had remained beneath the Emathian waves.
> (6.347–51)

So Lucan sees to it that "the protagonist of the 'last' epic in history, Lucan's Caesar, returns to the home city of the protagonist of the first epic of all."[41] It is a return, but more than just a return: in Book 7 Lucan will transform this birthplace into a place of ending and death, for Rome and for the epic story. And, by making Pharsalos preexist and give birth to the hero of the war in Ilium, Lucan makes the story of Pharsalia in a sense engulf the *Iliad*; Pharsalia both gave birth to and will conclude the epic story. Lucan's process of return to and enveloping closure of the Homeric story, developed in this Book 6 passage, is then neatly and powerfully captured in the name *Pharsalia* that he reveals at the site of Troy in Book 9.

This name, with the centering of action in Pharsalia that it announces, also succinctly captures the poem's polemical engagement with the *Annales*. Through reference to Rome's pontifical records, Ennius's title placed Rome and Roman tradition right at its center.[42] "Ennius' poem displays the partiality of its perspective in its very title," writes Elliott, who goes on to read the epic's Romanocentric title as a deliberate counter to Hellenocentric works of universal history.[43] Ennius's epic is about Rome and its expansion in time and space, with the city itself firmly positioned as central node. And if it was the aim of the *Annales* to move the center of universal action away from Greece and place it emphatically in Rome, then the *Pharsalia* pointedly reverses this movement, dislocating Rome's center to a wholly different and deadly umbilicus, Pharsalia. To be sure, as we saw earlier, Lucan marks his creation as the work of a Roman *uates*. But the poem's content, the Roman story, is uprooted. To Roman readers familiar with the Latin epic tradition and promised *Romana carmina* (1.66), the unveiling of the name *Pharsalia* in Book 9 forces upon them a hard and lasting truth: the Roman story has not only moved, but has gone off to its death.[44] Further still, this spatial dislocation is

---

[41] Masters (1992) 158.
[42] Elliott (2013) 275 and (2014) 227. On the authority gained by the title's reference to the pontifical records, see Gildenhard (2003) 97; Wiseman (2006) 526–9; and Elliott (2013) 71–3 and 265.
[43] Elliott (2013) 237–9, with the quotation at 237.
[44] So Bexley (2009) 466, in her treatment of the dislocation of the Roman center in the *Ph.*: "the paradox extends to the title of Lucan's epic: *Romana carmina* that sing of Roman destiny and yet are called the *Pharsalia*."

joined by a temporal one: while the title *Annales* announces the poem's presentation of Rome's year-to-year advance, the name *Pharsalia* also speaks to Lucan's presentation of Pharsalia as a fatal point in time, a day of doom.[45] The day and place of *Pharsalia* puts an end to the temporal and spatial march of *Annales*.

This discussion of 9.980–6 and the matter of the name of the poem is intended as introductory; many of the threads I have picked up here will be pursued further in the coming pages and chapters. In a similar way, while I have presented here a case for the name *Pharsalia* standing in assertive opposition to the titles *Iliad* and *Annales*, my ensuing consideration of the importance of Lucan's engagement with these poems should offer additional support for what to call the poem.

1.3. Beginning at and against the beginnings: 1.1–32

Another point of entry into the arguments explored in this study is the most natural—and necessary—one: the proem (1.1–7) and subsequent apostrophe to Roma and her citizens (1.8–32). I follow Book 1's most recent commentator in dividing up the lines in this way;[46] but, as will become clear from what follows, I think it is important to read 1.1–32 as a cohesive introductory unit, in which Lucan presents his poetic agenda of both destruction of and lament for epic's foundational texts. The first seven lines show straightaway the importance of Ennius and Homer as models:

bella per Emathios plus quam ciuilia campos
iusque datum sceleri canimus, populumque potentem
in sua uictrici conuersum uiscera dextra
cognatasque acies, et rupto foedere regni
certatum totis concussi uiribus orbis   5
in commune nefas, infestisque obuia signis
signa, pares aquilas et pila minantia pilis.

Of wars greater than civil throughout the Emathian fields and law given
over to crime we sing, and of a powerful people turned on its own innards

---
[45] See Joseph (2017a) and Chapter 3.
[46] Roche (2009) 10–11.

with a victorious right hand, of kindred battle-lines, and—after the
bursting of a pact for power—of a contest for shared wrong, fought with
all the strength of the shaken world, and of standards opposing enemy
standards, of matching eagles and of spears threatening spears.

The proem is one long sentence, with the verb *canimus* taking as its objects the series of markers of civil war and Roman self-destruction in lines 1–7. In rapid-fire fashion, Lucan makes it clear that this poem is about lawlessness (line 2) and unrelenting self-slaughter (lines 2–4 and 6–7), a Roman horror story that is both intimate and familial (lines 3–4) and global in its scale (line 5). The proem ends with a drawn-out image of mirroring battle lines (6–7), concluding with "spears threatening spears" (*pila minantia pilis*). A ninth-century commentary on the poem, the *Commenta Bernensia*, compares these lines with the otherwise unattested Ennian verse *pila retunduntur uenientibus obuia pilis* ("spears opposing arriving spears are beaten back"; *Ann.* 582).[47] These are the only two passages I have found in the Latin corpus that include a form of *pilum*, the heavy spear or javelin characteristic of Italian combat, paired with another form of *pilum*. Lucan's use of *obuia* to modify *signa* in the preceding phrase (1.5–6) also echoes Ennius's use of *obuia* in the same metrical position in *Ann.* 582.

Lucan has thus included, as the final, crowning element of the contents of his poem, an image of combat from Ennius's *Annales*. The choice is striking. Skutsch notes that previous editors placed this fragment amid Ennius's account of Rome's early war with Alba.[48] But he also mentions that both Spanish and Gallic soldiers used a *pilum*, and, moreover, that the term may be translated more generically as "spear." Whatever the case, a fundamental contrast between the contexts in the *Pharsalia* and the *Annales* is clear. Ennius most certainly included the detail in an account of Roman expansion (be it within Italy or against a Spanish or Gallic enemy), whereas Lucan puts the memorable image to use specifically and pointedly for the self-destructive practice of civil war.

Right at the outset of the poem, then, Lucan introduces himself as a poet who employs Ennius's images of Roman conquest but redirects them inward, onto themselves. The adaptation of the modifier applied to *pila* enhances this

---

[47] Noted by Skutsch (1968) 23 and (1985) 16 and Narducci (2002) 19–20.
[48] See Keith (2016) 161–2 on the possibility that Ennius represented Alba as both a proto-Rome and an anti-Rome.

transformation of the Ennian material. With *uenientibus*, Ennius had personified one side's spears, which "arrive" and in the syntax of the sentence are given the agency to beat back opposing spears. Lucan also uses a present active participle as a modifier, but his spears now threaten (*minantia*). They not only have life and confront each other, but they dare to *speak*, verbalizing the unspeakable *nefas* of civil war introduced in the preceding line (1.6).[49] And here in the proem these *pila* speak ominously of—indeed threaten the reader with—more self-destructive poetic inversions to come.

This unmistakable allusion anchors a connection with the *Annales* and compels the reader to look in the opening lines for further connections with Ennius's epic. For one, we note that the main character of the poem is not an individual hero but the collective "powerful people" (*populumque potentem*, 1.2) who had been the driving engine of the *Annales*.[50] And as Ennius did in his epic, Lucan straightaway places the character of the *populus* on a global stage. Within a few lines he zooms out from the central battle site of the "Emathian fields" (1.1) to announce that "all the strength of a shaken world" (1.5) will fight in this contest.[51] The world will fight and be fought for in the *Pharsalia*. In the address to Rome and her citizens that follows, the narrator decries the loss of global sway that will result from Rome's civil wars (1.9–23).[52] Here, in picturing Rome's potential imperial reach to all regions of the earth, Lucan figures space and time closely together. East and West are marked as the areas of day's arrival and night's dwelling (1.15), the South as the place where "midday burns with its flaming hours" (1.16), and the North as the domain of winter or, more precisely, the winter solstice (*bruma*, 1.17). What emerges is a picture of Roman conquest as simultaneously spatial and temporal, the two dimensions inextricably tied together. This passage also impresses upon the reader that the conquest of bodies of water was pivotal to Roman control of the world. "Land and sea" (*terrae . . . pelagique*, 1.13) were Rome's for the taking, and for three of the four locations Lucan names, he evokes bodies of water: the Black Sea in Scythia (1.18), the Araxes River in Armenia, and then, most enticingly, the Nile's source.

But the passage is a biting counterfactual. The result of the civil wars Lucan will narrate was the opposite of expansion, the opposite of the spatiotemporal

---

[49] See Henderson (1987) 140 on Lucan's personification of weapons.
[50] As I will explore in Chapter 3. Bowra (1966) 558–9 writes of the novelty of this collective main character in the epics of Naevius and Ennius.
[51] See Roche (2009) 96 on this progression.
[52] See Serena (2020) 111–13.

march that Ennius's epic had launched. Here in the *Pharsalia* is contraction, the redirection of the *populus*'s energy not outward but rather "turned on its own innards with a victorious right hand" (*populumque potentem | in sua . . . conuersum uiscera*, 1.2–3). The loss is not only of opportunities for foreign conquest, but also of Italy itself, a theme Lucan develops at 1.24–32, a picture of the contemporary Italian countryside a century after the Battle of Pharsalia as neglected, barely populated, and dilapidated. Readers have emphasized how the passage reads as a reversal of the anticipations of Italian growth and eventual prosperity at *Aeneid* 6.771–6 and 8.347–50.[53] The latter passage comes during Aeneas's visit to the future site of Rome, when the narrator, from his perspective in the first century BCE, describes the Capitoline Hill as "golden now, but once rough with woodland bushes" (*aurea nunc, olim silvestribus horrida dumis*, *Aen*. 8.348). Lucan's adaptation of Virgil's phrasing reads:

> horrida quod dumis multosque inarata per annos
> Hesperia est desuntque manus poscentibus aruis,
>
> . . . now that Hesperia is rough with bushes and has gone unplowed for
> many years; and hands are lacking, though the fields demand them.
> (*Ph*. 1.28–9)

In the aftermath of the civil wars, Italy has reverted to the rough, uncultivated state that Virgil pictured in *Aeneid* 8. This sense of reversion to a pre-Roman and pre-Virgilian state is accompanied by a gesture further back, to Ennius, as the word *Hesperia* evokes specifically Ennius's Italy. It first appears in *Annales* 1, in an ecphrasis beginning with the powerfully direct and forward-looking line "There is a place that mortals used to call 'Hesperia'" (*Ann*. 20: *est locus Hesperiam quam mortales perhibebant*).[54] The toponym is, as Nora Goldschmidt has put it, "Ennius' name for Italy."[55] The tense of *perhibebant* conveys that it was already an *old* name for the peninsula, as,

---

[53] See Roche (2009) 124–5.
[54] Cited by Macrob. (6.1.11) as the model for Virg., *Aen*. 1.530 (*est locus Hesperiam Grai cognomine dicunt* = *Aen*. 3.163). See Mayer (1986) 52–3 on Ennius's apparent introduction of the noun *Hesperia* into Latin. Elliott (2013) 92 writes that *Ann*. 20 "has a clear place in the construction of [the Roman epic] tradition by virtue of its use of language that becomes quasi-prescriptive in the Roman tradition for the introduction of that Homerising feature, the ecphrasis."
[55] Goldschmidt (2013) 132.

by Ennius's time, the term *Italia* had come to replace it.⁵⁶ Indeed, Homer and subsequent Greek authors had used the adjective ἑσπέριος to mean "western," and so to refer to the peoples of the western Mediterranean with this word (*LSJ* II; see, e.g., *Od.* 8.29). In *Annales* 1 Ennius made this Homeric word his own, transforming it into *Hesperia* and bringing it into Latin epic.

Whereas Ennius began the process of telling Hesperia's story in Latin epic, Lucan now narrates its devastation and end in the *Pharsalia*. While the elder poet channeled Homer to sing of Hesperia's growth and ascendancy on the world stage, Lucan—as we have seen in 1.9–32—is now chronicling Hesperia's failure to expand further and in fact its shrinkage, back into a primitive and lifeless state.⁵⁷ The *Annales* had figured Roman expansion as simultaneously temporal and spatial, charting Roman growth over the years and over the lands and seas. We saw that at *Ph.* 1.15–18 Lucan presents the reversal of that expansion in similar terms. In this light, it may also be significant that he describes *Hesperia* as "unplowed for many years" (*multosque inarata per annos | Hesperia*, 1.28–9). The phrase *multos...per annos* is not itself extraordinary,⁵⁸ but its alignment with *Hesperia* may underscore Lucan's gesture toward the *Annales*, as Roman time, conceptualized in the passing of years, and the pregnant space of Hesperia are construed together. But in place of that land's cultivation and expansion over time comes its collapse into a wasteland that lies uncultivated for many years.

I am suggesting that Lucan announces here at the outset of his poem an agenda of reversing the *Annales*' narrative of expansion, its *pila* repurposed for self-destruction, its collective *populus* now turned against itself,⁵⁹ its story of Hesperia's growth brought to a grim and ongoing end. And if he is holding up the *Annales* as an anti-model, then the names with which he concludes this introductory passage may also be significant:

non tu, Pyrrhe ferox, nec tantis cladibus auctor   30
Poenus erit: nulli penitus descendere ferro
contigit; alta sedent ciuilis uolnera dextrae.

---

[56] Skutsch (1985) 179.
[57] It is noteworthy that Lucan uses *Hesperia* 20 times and *Italia* just 7 times. Contrast the ratio of usage in the *Aen.*, in which *Italia* appears 44 times and *Hesperia* 13 times. See Hunink (1992) 31.
[58] Lucan uses it again at 5.69 and 5.472. See also, e.g., in hexameter, Lucr. 1.1029 and 5.95; Virg. *G.* 2.208 and 4.208, *Aen.* 1.31, 2.363, 2.715, 7.60, 9.85; and Sil., 4.678 and 14.84.
[59] Note *conuersum* in 1.3, with my further discussion in the ensuing pages.

You, fierce Pyrrhus, will not prove to be the cause of such great disasters,
nor will the Punic one. No other sword could go down so thoroughly: the
wounds that lie deep are from a citizen's hand.

Let us recall that this passage as a whole is addressed to Rome's citizens (1.8), and the narrator concludes it by underscoring the responsibility of these citizens' hands for the nation's destruction (at 1.32 as at 1.14). But rather than naming any culpable Roman individuals here—at this point in the poem Caesar, Pompey, and Cato all remain unnamed[60]—he calls to mind Pyrrhus and "the Punic one," Hannibal. Rome's defeat of these two generals, its most formidable enemies during the Republican expansion, was perhaps most famously told in Book 6 and then Books 7–9 of the *Annales*.[61] Paul Roche notes that *ferox* is an unexpected epithet for Pyrrhus, given that many sources emphasize his concern for justice and efforts at peacemaking. But he also notes that Ennius characterizes Pyrrhus's army as "the stolid race of the descendants of Aeacus; men more powerful in war (*bellipotentes*) than powerful in wisdom" (*Ann.* 197)[62] and thus suggests that the *Annales* is the source for Lucan's phrase *Pyrrhe ferox*.

Whether or not there is an Ennian allusion in that phrase, the evocation of Pyrrhus and then Hannibal may be a further development of the Ennian reversal I have suggested. It is not just that the events of Lucan's poem will undo the story of Rome's victories over these celebrated foes and the resulting expansion. In the case of Hannibal and Carthage, Lucan will narrate a pointed reversal and the vengeful victory of Carthage. This narrative turnabout is one particularly prominent theme in his narration of the halt of Roman sea prowess (recall 1.13 and 1.18–20), whose growth was central to the earliest Latin epic poems (as I will explore in Chapter 4). But beyond the theme of reversal of imperial sway, at 1.30–32 the narrator expresses remorse that Pyrrhus and Hannibal were *not* the ones to prevail over Rome: their victories would have been *less* devastating. Only Roman hands (1.32, as at 1.3) could have inflicted wounds

---

[60] So far only the ghost of Crassus has been named, at 1.11.

[61] On the (less than certain) placement of Ennius's account of the conflict with Carthage in Books 7–9, see Elliott (2013) 298–300 and (2014) 230. See Fantham (2006) on the afterlife of Ennius's account of the Pyrrhic War; and my discussion in Chapter 4 of the influence of Ennius's telling of the Hannibalic War.

[62] Roche (2009) 127–8. See too Pyrrhus's call to "not barter war but wage war" (*non cauponantes bellum sed belligerantes*) at *Ann.* 184. Prinzen (1998) 335 also regards Lucan's inclusion of Pyrrhus and Hannibal as Ennian.

this deep. Only a story like the *Pharsalia* could undo the Roman success story launched by the *Annales*.

I move now to the polemical engagement with Homer that runs concurrently through 1.1–32. That Lucan sought to evoke and contest the Smyrnaean bard head-on becomes clear from a number of structural and dictional features in these lines.[63] Both the *Iliad* and the *Pharsalia* open with a proem consisting of one seven-line sentence, followed in line 8 by a question initiated by the cognates *tis* / *quis*:

Τίς τ' ἄρ σφωε θεῶν ἔριδι ξυνέηκε μάχεσθαι;
Who of the gods brought them together to battle in rivalry? (*Il.* 1.8)

Quis furor, o ciues, quae tanta licentia ferri? (*Ph.* 1.8)
What was this madness, citizens, what was this great license of the sword?

Just like Homer, Lucan begs for an explanation for the strife and conflict that will follow in his poem.[64] But he looks for answers from humans, not the gods, a difference that runs in parallel with the adaptation of Ennius's *pila . . . pilis* in the previous line, as here too "the outward energy of epic is redirected back inwards, to the citizens who are the subject (and the audience) of the poem."[65] We will see that this type of redirection of energy, action, and violence from foundational texts back inward is pervasive in the *Pharsalia*, speaking to both the poem's content and, I will argue, its poetic agenda of closure of the epic tradition.

The *Iliad* and *Pharsalia* also both begin with a *propositio*, a word broadly characterizing the tale to come. Lucan chooses the sweeping *bella*, while the rage (*menis*, *Il.* 1.1) that Homer makes the driving force of the *Iliad* will be picked up by Lucan's *furor* in 1.8. Readers have drawn parallels between the wrathful personal feuds that drive the action of both epics, with the contention that the rage Achilles feels toward his Greek ally Agamemnon is akin to the madness that motivates Caesar against his countryman and kinsman Pompey.[66] But a contrast in the ultimate direction of these deadly emotions is again what distinguishes the poems: whereas Achilles's rage will in time

---

[63] See Conte (1988) 11–23 (= [1966]) and Roche (2009) 94–7.
[64] The faulting of *furor* and the plaintive, interrogative tone in 1.8 may also be influenced by Horace, *Epod.* 7.
[65] Feeney (1991) 275.
[66] See Lausberg (1985) 1582–3; Green (1991) 234–8; and Christophorou (2017) 355.

be directed outward toward Hector and eventually find resolution in his meeting with Priam in the *Iliad*'s final book, the *furor* of the *Pharsalia* continues its inward drive, among Rome's citizens. In the same way, while the *propositio bella* indicates that Lucan's poem follows squarely in the Iliadic tradition, the addition of *plus quam ciuilia* shows right away that the violence in this epic will not only be directed inward, upon its citizens, but will also be exponentially expansive—*plus quam*—in its spread.

Lucan's proem also announces the poem's engagement with Odyssean themes. Let us recall the opening three lines:

bella per Emathios plus quam ciuilia campos
iusque datum sceleri canimus, populumque potentem
in sua uictrici conuersum uiscera dextra

The two phrases *bella . . . ciuilia* and *populumque potentem* pick up on Virgil's *arma uirumque* (*Aen.* 1.1), itself an announcement that the *Aeneid* would incorporate both Iliadic battle narrative (*arma*) and the Odyssean tale of an individual man's (*uirum*) journey. So, while marking succession of Virgil's epic, Lucan's programmatic pair *bella . . . populumque* surely also heralds his engagement with both Iliadic and Odyssean themes.[67] A notable difference from the *Odyssey* as well as the *Aeneid* lies in the collective identity of Lucan's central hero. The singular and eponymous man of Homer's (*andra*, *Od.* 1.1) and subsequently Virgil's epics is expanded in the *Pharsalia* into the Roman people, the *populus Romanus* as a unit.

I argued earlier that Lucan's casting of the collective *populus* as his main character follows Ennius's practice, only to tell a self-destructive story that counters the Roman story of the *Annales*. That same phrase contains a pointed, anchoring inversion of the *Odyssey*'s hero, in the description of the Roman populace as "turned back on its own innards with a victorious right hand" (1.3). This jarring image of Roman suicide has at its center the perfect participle *conuersum*, meaning "thoroughly turned" or "turned back." It thus emerges, after *potentem* in 1.2, as a sort of second epithet for *populum*, announcing the inward-turning self-destruction of the Ennian story, but also recalling the definitive epithet for Odysseus introduced in the opening line of the *Odyssey* and then used throughout the poem: πολύτροπος, "much turned / much turning." In the launch of epic at Rome, Livius Andronicus had

[67] See the discussion by Lebek (1976) 18–36.

translated Homer's *polutropos* with *uersutus*, opening his *Odusia* with: *uirum mihi, Camena, insece uersutum* ("Tell me, Camena, of the 'turned' / versatile man," fr. 1).[68] Lucan's *conuersum* is an even closer translation of *polutropos*, with *con-* capturing the intensifying force of *polu-*, his Roman people cast as markedly Odyssean in the twists and turns they will endure. Moreover, *conuerto* is a literary-critical term used for the acts of both translation (*OLD* 9; see, e.g., Cic. *Opt. Gen.* 18 and *Fin.* 1.5; Sen. *Suas.* 7.12; and Suet. *Rhet.* 25) and interpretation (*OLD* 10; see esp. Pl. *Poen.* 1321; Cic. *de Orat.* 2.257; and Quint. *Decl.* 313).[69] With *conuersum* Lucan is being boldly explicit: he does not want the reader to miss this declaration of his "turning over" and transformation of Odyssean themes.

For the story of the Roman people in the *Pharsalia* is, like that of Odysseus, a tale "of many turns." And while Lucan does not apply a form of *conuerto* to the Roman people again, the "progression of adjectives and participles applied to the *populus Romanus* throughout *BC* is indicative of their dislocation from power to servitude."[70] Their course in the *Pharsalia* is one of travail, subjugation, loss, and death. Indeed, the sense of self-reflexivity in Lucan's phrase *in sua uictrici conuersum uiscera dextra* may well draw upon the ambiguity in the epithet *polutropos*, whose voice is famously difficult to pin down, as Odysseus both twists and turns much and is much twisted and turned.[71] While the morphology of *conuersum* is passive, it modifies a noun (*populum*) which itself is the agent of that turning against, which itself delivers the blow upon its own innards (*in sua ... uiscera*). Like Odysseus, but on a grander and more gruesome scale, Lucan's *populus* is simultaneously acting and acted upon. But there lies a fundamental difference in the ultimate destinations for Homer's and Lucan's heroes, the places where their many turns take them. As I will explore in Chapter 5, there are no successful *nostoi* in the *Pharsalia*, either individually or collectively. Lucan crafts the stories of each of his central characters, Caesar, Pompey, and Cato, as journeys without homecomings, odysseys without the fulfillment that Homer's Odysseus eventually attains. In a similar way, the Roman people are left lost and homeless, a theme

---

[68] For *uersutus* as an epithet for Odysseus, see too Hyginus, *Fabulae* 201.4.4, as well as Quint. 6.3.96, quoting an Odyssean pun by Cicero about a certain Lartius, described as *hominem callidum et uersutum*. See Hinds (1998) 61; McElduff (2013) 52-3; and Feeney (2016) 53-4 on Livius's *uersutus* as a marker of his process of translation and transformation.

[69] On *conuerto* see further McElduff (2013) 42-3.

[70] Roche (2009) 103.

[71] Loney (2019) 31 discusses the inclusion in the proem of the *Od.* of both active and passive verbs and verbal forms to characterize Odysseus.

introduced here at the poem's outset in the description of the contemporary Italian wasteland at 1.24–8, with its "homes maintained by no keeper" (*nulloque domus custode tenentur*, 1.26). The Roman populace's journey in this poem leads not to homecoming but to its opposite.

A prominent theme in the proems of both the *Iliad* and the *Odyssey*, which Lucan then stretches out to maximum effect, is the devastation of the broader community. The long relative clause at *Iliad* 1.2–5 details the bloody cost in human life brought on by Achilles's rage, and *Odyssey* 1.6–9 highlights Odysseus's failure to bring home his Ithacan companions. These communal sufferings carry through both poems, though each ultimately renders some resolution and, however briefly, a measure of peace for the heroes: Achilles in *Iliad* 22–24 and then Odysseus in *Odyssey* 22–24. In the *Pharsalia*, devastation of the larger community is all. The recklessness that destroyed Odysseus's companions (ἀτασθαλίῃσιν, *Od*. 1.7) recurs in the *Pharsalia* (note *iusque datum sceleri* at 1.2 and especially *tanta licentia* at 1.8), but here it does in the entire *dramatis personae*, heroes and all. The gore and human carrion pictured so memorably at *Iliad* 1.4–5 occupy the entirety of Lucan's proem and then his poem. Here there are no outlying individuals, escape hatches, or respites.

The unspeakable sufferings of the *Pharsalia* are definitively communal, as the phrase *commune nefas* in 1.6 makes clear. Here Lucan also introduces the mode of response to collective suffering that was integral to Homeric epic: communal, antiphonal lament. The address at 1.8–32 contains many of the hallmarks of the Homeric *goos* that we will see employed across the ensuing poem. First, there is the conventional address to the deceased (*ciues*, 1.8), which the narrator renews with variation at 1.21 (*Roma*). As in traditional *gooi*, there is a focus on contrasts, here between past imperial success (an undercurrent at 1.9–23) and present woe (1.24–9), a contrast cued by the familiar marker *at nunc* (1.24). These lines about the abiding devastation in Italy also express, in keeping with the conventions of lament, that the mourner (the narrator living under Caesarism some 100 years after Pharsalia) shares a common fate with his deceased addressees. Also captured in 1.8–32 is a clear sense of Rome's past might and magnificence—the praise of the dead that is conventional to lament. The narrator's lament, while decrying the decayed, deathly state of Rome and her citizens, at the same time imparts *kleos* to the deceased.[72]

---

[72] See my further discussion of this passage and of lament in the poem in Chapter 6.

The opening 32 lines as a whole, then, showcase the dialectic between communal self-destruction and the communal lament that must accompany, respond to, and process that destruction. And while the Homeric poems had introduced lament as a collective, antiphonal activity, Lucan boldly adds the voice of the narrator to this antiphony. He announces this agenda in the address to fellow citizens at 1.8–32 and, earlier still, when defining his poetic act in 1.2 with the word *canimus*, which immediately identifies the process of singing about the horrors of civil war as both personal and shared. The first-person plural form conspicuously distinguishes itself from Virgil's singular *cano* (*Aen.* 1.1)[73] and signals the plurality and broad inclusiveness of singing/lamenting voices in the coming work. At the same time, the present tense of *canimus* marks the experience and fate of the narrator as coterminous with that of his fellow mourners, the poem's characters. This blending of the narrator and the poem's characters in an expansive, lamenting "we," subjected to a common fate as Romans, will carry across the epic.

I have highlighted how the *Pharsalia*'s opening lines announce Lucan's engagement with and audacious break from foundational epic predecessors Ennius and Homer. But perhaps the most striking break comes in his omission of the Muse or Muses, the divine force that gives voice to the epic genre.[74] The *Iliad* and the *Odyssey* begin with invocations of the Muse, and the practice was followed, with variation, when epic came to Rome.[75] Livius opened his *Odusia* with an address to the Roman water divinity *Camena* (fr. 1); Naevius invoked the "nine harmonious sisters, daughters of Jove" (*nouem Iouis concordes filiae sorores*, fr. 1);[76] and Ennius explicitly embraced the Homeric tradition when transliterating the Greek *Mousai* and calling on the "Muses who beat great Olympus with their feet" (*Musae, quae pedibus magnum pulsatis Olympum, Ann.* 1) and invoking the Muse again in Book 10 (*Ann.* 322: *insece Musa*).[77] The second-century BCE poet Pompilius describes Ennius as a student of the Muses (*discipulus . . . Musarum*),[78] and poets in the later Latin epic tradition take up this discipleship. There is, to be sure,

---

[73] *Pace* Fratantuono (2012) 1, emphasizing continuity between Virgil's *cano* and Lucan's *canimus*.
[74] Feeney (1991) 275: "His proem is immediately startling for the comprehensiveness of its disavowal of inspiration."
[75] See the verses by Porcius Licinius (fr. 1 Courtney) on the arrival of the Muse at Rome: *bello Poenico secundo Musa pinnato gradu | intulit se bellicosam in Romuli gentem feram*. See further the discussion at 144 n. 8.
[76] Whether as Italic *Camenae* or as Greekizing *Musae* remains a matter of debate; see Skutsch (1985) 373 n. 4.
[77] He also refers to the Muses at *Ann.* 208, 293, and 487.
[78] See n. 59 in the Introduction.

ongoing variation and innovation: Lucretius will wait until the final book of the *DRN* to call on the Muses (6.92–5), though he opens by invoking Venus (1.1–61); Virgil leads with the assertive first-person *cano* and postpones the invocation itself until *Aeneid* 1.8 (*Musa, mihi causas memora*); and at the opening of the *Metamorphoses* Ovid does not call on the Muses explicitly, but on a broader collective of gods (*di*, 1.2; see the explicit invocation at 15.622). In the *Pharsalia*'s proem, there is nothing: no Muse, no gods whatsoever invoked—an absence made all the more conspicuous by the numerous evocations of Homer's, Ennius's, and Virgil's proems. The divine entity who was the vehicle for epic poetry, its constitutive source, its *prima origo*, is omitted, rejected. Lucan develops this rejection in his wry appeal to Nero and the Neronian principate as the source of his inspiration (1.63–6).[79] If anyone is an appropriate Muse for a Roman poem of this sort, it is Nero.

Lucan's first address is not to the Muse but to his fellow citizens. Line eight (*quis furor, o ciues, quae tanta licentia ferri?*) clearly recalls the questions posed to the Muse by Homer at *Iliad* 1.8 (see earlier discussion) and Virgil at *Aeneid* 1.8 (*Musa, mihi causas memora, quo numine laeso*).[80] Lucan's conspicuous redirection towards *ciues* underscores his move away from the stance of the distanced narrator through whom the Muses speak[81] toward a subjective, engaged interaction with fellow Roman citizens[82]—most significantly in the communal process of lament. More broadly, this rejection and silencing of the Muse marks a sort of point of no return for epic. In light of the generic demand to call for divine inspiration, which goes back—through the likes of Virgil, Ennius, Naevius, and Livius—to Homer himself, the move is impossible to miss or to forget, its signal of closing and ending a tradition as stunning as it is clear-cut. It is unsurprising that Statius would have Calliope herself notice the move.

---

[79] See O'Higgins (1988) 216; Feeney (1991) 300–1; Martindale (1993) 71; Leigh (1997) 23–6; Roche (2009) 7–10; and Hardie (2013a) 229 on how the address to Nero fits with the dark view of the principate across the poem. See also the balanced discussion by O'Hara (2007) 132–6, as well as Closs (2020) 126–7 on the self-destructive figure of Phaethon here.

[80] Roche (2009) 110–11, noting that the narrator's diction in 1.8 also builds upon Laocoon's words at *Aen.* 2.42 (*o miseri, quae tanta insania, ciues?*) and Ascanius's reproach of the Trojan women at 5.670–1 (*quis furor iste nouus? quo nunc, quo tenditis . . . heu miserae ciues?*). Servius on *Aen.* 1.8 regards Lucan's arrangement of material in his opening lines as an (inferior) inversion (*Lucanus tamen ipsum ordinem inuertit*) of the order of proposition-invocation-narration established by Homer.

[81] Conte (1988) 16; see too Thorne (2016) 100 on this declaration of subjectivity.

[82] Henderson (1987) 149: "This is not the Homeric-Virgilian appeal to the Muse, but horror of the inconceivable and programmatic collapse of reader into character into text."

1.4. The apparition of "Roma" rejected: 1.183–205

The rejection of the Muse in the *Pharsalia*'s opening lines, I am proposing, constitutes nothing less than a closing of epic, a declaration of Lucan's plan to silence and end the genre. With this move in mind, I want to close this chapter by reconsidering another early programmatic passage, Caesar's entrance into Italy and encounter with the *imago* of the goddess Patria/Roma at the Rubicon (1.183–205). This is the very first episode in the poem's narrative: Caesar's—and the epic's—first act is to cross over from Gaul with his army and invade Italy, formally initiating the war against his senatorial enemies. The appearance of an apparition at the Rubicon likely existed in one of Lucan's sources, as there are comparable episodes in both Plutarch's (*Caes.* 32) and Suetonius's (*Jul.* 32) *Lives* of Caesar; and the *prosopopoeia* of Patria was a figure that went back to at least Cicero.[83] Lucan leverages the scene as a showpiece for his polemical engagement with his epic predecessors. It begins:

iam gelidas Caesar cursu superauerat Alpes
ingentisque animo motus bellumque futurum
ceperat. ut uentum est parui Rubiconis ad undas,   185
ingens uisa duci patriae trepidantis imago
clara per obscuram uoltu maestissima noctem
turrigero canos effundens uertice crines
caesarie lacera nudisque adstare lacertis
et gemitu permixta loqui: 'quo tenditis ultra?   190
quo fertis mea signa, uiri? si iure uenitis,
si ciues, huc usque licet.'

Caesar had already conquered the chilly Alps in his march and had taken up in his mind huge undertakings and the war that was to come. As he came to the waves of the little Rubicon, the huge image of the Fatherland, trembling, seemed to be present, clear in the dark night, most mournful in her face, pouring out white hair from her towered head, her locks torn and arms bare, and, with a groan mixed in, she seemed to say, "Where further

---

[83] See *Cat.* 1.17–18 and 4.18, with Bernstein (2011) 261 and Narducci (2002) 194–207, on this and other depictions of *Patria* that may have informed Lucan; see Masters (1992) 1–10 and Kimmerle (2015) 221–32 and 262 on the metapoetics of this passage.

are you heading? To where are you taking my standards, men? If you are coming lawfully, if you are coming as citizens, you are permitted to come up to this point." (*Ph.* 1.183–192)

It is an arresting way for Lucan to open his story: Caesar's huge undertakings (*ingentisque . . . motus*) compel the huge figure (*ingens . . . imago*) of the apparition of Patria (or Roma, as Caesar will call her at 1.200) to stand in his way.[84] With the stakes high, Lucan heightens them further—for both his story and his poetic agenda—with a number of evocative echoes. Readers have focused on the recollection of *Aeneid* 2.268–97, where Hector's ghost appears to Aeneas and hands over leadership of the Trojan cause. Each apparition is "most mournful" (*maestissimus*, *Aen.* 2.270; *maestissima*, *Ph.* 1.187), visibly disheveled (*Aen.* 2.277 and *Ph.* 1.189), and groaning (a form of *gemitus* at *Ph.* 1.190 and *Aen.* 2.288).[85] Moreover, "in both cases a figure representative of the nation confronts the hero at the outset of a national disaster and warns him away from the fatherland."[86] But while Virgil's Aeneas heeds the advice of the apparition, Lucan's Caesar emphatically does not. After pausing on the bank of the Rubicon (1.192–4), Caesar addresses a number of deities (1.195–203)[87] and concludes by commanding Roma to favor his undertakings (*Roma, faue coeptis*, 1.200). Her prohibitions in 1.190–2 and her divine authority (he addresses her as *summique o numinis instar* in 1.199) are thus briskly brushed aside, and Caesar hastily moves his men across the river (1.204–5).

In order to understand the poetic statement that accompanies Caesar's bullying repudiation of the *imago patriae*, it is important to first grasp the metapoetic dynamics that are already operative in Lucan's model passage in *Aeneid* 2. There, in Hector's apparition to Aeneas, "the hero of the *Iliad* hands over to the hero of the *Aeneid*, just as the Roman Virgil takes over the epic mantle from Homer."[88] In that same moment Virgil signals his succession of Ennius, as Aeneas's dream of a weeping Hector also clearly recalls[89] Ennius's

---

[84] See Masters (1992) 1 and Day (2013) 120–4 on this encounter.
[85] See Conte (1988) 36–9; Roche (2009) 206–7; and Bernstein (2011) 261–2 on similarities in diction. The encouraging *imago* of Creusa (*Aen.* 2.771–95) offers another contrast with Lucan's Roma.
[86] Roche (2009) 206.
[87] Wheeler (2002) 371 notes that Caesar "anachronistically invokes the same Augustan gods (195–200) that Ovid prays to on behalf of Augustus at the end of the *Metamorphoses* (15.861–67)" and suggests that the parallel is programmatic of Lucan's use of Ovidian language and themes. Absent from Ovid's list, but paramount in Lucan's, is Roma herself.
[88] Hardie (1993) 102.
[89] Note esp. *Aen.* 2.271 (*uisus adesse*) echoing *Ann.* 3 (*uisus Homerus adesse* poeta). See Skutsch (1985) 155–6 on the inheritance of this Ennian passage in Lucr. and Virg.

dream of a weeping Homer, who appears at the outset of the *Annales* and passes his soul to a receptive and indeed dutiful (*o pietas animi, Ann.* 4 = Cic., *Acad.* 2.88) Ennius. The most detailed description of this celebrated[90] moment in the *Annales* is Lucretius's at *De Rerum Natura* 1.124–6:

> unde sibi exortam semper florentis Homeri
> commemorat speciem lacrimas effundere salsas
> coepisse et rerum naturam expandere dictis.

> there [Ennius] recalls that the appearance of Homer, ever flourishing, came to him and began to pour out salty tears and to expound with words on the nature of things. (*DRN* 1.124–6)

By using Aeneas's dream to recall this famous dream and the transfer of poetic authority that it signaled, Virgil suggests, in one fraught but forward-looking scene, his own succession of both Homer and Homer's Roman successor.[91]

Pharsalia 1.185–92 revisits this very same nexus of models but offers a radically different response to them. Lucan's Caesar dismisses the apparition's orders, and the coinciding metapoetic statement operates in parallel, flagging and rejecting the Virgilian adherence to the Homeric and Ennian traditions. For, as he evokes the *Aeneid* 2 passage and its Homeric-Ennian-Virgilian trajectory, Lucan points us directly to Ennius's celebrated moment of succession in the *Annales*. The description of Roma's epiphany (*ingens uisa duci patriae trepidantis imago . . . adstare*, 1.186 and 1.189) recalls both Virgil's *uisus adesse* (*Aen.* 2.270–1) and its model, Ennius's *uisus Homerus adesse* poeta (*Ann.* 3). Moreover, if, as Skutsch concludes, "Lucretius clearly follows Ennius's words very closely,"[92] then Lucan's word for Roma's act of mourning, *effundens* (1.188), follows not only Virgil's *effundere* (*Aen.* 2.271) but also Ennius's use of that same form to describe the apparition of Homer (*DRN* 1.125). But whereas Ennius's Homer and Virgil's Hector pour out tears, Roma pours out her "white hair" (*canos . . . crines*, 1.188), a marker of old age that underscores a contrast with Ennius's ever-thriving Homer, described at *DRN* 1.124 with the phrase *semper florentis*. Lucan may counter that phrase in yet another way through the description of Roma as *trepidantis*

---

[90] See Skutsch (1985) 147–67 on fragments and testimonia of the dream.
[91] Hardie (1993) 103
[92] Skutsch (1985) 155.

(1.186), a word analogous in form to *florentis* but contrary in meaning. The epithet *turrigero* (1.188), which brings to mind the compounds common in Ennius,[93] on its own might suggest Roma's vitality and promise[94] – but the word is surrounded by markers of aging, decrepitude, and grief. While Roma still wears a look of strength, she is hardly thriving, but old, in distress, and under attack.[95]

If at 1.185–92 Lucan is evoking not just *Aeneid* 2.268–97 but, together with it, the famous episode from *Annales* 1, then the metapoetic statement emerges as much broader and bolder. Ennius's achievement was to piously absorb Homer, make him flourish forever (recall *semper florentis Homeri*, *DRN* 1.124), and bring the conventions and grandeur of Homeric poetry to the story of Rome.[96] In the opening episode of Lucan's epic, Roma— metapoetically, "the story of Rome"—is not just weeping but trembling, old, helpless. Rome's story, dutifully brought into Homeric epic by Ennius and long prosperous in that tradition, is nearing its infirm end. And when we consider that the address of the city's deity as *Roma* may itself be an "Ennian touch,"[97] then a direct confrontation with the *Annales* emerges even more clearly. Poet and character march in lockstep in their impious attack on the "forbidden fields of Hesperia / the story of Hesperia" (*Hesperiae uetitis ... aruis*, 1.224; recall the programmatic *Ann*. 20): as Caesar rejects Roma's laws and traditions, Lucan rejects the continuation of the story of Rome, together with the process of epic succession that brought Homeric laws and traditions to the story of Rome. When Caesar dismisses the *imago patriae* (1.186), Lucan, far from exhibiting the poetic *pietas* of Ennius (*Ann*. 4), rejects *pater Ennius* and the entire patrilineal epic tradition.

Caesar's confrontation with the goddess at the Rubicon also and invariably reminds us of the exchanges and actions of earlier epic heroes. There is Aeneas's encounter with Tiberinus, who, very differently, encourages the arriving hero to cross his banks (*Aen*. 8.36–65). Homer's Achilles also comes to mind, as he and Lucan's Caesar share a brashness and ferocity; and in the latter's statement at the Rubicon, "Now let pacts (*foedera*) be far away from

---

[93] See Roche (2009) 139 on Lucan's not infrequent use of such compounds (*contra* Fantham [1992] 35).

[94] Servius (on *Aen*. 8.33) quotes this line as a case of *turrigerus* indicating "flourishing."

[95] Mulhern (2017) 449 suggests that the turret crown associates the deity with the look of Imperial, not Republican women.

[96] Elliott (2013), esp. 75–9, 249–51, 254–67, and 276–91.

[97] Thomas (2011) 141 on Horace's use of *o Roma* at *C*. 4.4.37, citing the *Scipio*, *Var*. 6 V. (= Cic., *De or*. 3.167 and *Fin*. 2.106).

here" (*procul hinc iam foedera sunto*, 1.226), we may hear an echo of Achilles's ruthless and repeated rejection of pacts (*orkia*) with Hector at *Iliad* 22.262-6. But when we look at Achilles's encounters at bodies of water in the *Iliad*, it is pointed differences from what transpires at the Rubicon that emerge, as Homer's hero, for all his celebrated strength and stubbornness, is either bested or obedient on these occasions. When he takes on the Scamander in *Iliad* 21, he is ultimately repelled by the river (21.248-71). And, most meaningfully for the set piece at the Rubicon in *Pharsalia* 1, there is Achilles's meeting with his divine mother Thetis on the seashore at *Iliad* 1.348-427. Carin Green has shown how this passage operates as a meaningful anti-model for *Ph*. 1.183-227. Whereas Achilles waits by the sea for Thetis (1.348-51), Caesar—after a moment of delay on the riverbank (1.194)—of course races over the Rubicon against Roma's orders. And while Thetis promises to speak to Zeus on Achilles's behalf (1.425-7), Caesar responds to Roma's prohibitions by turning to address Jupiter himself (1.195-8). In short, though similarities in character lead us to align these two headstrong heroes, Achilles's obedience to his divine mother meets a pointed contrast in Caesar's disobedience to his divine mother-city.[98] The identification of this Homeric inversion spotlights Caesar's act at the Rubicon as a repudiation of a maternal figure, with the result that multiple layers of Caesar's—and Lucan's—irreverence emerge: the dismissal of *Patria* and crossing of the Rubicon amount to a rejection of father(land) *and* mother, of tradition and source as figured in both genders, of the process of (poetic) continuation and regeneration through either and thus any line. In the same motion, by introducing and then irreverently rejecting what proves to be the poem's one and only embodied divinity,[99] this passage affirms the *Pharsalia*'s wholesale dismissal of divine characters, who, beginning with Homer and then returning to epic again and again, had endowed the genre itself with a patina of immortality.

Of Roma's futile appeal to the law (*si iure uenitis*, 1.191) at this critical moment, Green writes: "This terrible violation of Roman law is also, in Lucan's poetry, the violation of the epic story . . . Caesar has not come in accordance with the law, not with the law of Rome, nor with the law of epic."[100] Caesar himself spells this out in his declaration soon afterwards, "I am abandoning

---

[98] Green (1991) 238-9. Lausberg (1985) 1589 contrasts Achilles's obedience to Athena in *Il*. 1. See too Narducci (2002) 195.
[99] Ahl (1976) 211 and Masters (1992) 8 ("Lucan . . . is disobeying the sacred command of a divine figure, and is hence as impious as Caesar").
[100] Green (1991) 239. See too Spentzou (2018) 249-50 on Caesar the violator here.

the laws" (*iura relinquo*, 1.225), a credo applying equally well to Lucan's poetics. This entire opening episode reinforces the redirections, inversions, and rejections of foundational epic laws and codes that had been announced in the proem and the narrator's opening address.

As in the proem, here at the Rubicon the poetic mode of rejection and transgression, of violence against the tradition, is accompanied by the mode of lament. Let us recall that the vision of Roma, like Virgil's Hector and Ennius's Homer, is mourning: "trembling" (1.186), "most mournful in her face" (1.187), and "pouring out white hair from her towered head, her locks torn and arms bare" (1.188–9).[101] This moment of destructive rule-breaking, of seismic changes for Rome and the Roman epic story, demands lament too; and the conceit of Roma herself—the personification of the collective *populus Romanus*, both enactor and victim of the poem's violence—offering lamentation deftly captures the tensions constitutive of Lucan's story and his poetics of closure. As clearly as anywhere in the *Pharsalia*, here in the opening scene the central and characteristically male practice of violent action and the conventionally marginal, characteristically female practice of lament coexist in one image. The female Roma weeps, as the male-led state that she represents—its doomed greatness again emphasized in *ingens*[102] at 1.186 and then *magnae . . . urbis* at 1.195—is attacked. Suffering both acts of closure in the same moment, Lucan's Roma is tautly microcosmic of the poem itself.

It is also significant that Roma's tears evoke but redirect the tears in the model texts we have considered. Let us recall that Ennius's Homer and Virgil's Hector not only weep for their own deaths, but also pass something on.[103] The perpetuation of a regenerative tradition is in fact the purpose of their appearances. In the *Pharsalia*, Roma/"the story of Rome" weeps for herself too, but because she *fails* in her objective to preserve herself. Her tears at 1.186–90 are proleptic—she knows this is a point of no return (1.190–2)—and in this prolepsis we may think again of the Thetis of *Iliad* 1. The meeting between Achilles and Thetis ends with the goddess shedding tears (*Il.* 1.413) and uttering words of anticipatory lament[104] for her doomed son (1.414–18). She imagines the alternative, a griefless life away from war and glory, and in doing so touches on the interconnectedness of *kleos* and lament, how the

---

[101] Roche (2009) 207 compares the language used of the grieving matrons at 2.28–42.
[102] See Harrison (1991) 95 on *ingens* as "the archetypal epic epithet."
[103] Skutsch (1985) 155–7, arguing that Ennius's Homer was weeping out of distress, nevertheless concludes: "We should certainly not seek the cause of Homer's grief in the lack of a worthy successor" (156).
[104] If not a *goos* per se, Thetis delivers a more formal anticipatory *goos* at *Il.* 18.52–64.

one always accompanies the other. The Roma of *Pharsalia* 1, in her own anticipatory lament for the self-destruction imminent for herself/Rome/the Roman story, embodies this interconnectedness of martial glory and lament in a necessarily self-reflexive way; as in the images that Lucan highlights in his proem, Roma directs each of these expressions inward, upon herself. This junction of inward-turned actions—(self-)destructive thunder, alongside (self-)lament for that very same destructiveness—is characteristic of the contents and the poetics of Lucan's epic. In the coming pages we will see these modes interact frequently, beginning in the next chapter with his engagement with the *topoi* of violence that lie at the genre's core.

2
Toppling *Topoi*: Epic's Violence Directed against Itself

In an influential essay titled "The Law of Genre," Derrida writes of the coexistence in literary genres of laws and of a resistance to or "closing" of those laws. Of these two elements he states:

> They form what I shall call the genre-clause, a clause stating at once the juridical utterance, the precedent-making designation and the law-text, but also the closure, the closing that excludes itself from what it includes (one could also speak of a floodgate [*écluse*] of genre). The clause or floodgate of genre declasses what it allows to be classed. It tolls the knell of genealogy or of genericity, which it however also brings forth to the light of day. Putting to death the very thing that it engenders, it cuts a strange figure; a formless form, it remains nearly invisible, it neither sees the day nor brings itself to light. Without it, neither genre nor literature come to light, but as soon as there is this blinking of an eye, this clause or this floodgate of genre, at the very moment that a genre or a literature is broached, at that very moment, degenerescence has begun, the end begins.[1]

Derrida's understanding of genre provides a helpful entry point for my consideration in this chapter of Lucan's deployment of certain epic *topoi* of violence. The characterization of genre as "[p]utting to death the very thing that it engenders" invites a particularly straightforward application to epic, since acts of physical violence and the resulting deaths are constitutive of epic narrative; conventional scenes of violence exist as building blocks of epic storytelling. In this chapter I consider how Lucan goes to familiar *loci* of violence and ending in the epic tradition, which are already fraught and fragile places, and marks his own poetic violence toward the tradition. His gestures, we will

---

[1] Derrida (1980) 65–6, who goes on to regard any set laws of genre as sources of madness (see esp. 81).

see, enact the possibility for degenerescence and closure that is already latent in epic's beginning texts.[2]

Each of the passages I will consider—the mutilation of a warrior's face in Book 2, the violation of a grove in Book 3, and the bloodied but defiant battlefield stand of a warrior in Book 6—has a rich and fluid literary history, going back to the Homeric poems. Each episode bears out Hinds's understanding of the "mobility and renegotiability"[3] of *topoi*; and in each, Lucan deftly engages with a number of model texts. Crucially, in all three *loci* we observe close and cutting confrontations with both Homeric conventions and Ennian adaptations of those conventions. Lucan goes to these moments in the Homeric poems and the *Annales* as pivotal epic beginning-points, and he brings out the ends that are already present, the "degenerescence" already existing in them. In each, he redirects the violence central to these familiar episodes toward self-destruction: the genre comes to its end by mutilating, crashing upon, and slaughtering itself.

Fundamental to this argument is the reading of each of these passages as metapoetic. So throughout the chapter I will keep an eye on the metapoetic signposts that Lucan stakes in these *loci*. I address the passages in the order they appear in the poem; and we will see how Lucan builds on metapoetic motifs and positions established earlier. The first of these, the mutilation of Marius Gratidianus's face in Book 2, appears in an extended showpiece, the old man's speech about the civil bloodshed of the 80s BCE (2.68–232), a passage that comes early in the poem and is highly charged with metapoetic language;[4] the passage as a whole and its relationship to the surrounding poem require some unpacking, with which I begin now.

2.1. The *mise en abyme* of the old man's speech

A hallmark of Lucan's poetics is his use of delay and anticipation, his method of winding up tension until it unspools at Pharsalia in Book 7.[5] One of the most elaborate episodes of anticipation in the *Pharsalia* comes, paradoxically,

---

[2] See Gale and Scourfield (2018b) 14–15 on the centrality of violence in epic, amid a larger discussion of violence in Roman society and culture; and Spentzou (2018) on the *Ph.* as a "(post-)classic(al) locus of violence" (246), with a focus on responses to Caesar's acts of violence. I became aware of the study of violence in the *Ph.* by Nill (2018) after completion of this manuscript.

[3] Hinds (1998) 45.

[4] See Conte (1968) and the recent appraisals of the passage by Dinter (2012) 45–7 and 125–6; Ambühl (2010); Day (2013) 79–87; Walters (2013); and Alexis (2013) 86.

[5] See Henderson (1987) 133–4, with further bibliography at 158 n. 70; Masters (1992) 43; and Roche (2019) 2–4.

in the artifice of a flashback at the beginning of Book 2. Here, after Caesar has entered Italy but before his arrival in Rome, Lucan recounts the preemptive lamentations by groups of Roman women and men (2.16–66); then, in what is the longest speech in the poem (2.68–232),[6] a Roman elder recalls the horrors in the city during the purges by Marius and then Sulla in the 80s BCE. Lucan introduces the speech by writing:

> atque aliquis magno quaerens exempla timori
> "non alios" inquit "motus tum fata parabant
> cum post Teutonicos uictor Libycosque triumphos
> exul limosa Marius caput abdidit ulua."

> And one [older Roman], seeking precedents for this great fear, said, "No different were the movements that the fates were preparing then, when, after his Teutonic and Libyan triumphs, victorious Marius, now an exile, buried his head in the muddy sedge." (2.67–70)

The first words of the old man's speech establish a sense of repetition and sameness for the situations in 49 BCE and 87 BCE: Caesar's march back to Rome from Gaul was "no different" (2.67) from Marius's return to Rome from exile a generation earlier. This opening line sets the tone for the speech, which is full of language and imagery foreshadowing events in the poem's surrounding narrative of 49 and 48.[7] For example, there is the fundamental similarity in the focus on dueling duos of civil warriors (Marius and Sulla in the 80s, Caesar and Pompey in the 40s); and the elder's speech uses many of the motifs and typologies that the narrator will employ later in the poem.[8]

There is also much of the *poeta doctus* in this old man. In his characterization of Sulla, for example, he makes learned references to the villains Diomedes of Thrace, Antaeus of Libya, and Oenomaus of Pisa (2.162–5).[9]

---

[6] Fantham (1992) 91.
[7] See Conte (1968) 239–40; Grimal (1970) 88–9; Narducci (1979) 53; Henderson (1987) 129–33; Leigh (1997) 299–303; Fratantuono (2012) 65–6; and Dinter (2012) 125–6 on the sense of civil war's repetitiveness conveyed by the speech.
[8] His vivid images of slaughter in particular find repetitions elsewhere in the *Ph.*, most of all in Book 7. Note, e.g., interfamilial slaughter at 2.149–51 and 7.182–3, 7.453–4, 7.626–30, and 7.762–3; disrespect for corpses at 2.160–73 and 7.789–803; and the conceptualization of disasters in civil war as equivalent to numerous other disasters at 2.198–201 and 7.412–20.
[9] Fantham (1992) 110 notes that Lucan chooses not to include a "straight comparison" and identifies only Antaeus by name. He thus employs the Alexandrian method of requiring learned engagement from his readers.

The most recent commentator on Book 2 finds the speech's erudition to be out of place, writing that "[s]uch mythical comparisons are less appropriate to this speaker than to tragic figures or in direct narrative," and elsewhere states that the old man is "little more than a mouthpiece for information not otherwise accessible."[10] But the speaker and his studied speech surely have a more dynamic and meaningful relationship with the narrator and the surrounding poem.[11] And in light of the parallels in content, theme, and style between this speech and the *Pharsalia* as a whole—and we will observe many more in the coming pages—we might best understand the speech at 2.68–232 as a *mise en abyme*—a passage that is reflective of, and in fact representative of, the work as a whole. At the end of the speech the narrator will describe the old man as weeping, and as "mindful of the past and fearful of the future" (2.233: *praeteritique memor flebat metuensque futuri*). I will return to the matter of his tears later, but for now it is important to note that the phrase *praeteritique memor . . . metuensque futuri* is also an apt description of the poem's narrator, whose articulation of Pharsalia's transformation of the Roman past *and* future is central to the poem.[12] The character of the old man, who looks back on Rome's past as he fears for its present and future, is a textual doublet of the poet himself.

Near the end of the speech, the elder restates his point about the repetition of the horrors under Marius and Sulla in the ongoing events (2.223), but also fears there are worse things (*grauiora*, 2.225) and greater destruction (*maiore . . . damno*, 2.226) in store, before concluding with specific premonitions of the more destructive ambitions of Caesar and Pompey (2.227–32). He thus underscores the worseness of these civil wars, the *plus quam* foretold in the poem's opening line.[13] The reflection in 2.68–232 of the *Pharsalia* as a whole, it turns out, has a distorting and enlarging bend to it. And so, even as Lucan includes a doublet of himself here, he characteristically makes his own poetic effort—the larger poem that contains this miniature reflection—weightier, broader, greater.

---

[10] Fantham (1992) 110–11 and 91.
[11] See Ambühl (2010) 29 on the old man's "remarkable affinity with Lucan's primary narrator," and Alexis (2013) 86, also viewing the reflection of Caesar and Pompey in Marius and Sulla as a *mise en abyme*.
[12] See Chapter 3. See Lebek (1976) 39–40 on the modifiers in 2.233. Conte (1968) 242–5 compares the old man's speech with choral passages in tragedy, and the use of *aliquis* at 2.67 with *tis* speeches in Homer.
[13] See Henderson (1987) 130–1.

The *mise en abyme* of the old man's speech is also revealing of Lucan's relationship with his epic predecessors, as he engages closely with particular model passages at several points. At 2.113–14, for example, he states that during Marius's reign of terror, "the one hope for safety (*spes una salutis*) was to fix trembling kisses on a bloodied right hand," an inversion of Aeneas's statement about the Trojans' bravery during the fall of their city (*Aen.* 2.354 *una salus uictis, nullam sperare salutem*, "the one safety for the defeated was to hope for no safety"). The allusion highlights a stark contrast and so speaks to the subversion of Virgilian heroism that Lucan undertakes at several points in the poem.

The poem's engagement with Homer is also showcased here. As Elaine Fantham has noted, the rivers of blood running through Rome after Sulla's purges (2.209–20) recall Troy's famously bloody rivers in *Iliad* 21. Just like the Scamander at *Il.* 21.218–20, the Tiber becomes so full of corpses that it cannot flow into the sea (*Ph.* 2.211–13). Ultimately the Tiber throws the corpses onto the land (*Ph.* 2.217–18), as the Scamander had (*Il.* 21.235-8),[14] but a key difference lies in how each passage ends. In time, Hera quells the river's fury (*Il.* 21.377–84)—a motion toward the upcoming resolution of the rage that drove Achilles and the action of the poem as a whole. In the Sullan Rome recounted by Lucan's old man, "finally, [the Tiber] barely wrestled out into the Tyrrhenian waves and split the dark blue sea with torrents of blood" (*tandem Tyrrhenas uix eluctatus in undas | sanguine caeruleum torrenti diuidit aequor*, 2.219–20). The bloody Tiber is not quelled but spreading and strengthened, as brought out by the juxtaposition of the red blood with the blueness of the sea (*sanguine caeruleum*) and the contrast of the sea's calm plain (*aequor*) and the violent gushing (*torrenti*) of the river's blood.[15] So while *Iliad* 21 shows the horrors of the blood-red Scamander but also its ultimate quiescence, Lucan's old man pictures a bloodied Tiber bound to continue its flow outward. This gush of Roman blood from civil war then carries forward temporally to the events of Lucan's poem and also, then, spatially—to the bloodshed in Gaul, Spain, Greece, and Africa that will make up much of the contents of the poem.

---

[14] Fantham (1992) 118 notes these parallels. Ambühl (2010) identifies parallels with descriptions of the Ilioupersis, with a focus on Euripides's tragedies.

[15] Fantham (1992) 119.

2.2. Metapoetics in the mutilation of Marius Gratidianus

The old man's inclusion of a bloodied and still flowing Tiber is thus representative of Lucan's manner of taking what is resolved in Homer and opening it up, imploding it—a matter I will explore in detail in Chapter 5. Just prior to showcasing this break from the Smyrnaean bard, the old man includes another episode with a literary lineage going back to Homer. This is his description of the mutilation of Marcus Marius Gratidianus during the Sullan purges (2.173–93). Gratidianus was Marius's adopted nephew and de facto successor, and his prosecution of Sulla's ally Quintus Lutatius Catulus had led to the latter's suicide in 87 BCE. The episode of the Sullans' vengeful killing of Gratidianus in 82 became infamous and is recounted by a number of authors, both before Lucan (Sallust, Livy, Asconius, Valerius Maximus, and Seneca) and after him (Florus).[16] But no author gives it as much attention as Lucan, who commits twenty-one lines to the mutilation and makes it the gruesome climax of the old man's speech. The episode begins as follows:

> quid sanguine manes
> placatos Catuli referam? cum uictima tristis
> inferias Marius forsan nolentibus umbris   175
> pendit inexpleto non fanda piacula busto,
> cum laceros artus aequataque uolnera membris
> uidimus et toto quamuis in corpore caeso
> nil animae letale datum, moremque nefandae
> dirum saeuitiae, pereuntis parcere morti.   180
> auolsae cecidere manus exectaque lingua
> palpitat et muto uacuum ferit aera motu.
> hic aures, alius spiramina naris aduncae
> amputat, ille cauis euoluit sedibus orbes
> ultimaque effodit spectatis lumina membris.   185

What should I say about placation of the shades of Catulus? That was the time when a Marius was the victim and extended sad offerings to shades that were perhaps unwilling—unspeakable expiations to a tomb

---

[16] Sall., *Hist.* fr. 14 (Maurenbrecher) (= *Adn.* on *Ph.* 2.174); Livy, *Periocha* 88; Asconius, notes on Cic.'s *In Toga Candida* 75.5; Val. Max. 9.2.1; Sen., *De Ira* 3.18.1–2; and Flor. 2.9.26. Rawson (1987) argues that Sallust's account was the basis for *Ph.* 2.68–232.

that could not be satisfied; at that time we saw his limbs torn apart and as many wounds as he had body parts. And even though his entire body was bloodied, we saw no lethal blow strike his spirit, but we saw the dreadful practice of unspeakable savagery, and the withholding of death from the dying. His hands were torn off and fell; his tongue, though cut off, kept slithering and struck the empty air with a silent motion. One man cuts off his ears, another cuts off the vent-holes of his hooked nose, yet another scoops the eyeballs out of their hollow sockets and gouges out the eyes last, after they have seen the other limbs. (2.173–85)

After twice describing the act as "unspeakable" (*non fanda piacula* at 2.176 and *nefandae . . . saeuitiae* at 2.179–80), the elder goes into lavish detail about what happened to Gratidianus—a move that mirrors the narrator's own manner of singing what he himself identifies as *nefas*.[17] Appropriately in this poem about Roman self-destruction, Gratidianus's death is figured as both a homicide and a suicide; he is a sacrificial victim (*uictima*, 174), but in the syntax of 175–6 he makes the offering himself (*inferias Marius . . . pendit*).[18] The description that then follows includes the dismemberment of his limbs (181), tongue (181–2), ears (183), nose (183–4), and eyes (184–5)—cutting across and cutting out all of his senses.[19]

One reader of the poem has described this scene as "horror pushed to the extreme" and another as "arguably more horrible than anything found before it in Latin verse."[20] A nineteenth-century reader included this passage among examples of Lucan's "defects" on the grounds that "Lucan thinks fit to enlarge on the ghastly brutality of the deed step by step, quite needlessly."[21] He is right: the focus on the mutilation of Gratidianus's face is indeed a case of extraordinary narrative expansion; but passages like this have precedent in earlier literature,[22] and facial mutilation is not uncommon in epic battle scenes. Homer includes several death scenes with details of facial dismemberment,[23]

---

[17] See 1.6, 7.556–96 and *passim*.
[18] See Fantham (1992) 113; Bartsch (1997) 24 ("*he is both subject and object* of this sentence"); and Day (2013) 83–4.
[19] Conte (1968) 234 and Walters (2013) 117–18.
[20] Connolly (2016) 291 and Fratantuono (2012) 64. See too the superlatives of Ambühl (2010) 28; Day (2013) 80; and Thorne (2016) 108.
[21] Heitland (1887) lxxii.
[22] Note the ritual practices of *acroteriasmos* and *maschalismos* (with Aesch. *Cho.* 439 and Soph. *El.* 445).
[23] See, e.g., *Il.* 5.290–3, 13.615–18, 16.348–50, 23.395–7; *Od.* 18.86, 21.300–1, 22.475; and Kucewicz (2016) on the mutilation of the dead in Homer.

and, while Virgil is generally more reserved in his descriptions, Ovid includes comparable passages of facial mutilation in combat.[24]

The mutilation of Marius Gratidianus follows in this tradition, but Lucan innovates in extraordinary ways with what are already graphic details. For one, while the battle scenes in Homer and Ovid have a more kinetic quality to them, Lucan's "step by step" scene is ghastly in its static, deliberate,[25] and more inward-driven affect. A revealing example of this redirection of epic violence comes in the detail about Gratidianus's eyeballs, which were pushed out of their sockets and gouged out (*ille cauis euoluit sedibus orbes | ultimaque effodit . . . lumina*, 2.184–5) only after they had watched the mutilation of the man's limbs (*spectatis . . . membris*, 2.185). Homer had described how Menelaus pops out Peisander's eyeballs, which then fall into the dust (*Il.* 13.616–17), and Servius preserves a similar image from a battle scene in Ennius's *Annales: oscitat in campis caput a ceruice reuolsum | semianimesque micant oculi lucemque requirunt* ("The head, ripped off from its neck, gapes open in the fields, and the half-alive eyes twitch and look for the light," *Ann.* 483–4 = Servius on *Aen.* 10.396). This Ennian image appears to be adapted from Homer's in *Iliad* 13,[26] and it goes on to have a rich afterlife. Servius states that in the first century BCE, Varro Atacinus transferred the verse verbatim to his own poem (fr. 2 Courtney); Lucretius pictures a head severed by a scythed chariot that keeps its eyes open (*oculos patentis*) before its soul has departed (3.654–6);[27] and Virgil adapts Ennius's diction for his description of Larides's severed fingers at *Aeneid* 10.396 (*semianimesque micant digiti ferrumque retractant*).[28] At *Pharsalia* 2.184–5, Lucan's old man *doctus* seems to recall the long-remembered Homeric and Ennian model passages, and he zooms in on the mutilated eyes of the dying man, just as epic predecessors had.[29] But he achieves an entirely new effect. These eyeballs do not roll in the dust or look for

---

[24] See Adams (1980) on the "restrictiveness" (50) of Virgil in the depiction of the anatomy, to be contrasted with, e.g., Homer, Ovid, and Lucan. Ovidian examples of facial mutilation on the battlefield come at *Met.* 5.137–9 and 12.252–3.

[25] Most (1992) 397–400 finds that Lucan's scenes of wounding or killing are on average three to four times longer than those in Homer, Virgil, Silius Italicus, and Statius. Dinter (2012) and McClellan (2019) 115–69 offer extended studies of these frequent scenes of dismemberment.

[26] Elliott (2013) 101–2. Dinter (2012) 39 views the Ennian and Virgilian passages as "Latin successors" to *Il.* 10.457 and *Od.* 22.329, where decapitated heads are still speaking when they land in the dirt. Hunink (1992) 232 (on *Ph.* 3.612) also compares this set of passages.

[27] Kenney (1971) 166 and Segal (1990) 141–2 suggest an Ennian provenance.

[28] Elliott (2013) 102: "by virtue of having been repeated among different works of the pre-Vergilian epic tradition, the line had already acquired its own sort of quasi-formulaic status for Vergil to exploit."

[29] See Hardie (2009) 122 n. 156, noting his "suspicion that *Bell. Civ.* 2.181–5 is sustainedly Ennian-Lucretian."

the light, as in the *Iliad* and *Annales*, respectively. They look right at the violence being inflicted on Gratidianus's other body parts (recall *spectatis . . . membris*, 2.185). In the preceding lines, the old man had emphasized his own autopsy of Gratidianus's mutilation (*meque ipsum memini . . . lustrasse*, 169–71; *uidimus*, 178), and he will later depict Sulla's spectatorship of the carnage he ordered (*spectator sceleris*, 208). The shocking detail of Gratidianus's dying eyes viewing his own slaughter enhances the spectacular character of the scene—making it even more eye-popping. The image thus models for the Roman reader the act of focusing on this scene of Roman self-destruction. *This*, Lucan's old man tells us, is a moment worth looking closely at.

The detail of Gratidianus's popped-out but self-spectating eyeballs also directs the reader to the poetic action taking place. The mutilation here—unlike in the Homeric and Ennian model passages—is self-reflexive: Gratidianus had enacted it himself (recall *pendit* in 176), and now his eyes gaze upon the dismemberment that has occurred. The simultaneous adoption of the phrase *euoluit . . . orbes* from Seneca's description of Oedipus's self-blinding at *Oedipus* 967[30] affirms the specifically inward direction of the violence here. When we recall that *membra* can refer to units of words, the metapoetic import of this mutilation—with *spectatis . . . membris*—becomes clearer: Lucan's old man is compelling us to zero in on the dismemberment of the epic convention of mutilation, to observe the genre's self-mutilation.[31] Further still, in this conceit the model texts themselves—Homer, Ennius, the later tradition—are made to watch their own mutilation and death.

2.3. Cutting off Ennius's nose

The violent excision of Gratidianus's eyeballs thus exhibits the poet's familiarity with the Homeric and Ennian tradition of mutilation scenes, but also his interest in turning that violence back onto itself. Another detail at the center of this act reinforces and enriches the sense of textual self-mutilation: the cutting off of his nose. The slaughter of Gratidianus's limbs, tongue, eyes, and ears all appear variously in other accounts of his death, but no other source mentions his nose. Lucan is clearly adding this detail on his own.

---

[30] Conte (1968) 235.
[31] See similarly the analysis of Walters (2013) 121–2. And see, e.g., Horace's use of *membra* at *Sat.* 1.4.62, with McClellan (2019) 13–14.

Earlier epic mutilation scenes *had* included the severing of a man's nose, with Homer featuring this act most often, at *Iliad* 5.291, 13.616 (Peisander's death), and 23.395; and *Odyssey* 18.86, 21.301, and 22.475.[32] The inclusion of the detail by Lucan's old man is in this regard generically traditional.

At the same time, Gratidianus's severed nose evokes an unforgettable moment in Ennius's *Annales*. The words the old man uses of the mutilation (*spiramina naris aduncae | amputat*, 183–4: "another cuts off the vent-holes of his hooked nose") closely recall a line from Book 7 of the *Annales*. The Ennian line is preserved by the grammarian Priscian, who, in a discussion of forms of the noun *naris*, writes: *Ennius in vii Annalium 'sulpureas posuit spiramina Naris ad undas'* ("Ennius in the seventh book of the *Annales* writes, 'he placed vent-holes beside the sulfurous waves of the Nar,'" *Ann.* 222 = Priscian 2.223). The reference is to the Nar River in southern Italy, and Skutsch offers the explanation that "here Ennius may have meant to suggest that the holes in or near the river's banks were in fact the nostrils of Hell, thus giving an etymology of [the place-name] *Nar*."[33] Ennius, then, is describing a portal to and from Hell, or a "Plutonium," and the unstated but logical subject of *posuit* is the king of the Underworld himself. From the other fragments that Norden, followed by Skutsch, grouped with this passage (*Ann.* 220–1 and 223–6), it appears that Ennius had the Fury Discordia ascend to Earth through the portal at Nar.[34] The occasion would be the war against the Etruscan Faliscans in 241 BCE, which required Discordia to open up the gates of war that she had just closed after the completion of the First Punic War.

That Lucan's old man at *Pharsalia* 2.183 is recalling the Ennian line and its play on the etymology of the Nar seems to be beyond doubt.[35] The phrase "hooked nose" appears in several Latin authors, and Seneca uses the same expression (*naris aduncae*) at *Oedipus* 189.[36] But Lucan's inclusion of *naris aduncae* also seems to echo Ennius's *Naris ad undas* in the same placement in the hexameter. Most significantly, the collocation *spiramina naris* is found in only these two passages, and Lucan is the first writer after Ennius to use

---

[32] See Adams (1980) 50 and 55–6 on the mutilation of noses in epic battle scenes. He notes that Virgil includes a wounded nose only once (*Aen.* 6.497), arguing that he found the word "too undignified for epic" (50).

[33] Skutsch (1985) 399. This association between the Nar River valley and a portal to Hell is found in Virgil (*Aen.* 7.517; see O'Hara [1996] 190) and later poets.

[34] Norden (1915) 10–33 and 143–52; Skutsch (1985) 392–4.

[35] Noting the correspondence are Skutsch (1985) 399; Fantham (1992) 113; Hardie (2009) 122; Day (2013) 81–2; and Walters (2013) 117 ("a strong scent of Ennius").

[36] Ter., *Haut.* 1062, Hor., *Sat.* 1.6.5, and Suet., *Galba* 21.1 all apply *aduncus* to *nasus*.

any form of *spiramen*.³⁷ The evocation of the Ennian line seems clear. But why? Why in this conspicuous and climactic episode in the old man's speech, amid this "crescendo of mutilation,"³⁸ in a conventional epic locus, do we encounter—on the very face of the mutilated Marius Gratidianus—the gateway to Ennius's Underworld?

On a thematic level, the evocation of Ennius's Underworld speaks to a prominent theme in the *Pharsalia*: that Rome's civil wars brought Hell onto Earth.³⁹ The idea that Hell came up to Thessaly becomes prominent at Erictho's lair (6.434–830) and again on the plains of Pharsalia after the battle (7.764–76). Here, through the allusion to *Ann.* 222, Marius Gratidianus's mutilated face *is*, quite literally, a passageway from Hell. This mutilation and similar acts of civil war are what allow for, and in essence constitute, the passage of Hell onto Earth.

Along with this thematic import comes a powerful poetic statement. If the speech at 2.68–232 operates as a *mise en abyme* for the poem as a whole, then the Ennian allusion here in the passage's horrific climax highlights the importance of the *Annales* for the *Pharsalia*. Like the allusion in the poem's proem (1.6–7, evoking *Ann.* 582), this line works as an anchor for Lucan's engagement with Ennius. And just as in 1.6–7, the old man appears to take an Ennian scene and redirect it inward, back onto itself. In *Annales* 7, Discordia emerges from the portal to the Underworld to open the gates of war (*Ann.* 225–6), signifying the renewal of war with an external enemy (the Faliscans, it seems). Gratidianus's mutilated face becomes a portal from the Underworld, though the spirits that emerge are headed only for internal, civil war and Roman self-destruction. To this end, let us recall that at 2.174–6 Lucan fashions Gratidianus's death as both a homicide and a suicide; like Rome as a whole, Gratidianus releases the spirit of Discordia on himself.

The allusion at 2.183, then, signals Lucan's manner of picking apart and redirecting Ennius's words about Rome's expansive combat inward, toward self-slaughter. The metapoetic markers in the phrase *spiramina Naris aduncae | amputat* complement this sense. The Romans commonly understood the nose to represent the powers of discernment and sagacity (*OLD* s.v. *naris* 3). Ennius (*Ann.* 333) and Lucan (7.829), for example, apply the adjective *sagax*

---

³⁷ And, as Fantham (1992) 113 notes, this is the only passage in Latin literature where *spiramina* is used *proprie* of nostrils.
³⁸ Thorne (2016) 109.
³⁹ So similarly Day (2013) 81, building on Hardie (2009) 122: "from Gratidianus' corpse the ghost of Ennian *Discordia* emerges; Gratidianus' dismembered body comes to stand for the *discordia* of L's own fractured poem."

to *nar*—as an epithet of sorts: *nare sagaci*, "with a keen nose."[40] Each of those passages describes an animal's nose; but we also note, for example, Horace's appeal to being *neque naris obesae*, "not of an unrefined nose" (*Ep.* 12.3). The elder Pliny writes in the preface to his *Natural History* of "Lucilius, who was the first to put 'nose' (*nasum*) in a pen" (*NH* Pref. 7). By *nasum* Pliny, too, appears to mean "discernment" or "wit."[41] We see that the nose was understood to be a sort of control center of one's wit and refinement. In addition, derivatives of *spiro* such as *spiramen* could carry with them associations of inspiration (see, e.g., *OLD* s.v. *spiritus* 5).[42] The phrase *spiramina naris* can reasonably be translated not just as "the vent-holes of his nose" but also as "the sources of inspiration for wit."

Moreover, there is a lot packed into the verb that takes *spiramina naris* as its object, *amputat*. In 2.184 the old man uses it to mean "to sever altogether," just as at *Ph.* 3.612 and 6.176. But *amputat* also captures well the poetic act occurring here. The verb can mean both "to cut off" or sever (*OLD* 1) and "to prune" (*OLD* 2a), and it can be used figuratively of cutting short a speech or work of writing (*OLD* 3c). With *amputat* taking the Ennian phrase *spiramina naris* as its object, Lucan—through his doublet the old man—is making claims both to prune *and* to mutilate his model. He will snip at Ennius—selectively reading, adopting, and adapting his diction and themes, but at the same time he will assail Ennius in disruptive and radical ways.[43] When we look at *Ph.* 2.183–4 alongside *Ann.* 222, the potency and aggressiveness of the verb *amputat* are brought out by the contrast with Ennius's *posuit*, which marks the constructive act of placing or establishing.[44]

The image of "cutting off a nose" becomes even more metapoetically pointed when we recall that Ennius had fashioned himself as a poet of great refinement. He holds up his learnedness and taste in, for example, the *Annales*' second proem at the outset of Book 7. There he distinguishes himself from predecessors who had written rustic verse (*Ann.* 206–7), styles himself as "a student of the word" (*dicti studiosus*, *Ann.* 209), and expostulates on the origins of *sapientia*, or "taste" (*Ann.* 211–12).[45] Ennius was a self-styled

---

[40] A phrase also appearing at Sen., *Phaedra* 39.
[41] See also Catull. 13.13–14 and the suggestion at Ov., *Fast.* 5.375–9.
[42] See, e.g., Hor., *C.* 2.16.38, of the "fine inspiration of the Greek Muse" (*spiritum Graiae tenuem Camenae*) that the author has.
[43] Hunink (1992) 232 (on *Ph.* 3.612) describes *amputo* as "a striking, harsh word, used mainly by prose writers."
[44] I am thankful to Isabel Köster for this point.
[45] Hor. also describes Ennius as *sapiens* at *Epist.* 2.1.50. On *Ann.* 211–12 and Ennius's *sapientia*, see Habinek (2006). On his self-aware learnedness and Hellenistic poetics, see Dominik (1993) 38–48;

philologist—and Lucan comes at him with a deft philological move of his own. The act of poetic violence in *Ph.* 2.183-4—the act of *amputat*—comes in the radical reapplication of Ennius's words, such as *spiramina naris*, but also, metapoetically, in the assault on Ennius's self-fashioning as a poet of taste and wit. In sum, with this trenchant act of poetic disfigurement, here in this self-consciously spectacular episode in the poem (recall *spectatis ... membris*), Lucan signals that he is "cutting off the inspiration for the wit" of his predecessor—that is, cutting short and cutting down the venerable and refined forefather of Latin epic.

Further, the cutting off of a nose can at the same time be symbolic of the act of castration. Lucan's contemporary Martial twice describes husbands cutting off the noses of their wives' lovers (2.83.3 and 3.85.1).[46] In the latter epigram he describes the lover as "your Deiphobus" (3.85.4), the son of Priam who had taken Helen after Paris's death and whose nose was then severed by the avenging Menelaus (*Aen* 6.494-7 and 6.525-9). This is presumably done, as in Martial, in an act of symbolic castration to punish Deiphobus for his tryst with Helen. Given the association between nasal mutilation and castration that comes out in these passages, and given our knowledge that Lucan alone opted to include the nose in Gratidianus's mutilation scene, is this a further layer of meaning in the metapoetic act in *Pharsalia* 2.183-4? With the image *spiramina naris aduncae | amputat*, is Lucan's old man signaling a Saturn-like castration of Latin epic's Caelus-like father figure?

When we see that Lucan has placed an Ennian phrase on Marius Gratidianus's face, as an object of poetic and metapoetic violence, other details in this scene read as complementing and reinforcing this poetic statement. As we have seen, the subsequent detail of Gratidianus's spectating eyes (2.184-5), a grotesque adaptation of similar moments in the *Iliad* and *Annales*, serves to command special attention to the scene and the gesture of narrative and textual dismemberment that is occurring. The immediately preceding lines, which detail the removal of Gratidianus's hands and tongue, are also of particular interest. Seneca is the only earlier author to specify the

---

Gildenhard (2003) 103; and Feeney (2016) 159-60 (glossing *studiosus dicti* as synonymous with *philologus*), with the cautious assessment of Goldberg (1995) 90-92. Casali (2006) 124-6 argues for Virgil's one-upmanship of Ennius as *studiosus dicti*.

[46] Adams (1980) 60 notes "the removal of the nose as a castration symbol" and points to the Deiphobus story, as well as Mart. 2.83 and 3.85. Ambühl (2010) 27-8 compares Lucan's Gratidianus with the more "tactfully" described Deiphobus in *Aen*. 6.

dismemberment of the hands and tongue in that act of mutilation (*De Ira* 3.18.1),[47] and while Lucan was likely familiar with his uncle's account, he develops the details much further. Here again are the lines, together with the subsequent verses on the severing of the nose:

auolsae cecidere manus exectaque lingua
palpitat et muto uacuum ferit aera motu.
hic aures, alius spiramina naris aduncae
amputat

His hands were pulled off and fell; his tongue, though cut off, kept
slithering and struck the empty air with a silent motion. One man cuts off
his ears, another cuts off the vent-holes of his hooked nose. (2.181–4)

Gratidianus's hands are pulled apart (*auolsae*) and fall (*cecidere*), thus experiencing their own poignant death. The image recalls the droop of the artist Daedalus's weary hands at *Aeneid* 6.33, described with the same phrase *cecidere manus*, though here Gratidianus's hands undergo a literal fall to death.[48] And, in a description influenced by Ovid's narration of Philomela's silencing (*Met.* 6.557–60),[49] the man's tongue is cut off (*exsecta*); though it keeps wagging (*palpitat*), its movement now makes no sound (*muto ... motu*, 2.182).

At the historical level, the removal of Gratidianus's hands and tongue are fitting, given his status as a prominent orator.[50] At the metapoetic level these details work together, as the poetic mutilation of Ennius's verse and cutting off of his discerning nose in 2.183–4 are joined by the severing of both the bodily instruments of the writer, the hands, and the mechanism of speech itself, the tongue. This figure who wears Ennius on his face—and has that face defiled—thus also loses the power to write and speak. The evocations of the Virgilian Daedalus's artistic failure and a moment of silencing in the typically garrulous Ovid complement the metapoetic gesture toward Ennius: Marius Gratidianus emerges as a sort of composite textual representative of the epic tradition—a composite that is systematically pulled apart

---

[47] The detail of cracked hands also appears in the later account by Florus (2.9.26), who frequently adopted Lucanian language (Goodyear [1982] 664 and Leigh [2007] 492) and so may have drawn it from Lucan.
[48] Dinter (2012) 47. See also Day (2013) 84–6 on the "agglomeration of detail" (86) here.
[49] See Conte (1968) 235 n. 19 and Dinter (2012) 41–3 and 46, describing the removal of Philomela's tongue as "a sequence loaded with metapoetics" (46).
[50] Dinter (2012) 46–7, pointing to Cic., *Brut.* 223.

68　THUNDER AND LAMENT

and dismembered. The image of mutilation that is so innate to epic battle narrative is transformed into one of comprehensive, silencing self-mutilation; the inevitable "degenerescence" of the genre is palpably visualized.

2.4. Gratidianus and the collapse of Ennian space and time

We have observed how the elaborate tableau of Marius Gratidianus's mutilation, placed within the *mise en abyme* of the old man's speech, provides a prominent, indeed spectacular, venue for Lucan's poetic statement about his manner of engagement with the epic tradition, with a severance of Ennius right at the center, in the middle of the victim's face. The Ennian intertext in 2.183–4 may also operate as an anchor for further, complementary interaction with the *Annales* in this passage, both in particular phrases and images in the coming lines, and in broader themes that the passage explores.

A few lines after the vignette of Gratidianus's mutilation, the old man moves to describe the massacre of Sulla's opponents in the Campus Martius:

> tum flos Hesperiae, Latii iam sola iuuentus,
> concidit et miserae maculauit ouilia Romae.
> **tot simul infesto iuuenes occumbere leto**
> saepe fames pelagique furor subitaeque ruinae
> aut terrae caelique lues aut bellica clades,　　　200
> numquam poena fuit. densi uix agmina uolgi
> inter et exangues immissa morte cateruas
> uictores mouere manus.

Then the flower of Hesperia, now the only youth of Latium left, fell to the ground and polluted the voting spaces of wretched Rome. Often famine or the fury of the sea or sudden crashes or the plague of the earth and sky or wartime disaster resulted in so many young men falling to unbeatable death at the same time—never before was it execution. Inside the battle-lines of the packed mob and the crowds made bloodless by death's entrance, the victors could scarcely move their hands. (2.196–203)

This picture of bloodshed in Rome includes a number of words and phrases that recall—but reverse—moments in the *Annales*. In a pair of lines that

Priscian assigns to *Annales* 15, and that editors have placed during the Roman siege of Ambracia in 189 BCE, Ennius writes:

occumbunt multi letum ferroque lapique
aut intra muros aut extra praecipe casu

Many men fell to death by sword or by stone, either inside the walls or outside, in a headlong fall (*Ann.* 389–90)

The phrasing by Lucan's old man in 2.198 (*tot simul infesto iuuenes occumbere leto*) appears to build upon Ennius's phrasing in *Ann.* 389–90. Most notable is the use of *occumbere* with a form of *letum*. This collocation (instead of the more common *occumbere* + a form of *mors*) becomes popular in descriptions of battlefield deaths after Lucan, appearing in Statius's *Thebaid* (1.595 and 5.693), Valerius Flaccus's *Argonautica* (1.633), and Silius's *Punica* (13.380). But Lucan is the first epic poet after Ennius to construe *occumbere* with *letum*, a more "elevated" synonym of *mors*.[51] Furthermore, Lucan's old man, like Ennius, emphasizes the great quantity of those falling to their death (note *multi* in *Ann.* 389 and *tot* in *Ph.* 2.198); but he outdoes Ennius by intensifying the deathly image with the inclusion of *simul* ("all at the same time") and by modifying *leto* with *infesto* ("unbeatable"). The series *tot simul infesto* piles up to overwhelm the dying young men in Sulla's Rome—and to highlight the Lucanian expansion of his model.

The old man emphasizes the youth of those slaughtered in the Campus Martius three times: with the word *iuuenes* in 2.198, the phrase *Latii iam sola iuuentus* at 2.196, and, in the same line, as the very first words of this episode, the expression *flos Hesperiae*. Commentators on the passage point to Virgil's use of the pair of *flos* and *iuuentus* at *Aeneid* 8.499–500, where Etruscan warriors are described as "the chosen youth of Maeonia, the flower and strength of an old race of men" (*o Maeoniae delecta iuuentus,* | *flos ueterum uirtusque uirum*). But we should also note that Servius views Virgil's use of *flos* at *Aen.* 8.500 as "Ennian";[52] and indeed Cicero (*Brut.* 58) preserves a fragment of Ennius characterizing the esteemed orator and consul for 204 BCE, Marcus Cornelius Cethegus, as "the picked flower of the people" (*Ann.*

---

[51] Skutsch (1985) 555. The one author prior to Lucan I found to use *occumbo* with *letum* is Seneca at *Phaedra* 997 (*leto occubat*).
[52] Serv. D. on *Aen.* 8.500: *Flos ueterum—Ennianum.*

308: *flos delibatus populi*).⁵³ Flower imagery, to be sure, is common in all genres and certainly in epic.⁵⁴ But Lucan employs it rarely;⁵⁵ here, in proximity to other Ennian intertexts, we might consider whether the phrase *flos Hesperiae* is another evocation of the world of the *Annales*. Let us recall that Ennius seems to have introduced the word and thus the idea of *Hesperia* into Latin in Book 1 of his epic (*Ann.* 20). In Chapter 1, I argued that Lucan evokes *Hesperia*'s emergence in the *Annales* when presenting the country's decay and death in the *Pharsalia*'s opening lines (1.28–9). The sacrilegious slaughter of the "flower of Hesperia" here at 2.196–201 may pick up on and perpetuate the poem's imagery of the decay and loss of Ennius's *Hesperia*. The *Annales* had celebrated excellent Roman *exempla* such as Cethegus, as well as, more generally, "the best Roman youth, with beautiful spirits" (*optima cum pulcris animis Romana iuuentus*, *Ann.* 563). Lucan's poem—as captured in microcosm here in the old man's speech—narrates the end of this line, the wilting and the fall to the ground (*concidit*) of the *flos Hesperiae*.⁵⁶

It is important to note that the intensification of the Ennian model in *tot simul infesto iuuenes occumbere leto* (2.198) is joined by a meaningful relocation of the scene of death. The siege of Ambracia was of course abroad, in Epirus, and it seems likely that in *Ann.* 390 Ennius is referring to the death of the city's defenders inside the city walls (*intra muros*) and the death of the Roman attackers outside (*extra*) the walls;⁵⁷ this battle was a rather straightforward contest of "us vs. them." The deaths in *Pharsalia* 2.196–203 are all Roman, all occurring within the city's walls. The old man in fact describes the slaughter of these youths as a pollution (*maculauit*)⁵⁸ of the most interior of spaces, the sacred ground of the voting enclosures in the Campus Martius (2.197). The ensuing lines describing the bloodshed in the Campus go further within, to a place "inside (*inter*) the battle-lines of the packed (*densi*) mob and the crowds made bloodless by death's entrance" (2.201–2). And so, while the Ennian passage shows a natural contrast between action inside (*intra*) and out (*extra*), the Lucanian passage contains only interior space. As

---

⁵³ See Elliott (2013) 54–7 and 156–61 on Ennius's grandiose depiction of Cethegus (to which I return in Chapter 3).
⁵⁴ See Fratantuono and Smith (2018) 564–5 (on *Aen.* 8.500); and Dué (2020): "the comparison of a dying warrior to a flower is an ancient theme at the core of the Greek epic tradition."
⁵⁵ His only other use of *flos* is at 6.562; see too *floriferi* at 9.290 and a form of *floreo* at 10.164. By contrast, *flos* and its derivatives in *flor-* appear sixteen times in the *Aen.*
⁵⁶ See my discussion in Chapter 3 of the comparable image of *Hesperiae segetes* (*Ph.* 7.403).
⁵⁷ Skutsch (1985) 555.
⁵⁸ See Leigh (1997) 302 n. 15 on the many evocations that *maculauit* activates.

in the anchoring intertexts at 1.6–7 and in the preceding lines at 2.183–4, we observe again a redirection of Roman violence from outward and expansive in the *Annales* to inward and self-destructive in the *Pharsalia*. While the *Annales* is a "poem faced primarily outwards from Rome" with a "centrifugal thrust,"[59] the *Pharsalia* directs that movement inward, at and against itself.

The cluster of Ennian intertexts in 2.196–203, I am suggesting, accompanies and underscores the violent intertextual statement made on Marius Gratidianus's mutilated face just previously at 2.181–4. Additional features of Gratidianus's death scene and the old man's speech as a whole complement the Ennian intertextuality and bolster Lucan's poetic statement. To conclude my treatment of this passage, I will consider how a few broader elements may underwrite Lucan's claims about his relationship with Ennius and the epic tradition as a whole.

The death of the historical Gratidianus occurred some ninety years after the conclusion of the *Annales*' narrative; he may seem to be an odd choice as a textual representative for a poetic claim about Ennius and the Latin epic tradition he represented. Yet it is important to emphasize that his murder was a *locus classicus* of debased and degenerated Roman conduct. Told and retold in sources, it stood out as a disgraceful act even among all the horrors of the Republic's bloody decline, and Lucan's old man includes several details that mark Gratidianus's death scene as symbolic of something greater. For one, the observation in 2.190–1 that Gratidianus's face was destroyed (*perdere*) and disfigured (*confundere*) and thus made unrecognizable calls to mind, as Martin Dinter has observed, the time-honored use of the *imago* at Roman funeral processions. The violent act cuts off not only his facial features but his ability to project tradition forward—and in turn speaks to the halting of the Republic itself.[60] The sense of Gratidianus's death as microcosmic of broader Roman disaster is also underscored by the double simile at 2.187–90, coming right after the details of the mutilation:

> sic mole ruinae
> fracta sub ingenti miscentur pondere membra,
> nec magis informes ueniunt ad litora trunci
> qui medio periere freto.

---

[59] Elliott (2014) 226 and 228.
[60] Dinter (2012) 46–7. Fantham (1992) 112: "The act serves to represent civil war and Sulla's cruelty."

In this same way broken limbs are disfigured under great weight by the fall of massive buildings; and trunks of those who died in the middle of the sea do not return to shore more deformed than this.

The comparisons with those dismembered by crashing buildings and those deformed in shipwrecks form a potent pair: an image of urban disaster joined by one of maritime disaster. The mutilation of Gratidianus is aligned through these similes with death on land *and* at sea, at home and abroad. We have seen how Lucan's old man redirects Ennian diction from its outward and productive impetus in the *Annales* back inward, onto itself, toward Roman self-destruction. These similes reinforce and in fact bring specificity to this point. To Lucan the self-mutilation of the Republic entailed Roman loss on land and sea, a closure of the expansion on land and sea that Ennius's epic had put at its center.[61] The *Annales* had showcased the fullness of Roman power, in ships and land marches—a might neatly captured in *Ann.* 518 (= Servius on *Aen.* 6.545): *nauibus explebant sese terrasque replebant* ("They unloaded themselves in full from the ships and then filled up the lands"). Lucan's poem tracks the emptying of the fullness of Roman sway, the ruin on land and wreck at sea evoked in this passage.

Earlier in his speech, the old man had condemned the cowardice shown during Marius's reign of terror and addressed the Romans as *degener o populus* (2.116: "O you degenerate people"). We recall that Lucan uses the pair *potentem* and *conuersum* to characterize the Roman people in his proem, but *degener* also makes for a fitting epithet: throughout the *Pharsalia* he depicts the populace as growing backward (*degener*), regressing, shrinking, collapsing into degenerescence and death—a trajectory counter to Ennius's narrative of Roman launch and advance.[62]

I conclude my analysis of the old man's speech by considering again its narrative frames. He is introduced as one of many parents who were lamenting conditions at Rome, and who hate that "their years have been preserved for the return of civil wars" (*seruatosque iterum bellis ciuilibus annos*, 2.66). Instead of the advance and forward movement of years, these Romans are seeing their years held back (*seruatos*) and sent again (*iterum*) into civil war. This conception of Roman time and movement as not advancing but

---

[61] Points of focus in Chapters 3 and 4.
[62] See Hardie (1993) 89–90 on *degener* at *Aen.* 2.549 as a metapoetic marker.

contracting and moving inward is what that the old man goes on to articulate in his speech, with, I am proposing, Ennius's *Annales* as a conspicuous counterpoint. This is a master trope of the *Pharsalia* as a whole, shrinking—and indeed cutting off, mutilating—the Roman spatial and temporal advance that Ennius's epic had set off.

Alongside this poetic violence against epic's beginnings, the other stylistic hallmark of Lucan's engagement with the epic tradition, lament, can also be heard. Let us recall that the speech follows closely upon the lamentations of Roman citizens at 2.16–66. The disposition of the grieving elders (*miseros ... parentes* in 2.64) is then matched by the lamentable memories from the Marian-Sullan past that the old man recalls. Then, too, there were lamenting elders (*miserorum ... parentum.* 2.167), to go with infants (*infantis miseri*, 2.107) and indeed a whole city suffering the same mournful lot (*miserae ... Romae* in 2.197 and *miseri ... uolgi* in 2.208). The content of this speech—like the content of the surrounding poem—generates lament, from the old and the young, from all of Rome.

So it should not be surprising that Lucan defines the old man's speech in precisely this manner. At its conclusion we read: *sic maesta senectus | praeteritique memor flebat metuensque futuri* (2.232-3: "in this way mournful old age, mindful of the past and fearful of the future, wept"). The speech as a whole is an act of lament, of weeping—*flebat*. Even as the speech highlights Lucan's violent, closural break from the epic tradition and in particular from Ennius's outward-looking, expansive Roman story, it also laments that break, showcasing the poem's manner of double response to the end of the Roman story and the concomitant closure of the epic genre. At the same time, the fact that Lucan couches the old man's speech as a *mise en abyme* suggests that the lament is a reproducible process, open to additional, complementary mourners. Though the epic story of Rome comes to a gory, violent end, the ongoing process of lamenting that end carries on with this poem.

2.5. Razing the leafy wood

I turn now to consider an act of metapoetic violence in the following book, during Lucan's account of Caesar's siege of Massilia in Book 3. Just as the anchoring poetic statement in Book 2 is couched within a conventional epic scene (a mutilation in combat), in Book 3 the statement comes in the conventional scene of chopping down a grove.[63] An episode of this sort first appears in *Iliad* 23, the preparations for Patroclus's funeral pyre (23.114–22). In the woods of Mount Ida, the Achaeans "at once began eagerly to cut down the high-crested oaks with the long-edged bronze, and with a great crash the trees kept falling"[64] (*Il.* 23.118–20: αὐτίκ᾽ ἄρα δρῦς ὑψικόμους ταναήκεϊ χαλκῷ | τάμνον ἐπειγόμενοι· ταὶ δὲ μεγάλα κτυπέουσαι | πῖπτον). Scenes of the felling of groves, including similar details, then appear in the *Annales* (175–9), the *Aeneid* (6.179–82 and 11.135–8), Ovid's *Metamorphoses* (8.741–76), the *Pharsalia* (3.394–452), Statius's *Thebaid* (6.90–106), and Silius's *Punica* (10.527–34).

Each iteration of the *topos* has distinct features; there is, in Hinds's formulation, great "mobility" in the use of this familiar scene. An element connecting many of the passages is that the *topos* lends itself in very specific ways to metapoetics and statements of poetic self-fashioning. Lucan's grove has been visited by a number of scholars, but the scale and potency of his poetic statement here—and in particular his strike at the representatives of the beginnings of the tradition—merit further attention.

Before coming to the Massilian grove, let us consider in brief the deforestation scenes at *Annales* 175–9 and *Aeneid* 6.179–82. Macrobius (*Sat.* 6.2.27) is our source for the Ennian passage, which he cites as a model for the Virgilian one:

Annales 175–9
Incedunt arbusta per alta, securibus caedunt,
Percellunt magnas quercus, exciditur ilex,
Fraxinus frangitur atque abies consternitur alta.
Pinus proceras peruortunt: omne sonabat
Arbustum fremitu siluai frondosai.

They proceed through the high forest, with axes they fell it, they strike down the great oaks, the holm oak is cut down, the ash is broken and the high fir is laid low. They overturn the lofty pines: the whole forest resounds with the roar of the leafy wood.

---

[63] On the desecration of the grove in Lucan, see Phillips (1968); Hunink (1992) 167–70; Masters (1992) 25–9; Thomas (2001) 85–9. See Sklenář (2003) 129–32; Williams (1968) 263–7; Thomas (1988b); Hinds (1998) 10–14; and Nethercut (2019) 201–6 (noting further examples and permutations of the *topos*) on the *topos* more generally. Westerhold (2013) looks at Ovid's adaptation of the scene at *Am.* 3.1.1–6.

[64] Trans. by A. T. Murray and rev. by W. F. Wyatt (with some adjustments).

Aeneid 6.179–82
itur in antiquam siluam, stabula alta ferarum;
procumbunt piceae, sonat icta securibus ilex   180
fraxineaeque trabes cuneis et fissile robur
scinditur, aduoluunt ingentis montibus ornos.

They enter an ancient wood, the deep dwelling place of beasts. Pine trees fall down, the holm oak, struck by axes, resounds, and beams of ash and the splittable strength of oak are cut down, they roll out huge ash trees from the mountains.

A first thing to observe is that Ennius's grove emerges as a significant expansion of the Iliadic model. While including Homer's mighty oaks (*Il.* 23.118), Ennius augments the grove and gives it more personality[65] with the addition of the pine, holm oak, ash, and fir—a plurality that will be common in later scenes in Latin epic. The Virgilian grove includes a similar diversity of trees and shares much in basic conceit and language (notably *alta, ilex, fraxineae*) with the Ennian passage,[66] while Virgil innovates in, for example, the greater variety of expression and meter. In an influential reading of the latter passage, Hinds argues that the opening phrase *itur in antiquam siluam* (*Aen.* 6.179) "can be argued to invoke its archaic model with a programmatic gesture of reflexive annotation in its opening phrase." As Aeneas and his men enter the ancient grove, so too Virgil enters a *locus* once inhabited by the "ancient" poet Ennius. The *Annales* is thus "figured as a harvest of mighty timber from an old-growth forest,"[67] for the *Aeneid* to draw upon. A key part of Hinds's analysis is the reading of the word *silua* to mean both "forest, wood" (*OLD* 1) and also "the raw material of a literary work" (*OLD* 5b).[68]

The rich texture of the word *silua* is critical to our understanding of Lucan's poetic agenda in *Pharsalia* 3.394–452. In his discussion of the passage, Masters also comments on the poetic dynamism of the word and aptly concludes that in the Lucanian passage "deforestation becomes a metaphor for the plundering of poetic material from another source ... it enacts on the

---

[65] Williams (1968) 263: "The effect is ... to personalize the fate of each type of tree."

[66] On meaningful stylistic differences in *Il.* 23.114–22, *Ann.* 175–9, and *Aen.* 6.179–82, see Williams (1968) 263–5; Skutsch (1985) 342; and Goldberg (1995) 83–5.

[67] Hinds (1998) 13.

[68] Hinds (1998) 12–13, pointing to Cic., *Orat.* 12 and Suetonius, *Gram.* 24. See further Coleman (1988) xxii–xxiii, Wray (2007), and Newlands (2011a) 6–7 on the textures of the word *silua*. The Greek cognate *hulē* has many of the same resonances.

plane of epic action what it represents on the plane of literary activity."[69] This insight is on target, but Masters stops short of tracking Lucan's uses of *silua* here—and what precisely we may conclude from them. That Lucan would be sensitive to the literary valences of the word *silua* should not be surprising. His late-antique biographer Vacca tells us that he wrote a ten-book collection of *Silvae*, which may have served as a model for Statius's collection of the same name.[70] The seven appearances of the word in his narrative of Caesar's deforestation of the Massilian grove thus merit close attention. Lucan's most pronounced statement comes at 3.440–5, but that climactic passage is anticipated by a series of earlier gestures. The episode is introduced with the statement: *tunc omnia late / procumbunt nemora et spoliantur robore siluae* (3.394–5: "then all the forests, far and wide, fell down, and the woods were plundered of their strength"). Then follows an extensive description of the grove's antiquity and mysterious divine presences (3.399–425); neither wind nor thunder, we learn at 3.408–10, had been able to fell these woods (*siluas*, 3.409). But then comes Caesar, who "orders this wood to fall to the strike of steel" (3.426: *hanc iubet inmisso siluam procumbere ferro*). After his troops' initial hesitation, Caesar takes the lead, saying, "Now may none of you doubt that I have razed this wood; believe that I have done this unspeakable thing!" (*iam ne quis uestrum dubitet subuertere siluam, | credite me fecisse nefas*, 3.436–7). At the level of the epic's action, these statements announce that Caesar's devastation of the grove will be complete.

If we read *silua* to also indicate "textual material," then Lucan here is declaring a wholesale destruction of the models that preceded him. The verbs *spoliantur* (3.395), *procumbere* (3.395 and 3.426), and *subuertere* (3.436) capture that assault with great variety. The last of these, *subuertere*, is commonly used of the metaphorical subversion of written or spoken words (the law, another's argument; see *OLD* 3). And so, in the same way that Caesar's act of undertaking the unspeakable (*nefas*) speaks to the poet's own brazen and transgressive efforts, the choice of *subuertere* with *silua* seems to mark rather explicitly his act of undercutting earlier textual material. The scale of his poetic violence comes out when he writes at the outset of the passage that the *siluae* to be plundered are from "all the forests, far and wide" (*omnia late... nemora*, 3.394–5). The word *silua* already contains a sense of plurality and variety,[71] but the plural form *siluae* in 3.395, together with the reference

---

[69] Masters (1992) 27. See also Nethercut (2019) 205.
[70] Coleman (1988) xxii.
[71] Coleman (1988) xxiii.

in the same line to *all* the forests, enhances the notion of the vast scale of the attack. Lucan is re-entering and violating not one, but all the woods—the entire epic tradition. Readers of the passage have focused on its adaptation of the deforestations at *Aeneid* 6.179–82 and *Metamorphoses* 8.741–76, and in what follows I will address those model passages, each at play in the poet's "mobile" engagement with the *topos*.[72] But if it is Lucan's ambition to cut down the tradition as a whole—*omnia late . . . nemora*—he must take on and topple Ennius and Homer too.

Lucan's contemporary Quintilian would conceive of Ennius's place in the literary tradition with precisely the image of a sacred grove: "We must revere Ennius as we do groves that are sacred from their age" (*Ennium sicut sacros uetustate lucos adoremus, IO* 10.1.88). Though sure to involve Ennius in his grove, Lucan does not approach in reverence. The revealing lines come at the culmination of the passage, when the trees fall. Here again is the Ennian passage, followed by the climactic lines from *Pharsalia* 3:

Annales 175–9
Incedunt arbusta per alta, securibus caedunt,
Percellunt magnas quercus, **exciditur ilex**,
Fraxinus frangitur atque abies consternitur alta.
Pinus proceras pervortunt: omne sonabat
Arbustum fremitu **siluai frondosai**.

Pharsalia 3.440–5
procumbunt orni, **nodosa inpellitur ilex**,
siluaque Dodones et fluctibus aptior alnus
et non plebeios luctus testata cupressus
tum primum posuere comas et **fronde carentes**
admisere diem, propulsaque robore denso
sustinuit se silua cadens.

Ash trees fall down, the knotty holm oak is forced down, and the wood of Dodona, the alder that is more suited for the sea, and the cypress that

---

[72] Thomas (1988b) 268–9 and (2001) 85–9 argues that the presentation of Caesar at the grove draws on (and affirms) Virgil's depiction of Aeneas as a grove violator. Phillips (1968) proposes that Lucan took the idea for the episode wholesale from Ovid, *Met*. 8.741–76. Keith (2011) 124–7 considers Lucan's adaptation of imagery from the passage in *Met*. 8 as well as scenes from Theban myth in *Met*. 3.

is a witness to non-plebeian grief then for the first time let down their
hair and, losing their leaves, let in the day. And the toppled wood, falling,
upheld itself with its dense timber.

After carefully preparing us for this moment over the preceding forty-five lines, now it is happening: the old oaks and pines and ashes are going down. The *silua* of the other sort is toppling, too, and the first line of this description operates quite conspicuously as a marker of engagement with key models. The frame *procumbunt . . . ilex* in 3.440 evokes the identical frame at *Aeneid* 6.180,[73] a signal that Lucan is following Virgil onto this ancient Ennian ground. But in this same line, Lucan announces that he is engaging with the *Annales* in his own ways. His line-end *inpellitur ilex* closely recalls Ennius's line-end *exciditur ilex* (*Ann.* 176), in both the form—-*itur ilex*—and the metrical echo. A noticeable difference lies in Lucan's addition of the uncommon epithet *nodosa*, meaning "knotty," a condition that comes with growth and so perhaps speaks to the oak's age.[74] Also striking is the replacement of *exciditur*, a verb of cutting *proprie*, with *inpellitur* (with the identical morphological characteristics). This verb of pushing aside/forcing out is all the more eye-catching because *inpello* is used nowhere else of trees. With his crafting of 3.440, then, Lucan is pursuing Virgil's path into the grove—but also marking his own forceful thrust aside (*inpellitur*) of the knotty (*nodosa*), overgrown, conventional Ennian imagery. This dynamic in 3.440, I propose, operates as an allusive anchor for the engagement with Ennius across the passage.

Like Virgil at *Aeneid* 6.179–82 (and 11.135–8) and Ennius at *Ann.* 175–9, Lucan includes five different varieties in his miniature catalog of felled trees. Each poet includes an oak, holm oak, ash, and pine tree. But Lucan departs from these models with conspicuous *variatio*, referring to the oak not with the nouns *quercus* or *robor*, but with the phrase *silua Dodones* (3.441), a reference to Jupiter, who kept an oracle at Dodona in Epirus. And he alone includes not the broader term for a pine (*pinus* or *picea*) but a more specific type, the weeping cypress (*cupressus*, 3.442). We shall see later that each of these conspicuous innovations is meaningful.[75] Like Virgil, Lucan uses a variety of verbal expressions for the trees' toppling (*procumbunt, inpellitur,*

---

[73] Thomas (1988b) 268–9 and (2001) 85–6; Masters (1992) 26.
[74] There may be an association with old age in Lucan's one other use of *nodosus*, at 8.672–3, of Pompey's knotty bones (*nodosaque . . . ossa*) that are being cut by his assassin Septimius.
[75] See Fratantuono (2012) 113 on Lucan's careful description of these trees.

posuere comas et . . . admisere diem in 3.340–4).[76] This morphological and syntactic variation—even unruliness—stands in stark contrast to the "weighty symmetry"[77] of Ennius's verses, where three third-person plural present active verbs of the humans' actions (*incedunt, caedunt, percellunt*) are followed by three third-person singular present passive verbs of the trees' axing (*exciditur, frangitur, consternitur*). Any sense of order that the Ennian passage conveyed is undermined by the more chaotic toppling and tumbling of trees in Lucan's grove.

While clear similarities point the reader of *Ph.* 3.440–6 back to *Annales* 175–9, one finds further details that complicate, destabilize, and push aside (recall the conspicuous *inpellitur*) the earlier, overgrown (*nodosa*) model. Another pointed difference comes in how the passages end. Like Ennius at *Ann.* 178–9 (*omne* to *frondosai*),[78] Lucan concludes with a description of the grove as a whole (*propulsaque* to *cadens*), but with a difference that is significant at the narrative and metapoetic levels: he pictures the wood as not just falling, but falling onto itself (*propulsaque robore denso | sustinuit se silua cadens*, 3.444–5). With this in mind, it is worth considering, however speculatively, the context of the Ennian fragment. Macrobius tells us that it comes from *Annales* 6, and while some assign it to an account of the construction of the Roman fleet, others have placed it amid preparations for a funeral pyre after a Roman battle against Pyrrhus.[79] Such a context would be consistent with those at *Iliad* 23.114–22, *Aeneid* 6.179–82 and 11.135–8, *Thebaid* 6.90–106, and *Punica* 10.527–34. Elliott is cautious about placement in a specific spot in *Annales* 6, but, with the model in *Iliad* 23 in mind, reads it as unmistakably part of a narrative of Roman aggrandizement, progress, and destiny: "Whatever action framed this passage . . . the recurrence of the vignette retrospectively illuminated its role in its earlier, Homeric context, by revealing [the *Iliad* 23 passage] as a simple precursor to an eventual Roman destiny."[80]

The Lucanian passage operates in a pointedly opposed way. While the *Annales* passage contributes to Ennius's narrative of Roman expansion (be it in the war against Pyrrhus, the development of Rome's fleet, or another

---

[76] Note the variety at *Aen.* 179–82 in *procumbunt* (6.180), *sonat* (6.180), *scinditur* (6.182), and, with the Trojans as subject, *aduoluunt* (6.182).

[77] Skutsch (1985) 342.

[78] And unlike Virg. at *Aen.* 179–82 and 11.135–8.

[79] See Skutsch (1985) 341 (following Vahlen) and Flores et al. (2002) 122–3.

[80] Elliott (2013) 290, in her broader argument about the aims of Ennius's Homerizing passages (233–94). See Dominik (1993) 44 for a concise discussion of Ennius's adaptations of Homer.

endeavor), the chopping down of the Massilian grove stands as another textual representation of inward-facing Roman self-destruction. For one, since Lucan had compared Pompey to an old oak in the poem's prologue (1.136–43), Caesar's razing of this grove seems to pick up on that image of violent conflict at the center of the poem's story.[81] But this act does not spell doom for Pompey's side alone. There was a strange and terrifying sacredness to the grove (3.402–17), and Lucan writes that Caesar's men "believed that, if they were to strike the sacred oaks, the axes would come back at their limbs (*in sua . . . membra*)" (3.430–1). During the felling itself, he emphasizes the irreverence of the act by referring to the oak as the *silua Dodones* (3.441)—it is as though the men are chopping down the famed grove at Jupiter's oracle in Dodona.[82] Further, evocations of Erysichthon's violation of Ceres's grove at *Metamorphoses* 8.741–76[83] lead the reader to expect the same punishment for Caesar and his men as Erysichthon received. Yet the axes do not fly back at the violators, who leave the grove unpunished. What happens is more powerful: "the toppled wood, falling, upheld itself with its dense timber" (3.444–5: *propulsaque robore denso | sustinuit se silua cadens*). The falling trees strike back not at Caesar's men but at *each other*, an image neatly capturing the condition of civil war, of violence directed not outward but inward, onto itself.[84] Vincent Hunink observes that the "image recalls a gruesome motif in Lucan's battle scenes, where the same thing happens to corpses,"[85] noting the descriptions of the dead in the Tiber at 2.209–20 and in Africa at 4.787. Like the self-defeating Romans of the surrounding narrative, the trees in the Massilian grove are dead, but still standing. Here in one image is Lucan's story of Rome, which dies at Pharsalia—crashing into and against itself, its *membra* hacked in this way—but still exists. Masters comes to a somewhat different conclusion, arguing that the grove is a "model of the civil war, where what falls rises again."[86] He points to the statement at 3.417–19 that "legend used to relate (*fama ferebat*) . . . that yews that had fallen down rose up again." But this reading overlooks the meaningful use of tense in that statement: legend *used to* relate (*ferebat*) the story of the trees' resurrection

---

[81] See Ahl (1976) 199 and Masters (1992) 27–8.
[82] Referenced again at 6.426–7. See Sklenář (2003) 129–32 on this defilement.
[83] See Phillips (1968) and Keith (2011) 127, as well as Murray (2004) on Ovid's own reworking of the Erysichthon scene in Callim., *Hymn* 6, and a deforestation scene at Ap Rhod., *Argon.* 2.468–90.
[84] Hunink (1992) 183 contrasts Ov., *Met.* 8.775–6, where the trees collapse in a normal way (*multam prostrauit pondere siluam,* 8.776).
[85] Hunink (1992) 183.
[86] Masters (1992) 28.

and the grove's regeneration. After Caesar's onslaught, there is no more life in this grove. The *fama* of Lucan's epic is telling a different story.

This stroke of finality in the clearing of the grove is also operative on the metapoetic level.[87] The process of epic inheritance is crashing down, as the climactic statement at 3.444–5 conveys: here the epic material (*silua*) dies, falling (*cadens*) onto itself. It—the *topos* of the grove deforestation and the epic genre more broadly—still stands on its own strength, but after Lucan's acts of incursion and violence, it is a fallen thing, a dead thing.[88] Additional contrasts with *Annales* 175–9 confirm this notion of poetic finality. Ennius's details had brought out the grove's/epic's vitality and possibility for regrowth. The statement *omne sonabat | arbustum fremitu siluai frondosai* (*Ann.* 178–9) emphasizes the wood's vibrant sound (*sonabat, fremitu*) and abiding lushness (*siluai frondosai*). In a departure from not only Ennius but also Homer (*Il.* 23.119), Virgil (*Aen.* 6.180 and 11.135),[89] and Ovid (*Met.* 8.770–3),[90] Lucan's trees do not make a sound. Their surprising silence is accompanied by a marked loss of foliage. Readers have discussed how "extraordinary" and even "outlandish" Ennius's spondaic line-end *sīluāī frōndōsāī* is.[91] It is reasonable to suggest that Lucan also found the line to be extraordinary, and his line-end *fronde carentes* ("leafless," 3.443) highlights a conspicuous break: whereas to Ennius the genre was fresh, generative, boisterous, and capable of providing material for regrowth, in the *Pharsalia* it is made silent, leafless, and lifeless. The tradition of epic inheritance and evergreen potential is being cut short, chopped down. To mark this poetic act as complete, Lucan must include the final deforestation of Ennius's ancient and oft-visited *silua frondosa*.

2.6. A grove and a genre grieve

Lucan departs from his models by moving his deforestation scene away from the familiar context of preparations for a funeral pyre.[92] But at the same

---

[87] *Contra* Masters (1992) 28–9 ("the poem too is a repetition, a resurrection of other poems through this very process of 'deforestation'; and in the future it will itself be part of the same process").

[88] Again there is a parallel with the simile at 1.136–43 comparing Pompey with an old oak standing only on its own weight (1.139).

[89] See Williams (1968) 264 on the trees' variety of sounds.

[90] Where a nymph cries out from within the tree (*redditus e medio sonus est . . . robore*, 8.770).

[91] See Goldberg (1995) 85 and Williams (1968) 263, respectively.

[92] But see the creative suggestion by Masters (1992) 26: "Lucan is definitely playing on these funerary connotations: for the pile of wood making up the rampart *does* eventually burn, and becomes one of a succession of ersatz funeral celebrations."

time, he brings the voice of grieving to the Massilian grove in a more intimate and profound way. As the trees are being cut down and falling upon one another, Lucan makes the grove itself mourn. While Ovid had noted the mourning of Ceres's nymphs after Erysichthon's violation of her grove (*Met.* 8.778–9), Lucan grants this process to the trees themselves. Here once again are the lines:

> procumbunt orni, nodosa inpellitur ilex,
> siluaque Dodones et fluctibus aptior alnus
> et non plebeios luctus testata cupressus
> tum primum posuere comas et fronde carentes
> admisere diem, propulsaque robore denso
> sustinuit se silua cadens. (*Ph.* 3.340–5)

Instead of the more general pine familiar from Ennius's and Virgil's groves, Lucan includes "the cypress that bears witness to non-plebeian grief" (*non plebeios luctus testata cupressus*). A scholiast on the *Pharsalia* notes that the cypress was associated with death because it does not regenerate after being cut down.[93] In the ancient world it was commonly used at funerals, particularly those of the wealthy (thus Lucan's detail *non plebeios*). Here the inclusion of the cypress serves two functions: it marks the finality of the axing—this wood, this *silua*, will not grow again—and it brings the emotion of grief (*luctus*) to the deforestation.

After the explicit mention of the cypress's grief, that tree, together with the oak and alder, "then, for the first time, let down their hair and, losing their leaves, let in the day" (3.443–4). At the plainest level, these lines convey that the dark grove shed its leaves and thus admitted daylight for the first time,[94] but Lucan is also projecting onto the trees a physical gesture closely associated with lament: letting down and tearing out one's hair. The metaphor of *comae* for "leaves" is a common one,[95] but the use here, just after the explicit reference to the cypress's participation in grieving, compels the reader to think of

---

[93] *Commenta Bernensia* on 4.442: *cupressus et tamarix ideo mortuis ponitur, quod excisa non renascatur, aut quod infelices sint id est steriles.* See Ov., *Met.* 10.106–42 on Apollo's conversion of the grieving youth Cyparissus into the cypress tree; and Connors (1992) on the association of the cypress with death.

[94] See Hunink (1992) 183 (on 3.443), responding to the pedantic concern of Shackleton Bailey (1987) 78 that some of the trees are deciduous and so would have shed leaves each year (and so not "for the first time").

[95] See 4.128, 6.44, and 9.428, with Hunink (1992) 183 (on 3.443), who notes the appearance of the metaphor at Homer, *Od.* 23.195, and in a number of Latin texts.

hair *proprie*. In the previous book, Lucan had described the Roman matrons' act of tearing up and letting loose their hair (*lacerasque . . . | attonitae fudere comas*, 2.31-2; see too 2.39) in preemptive lament for Rome's fall. In Book 9 he will recount a similar gesture from Pompey's widow Cornelia, who "loosened and let her hair fall onto her face" (*solutas | in uoltus effusa comas*, 9.172-3). The dying trees in the Massilian grove show this same expression of grief, and Lucan dwells on the gesture by envisioning it twice, with the matching phrases *posuere comas* and *fronde carentes*. Then, the first detail that Lucan includes after the grove's fall, in the same line, is that the Gauls who witnessed the fall groan in grief (*gemuere*, 3.445). A few lines later, Caesar's men seize wagons from nearby Gauls to haul the timber (3.450-1), and farmers weep (*fleuere*, 3.452) for the harvest that they will lose without the use of their oxen. The trees' lamentation, we see, spreads quickly to the neighboring community. And so this act of violent defilement is met by a sort of antiphony of lament, the kind of multivocal expression that carries through the poem, with characters, narrator, and even the Roman reader participating in the process. The involvement in the lament of both the victim of the violence (the grove itself) and the witnessing community members (the neighboring Gauls) may reflect the larger poem's presentation of both Rome/Roman characters and the broader "we" of the poem's Roman readers as participants in the antiphony.

The material (*silua*) of epic that was leafy and generative in Ennius (*siluai frondosai*) collapses on itself and is made dead by Lucan. There had been many iterations of the grove's fall, going back to *Iliad* 23, and many regenerations, including Ennius's influential inheritance of that grove into Latin epic. This *silua*, this epic material, had long been rich and productive. But in Lucan's grove, *then for the first time* (*tum primum*, 3.443) the trees lamented, knowing now that their loss of leaves and of life was final. There is thus both novelty and finality in the metapoetic marker *tum primum*. In Lucan's poem—for the first and also the last time—the fallen wood expresses lament, heralding and grieving a poetic end.

2.7. Scaeva in and against the epic tradition

Up to this point in the chapter, I have looked at Lucan's use of two conventional scenes of violence as vehicles for statements about his polemical closural poetics: the self-mutilation of Gratidianus in Book 2 as a showcase for the *Pharsalia*'s disfigurement of the genre, and the violent self-collapse of the grove in Book 3 as representative of the collapse of the epic tradition. I conclude the chapter by considering Lucan's comparable inversion of another stylistic warhorse of the genre, the individual hero's courageous stand against many enemies on the battlefield. A scene of this sort, with particular conventional details, had a literary lineage going back to the *Iliad* and appears regularly in subsequent epic. During his account of the Battle of Dyrrachium in Book 6, Lucan blows up this familiar scene into over 120 lines (6.140–262). The hero in his version, the Caesarian centurion Scaeva, is a veritable emblem of the civil war as a whole, a Roman "ready for every unspeakable deed" (*pronus ad omne nefas*, 6.146). Scaeva is in many ways, as John Henderson has put it, Lucan's "finest creation,"[96] and this brawling, braggadocious, and relentless embodiment of *uirtus* in vain[97] has led many readers to identify him as an icon of the work as a whole.[98] We will see here how Lucan uses Scaeva's outsized battle stand as a venue for a sweeping poetic statement about the epic genre, with, again, pointed, piercing aim at the predecessor who brought Homeric epic into Latin.

The key *locus* for observing continuities and breaks from his epic predecessors is 6.184–95. After introducing Scaeva (6.140–48), giving him a spirited speech to encourage his lagging fellow Caesarians (6.149–65), and then narrating his battlefield position on a growing heap of corpses (6.166–83), Lucan zooms in on the attack on Scaeva from all sides:

> tunc densos inter cuneos conpressus et omni
> uallatus bello uincit, quem respicit, hostem.   185
> iamque hebes et crasso non asper sanguine mucro
> perdidit ensis opus, frangit sine uolnere membra.   188
> illum tota premit moles, illum omnia tela,
> nulla fuit non certa manus, non lancea felix;   190
> parque nouum Fortuna uidet concurrere, bellum
> atque uirum. fortis crebris sonat ictibus umbo,
> et galeae fragmenta cauae conpressa perurunt
> tempora, nec quidquam nudis uitalibus obstat
> iam praeter stantis in summis ossibus hastas.   195

---

[96] Henderson (1987) 125.
[97] Sklenář (2003) 58.
[98] On Scaeva, see Johnson (1987) 57–60; Leigh (1997) 158–90; Gorman (2001) 277–9; Sklenář (2003) 45–58; Hömke (2010); Seo (2011) 209–11; and Fratantuono (2012) 226–31, noting that "the midpoint of the epic falls somewhere during the Scaeva episode" (231). Conte (1988) 43–112 offers an interpretive commentary on the full passage.

Then, packed into the dense ranks and surrounded by the whole war,
he defeats whichever enemy he lays his eyes on. Now dull and no longer
sharp because of the clotted blood, his sword-point has lost the ability to
do a sword's work—it breaks limbs without wounding them. On him the
whole force presses, on him all the weapons; there wasn't one errant hand
or one unlucky lance. Fortune witnesses a new pair of equals clashing: war
and a man. The stout boss of his shield resounds with constant blows, and
the crushed pieces of his hollow helmet burn up his temples, and nothing
stands in the way of his naked vitals except the spears sticking onto the
tops of his bones (6.184–95)

Many of the details here have close parallels in three comparable scenes
in earlier epic: Ajax's stand against a throng of Trojans near the Achaean
ships at *Iliad* 16.102–11; the heroics of a Roman military tribune[99] against
Histrian attackers at the siege of Ambracia in 177 BCE in *Annales* 15 (391–
8); and Turnus's holdout against enemies inside the Trojan camp at *Aeneid*
9.806–14. These three episodes have long been aligned and studied together,
first by Macrobius (*Sat.* 6.3.2–4), who excerpts them in an effort to demon-
strate that many passages in Virgil were not adapted from Homer but "taken
from our own authors, who had first drawn them from Homer for their own
poems" (*a nostris auctoribus sumpta qui priores haec ab Homero in carmina
sua traxerant*, 6.3.2).[100] The example of *nostri auctores* that Macrobius cites is
Ennius. To him it is clear that Ennius's Latin adaptation of the Homeric pas-
sage served as the chief model text for Virgil.

A great number of correspondences exist between the description of
Scaeva at 6.184–95 and the scenes in the *Iliad*, the *Annales*, and the *Aeneid*.
I reprint the passages here, keeping Macrobius's order:

Iliad 16.102–11
Αἴας δ' οὐκέτ' ἔμιμνε· βιάζετο γὰρ βελέεσσι·
δάμνα μιν Ζηνός τε νόος καὶ Τρῶες ἀγαυοὶ

---

[99] Identified by Macrobius (6.3.3) as one Gaius Aelius.
[100] In the preceding lines, at 6.2.32, Macrobius writes that the passage on Pandarus's and Bitias's opening of the gates of the Trojan camp (*Aen.* 9.672–755), just prior to Turnus's efforts in *Aen.* 9, is also taken from a passage in *Ann.* 15, one describing the escape of two Histrians from their besieged stronghold. See Skutsch (1985) 558; Goldberg (1995) 87–88; and Elliott (2013) 226–8 and 284–7 on Ennius's artful departures from Homer. See also Goldschmidt (2013) 180–87, suggesting that the story of Horatius Cocles (and possibly Ennius's account of Cocles) lies behind Turnus's fight in *Aen.* 9.

βάλλοντες· δεινὴ δὲ περὶ κροτάφοισι φαεινὴ
πήληξ βαλλομένη καναχὴν ἔχε, βάλλετο δ' αἰεὶ   105
κὰπ φάλαρ' εὐποίηθ'· ὁ δ' ἀριστερὸν ὦμον ἔκαμνεν,
ἔμπεδον αἰὲν ἔχων σάκος αἰόλον· οὐδ' ἐδύναντο
ἀμφ' αὐτῷ πελεμίξαι ἐρείδοντες βελέεσσιν.
αἰεὶ δ' ἀργαλέῳ ἔχετ' ἄσθματι, κὰδ δέ οἱ ἱδρὼς
πάντοθεν ἐκ μελέων πολὺς ἔρρεεν, οὐδέ πη εἶχεν   110
ἀμπνεῦσαι· πάντῃ δὲ κακὸν κακῷ ἐστήρικτο.

But Ajax no longer held his ground, for he was hard pressed with missiles; the mind of Zeus was subduing him as were the lordly Trojans with their missiles; and terribly did the bright helmet about his temples ring continually as it was struck, for it was constantly struck on the well-made cheekpieces, and his left shoulder grew weary as he ever firmly held his flashing shield; nor could they beat it back about him, though they pressed him hard with missiles. And he was constantly distressed by painful breathing, and down from his limbs everywhere abundant sweat kept streaming, nor could he catch his breath at all, but on every side evil was heaped on evil. (Trans. by A. T. Murray. Rev. by W. F. Wyatt)

<u>Annales 391–8</u>
undique conueniunt uelut imber tela tribuno:
configunt parmam, tinnit hastilibus umbo
aerato sonitu galeae: sed nec pote quisquam
undique nitendo corpus discerpere ferro.
semper obundantes hastas frangitque quatitque: 395
totum sudor habet corpus multumque laborat,
nec respirandi fit copia: praepete ferro
Histri tela manu iacientes sollicitabant.

From all sides the weapons come at the tribune like rain: they pierce his shield, and its boss rings from the spears, to go with the bronze din of his helmet. But no one, though striving with their steel from all sides, is able to tear apart his body. The spears that are coming at him in waves—each time he breaks and brandishes them. Sweat takes hold of his whole body, and he toils greatly, and there is no room to breathe. With their swift-winged steel the Istrians hurl weapons from their hands and continue to come at him.

Aeneid 9.806–14
ergo nec clipeo iuvenis subsistere tantum
nec dextra ualet, iniectis sic undique telis
obruitur. strepit adsiduo cava tempora circum
tinnitu galea et saxis solida aera fatiscunt
discussaeque iubae, capiti nec sufficit umbo   810
ictibus; ingeminant hastis et Troes et ipse
fulmineus Mnestheus. tum toto corpore sudor
liquitur et piceum (nec respirare potestas)
flumen agit, fessos quatit aeger anhelitus artus.

Therefore, with neither shield nor sword arm can the soldier hold his own: with such a hail of missiles is he overwhelmed on all sides. Round his hollow temples the helmet echoes with ceaseless clash; the solid brass gapes beneath the rain of stones; the horsehair crest is torn from his head, and the shield's boss withstands not the blows: the Trojans and Mnestheus himself, of lightning force, launch a storm of spears. Then all over his body flows the sweat and runs in pitchy stream, and he has no breathing space; a sickly panting shakes his wearied limbs. (Trans. by H. R. Fairclough. Rev. by G. P. Goold)

In looking at the passages alongside *Pharsalia* 6.184–95, we identify several shared elements. Each author emphasizes, at the outset of the clash, the plurality of the attacks on the hero.[101] Homer writes that Ajax "is hit hard by missiles" (βιάζετο γὰρ βελέεσσι, *Il.* 16.102), and then Ennius (*Ann.* 391: *undique conueniunt . . . tela tribuno*) and Virgil (*Aen.* 9.807–8: *obiectis sic undique telis* | *obruitur*) similarly describe weapons coming at their heroes from everywhere. After stressing the great number of attackers at 6.184–5, Lucan unpacks and expands the Ennian and Virgilian image of "weapons coming from everywhere" with a list at 6.189–90, including not just the "full force" of the enemy and every weapon coming at him (*illum tota premit moles, illum omnia tela*, 6.189), but also individual hands and spears (*nulla fuit non certa manus, non lancea felix*, 6.190).

In each of the Latin passages, there is an emphasis on, specifically, the abundance of spears hurled at the hero (*Ann.* 395, *Aen.* 9.811–12, and *Ph.* 6.195). Each author also concentrates on the sensation within the hero's

---

[101] Noted by Conte (1988) 27 in his discussion of the four passages together (25–8).

helmet, at *Iliad* 16.104–5 (δεινὴν δὲ περὶ κροτάφοισι φαεινὴ | πήληξ βαλλομένη καναχὴν ἔχε), *Annales* 393 (*aerato sonitu galeae*), *Aeneid* 9.808–9 (*strepit adsiduo caua tempora circum | tinnitu galea*), and *Pharsalia* 6.193–4 (*et galeae fragmenta cauae conpressa perurunt | tempora*). Whereas each of his predecessors describes a ringing sound, Lucan uses similar language but also visualizes the warrior's experience within the helmet, with the searing image of pieces of the helmet burning away (*perurunt*) at Scaeva's temples. Finally, in another detail common to the four passages, each author focuses on the centrality of the hero's shield in the action, at *Iliad* 16.107 (ἔμπεδον αἰὲν ἔχων σάκος αἰόλον), *Annales* 392 (*configunt parmam, tinnit hastilibus umbo*), *Aeneid* 9.810 (*capiti nec sufficit umbo | ictibus*), and *Pharsalia* 6.192 (*fortis crebris sonat ictibus umbo*).

Scaeva's act of defense against a charge of many clearly responds to and builds upon this tradition as a whole. In his discussion of the reversal of Homeric and Virgilian heroism in the passage, Sklenář aptly writes that "Scaeva is aware of his own intertextual identity and able to control certain of its features."[102] In this way he is like the old man as *poeta doctus* in Book 2; Scaeva knows of his metatextuality, and Lucan even embeds this awareness of his own metatextuality into the passage. Soon after the densely intertextual lines 6.184–95, the poet writes of Scaeva:

>   tot uolnera belli
> solus obit densamque ferens in pectore siluam
> iam gradibus fessis, in quem cadat, eligit hostem.
>
> He alone takes on so many wounds, and, bearing a thick forest on his chest,
> now with weary steps he chooses which enemy to fall upon. (6.204–6)

With the phrase *tot uolnera belli | solus obit*, Lucan succinctly defines the scene-type of the one-against-many battlefield stand, seemingly signposting Scaeva's embrace of the *topos*. He then writes that his hero bears "a thick forest" (*densam . . . siluam*) on his chest. The metaphor captures just how many spears are stuck in Scaeva, but also, given the literary resonances of *silua*, how rich and varied Scaeva's literary pedigree is. Lucan's hero carries with him—wears on his chest—the history of this grisly *topos*.

---

[102] Sklenář (2003) 54, who at 49 acknowledges but downplays the significance of the Ennian model: "Though Ennius' tribune is doubtless among his ancestors, Scaeva ultimately represents the triumph of Thersites' line over that of Achilles as Aeneas."

He also makes it his own. The poet underscores the newness of Scaeva's take on the *topos* at the center of the description at 6.184–95: *parque nouum Fortuna uidet concurrere, bellum | atque uirum* (6.191–2: "Fortune witnesses a new pair of equals clashing: war and a man"). Scaeva is something new, strange, never before seen: "That a single man should fight against an entire army is unprecedented (*nouum*) both in actual warfare and in epic."[103] And while Lucan's models all emphasized the magnitude of the attacking army, Lucan expands the scale of the enemy to be coterminous with the war itself. In other words, what is new about Scaeva is that he is equal to and in a real sense *is* the war—*parque . . . bellum | atque uirum*.

Scaeva is a walking, talking incarnation of the violence of civil war, beaten to a pulp—but he brings it on himself. Earlier in the passage he had personally explained his manner of fighting when instructing his comrades about facing the enemy: "Smash their weapons with the thrust of your chest (*pectoris inpulsu*), and beat back their steel with your throats (*iugulis*)" (2.160–1). *This* is how to fight: with your self, your actual chest and throat and person. We soon see this method of combat in action, when "all of the ruins provide the man with weapons; he threatens the enemy with wood beams, with masses of block, and with *himself*" (2.172–3: *totaeque uiro dant tela ruinae, | roboraque et moles hosti seque ipse minatur*). The juxtaposition of the reflexive *se* and then the intensive *ipse* strengthens the emphasis on Scaeva as an embodiment of self-reflexive attack, and thus of the inward-directed violence of civil war.

So while the heroes in Lucan's model passages all take on foreign enemies, Scaeva practices violence not just on fellow Romans but, in the same process, on himself. In the final lines of the passage the narrator explicitly draws this contrast, after describing the acclaim Scaeva's fellow Caesarians give to him:

>   felix hoc nomine famae,
> si tibi durus Hiber aut si tibi terga dedisset
> Cantaber exiguis aut longis Teutonus armis.
> non tu bellorum spoliis ornare Tonantis   260
> templa potes, non tu laetis ululare triumphis.
> infelix, quanta dominum uirtute parasti!

---

[103] Sklenář (2003) 51. See also Hömke (2010) on the uniqueness of the Scaeva passage as a whole, "a pointed rejection of the validity of [the] epic structure" (96) of the *aristeia*.

You would have been fortunate in this claim to fame, if a stout Iberian or a Cantabrian or a Teuton with his long weapons had fled from you. You cannot decorate the temple of the Thunderer with the spoils of war; you cannot sing aloud in celebratory triumphs. Unfortunate one, with what courage you made the way for a master! (6.257–62)

To Lucan the defining characteristic of Scaeva's fighting is its direction, moving not against foreign enemies such as the Iberians, Cantabrians, or Teutones, but against Romans, with his own throat and heart as both tool and target of the violence (2.160–1).

Lucan's presentation of Scaeva as a self-destroying Roman civil warrior invites us to look more closely at the one other iteration of this *topos* with a Roman fighter at its center, Ennius's depiction of the Roman tribune fighting at Ambracia at *Ann.* 391–8. A number of particular points of contact connect the passages. Conte has called attention to the close correspondences between the line-ends of *Ph.* 6.192 (*fortis crebris sonat ictibus umbo*) and *Ann.* 392 (*tinnit hastilibus umbo*).[104] A description of the boss of the shield emitting a sound appears in only these two passages,[105] and, as Conte notes, Lucan's *sonat ictibus umbo* aligns with Ennius's *tinnit hastilibus umbo* in both meter and in the progression of verb → ablative plural → nominative. The echo is clear, though Lucan amplifies the sound: instead of ringing (*tinnit*), Scaeva's boss resounds (*sonat*). And, prior to the allusive line-end, Lucan piles on the adjectives *fortis* ("stout," of the boss) and *crebris* ("frequent," of the blows to the shield). This expansion of Ennius is in keeping with the expansions of each model text in 6.184–95 considered earlier (the detailed enumeration of the many weapons coming at Scaeva, and the visualization of the horrific effects within the helmet).

An additional detail that Lucan appears to build upon for his own purposes is that of the image of rain. At *Ann.* 391 the weapons fall on the tribune *uelut imber*, an image also in *Ann.* 266 (*ferreus imber*) and that Skutsch has suggested Ennius may have introduced into Latin.[106] Lucan does something

---

[104] See Conte (1988) 28 and 85, where he suggests that in both *Ann.* 392 and *Ph.* 6.192 the series of short words captures the battery of blows on the shield.

[105] At *Aen.* 9.810–11 the boss of Turnus's shield cannot stand the blows (*nec sufficit umbo | ictibus*) but makes no sound.

[106] Skutsch (1985) 445–6 on *Ann.* 266, which Macrobius (6.1.52) cites as the model for *Aen.* 12.284 (*ac ferreus ingruit imber*), demonstrating the memorability of Ennius's phrase. Rossi (2004) 139 n. 40 also suggests that *Ann.* 266 is the model for *Aen.* 12.284 as well as *Aen.* 9.668–9.

much more jarring with rain imagery. After another forty lines of Scaeva's gory, self-immolating fighting, he writes that "madness had destroyed his face; his visage appeared deformed by a rain of blood" (6.224–5: *perdiderat uoltum rabies, stetit imbre cruento | informis facies*). Lucan sticks the figurative language of *imber* that Ennius had used of war's weapons right onto his hero's bloodied face, a fitting turn for this warrior who leads with his throat— and, perhaps, a *second* time in which Lucan chops up an Ennian image and places it onto a bloodied civil warrior's face. And by making his a rainstorm of blood, Lucan highlights—as often in this passage (see too 6.145, 186, 226, and 250)—how much blood and thus life is pouring out of this warrior. The *topos* of the hero's one-against-many stand, we might suggest, is being drained of blood—losing its form (note *informis*) and its life.

Perhaps the most revealing adaptation of *Annales* 391–8 comes in the picture on which Lucan pauses at 6.194–5, just before a narratorial address to Scaeva's attackers. It is an unforgettable sight: "nothing stands in the way of his naked vitals except the spears sticking onto the tops of his bones (*stantis in summis ossibus hastas*)" (6.194–5). Ennius had also zeroed in on his hero's reception of numerous spears at *Ann.* 395 (*semper obundantes hastas frangitque quatitque*), where his tribune takes on the flow of spears with daring and bravado, quickly snapping and then brandishing them in the rhyming pair *frangitque quatitque*.[107] But the swagger of the Ennian hero is exceeded by Lucan's Scaeva, who does not hold out and brandish the spears but *wears* them; they stick out of his bones as the only attire covering his naked body. Again a contrast is clear between outward projection of violence in Ennius and self-directed, inward absorption of it in Lucan. The passage goes on for another seventy lines, and we never read that Lucan's hero removes the spears sticking into him. The enemy's weapons become part of him, they become him.

Before making some final suggestions about the connections between Scaeva and Ennius's tribune, I want to return in brief to our source for *Annales* 391–8. In his consideration of the original Homeric passage and then the Ennian and Virgilian iterations of this *topos*, Macrobius oversimplifies things when claiming that the Ennian adaptation of *Iliad* 16.102–11 was the sole model for Virgil at *Aeneid* 9.806–13. It is surely more accurate to say

---

[107] As opposed to Virgil, who at *Aen.* 9.811–12 describes the onslaught of spears on Turnus from the perspective of the attackers.

that Virgil reworks both Homer and Ennius, just as Lucan draws on familiarity with all of these models when crafting Scaeva. But Macrobius's observation provides a key perspective on both this passage and the argument of this study as a whole. To Macrobius the *Annales* occupied a critical, principal place as *the* text that transformed Homeric epic into Roman epic, bringing Homeric imagery and themes to the Roman story.[108] It is in passages such as *Ann.* 391–8 that Homer is, in Ennius's own celebrated image, reborn in the Roman poet. It is not possible (or important) to determine with any confidence the historical identity of Ennius's tribune, or whether there was actually such an episode at Ambracia in the year 177 BCE. What matters is the authoritative standing that the tribune takes on. Elliott has written that "Ennius' tribune mattered because, as the poet made him, he instantiated Roman potential for stepping into Greece's shoes."[109] The tribune in *Ann.* 391–8 emerges as a Homeric-style hero, another Ajax, but made Roman, unmistakably fighting and toiling (recall *multumque laborat* at *Ann.* 396) for Roman conquest and expansion.

Lucan's Scaeva self-consciously engages with, expands, and contorts inward the efforts of this principal and dutiful (recall *Ann.* 4) receiver of the Homeric tradition, this crucial textual conveyor of the Homeric story into the Roman story. Scaeva pointedly takes on more and more varied weapons (6.189–90), with a boss that echoes but resounds more loudly and memorably than the Ennian tribune's (6.192). Crucially, the rainstorm of war and cascade of spears that beset but did not deter Ennius's tribune are now worn by Scaeva on his face and in his bones—the external and externalized violence of war now physically internalized. The war Scaeva fights does not proceed outward in expansion, as the fighting in *Annales* 15 and across that poem had, but moves inward, onto and even into himself.[110] Like the self-slaughtering Marius Gratidianus in Book 2 and the falling grove in Book 3, Scaeva is iconic of the collapse onto itself of both Rome and Roman epic. *Pila minantia pilis* once again. The forward movement of Rome—and of the genre that narrates that movement—here too rushes and crashes onto itself.

But Scaeva does not die. He does not even grow weary. Perhaps the most remarkable difference between Scaeva's battle scene and those of the

---

[108] As Elliott (2013) shows in her seminal work.
[109] Elliott (2013) 228. See too 287.
[110] Goldschmidt (2013) 186–7 reads Scaeva alongside Ennius's heroes as a marker of "the breakdown of the stability of exemplary interpretation and the possibility of exemplary behavior" (187).

one-against-many heroes in the *Iliad*, *Annales*, and *Aeneid* comes in the toll it takes on him, or, rather, *doesn't*. The earlier poets express the toll on their heroes with the same two details: sweat pouring over the hero's whole body (*Il.* 16.109–10; *Ann.* 396; *Aen.* 9.812); and the hero's shortness of breath (*Il.* 16.109 and 110–11; *Ann.* 397; *Aen.* 9.813 and 814). The recurrence in each passage of these two elements, beside one another, demonstrates how fixed their inclusion had become. Lucan leaves both out, an eye-catching omission in light of how many common details he does include.

When his steps do grow tired (6.206: *iam gradibus fessis*), he continues to brawl for another forty-five lines, until Pompey's army retreats. Herein lies another difference from the Homeric and Virgilian model passages, in which Ajax and Turnus are the ones to retreat. It is impossible to know what the Ennian tribune's next steps were, though the fragment ends with him fatigued and the Histrians on the offensive (*Ann.* 395–7). Scaeva, to be sure, is not the one to relent. As his Pompeian enemies flee, the narrator says to his hero: "Now that Mars has been led off, you collapse; for, after your blood was drained, the battle gave you strength" (6.250-1: *subducto qui Marte ruis; nam sanguine fuso | uires pugna dabat*). A paradox about Scaeva is clarified: not only does he not sweat or lose his breath, *the fight gives him strength*. It may be that no weapon misses him (6.189–90), that he wears a veritable suit of enemy spears in his bones (6.194–5), and that his face is deformed by a rainstorm of blood (6.224–5), but all this keeps him going. Scaeva lives on death: dead by any reasonable metric, he survives. On the metapoetic level, the "dense wood" of the epic tradition that Scaeva wears on his chest (recall 6.205: *densamque ferens in pectore siluam*) lives on, the violence of the genre absorbed into Lucan's creation Scaeva and into his poetic creation as a whole.[111]

In this chapter we have traced Lucan's manner of revisiting constitutive *topoi* of the epic genre that are, crucially, scenes of violence—a mutilation in battle, the chopping down of a grove, a warrior's one-against-many stand. Lucan's agenda in each passage is to redirect the violence already present in these foundational texts back upon the Romans in his narrative and back against the genre itself—revealing that the violent end was always immanent, exposing the truth that "at the very moment that a genre or a literature is broached, at that very moment, degenerescence has begun, the end begins."[112] We have seen that an essential foil for Lucan in this effort is Ennius,

---

[111] In the Conclusion, I will discuss the significance of Scaeva's return at 10.543-4 and survival as a "living dead thing"—and what his survival says about the *Ph.* and the death of epic.

[112] Derrida (1980) 66.

94 THUNDER AND LAMENT

the poet who, as Elliott puts it, Homerised the Roman story and staked a foundational beginning-point for that story. With the anchoring passages of this and the previous chapter in mind, we turn now to observe the *Pharsalia*'s engagement with—and closure of—the *Annales*' story on a broader scale.

3

The *Pharsalia* and the End of the Ennian Story

3.1. Two sunrises in Latin epic

Book 7 is the main event of the *Pharsalia*. The first six books build up the tension for the time and place that will decide Rome's fate, and we at last arrive there in Book 7 with the Battle of Pharsalia.[1] Lucan opens the book with a description of the sunrise or, rather, of the sun *resisting* its rise on the morning of the battle (7.1–6). In crafting these striking opening lines, he draws on a number of models, including Ovid's description of the sun's work in *Metamorphoses* 2 and Seneca's depictions of hesitant suns in his tragedies *Oedipus* and *Thyestes*.[2] On a broader generic scale, this opening tableau evokes and upturns one of the most familiar conventions in epic, a description of the rising sun. Beginning with the Homeric poems, the recurrences of sunrise and sunset, the day's beginning and end, are in many ways the timekeepers of the genre, markers of both pace and order.[3] By beginning Book 7 with the formal convention of the sunrise, Lucan conspicuously marks the ensuing events as taking place in what we might call "epic time." Engagement with the genre and its traditions is held up high to the reader as the poem's main event gets underway.

---

[1] On Lucan's strategies of delay leading up to Book 7, see Masters (1992) 43; Joseph (2017a) 113–19; and Roche (2019) 3–4. On delay in the poem generally, Henderson (1987) 133–4.

[2] Roche (2019) 57–9 notes the parallels with Ov. *Met.* 2.70–3 and Sen. *Oed.* 1–5 and *Thy.* 784–7. Hübner (1976) and Narducci (2002) 51–4 also compare the passage with episodes in Greek and Roman tragedy. Lanzarone (2016) 69–71 gathers other Latin passages describing eclipses. Chaudhuri (2014) 166–9 discusses how 7.1–6, like Virg., *G.* 1.466–8 and Ov., *Met.* 2.381–93 and 15.785–6, and Sen., *Thy.* 784–7, is associated with an act of divinization (in Lucan's case the apotheosis of the Caesars). See also Saylor (1990) 299 on the relative absence of "good" sunlight in the poem.

[3] See Kirk (1985) on *Il.* 2.48–9, Horsfall (2003) on *Aen.* 11.1, and Wolkenhauer (2020), including sunrise as an example of the periphrases of time that are markers of epic (229: "The periphrasis prepares the audience for new events; the rising of the sun connects to narratives of departure, hope, and new beginning").

However, just as with the epic *topoi* that we considered in the previous chapter, here Lucan delivers a halting, violent poetic strike at this convention. We might say that this epic commonplace, the description of the beginning of the day, is the most primal of them all, the earliest of epic beginning-points; and here again Lucan forcefully pushes back:

segnior Oceano quam lex aeterna uocabat,
luctificus Titan numquam magis aethera contra
egit equos cursumque polo rapiente retorsit,
defectusque pati uoluit raptaeque labores
lucis, et attraxit nubes, non pabula flammis
sed ne Thessalico purus luceret in orbe.

The sorrow-bringing Titan drove his horses slower than eternal law was beckoning him from the Ocean, never more in opposition to the sky; and he twisted back his course, though the pole had hold of him; and he desired to suffer eclipse and the toils of stolen light; and he dragged clouds toward himself, not as fodder for his flames but so as to not shine purely on the world of Thessaly. (7.1–6)

The sun uses all its powers not to rise on the day of Pharsalia. He drives against (*contra* | *egit*) the sky and thus against eternal law; he twists back his course (*retorsit*, Lucan's only use of the strong visual verb *retorqueo*); he even desires (*uoluit*) an eclipse and the pains that come with it; and he forcefully drags clouds toward himself (*attraxit*, another vivid compound verb). The personification of the sun as Titan contributes to the poignancy of the scene, making it easier for us to envision his struggle against nature's laws.[4] Twice in Homer's poems the order of the day is altered, at *Iliad* 18.239–40, where Hera ends the day's fighting by forcing the unwilling sun to set, and *Odyssey* 23.241–6, where Athena holds back Dawn in order to give Odysseus and Penelope time together before sunrise.[5] A critical difference in Lucan's epic is that on the day of Pharsalia the sun himself—not a separate deity commandeering him—wants to halt his own activity.

---

[4] See Tucker (1983) 146 and Dinter (2012) 14–15 on Lucan's frequent personification of the sun (and as *Titan* sixteen times). The analysis here of the diction in 7.1–6 first appeared in Joseph (2017a) 120–1.

[5] See Edwards (1991) 174, on *Il.* 18.239–42; and de Jong (2001) 560, on *Od.* 23.241–6.

Elsewhere in the poem the sun rises and sets without event,[6] and dawn commonly precedes Caesarian action and success.[7] And so this occasion is conspicuous: *here*, on the critical day of Pharsalia, the sun resists the drive toward Caesar's success, here "the cosmic order of time itself is turned upside down,"[8] even if the effort is ultimately in vain. We saw in Chapter 1 that Caesar's resistance to the laws at the Rubicon cues us to witness Lucan's own rule-breaking poetic endeavor. Here too the sun's pushback against eternal law (*lex aeterna*, 7.1) is at the same time a pushback against the law of epic, the law dictating the order of the day and of epic's movement forward.

What is more, again a violent action of opposition (recall *contra* | *egit*, 7.2–3; and *contorsit*, 7.3) is accompanied by an expression of lament. In what reads as a sort of perversion of the adjective *lucifer* ("light-bringing"), the sun is given the epithet *luctificus*, meaning "bringing sorrow or lamentation." This is Lucan's only use of the adjective,[9] which conveys that—on the planes of both the poem's action and the poet's action toward the epic tradition—this sunrise will bring both violence and the attendant lamentation, the rightful sadness for the end that is near.

As Lucan himself puts it, a sunrise of this sort was unprecedented: never before (*numquam*, 7.2) did the sun fight itself more strenuously than on that day. This choice to begin the climactic book of the *Pharsalia* with an act of vigorous opposition to the epic convention of the sunrise marks a conspicuous departure from Homer and, to be sure, Virgil.[10] But this book-opening must also call to mind what is surely the most significant sunrise in Latin epic: Ennius's description of the sunrise on the day of Romulus's ascent to become the first king of Rome. This extraordinary (and much discussed) passage is preserved in the long fragment from *Annales* 1 that Cicero includes in a discussion of divination practices at *De Divinatione* 1.107. The character of Cicero's brother Quintus, making the case that divination was trusted and practiced in Rome's early history, quotes the following twenty lines in full:

curantes magna cum cura tum cupientes
regni dant operam simul auspicio augurioque.

---

[6] See the sunrises at 2.719–20, 3.521, 4.125, 4.529, 4.734, 5.700–1, 8.202, 8.778–9, 9.1006, and 10.434; and the sunsets at 3.40, 4.280–4, 4.472–3, 5.424, and 8.159–61. See further König (1970) 459–60.
[7] König (1970) 467–71 and Saylor (1990) 299.
[8] Wolkenhauer (2020) 237.
[9] See Roche (2019) 58–9 on *luctificus* in earlier authors, incl. Virg. of the infernal Allecto at *Aen.* 7.324 (with Joseph [2017a] 120–1) and Sen. of the sun's flame at *Oed.* 3 (*flamma ... luctifica*).
[10] Dinter (2012) 14 contrasts Virgil's and Lucan's suns: "Virgil's sun habitually displays a peaceful and inconspicuous elegance in signifying the passing of time."

in Murco Remus auspicio sedet atque secundam
solus auem servat. at Romulus pulcer in alto   75
quaerit Auentino, servat genus altiuolantum.
certabant urbem Romam Remoramne uocarent.
omnibus cura uiris uter esset induperator.
expectant ueluti consul quom mittere signum
uolt, omnes auidi spectant ad carceris oras   80
quam mox emittat pictos e faucibus currus:
sic expectabat populus atque ore timebat
rebus utri magni uictoria sit data regni.
interea sol albus recessit in infera noctis.
exin candida se radiis dedit icta foras lux   85
et simul ex alto longe pulcerrima praepes
laeua uolauit auis. simul aureus exoritur sol
cedunt de caelo ter quattuor corpora sancta
auium, praepetibus sese pulcrisque locis dant.
conspicit inde sibi data Romulus esse propritim   90
auspicio regni stabilita scamna solumque.

Being careful then with great care, each desiring a kingdom, they together take the auspices and augury. On the Murcus Remus sits in wait for a sign and watches alone for a favorable flight; but handsome Romulus on the high Aventine seeks and watches for the high-soaring race. They were competing over whether to call the city Roma or Remora. All men were anxious over which would be their ruler. They wait, as when the consul prepares to give the signal, everyone eagerly looking to the starting gates for how soon he sends the painted chariots from the barrier: so the people were waiting; visible on each face was a concern for their affairs, to which one the victory of supreme rule would be given. Meanwhile the sun had set into the depth of night. Then struck by rays the shining light showed itself openly, and at once on high from far away a beautifully winged leftward flight advanced. Just as the golden sun arises, there comes descending from the sky a dozen blessed bodies of birds, settling themselves on fine and favorable seats. Thus Romulus sees that given to him alone, established by auspices, were the bulwark and realm of a kingdom. (*Ann.* 72–91; trans. by Goldberg and Manuwald [2018], with some adjustments)

This is a dazzling passage, with "a power that commands respect and admiration."[11] The diction and style point artfully and dramatically to Remus's defeat and Romulus's ascent. Moreover, while shining a particular light on the fratricide, this early episode is also revealing of fundamental elements and themes of the *Annales* as a whole. The passage's "actors well represent the dominant male, political and military cast of the poem,"[12] and it also speaks to the poem's dynamic, expansive sweep of Roman time and space. The simile at *Ann*. 79–81 comparing the spectators of the twins' contest with contemporary spectators at the Circus Maximus, in the same location in the city, serves to emphasize spatial and temporal continuities in Roman history, and indeed to merge this moment of foundation with Ennius's own time. Here "place functions . . . as a linch-pin connecting different temporal strata by highlighting the unities among them."[13] The Rome of this scene is sempiternal, ever mighty, even as it is ever growing.[14] The lasting power and interest in this passage are attested not only by the long quotation by Cicero, but also by Aulus Gellius's citation from it (quoting *Ann*. 89 in a discussion at *Att*. 7.6.9), and by later adaptations of the scene by Virgil and Ovid.[15]

This is a foundational moment in this foundational poem, and Ennius highlights its importance by paying close attention in *Ann*. 84–9 to the day's extraordinary sunrise. After Romulus and Remus have taken their positions on the hills, the white sun (*sol albus*) sets in 84, and then straightaway (*exin*) in 85 bright light (*candida . . . lux*) glowing from beneath the horizon appears, and with it a fortuitous flock for Romulus. Then, when the golden sun (*aureus . . . sol*) itself rises in 87, the full array of birds comes into view (88–9). Scholarly discussion of these lines has focused on efforts to explain what some perceive as "two suns," with proposals that the *sol albus* of 84 is different from the *sol aureus* of 87, and that the former must be the moon or the morning star. A presumed problem is that the sunset and sunrise in 84–7 occur too quickly.[16]

---

[11] Goldberg (1995) 105. See too Williams (1968) 685–6 and Fisher (2014) 57–86, an extensive discussion of the diction and composition of the passage.
[12] Elliott (2014) 240; see also 245.
[13] Elliott (2014) 245. On the dynamics of time and space in this passage, see also Goldberg (1995) 105–9; Goldschmidt (2013) 71–8 (75: "Ennius' epic was powerfully tied up with *lieux de mémoire* in and around the city"); and Fisher (2014) 85–6; further, the essays in Fitzgerald and Spentzou (2016) on other literary conceptions of Roman space and the layers of memory that may come with them.
[14] Goldberg (1995) 108: "The legendary, the historic, and the contemporary are treated as a unit."
[15] Skutsch (1985) 223 writes of the influence on Virg., *Aen*. 12.716ff. and Ov., *Met*. 9.46ff. See also Tarrant (2012) 273.
[16] Skutsch (1985) 231 summarizes this position ("the coming of light in the very next line seems to follow the setting of the sun too closely and too abruptly") but ultimately does not find the passage to be problematic. On the two suns, see also Meunier (2012) 103–14; Fisher (2014) 68–70 (with 179, n. 15); and Wolkenhauer (2020) 232–4.

To be sure, the sequence is peculiar. But this is the point: Ennius is putting extraordinary focus on the speed and the brightness of that day's sunrise. Immediately after emphasizing the darkness of the night in 84 with the vivid phrase *infera noctis*, he marks the speedy (*exin*) appearance of light, which bursts out (*icta foras*) with brightness (*candida*); moreover, the sun has agency in its appearance (*se dedit*). The light in line 85 is not the sun itself, but the light of its reflection over the horizon[17]—giving the strong impression that the sun is eager to make its light shown on that day. When the sun itself rises in line 87, it is not just bright but golden (*aureus*), and its appearance comes simultaneously (note *simul* in 87) with the flight of the birds marking the kingdom for Romulus.[18] So we see that Ennius's achievement in these lines is to employ the Homeric convention of the sunrise but to accelerate and intensify its significance in new and daring ways. In doing so, he illuminates the day of Romulus's ascent as central, essential to Roman history, a day that the sun wants to speed up.

Lucan's sunrise at 7.1–6, we have seen, operates in precisely the opposite way, with the opposite effect. While the dawn at *Annales* 84–9 is striking (and even perplexing to many) in its speed, the daybreak at the outset of *Pharsalia* 7 arrests the reader through its slowness, through the sun's reluctance to shine. The first word of the passage and of Book 7 is "slower" (*segnior*), marking, as I proposed earlier, a departure from the sunrises dictated by the eternal law (*lex aeterna*) of epic. The willful resistance that then plays out in the sun's actions in 7.2–6 sharply contrasts with the rapidity and assertiveness of the sun's light in *Ann.* 85. The sun at Pharsalia wants to conceal its own light, to *not* be "pure" (*purus*, 7.6), another departure from the brightness (*candida*, 85; *aureus*, 87) of the sunlight over the hills of Rome on the day of Romulus's rise.

There is also a marked difference in the spaces that are central to these two scenes of sunrise. In *Ann.* 72–91, Ennius focuses on interior Rome, the space on and between the hills, as the locale of this foundational moment, but also as the gathering place for the *populus* (*Ann.* 82) in both mythical and contemporary times. The Rome of these lines is the home base for the Roman community, the central locus of action and of meaningful change.[19] In *Pharsalia*

---

[17] Skutsch (1985) 233. See too Wolkenhauer (2020) 233 on the use of color here as "time-giving."

[18] Williams (1968) 686 writes that the abundance of temporal adverbs and conjunctions here "halts the narrative into a jerky and over-emphatic progression."

[19] Goldberg (1995) 107–8 and Elliott (2014) 245 emphasize the sense of Roman community generated here.

7, Lucan has the sun cover himself "so as to not shine purely on the world of Thessaly" (*sed ne Thessalico purus luceret in orbe*, 7.6). As the application of the adjective *Thessalicus* to *orbis* reveals, the world now belongs not to Rome but to Thessaly, the site of Caesar's imminent victory over Rome. The focus on the sun's rise here—far from the interior Rome of that foundational moment in *Annales* 1—neatly highlights how the Roman center has moved.

Another difference between these pivotal dawns is one rooted in a fundamental similarity. The rise of each day marks the ascent of a monarch, with each ascent made possible through the bloodshed of kin. But the slaughter in *Annales* 1 is productive, indeed foundational, as the final lines of the fragment indicate: "Thus Romulus sees that the bulwark and realm of a kingdom (*regni . . . scamna solumque*) were given to him alone, established by auspices (*auspicio . . . stabilita*)" (*Ann.* 90–1). This day—including, necessarily, the slaughter of Remus—marks for Rome a stabilizing beginning-point in time; and the day's events occur in a marked beginning-space, which becomes "the bulwark and realm of a kingdom." Leadership of the enterprise will go to Romulus, who will continue to be associated with the light of the sky: in the collective prayer at *Ann.* 106–9 (= Cic., *Rep.* 1.64), the Roman people address him as "heavenly Romulus" (*Romule die, Ann.* 106)[20] and then state, "You have led us into the realms of light" (*tu produxisti nos intra luminis oras, Ann.* 109). As we proceed in *Pharsalia* 7, on the other hand, the light of that day reveals that the fight against Caesarism is doomed (7.214–17); further, "this bloody light" (*hac luce cruenta*, 7.427) on the day of Pharsalia is blamed for the collapse of Roman spatial dominance.[21]

Even as he highlights Romulus's role on that dawn, Ennius also makes the Roman *populus* present and party to this foundational event (*Ann.* 82–3). This is a communal beginning-point and beginning place, and the conceit of Ennius's image gives the impression that the Roman people are present for the extent of the episode, from dusk until (accelerated) dawn. As I will explore over this chapter, the slaughter on the day of Pharsalia marks a conclusive end to Roman might in time and space, and at the same time an end to Rome's communal efforts toward domination. The sunrises of *Ann.* 84–9 and then *Pharsalia* 7.1–6 mark opposing ends, in temporal as well as spatial terms, of the collective Roman story.

---

[20] See Skutsch (1985) 210 on *dius* as "of the sky."
[21] See later in this chapter on the context of 7.427.

3.2. Rome pays in blood—her own

A further connection between Ennius's Romulus and Lucan's Roman actors reinforces the contrast between foundation in *Annales* 1 and closing in *Pharsalia* 7 that I am proposing. Macrobius (6.1.15) and Servius (on *Aen.* 9.422) preserve a separate Ennian fragment that is commonly placed after *Ann.* 72–91 and understood to contain the words of Romulus, just after Remus crosses the new city's wall and just before the fratricide. The fragment reads:

> nec pol homo quisquam faciet impune animatus
> hoc nec tu: nam mi calido dabis sanguine poenas
>
> No living man, by Pollux, will do this with impunity, and you will not either: for you will pay me the penalty with your warm blood. (*Ann.* 94–5)

Elliott has written of the diction here that "this language marks crucial moments of the narrative and was therefore designed to be memorable."[22] And it was long remembered: Macrobius and Servius quote these lines as the model for *Aeneid* 9.422, the threat that the Rutulian Volcens makes to Euryalus: *tu tamen interea calido mihi sanguine poenas* ("but meanwhile you will pay me the penalty with your warm blood"); and Aeneas's final, punishing words to fellow proto-Roman Turnus (*Aen.* 12.948–9: *Pallas | immolat et poenam scelerato ex sanguine sumit*) may also evoke Romulus's words to Remus.[23] Virgil employs the line-end *sanguine poenas* four other times in his epic (7.595, 7.766, 10.617, 11.592), as do Ovid (*Fasti* 4.239) and Silius (6.299).[24]

Lucan also found Romulus's words in *Annales* 1 to be memorable and capable of powerful effect. At the end of Book 4, the narrator turns from addressing Curio to decry the self-destructive warmongering of all the Roman leaders in his poem:

> ante iaces quam dira duces Pharsalia confert,
> spectandumque tibi bellum ciuile negatum est.

---

[22] Elliott (2013) 128.
[23] See Tarrant (2012) 8 and 340, finding that Aeneas's words "unmistakably echo" (8) those of Ennius's Romulus.
[24] Skutsch (1985) 241.

has urbi miserae uestro de sanguine poenas
ferre datis, luitis iugulo sic arma, potentes.

You are dying before dreadful Pharsalia brings the leaders together; and beholding civil war has been denied to you. You all are paying this penalty to the mournful city with your own blood. You, powerful ones, pay for wars with your throats. (*Ph.* 4.803–6)

In a move that is conspicuous though not atypical of the narrator's impassioned manner, he moves quickly from the second-person singular address to Curio (*iaces*, 4.803) to second-person plural verbs (*datis*, *luitis*, 4.806), spoken to the collective "powerful ones" (*potentes*). The statement in 4.805–6 is thus a general indictment of all those in power in the civil wars—Curio, Caesar, Pompey (who are mentioned together as *gener atque socer* in the immediately preceding lines, at 4.802), and the rest. The correspondences between Lucan's *uestro de sanguine poenas* | . . . *datis* (4.805–6) and Ennius's *dabis sanguine poenas* (*Ann.* 94) have led Paolo Asso to conclude: "By going all the way back to the earliest historical legends of Rome, the Ennian intertext fills L.'s apostrophe to the *potentes* with profoundly complex ideological, political, and religious/ancestral implications."[25] Yet there may be something more precise to the allusion. In *Ann.* 94 Romulus declares that the individual Remus will pay (*dabis*) the penalty to the prevailing Romulus (*mi*), whose new city of Rome will of course move forward. In *Pharsalia* 4, Lucan moves conspicuously to the plural *datis*, with the collective *potentes* as subject; and the dative receiver of that penalty becomes, in Lucan's formulation, not an individual (like Ennius's *mi*) but the collective city (*urbi*). Crucially the city is not at all victorious, like the Romulus of *Annales* 1, but in fact *mournful* (*miserae*). Rome does not gain from the spilling of the leaders' blood. There are no beneficiaries in the fratricidal slaughter of the *Pharsalia*; the inseparable and simultaneously reached outcome of this violence is, once again, grief and lamentation.

The Ennian intertext and inversion at *Ph.* 4.805–6, while anchoring the argument that Lucan was familiar with the account of Romulus's ascent in *Annales* 1, at the same time complements the contrast in the sunrises of *Ann.* 84–9 and *Ph.* 7.1–6. The sun in *Pharsalia* 7 fights its rise, a futile repudiation of the momentous events of that day—and a reversal of its acceleration

---

[25] Asso (2010) 288. See my discussion in Chapter 4 of this passage as a lament for Curio.

and validation of Romulus's day of ascent in *Annales* 1. The subversion of *Ann.* 94 in 4.805–6 is corollary but also more explicit: here Lucan gives the lie to the Romulan and Ennian myth that Roman self-slaughter is—or at least still can be—productive for Rome. Twice elsewhere in the poem he refers to the myth, each time with a similarly jaundiced eye. To him, the story of Romulus's accession is less a starting-point of Roman success than a marker of Rome's inability to share power without bloodshed (1.93–5) and, later, of her affinity to tyranny (7.437–9).

Lucan is telling the Roman story in a whole new way—a damning, crushing, closing way. I have begun this chapter with the sharp opposition of *Ph.* 7.1–6 and *Ann.* 84–9, together with the complementary contrast at *Ph.* 4.805–6 and *Ann.* 94, because I think this opposition is representative of a closural poetic program that runs throughout the poem. The dynamic of the *Pharsalia*'s shrinking and closing of the *Annales*' conceptions of Roman time and space will be my focus in this chapter, a reading that builds on my arguments in Chapters 1 and 2 for Lucan's hostile, violent engagement with Ennius in crucial passages. With the allusions that I examined in those chapters understood as anchors for a polemical intertextual program, this chapter looks at Lucan's engagement with the *Annales* on a larger, ongoing, structural scale, as a code model for the *Pharsalia*.

Readers of the *Pharsalia* has been attentive to Lucan's presentation of the collapse of Roman global sway, though they often pin it as a specifically anti-Virgilian poetic endeavor.[26] Virgil's highly influential conception of the Roman foundation story certainly stands as an important foil to Lucan's tale of Roman self-destruction. But the author of the *Pharsalia* also makes it clear that his epic covers very different ground from Virgil's. Charles Tesoriero has argued that Lucan conspicuously and provocatively places his narrative *prior* to the time of composition of the *Aeneid*, offering an account of Julio-Claudian origins that stands as "an alternative history"[27] to the story of Aeneas → Augustus presented by Virgil. Moreover, the story of the advance toward global domination of the collective *populus Romanus* was not the

---

[26] Hardie (1986) 381: "the Virgilian model is primary; the major difference is that whereas the *Aeneid* is a poem about the creation of a universe, the *Bellum civile* is about the destruction of a universe. In this and other respects Lucan is revealed as an anti-Virgil"; see similarly Hardie (1993) 90–1. Quint (1993) 157 writes that Lucan "cannot fully free the *Pharsalia* from its secondary dependence on the model of Virgil's imperialist epic"; and Leigh (1997) 21, writing of "Roman epic, where fate is nationalized and history represented as an onward path leading to the goal of Roman domination," cites the *Aen.* as model text in this paradigm.

[27] Tesoriero (2005) 203. Prinzen (1998) 334 remarks in brief on Lucan's ambitions to compete with pre-Virgilian epic, namely the *Annales*.

principal matter of the *Aeneid*, which centers its story around—and gives its title to—an individual leader. If Lucan was aiming to make the self-destruction of the Roman people central to his epic (see 1.2–3, with my discussion in Chapter 1), then it was necessary for him, while certainly assailing much of the *Aeneid*'s diction, structure, and Roman imagery, to also move past the *Aeneid*'s version of Roman history and engage with the epic that first clocked and mapped the global advance of the *populus Romanus*, the *Annales*. On several occasions he evokes the *Aeneid* and the *Annales* alongside one another, as joint anti-models. But it was Ennius's epic that launched and formed the master trope of the *res publica*'s movement across time and space. To that foundational poetic enterprise—and Lucan's closure of it—I now turn.

3.3. Roman time and space in the *Annales* and the *Pharsalia*

In his second-century CE commentary on the works of Horace, Porphyrio writes that at *Satires* 1.2.37, Horace is twisting a passage from the *Annales* for his own humorous ends. The Ennian lines, which are not attributed to any particular book, read:

audire est operae pretium procedere recte
qui rem Romanam Latiumque augescere uoltis

It is important to listen to those who want the Roman state to advance forward in a direct way and for Latium to continue to grow. (*Ann.* 494–5 = Porph. ad Hor. *Sat.* 1.2.37)

It is not possible to identify the speaker of these lines, whether a character in the poem or the narrator, but the quotation captures a fundamental feature of Ennius's epic: its focus on the forward progress (*procedere recte*) and continual growth (*augescere*) of Rome over time. Lucilius, writing around fifty years after Ennius, understood the *Annales* to have one coherent theme (*una . . . θέσις Annales Enni*),[28] and this was it. Elliott has explored this unity in depth, bringing to light the extent to which the *Annales* present Rome

---

[28] Lucil. 343M. Bowra (1952) 558 writes of this unity of theme in Naevius and Ennius: "the rise of Rome from humble beginnings to world-wide power is after all one theme, and only one."

as "the hub of space and time, the primary focus of the cosmos in all its aspects,"[29] and at the same time how "the poem faced primarily outwards from Rome,"[30] attentive to the city's growth abroad through war. She notes that approximately 44% of the 292 surviving lines that can be placed with some confidence in the narrative of the Republic (*Annales* 4–18) describe the preparations, actions, or consequences of war, and that only about 11% of these lines treat domestic matters.[31] The fragmentary state of the *Annales* of course imposes serious limitations on our analysis, but we can say with confidence that this is a poem about Rome's outward expansion, her global expansion. At the same time, Ennius figures his poem as not just narrating but accompanying Rome's global reach, when stating at the outset of Book 1: "Across a wide range of peoples my poem and its contents will be heard and will be famous" (*Ann.* 12–13; see Ch. 1).[32] Moreover, Ennius does not limit Roman expanse at worldly boundaries: the inclusion in the *Annales* of a variety of terrestrial and celestial elements and, crucially, providential supernatural forces results in the impression that his Rome is "the focus of the cosmos at large."[33]

It is important to keep in mind that, while Ennius's depiction of Rome as a global power is not unique, it is *formative*, holding a crucial, primary place in this narrative and its development in Latin literature. The presentation across eighteen books of Rome's growth in space and time from Aeneas's flight from Troy to the city's continuing conquests abroad during the author's own lifetime was a wholly new and extraordinarily ambitious project. This was "a work greater in scale and aspiration than any earlier Roman poem, and it changed forever the way Romans viewed themselves, their history, and their destiny."[34] Scholars have proposed that the *Annales* stands as the model for later universalizing accounts of Roman history in prose and poetry,[35] and for annalistic historiography in prose. And it was Ennius's "story of Rome" that Virgil, as Goldschmidt argues, aimed to preempt and push aside in his own temporally and spatially sweeping project of the *Aeneid*.[36]

---

[29] Elliott (2013) 234, echoed by Feeney (2016) 172.
[30] Elliott (2014) 226.
[31] Elliott (2014) 225–6. The appendices at 249–64 gather and sort the evidence.
[32] See Elliott (2013) 275–6, writing at 276 of Rome's and the poem's "centrifugal thrust."
[33] Elliott (2013) 247; and see the full discussion at 252–72. Later in this chapter I will discuss further Ennius's presentation of divine providence, alongside Lucan's exclusion of it.
[34] Goldberg and Manuwald (2018) 103.
[35] Elliott (2013), esp. 292–4.
[36] Goldschmidt (2013).

While the *Annales*, then, begins the process of telling Rome's ever-advancing global story, the *Pharsalia* delivers that story's end. Here Conte's concept of the relationship between epic code and epic norm—and, specifically, of what he understands to be the Latin epic norm—may be helpful. In a discussion that focuses on the *Aeneid*'s place in the epic tradition, he writes:

> The code appears as an open system of categories, behavior patterns, and linguistic models. The norm orients the code according to a definite ideological set, by adding "connotative"—historically contextualized—meanings to the epic sense of that system. . . . Thus while the code itself is noncommittal, the Latin epic norm establishes that the substance of its contents should, in particular, be identified with the supremacy of the state as an embodiment of the public good, with the acceptance of divine will as providential guidance, and with the historical ratification of heroic action.[37]

Though his discussion of the fragments of early Latin epic is limited, Conte aligns this "Latin epic norm"—that is, the pro-Roman ideological layer applied to the conventions of the epic code—with the epics of Naevius and Ennius. He goes on to explore how Virgil breaks from that norm with the "polycentric" *Aeneid*, in which he "remodels the field of signification of the *epic norm* . . . [and] disturbs its inflexible absoluteness and introduces relativity."[38] But while Virgil complicated the genre with the multiple perspectives he included in the *Aeneid*, Lucan dismantles Latin epic entirely, both the generic conventions (the code) and the Roman ideology (the norm) that accompanied and mediated it.[39]

Lucan's presentation of the undoing of state ideology and loss of Roman power over space and time comes out most clearly in the narratorial statements in the climactic Book 7, which we will consider later in this chapter. But he keeps our attention on the theme of Rome's global collapse throughout the work. The proem announces that "all the strength of the shaken world" (*totis concussi uiribus orbis*, 1.5) will be at play in the poem.[40]

---

[37] Conte (1986 [1974]) 143–4.
[38] Conte (1986 [1974]) 152.
[39] So Conte (1986 [1974]) 167 n. 17 writes that post-Virgilian epic such as the *Ph.* "appears to be the necessary outcome of the process started by Virgil."
[40] See similarly 1.69. Roche (2009) 106 reads Lucan's use of *orbis* 132 times (compared with 77 in all of Virg.) as a marker of "the poem's promotion of the war's global and universal ramifications." On Lucan's geopoetics, see too Henderson (1987) 151–3; Fantham (1992) 76–7; Leigh (2000); Bexley (2009) and (2014); Pogorzelski (2011); Myers (2011); Manolaraki (2013); Rimell (2015) 240–52; and Serena (2020).

Book 1 then concludes with a series of marvels, portents, and prophecies about the coming war from around the known world and the cosmos (1.522–695), leading Lucan to open Book 2 with the statement, "And now the angers of the gods were apparent, and the universe (*mundus*) gave clear signs of war" (2.1–2). In Book 3 he presents Pompey's army as assembled from around the world (*totum . . . per orbem*, 3.169), with the result that "Pharsalia extended the world [to Caesar], to be conquered at the same time" (3.297).

The actors in Lucan's epic come from across the globe. Moreover, as in Ennius's epic, the world is their stage, a condition reflected not just in the poem's rhetoric but in its narrative expanse from Gaul (Books 1 and 3) to Italy (Books 1–3 and 5), Spain (Book 4), Illyricum (Book 4), Libya (Books 4 and 9), Greece (Books 6–7), Asia (Books 8–9), and Egypt (Book 10), alongside countless other geographical references. Crucially, however, this is a story of a shaken and lost world, of Roman movement heading not outward as in the *Annales* but—as we saw in the anchoring *loci* in Chapter 2—inward, into and against itself. The consequence of the resulting internecine collision is not only the halting of Roman imperial efforts (a theme explored prominently at 1.9–23, 3.154–68, and 7.419–31),[41] but also the movement of the Roman center itself. While in the *Annales* "the City functions as a centripetal force drawing all of time and space, all human and divine affairs, into relationship with each other,"[42] halfway through the *Pharsalia*, the city ceases to be a center at all, as the poem systematically moves away from Rome toward new centers of action. What ultimately replaces the city as "the bleakly ironic center point of Rome's destiny"[43] is Pharsalia. Lucan's Roman story—his story of the end of Rome—builds up to and functionally ends at Pharsalia. This dislocation is announced in the poem's opening line with the identification of the Emathian fields as the epic's main stage.[44] In Book 7, Pharsalia's centrality in the Roman story, as her death-place, is confirmed: "*here* Rome dies" (*hic Roma perit*, 7.634), declares the narrator. In the apostrophe to Thessaly that concludes the book (7.847–72), he will describe that land as "the tomb of the Roman people" (*Romani bustum populi*, 7.862).

Moreover, while Ennius had presented Rome as the hub of both space *and* time, with spatial and simultaneous temporal growth advancing out from the

---

[41] See Chapter 1 (1.9–23), Chapter 4 (3.154–68), and later in this chapter (7.419–31).
[42] Elliott (2013) 268.
[43] Bexley (2009) 464. See similarly Masters (1992) 95; Pogorzelski (2011); and Dinter (2012) 69–70.
[44] See Roche (2009) 100. The lengthy Thessalian excursus (6.333–412) is another means of putting emphasis on Pharsalia as the poem's, and Rome's, central node.

city, in a comparable but contrary way Lucan figures Pharsalia as a space and time of Roman death. The poem's first, programmatic simile compares the collapse of Rome with the dissolution of the universe into chaos (1.72–80),[45] when "with the frame broken, the final hour of the universe will have closed so many ages, seeking again primordial chaos" (1.72–4). This focus on one moment in time, the "final hour of the universe" (*mundi suprema hora*) as destructive of many ages (*saecula tot*), anticipates the concentrated exploration of this theme in Book 7, where Lucan configures Pharsalia as both a place that destroys Rome and a day that consumes and ends all the years of Roman time. In the same gesture, I will argue presently, he positions his Pharsalia as closing the book on Ennius's *Annales*.

3.4. Days of doom and of development

At the outset of this chapter we observed how Lucan highlights the unprecedented significance of the day of Pharsalia with his focus on the sun's tormented and reluctant rise, a jarring disruption of the sunrise so familiar from earlier epic. At the same time his depiction of the day of the battle as a fatally decisive one is another adaptation of an epic *topos*,[46] as the motif of a single doomsday for each hero is a hallmark of Homeric epic, is picked up by later epic poets, and takes on permutations in a number of other genres.[47] While Lucan also highlights the final moments of several individuals, the narrator and the poem's characters give particular attention to the all-consuming (*quo cuncta perirent*, 7.91–2), deadly (*funesta*, 7.427), and finalizing (*summa*, 7.195) doomsday of Rome herself. Throughout the first six books there is recurrent foreshadowing of that day's destructive powers,

---

[45] On Lucan's use here of imagery drawn from the Stoic cosmological concept of a final conflagration, see Lapidge (1979) 359–70; Johnson (1987) 14–18; Roche (2005) and (2009) 147–8; and Closs (2020) 124–6. See further, Feeney (1991) 283–4; Sklenář (2003) 3–11; Pandey (2014) 122–4; and Kaufman (2020) on Lucan's tendency to subvert Stoic concepts. See D'Alessandro Behr (2007), esp. 8–15 and 159–61, for a reconsideration of the seriousness of Lucan's Stoicism, with a focus on the text's didactic elements.

[46] See Ahl (1976) 331; Conte (1988) 33–5; Stover (2012) 33–7; and Joseph (2017a).

[47] See e.g. *Il*. 8.72, 15.613, 19.294, 21.100, 21.111–13, 22.212; and *Od*. 8.525 and 10.175, with Kirk (1985) on *Il*. 4.164 and de Jong (2012) on *Il*. 22.212. In the *Aen*. see, e.g., 10.467, 11.28, and 12.150. On the *topos*'s development in other genres, see Handley (1965) on Menander, *Dysc*. 186f. On its use of cities in historiography, see, e.g., Polyb. 38.22 (= App., *Pun*. 132) and Diod. Sic. 32.24, of Carthage in 146 BCE, both quoting *Il*. 4.164–5 / 6.448–9; Livy 5.21.5 (Veii) and 22.61.10 (Cannae); Vell. Pat. 2.86.1 (Actium); and Tac., *Hist*. 5.2.1 (Jerusalem).

in Book 7 comes his "obsessive"[48] focus on the deadly day, and in the final three books are numerous post-bellum reflections on the day's catastrophic consequences.[49]

In a number of these passages, Lucan draws closely on Virgilian and Homeric imagery for doomsdays. For example, on the morning of the battle we read that, for the Pompeian troops, "it was clear that the day had come (*aduenisse diem*) that would establish (*conderet*) the fate of human affairs for all times" (7.131–2), an inversion of the statement in *Aeneid* 7 that "the day has come on which [the Trojans] are to establish their deserved walls" (7.145: <u>aduenisse diem</u> *quo debita moenia* <u>condant</u>).[50] The arrival in the *Aeneid* of the day that establishes the Roman civilization is replaced in the *Pharsalia* by the arrival of the day establishing its end. Soon afterward, an Italian augur intones "the last day has come" (*uenit summa dies*, 7.195), echoing the Trojan priest Panthus's declaration in *Aeneid* 2 that "the last day has come, and the inescapable time for Dardania" (*Aen.* 2.324–6: *uenit summa dies et ineluctabile tempus | Dardaniae*)—which itself had completed the prediction made in the *Iliad* by both Agamemnon and Hector that "the day will come when holy Ilium will be destroyed, as well as Priam and the people of Priam of the ashen spear" (*Il.* 4.164–5 and 6.448–9). So at 7.195, Lucan's auger draws powerfully on this Virgilian and Homeric backdrop, with the striking difference that, for the Roman reader, Troy's final day is also productive, pointing toward Rome's first day; the arrival of the *summa dies* in Lucan's epic brings only destruction.[51]

The engagement with the fall of Troy in the *Aeneid* and, through it, the *Iliad* enhances the sense of the greater, crushing finality of Rome's doomsday in the *Pharsalia*. But the Trojan reference point is perhaps not the most salient one in this poem about the end of the Roman Republic and what it represented; indeed we can appreciate Lucan's focus on that single destructive day more fully by also reading it alongside Ennius's use of the unit of the day in the *Annales*. An impressive number of fragments capturing sunrise (*Ann.* 571 and 572, along with 84–9) and sunset (*Ann.* 348, 415–16, and 419) survive, with

---

[48] Conte (1988) 35: "L'idea del giorno fatale viene martellata ossessivamente per tutto il settimo libro della *Farsaglia*."
[49] See Joseph (2017a) 113–19 on the anticipations of the doomsday in Books 1-6, 120–8 on references in Book 7, and 128–30 on those in Books 8–10.
[50] See Heitland (1887) cxxi; Conte (1988) 34–5.
[51] See Conte (1988) 33–9; Stover (2012) 28–37; and Joseph (2017a) 112–13. Von Albrecht (1970) 275 and 283, and Lausberg (1985) 1587–8 also consider in brief this nexus of passages.

a great variety of expression (and beauty).[52] It is clear that the sun's rhythms, moving the day and the story of Rome forward, formed a constitutive part of the narrative of the *Annales*. It is also clear that Ennius presented that forward march of Roman time as inexorable and pushy. The hasty, even transgressive movement of the sun at *Ann*. 84–9 is our best example of this. But note also the verbs Ennius uses of the advance of day and night: the sun casts open (*patefecit*, 572) the sky and rushes into (*obruit*, 416) the Ocean, while the morning star flees (*fugit*, 571) the sun's running (*cursum*, 571); and the night, like the Roman state itself—recall *procedere* in *Ann*. 494—marches forward (*processit*, 348). Ennius's days and nights—his calendar—are on the move, as are his seasons. In a fragment quoted by three sources and thus appearing to be particularly well remembered, Ennius writes: *aestatem autumnus sequitur; post acer hiems it* (*Ann*. 420: "autumn follows the summer; next comes harsh winter").[53] Skutsch reads the line as a reflection of "the irreparable lapse of time,"[54] but he may be putting too gloomy an overlay on the Latin. What the line conveys is rapid forward movement, going swiftly, almost—as at *Ann*. 84–9—impossibly swiftly, from one season to the next and then the next. The juxtaposition of *aestatem* and *autumnus* at the beginning of the line and the monosyllable *it* at the end reflect that swiftness: winter stays on the move and will soon pass into spring—and another year.

This attention to, or, in Skutsch's words, "loving care" for the movement of time is fundamental to the project of the *Annales*, a work that the grammarian Diomedes tells us "included the deeds of nearly every year in order" (*singulorum fere annorum actus contineant*).[55] While focusing on the forward movements of the sun and the seasons, Ennius also concentrates on the power of one day, at *Ann*. 258–60, 382–3, and 406. These fragments share some basic characteristics with the nexus of passages in *Iliad* 4 and 6, *Aeneid* 2, and *Pharsalia* 7, but Ennius incorporates the motif into his story in a distinct way.[56] Macrobius (*Sat*. 6.2.16) preserves the first of these, which he compares with *Aen*. 11.425–7 and places in *Annales* 8:

---

[52] Skutsch (1985) 711: "Daybreak and the approach of night were apparently described with loving care." Goldschmidt (2013) 80, on models for the sunrise at *Aen*. 7.25: "The formulaic description of the breaking dawn is an Ennian feature, possibly with a direct Ennian source as well as its Apollonian and Odyssean precedents." See also the more general statement about the movement of the heavens at *Ann*. 205.

[53] Priscian, *GL* II, p. 152.17–53.10, and Servius on *Aen*. 6.685 preserve the fragment. *Explan. in Donat. GL* IV, p. 491.26–7 quotes *post acer hiems*.

[54] Skutsch (1985) 583.

[55] Diom., *GL* I, p. 484, explaining the work's title. See my discussion of the title in Chapter 1.

[56] Skutsch (1985) 440 and 546.

> multa dies in bello conficit unus
> et rursus multae fortunae forte recumbunt
> haud quaquam quemquam semper fortuna secuta est

> One day brings about many things in war, and many fortunes by chance tumble again; and no one fortune has followed anyone at all times. (*Ann.* 258–60)

Editors have speculated that a line is missing between 258 and 259, on the grounds that a line capturing good fortune belongs there, to contrast with the misfortune conveyed in 259.[57] Whatever the case, a key takeaway is that the "one day" (*dies . . . unus*) on which Ennius's speaker focuses is an indefinite one. It is not a specific, seismic point in time like the *summa dies* of *Aeneid* 2 and then *Pharsalia* 7, but rather one of many days among the ups and downs of the Hannibalic War that filled Books 7–9. Like that war and like Roman history more broadly, that day occasioned good and bad fortune—but in a movement forward.[58] A comparable expression is found in *Ann.* 406, which Gellius (9.14.5) quotes for the peculiar use of the form *dies* as a genitive: *postremo longiqua dies confecerit aetas* ("in the end the long age of the day will bring about [object not specified]").[59] While the object and thus the translation of *confecerit* are uncertain, here again we see Ennius imagining "the day" as inherently part of a longer historical view. The statement in *Annales* 382–3, preserved and placed in Book 14 by Priscian (GL II, p. 501.10–16), also seems to place the "one day" within a larger Roman narrative:

> nunc est ille dies quom gloria maxima sese
> nobis ostentat, si uiuimus siue morimur.

> Now is that day when the greatest glory shows itself to us, whether we live or die. (*Ann.* 382–3)

---

[57] Skutsch (1985) 440. This is the sense of the adaptation at *Aen.* 11.425–7, where Turnus speaks about the possibility of bad fortune turning to good. Skutsch, pointing to Livy 22.41.2f, speculates that the speaker is Aemilius Paulus. Giusti (2018) 237–9 proposes connections between *Ann.* 258–60 and Dido's words at *Aen.* 4.433–4, as well as Hannibal's words at Livy, 30.30.21.

[58] Elliott (2013) 130 accordingly translates the phrase as "the passing of days."

[59] See Skutsch (1985) 568 and Goldberg and Manuwald (2018) 322–3. Editors have placed *Ann.* 406 just after a fragment that Macrob. (6.1.17) places in *Ann.* 16, about kings' construction of physical memorials (*Ann.* 404–5); and so Goldberg and Manuwald (2018) 323 translate *confecerit* as "will destroy," with the physical memorials as the understood object.

It seems clear that these lines are drawn from the pre-battle speech of a military commander.[60] And while there is pointed emphasis on the moment (*nunc... quom*), what emerges from the commander's words is that the effort on that one day is shared by a collective "we" (note *nobis*, *uiuimus*, and *morimur*), and that communal glory is deemed the greatest (*maxima*) kind. There will be survival and death, victories and losses, prosperous days and days of defeat, but in Ennius's Roman story, such days—one way or the other—are part of collective growth and advance.

The unit of the day, we see, appears to be a core building block in the *Annales*' presentation of Roman progress through time and space. And with Ennius's use of the day in mind, we might make more of the declaration on the morning of Pharsalia that "it was clear that the day had come that would establish the fate of human affairs for all times, and that the thing being contested in that war was what Rome was to be" (7.131–3: *aduenisse diem qui fatum rebus in aeuum | conderet humanis, et quaeri, Roma quid esset, | illo Marte, palam est*). Tim Stover has aptly written that "this *summa dies* in Lucan sees more than the collapse of a single nation. The fate of the entire world is to be decided on this 'final day' of the new Troy."[61] But the formulation at 7.131–3, with Pharsalia's destructive consequences limitless in both space (*rebus... humanis*) and time (*in aeuum*), surely strikes a contrast with not just the Virgilian conception of Rome as the new Troy, but also the broader, foundational Ennian motif of Rome as global and epochal hub. Lucan's space-and-time consuming day of Pharsalia, the one day when "everything dies" (*cuncta perirent*, 7.91), emerges as a halting temporal foil to the ever advancing, cumulatively and communally productive days that maintained the march of the *Annales*.

3.5. Bringing it all back, Rome

We shall see how this program of polemical opposition to the *Annales* develops in the coming pages, in my focus on the narrator's statement at 7.387–459, a passage that begins as the battle lines are finally about to collide and that lies at the heart of Book 7[62] and the poem. Here, in an action that "is in violation of any traditional conception of epic narration,"[63] the

---

[60] Skutsch (1985) 546 weighs options in the early second c. BCE but comes to no conclusion.
[61] Stover (2012) 34.
[62] The halfway point of Book 7 is 7.436–7, during the narratorial statement.
[63] Leigh (1997) 93.

narrator bursts in to explain, over seventy-three lines, what Pharsalia was and—I will argue—what the *Pharsalia* is. By placing this grand statement about Pharsalia's momentous consequences not in a character's voice but in that of the narrator writing from the perspective of the Neronian age (see my discussion in Chapter 6), Lucan seems to invite us to read the passage as revealing of his own literary effort and ends, as important for conceptualizing his epic project and *its* consequences. The statement concentrates on three main aspects of Pharsalia's destructiveness: (1) the devastation of the Roman people (7.387–407), (2) the loss of Roman power in time and space (7.407–45), and (3) the concomitant loss of divine providence for Rome and Rome's vengeance through the apotheosis of the Caesars (7.445–59).[64] These three elements closely complement one another in the unified ideology that Conte calls the epic norm: Roman expansion in space and time was reliant on the providential oversight of the gods and the communal actions of the Roman people. That was the story and the ideology created and formalized in Ennius's *Annales*, embraced by later authors, and, here in this one trenchant passage in the *Pharsalia*, systematically pulled apart.

I begin my treatment of the passage with its central tableau, where the narrator conceptualizes the loss of Roman temporal and spatial might:

> Pharsalia tanti
> causa mali. cedant feralia nomina Cannae
> et damnata diu Romanis Allia fastis.
> tempora signauit leuiorum Roma malorum,   410
> hunc uoluit nescire diem. pro tristia fata!
> aera pestiferum tractu morbosque fluentis
> insanamque famem permissasque ignibus urbes
> moeniaque in praeceps laturos plena tremores
> hi possint explere uiri, quos undique traxit   415
> in miseram Fortuna necem, dum munera longi
> explicat eripiens aeui populosque ducesque
> constituit campis, per quos tibi, Roma, ruenti
> ostendat quam magna cadas. quae latius orbem
> possedit, citius per prospera fata cucurrit?   420
> omne tibi bellum gentis dedit, omnibus annis
> te geminum Titan procedere uidit in axem;

---

[64] Leigh (1997) discusses the "architectonic unity" (86) and the "consistent sweeping movement" (93) of the passage; and see the summary by Roche (2019) 159.

> haud multum terrae spatium restabat Eoae,
> ut tibi nox, tibi tota dies, tibi curreret aether,
> omniaque errantes stellae Romana uiderent.   425
> sed retro tua fata tulit par omnibus annis
> Emathiae funesta dies.
>
> Pharsalia was the cause of such great evil. Let the savage names of Cannae and Allia, long condemned on the Roman calendar, give way. Rome marks the dates of lesser evils; *this day* it has wished to not know. O the sad fates! Pestilential air, widespread diseases, debilitating famine, cities subjected to flames, quakes that bring full civilizations crashing down—all [such disasters] could be filled up by these men whom Fortune dragged down from everywhere into miserable death—taking away the gifts of a long age, even as she shows the gifts and places nations and generals in the fields. Through them she may show to you while you crash, Roma, how great you are as you fall. Who had possession of the world more broadly, and who ran more quickly through prosperous fates? Each war gave nations to you, and every year Titan saw you advance toward both poles; just a small stretch of Eastern land remained. The result was that the night was yours, the entire day was yours, the sky revolved for you, the wandering stars saw that all things were Roman. But your fates have been brought back by a day equal to all those years, the deadly day of Emathia. (*Ph.* 7.407–27)

The passage captures how extensive Rome had been in space and time—and how one place and one time ended it all. The conception of Pharsalia as not just a fraught place but also a marked day, a *dies nefastus*, is made explicit in 7.408–9 in the image of the notorious losses at Cannae in 216 BCE and the Allia River in 390 BCE giving way on the calendar to Pharsalia, a day that Rome would "prefer not to know" (*hunc uoluit nescire diem*) but that now dominates the Roman calendar. Geographical and temporal progression had moved in sync: the many nations Rome could parade forward on that day (7.417–18) *were* the "gifts of a long age" (*munera longi | . . . aeui*, 7.416–17). This linkage comes out again when the narrator asks Roma, "Who had possession of the world more broadly, and who ran more quickly through prosperous fates?" (7.419–20). Roma had conquered space and time together, with unequaled breadth (*latius*, 7.419) and speed (*citius*, 7.420). Mention of the sun bearing witness (*Titan . . . uidit* in 7.422) to Roman expansion toward both poles (*geminum . . . in axem*) over all those years (*omnibus annis*) compels us to think of his forceful and unprecedented opposition to this one day in the book's opening lines. The elevation of Rome's spatiotemporal reach to the super-terrestrial level is then played out in 7.424–5, as the repetition three times in 7.424 of *tibi*, a possessive dative addressed to Roma, emphasizes the sway over time (*nox, dies*) and space (*aether*) that she once held.[65] Even the stars (*errantes stellae*, 7.425), like their kin the sun (recall *uidit*, 7.422), were witnesses (*uiderent*, 7.425) to Roman might—seeing that "all things were Roman" (*omnia ... Romana*). The forms of *omnis* pile up (four times in 7.421–6) to accentuate how all-encompassing Roman might was.

But Pharsalia ended all this. In 7.426–7 the poet concisely captures its hostile space-time takeover. Following the pointed adversative *sed* comes the adverb *retro*, the object *tua fata* ("your fates," that is, "you, Rome"), the descriptive phrase *par omnibus annis* ("equal to all those years"), and then, dramatically suspended in hyperbaton and enjambment, the subject *Emathiae funesta dies*, the "deadly day of Emathia." This is the moment and these are the consequences the poet has been anticipating since setting the stage of the Emathian fields in the epic's opening verse. That place and that day sent back (*retro ... tulit*) Rome's fates; that one day equaled (*par*) and indeed brought a deadly end (*funesta*) to all the years (*omnibus annis*) that preceded it.

The passage delivers an unequivocal statement about the potency and consequences of Caesar's victory at Pharsalia, with the narrator elaborating in the following lines (7.427–31) on how "this bloody day" (*hac luce cruenta*, 427) thwarted further Roman expansion. The takeaway at the level of the poem's action and argument is clear: Pharsalia halted Roman reach in space and time. Entwined with this thematic and historical argument is a literary one. Readers have focused on the departure of Lucan's cataclysmic Roman story from the "Virgilian plot of imperial destiny, unity, and historical continuity."[66] And indeed, he presents the day of Pharsalia as a closure of the "new day" for the Trojan/proto-Roman race that Virgil had developed in the *Aeneid*. Pharsalia moves the fates that Virgil's Jupiter had promised would stay unmoved (*Aen.* 1.257–8); it fixes crushing limits on the *imperium* he had designated as limitless (*Aen.* 1.278–9). But if the story of the deadly day of Emathia is to bring Roman fates all the way back (*retro*, 7.426), then it must also take aim at the epic that launched this narrative, the *Annales*.

---

[65] See Pogorzelski (2011) 154–7, on the loss of empire expressed in these lines, and Reed (2011) 24–8 on the motif of imperial contraction in the poem.
[66] Quint (1993) 157. Leigh (1997) 94 also identifies the *Aen.* as the principal target of Lucan's "assault" in 7.387–459. Reed (2011) 23 compares Lucan's "assertiveness" in this passage with Ennius's.

The "anti-Virgilian rhetoric"[67] of Lucan's conception of Roman space and time is also—and, once again, more fundamentally—anti-Ennian. Earlier I considered the *Annales*' presentation of Roman time (night and day, individual days, the seasons, and, ultimately, years) as on the move, a dimension that accompanies and allows for Roman spatial expansion. Ennius's epic had charted "the Roman state advancing forward and Latium continuing to grow" (*procedere recte* | ... *rem Romanam Latiumque augescere*, Ann. 494–5), moved along by sunrises that hastened and accompanied that advance. Here at the heart of the *Pharsalia*, Lucan employs the same evocative verb, *procedere*, in a description of what *used to happen*, namely the sun's tracking of far-reaching Roman advance (*te geminum Titan procedere uidit in axem*, 7.422). The rising and setting sun no longer accompanies Roman progress.

With Ennius in mind, let us take another look at the clinching statement at 7.426–7:

sed retro tua fata tulit par omnibus annis
Emathiae funesta dies. (7.426–7)

That one day reversed Rome's fates, equaling and bringing death to all those years. A poetic statement operates in parallel with this thematic one: the story of that deadly day, the *Pharsalia*, goes back to (*retro*) and reverses *tua fata*,[68] that is, what has been said about Rome in the past (on the etymology of *fatum* from *fari*). As the modifiers *par omnibus annis* and *funesta* succinctly capture, the story of the Emathian day, the *Pharsalia*, matches (*par*) but also morbidly brings to an end (*funesta*) the *Annales*' story of all those years of advance and the yearslong eminence of the epic poet who first earned the "crown of perennial leaves" (*primus ... perenni fronde coronam*, Lucr. 1.117–18).

3.6. With the gods not on our side

The narrator follows the (de-)crowning statement at 7.426–7 with an elaboration on the halt of Roman expansion in the East (7.427–31), which segues into a reflection on Rome's loss of *libertas* (7.432–45). Then, after stating that

---

[67] Quint (1993) 157.
[68] Rossi (2000) 584 reads 7.426–7 as a counterpoint to the story of Roman progress out of strife in *Aen.* 12.

our lot as Romans (*sors... nostra*) is the worst of all (7.444–5), the narrator breaks in mid-line to take on the topic of the Romans (*nobis*, 7.445[69]) and the gods:

>   sunt nobis nulla profecto   445
> numina: cum caeco rapiantur saecula casu,
> mentimur regnare Iouem. spectabit ab alto
> aethere Thessalicas, teneat cum fulmina, caedes?
> scilicet ipse petet Pholoen, petet ignibus Oeten
> inmeritaeque nemus Rhodopes pinusque Mimantis,   450
> Cassius hoc potius feriet caput? astra Thyestae
> intulit et subitis damnauit noctibus Argos:
> tot similis fratrum gladios patrumque gerenti
> Thessaliae dabit ille diem? mortalia nulli
> sunt curata deo.   455

For us, truly, there is no providence: when the ages are stolen away by blind chance, we are lying when we say that Jove is governing things. Will he watch the Thessalian slaughter from the sky above while holding on to his thunderbolts? Will he actually attack Pholoe, will he use his flames to attack Oete and the grove of undeserving Rhodope and the pines of Mimas, and will Cassius, rather than him, strike at this head [of Caesar]? He brought the stars upon Thyestes and condemned Argos with sudden nighttime. Will he grant daylight/the day to Thessaly, which bears so many kindred swords of brothers and fathers? Mortal affairs have been cared for by no god. (7.445–55)

This passage on the gods' and specifically Jupiter's indifference to Roman affairs has been the focus of much discussion, with one scholar describing the leading words *sunt nobis nulla profecto | numina* as a "devastating pronouncement" and another as a "stunning statement" that generates "shock."[70] The narrator's assertions on the absence of providence for Roman affairs are indeed powerful in their blunt directness: the enjambed statement *sunt nobis nulla profecto | numina* is matched ten lines later by the similarly arresting

---

[69] Roche (2019) 172: "for us Romans" (*contra Comm. Bern.* ad loc.).
[70] Feeney (1991) 281 (calling this passage a "climactic point" at 282) and Fratantuono (2012) 288 and 289, respectively. On the passage, see also Ahl (1976) 280–1; Johnson (1987) 88–90; Bartsch (1997) 111–13; Leigh (1997) 93–4 and 98–9; and Day (2013) 168–71.

mortalia nulli | sunt curata deo, in a sort of ring composition that reinforces the point.[71] But what he says in fact follows naturally from what precedes in the narratorial statement, and here again the passage's Ennian backdrop comes into view.

The involvement of the Olympian gods in the action of epic poetry was a constitutive component of the genre.[72] The Olympians begin their participation in epic narrative in the Homeric poems and enter Latin epic straightaway in Livius's *Odusia* and Naevius's *Bellum Punicum*. A major development seemingly begun by Naevius and then elevated to a grander scale in Ennius's *Annales* is the transformation of the Homeric Zeus into Jupiter, the providential state god of Rome, a project captured in the adaptation of *Iliad* 8.31 (ὦ πάτερ ἡμέτερε Κρονίδη, ὕπατε κρειόντων, "O father of ours, son of Kronos, highest of the lords") in *Ann.* 444 (*o genitor noster, Saturnie, maxime diuum*, "O father of ours, son of Saturn, greatest of the gods"). In this translation and in the *Annales* as a whole, a hallmark of the epic code takes on the norm of Roman ideology, as "Zeus is now Jupiter Optimus Maximus, and the world he rules is now a Roman world."[73] Testimonia such as Servius's remark on *Aen.* 1.20 that "in Ennius, Jupiter is brought in to promise the Romans the destruction of Carthage" confirm that the involvement of the gods stretched across the *Annales*.[74] The enduring influence of Ennius's Jupiter is seen in Virgil's adoption of Ennian language for the pro-Roman Jupiter of the *Aeneid*.[75]

Divine providence is inseparable from the story of Roman conquest in space and time that the *Annales* began. So, when at 7.407–45 Lucan's narrator pronounces the defeat of the old Roman epic story by the place and day of Pharsalia, the gods have to go too. More precisely, their providence,

---

[71] See Fratantuono (2012) 289 and Roche (2019) 172 on the enjambment, and Lanzarone (2016) 366–7 on the ring composition.

[72] Feeney (1991).

[73] Feeney (1991) 128. He also notes the apparent adaptation of the Homeric epithet in Naev. fr. 15 (Blänsdorf) (= Varro, *Ling.* 7.51). See too Feeney (1984) on Virgil's adaptation of Ennius's Juno, as well as Goldberg (1995) 161–2 and Elliott (2013) 263–72 on Ennius's process of "re-casting the Homeric gods, replaced in their hexametric setting, as the major and minor divinities of Rome, supervising the full panorama of Roman history" (272).

[74] See Elliott (2013) 45–51 and 303–7 (Appendix 2) on the involvement of the gods throughout the *Ann.*

[75] See Goldschmidt (2013) 128 n. 89 on Jupiter's council in *Aen.* 10 being "permeated with Ennian language"; and *Aen.* 12.565 (*Iuppiter hac stat*) with *Ann.* 232 (= Macr. 6.1.19: *nunc Iuppiter hac stat*), a line that Skutsch (1985) 412–13 (following others) attributes to Hannibal. Whatever the attribution, Virgil's adaptation shows that he drew on Ennius's language of Jovian providence for his own Roman narrative.

their assent (*numina*) and support must go: *sunt nobis nulla profecto | numina*. This and the following statements, though powerfully put, are natural and indeed necessary corollaries of the preceding statements about Rome's temporal and spatial collapse.[76] The narrator makes this explicit in 7.446–7, when saying that the loss of the ages (*saecula*) of Roman time are proof that "we are lying that Jove is governing things" (*mentimur regnare Iouem*, 7.447). He draws this connection again when asking, "Will [Jupiter] grant daylight/ the day to Thessaly, which bears so many kindred swords of brothers and fathers?" (7.453–4). He knows the answer: the gods do not care (*mortalia nulli | sunt curata deo*, 7.454–5).

This expression of the absence of divine providence for "us Romans" comes up several times earlier in the poem. In Book 4 the narrator claims that Rome would have been fortunate "if concern for our liberty were as pleasing to the gods as our punishment is" (4.807–8). Here he couples regret about the loss of providence for Rome (*libertatis superis . . . cura*) with the identification of its opposite, the gods' hostility (*uindicta*) toward Rome, a charge also made in the extended prologue at 1.128 (of their favor of Caesar; cf. 4.254–5) and earlier on the day of Pharsalia at 7.58–9. Book 2 opens with the declaration that "now the anger of the gods was clear" (*iamque irae patuere deum*, 2.1) and an incrimination of the *rector Olympi* (2.4); but then, echoing the seer Nigidius Figulus at the end of Book 1 (1.642–5), the narrator backs up to consider whether affairs result from a divinely set order (2.7–11) or merely from chance (2.12–13).[77]

These ostensibly scattered deliberations about the divine have been the subject of much discussion, with scholars comparing a number of texts that give voice to atheistic or anti-theistic views, or reading the passage as a reflection of Lucan's "fractured voice."[78] But understanding the context in Book 7 together with the Ennian backdrop that was formative of the conceit of the

---

[76] In this regard, Lucan's observation about the randomness of thunderbolts differs from Lucretius's at 6.387–95 in that Lucan focuses on the gods' abandonment of Rome in particular, not all of humanity. See Day (2013) 170 on additional contrasts.

[77] See Pandey (2014) on the points of contact between Figulus and the narrator here.

[78] See Narducci (2002) 58–70, with a focus on the anti-theistic voices in Seneca's tragedies; and Feeney (1991) 282 on "[t]his fractured voice, unsystematic and at odds with itself"; he goes on at 283–4 to discuss "the obvious, purposeful, and shocking . . . elimination of Providence" over "mankind." I differ in reading the narrator's focus as falling principally on the elimination of providence over *Rome* (which had expanded into a global entity). Bartsch (1997) 113–14 writes of the narrator's "ideology in cold blood" with respect to the gods: "the narrator *enacts* belief even as he acknowledges the lack of any grounds on which to hold that belief" (113).

gods in Latin epic is clarifying. Roman progress in space and time has ended, and an essential corollary is that Jupiter Optimus Maximus and the other gods are no longer on Rome's side. On the plane of the epic tradition, the *Annales* had made divine stewardship basic and inseparable from the story of Rome's growth in time and space; and the *Pharsalia* now charts the separation of the gods from that story—in Conte's terms, the removal of a crucial element of the epic norm—and in turn the dissolution of that story.

The narratorial statement as a whole then concludes with a wry remark about the gods, namely that Rome will be able to exact vengeance on them after Pharsalia:

> cladis tamen huius habemus
> uindictam, quantam terris dare numina fas est:
> bella pares superis facient ciuilia diuos,
> fulminibus manes radiisque ornabit et astris
> inque deum templis iurabit Roma per umbras.

But we have revenge for this disaster, as much as it is right for the gods to give to those on earth: the civil wars will make deified men equal to the gods above, and Rome will adorn shades of the dead with lightning bolts and beams and stars, and in the temples of the gods she will swear by their shades. (7.455–9)

Romans' vengeance against the gods comes in their worship of the deified Caesars. This darkly humorous statement about the imperial cult at the same time contributes to the passage's retrogression and eradication of the Roman story begun by Ennius. The process of making mortals equal to those in heaven (7.457) and then adorning their shades with celestial markers (7.458) amounts to a total disruption of the order that had maintained that story. The Roman march through time and space relied, as we have seen, on the supervision of the providential gods, as well as the execution of that march by the collective effort of humans. The onset at Pharsalia of autocratic Caesarism and the apotheosis of the Caesars imploded that order: the gods as panoramic overseers and humans as day-to-day actors were no longer distinct, their roles now intermingled and confused. With the constituent parts of the story no longer in place, its order now disordered, the story itself had lost its legitimacy and point.

3.7. The slaughter of the *populus Romanus*

We see that Lucan concludes the narratorial statement by highlighting the disruptive transformation of the divine-human order. In doing so, he loops back to the theme he had explored at the start of the passage (7.387–407): the tremendous loss at Pharsalia of present and future Roman life. With 7.387–459 as a whole, then, the poet reveals that the moment it becomes possible for a human (the conquering Caesar) to become a god is the very same moment the collective actor in the Roman story, the *populus Romanus*, is eliminated. In this section I look more closely at the narrator's conception of the degeneration (recall the evocative *degener o populus* at 2.116)[79] and death of the communal Roman people, a motif running in counterpoise to Ennius's formative story of the Roman popular collective.

When Book 7 reaches its grisly end, the narrator will call Thessaly "the tomb of the Roman people" (*Romani bustum populi*, 7.862), and it is at 7.387–407 that he develops that death and burial most fully. The slaughter is sweeping in time and space, totalizing, a scope that comes across clearly at 7.389–92:

> gentes Mars iste futuras
> obruet et populos aeui uenientis in orbem   390
> erepto natale feret.

> Mars on that day will destroy races yet to come and will carry off peoples of an age coming into the world—their births ripped away.

While at 7.421–7 Lucan tracks Pharsalia's retroactive destruction of years past, here we see the movement *forward* of that day's destructive power: even those not yet born will be laid low at that battle.[80] In a striking move, he imagines Mars, the father of Rome's first king, delivering the blow to the Roman people. While not every appearance of the word *Mars* evokes the god and his myth,[81] the context here, with *gentes* frontloaded in hyperbaton, surely

---

[79] See my discussion in Chapter 2 of this phrase, ominously uttered by Lucan's doublet, the learned old man.

[80] Leigh (1997) 98: "The notion of futurity serves as the leitmotif of the passage, but only a futurity cruelly conditioned and closed." See too Gowing (2005) 92–4.

[81] In his 55 uses of *Mars* or related forms (*Mars* 52 times, *Mauors* twice, *Martius* once), Lucan, like other authors, frequently uses the word as a metonym for "war." He uses it in the nominative only four other times (of the god at 6.579 and 7.569 and the planet at 1.663 and 10.206).

THE *PHARSALIA* AND THE END OF THE ENNIAN STORY 123

leads us to think of the divine father figure from the city's birth narrative—who is now rendering the end of births (*erepto natale*) for Rome.[82] And while the birth of Mars's sons was a rustic, local affair, Lucan's Mars now closes off Roman sway on not just a temporal but also a vast global scale, dimensions formulated together in the phrase *aeui uenientis in orbem*. The appearance of Mars may point us again to the *Annales*, the text that seems to have introduced him into the Latin epic story. We know from *Annales* 34–50 (Ilia's dream of Mars's rape of her)[83] and *Annales* 99–100 (a prayer to Mars and Quirinus) that Ennius made the violent god's role central to his story of the Roman race's origins. So when Lucan pictures a Mars poised to end that story by destroying (*obruet*) the Roman race for all time, we may see another closural gesture toward the *Annales*.

From this image of Mars's destruction of his own progeny, the narrator moves to describe the once prosperous towns in Latium that are now in ruins (7.392–4), as well as the abandoned countryside (7.395–6). He sums up his diagnosis of Rome's depopulation by stating:

non aetas haec carpsit edax monimentaque rerum
putria destituit: crimen ciuile uidemus
tot uacuas urbes. generis quo turba redacta est
humani! toto populi qui nascimur orbe   400
nec muros inplere uiris nec possumus agros:
urbs nos una capit. uincto fossore coluntur
Hesperiae segetes, stat tectis putris auitis
in nullos ruitura domus, nulloque frequentem
ciue suo Romam sed mundi faece repletam   405
cladis eo dedimus, ne tanto in corpore bellum
iam possit ciuile geri.

It was not time that carved up, ate, and left behind these decaying monuments of achievement. It is civil crime that we see in so many vacant

---

[82] An effect that commentators seem not to have noted and which numerous translators elide by translating *Mars* here in metonymy as "battle" or "fight" (Fox [2012] 193 is an exception: "That work of Mars"). See Fratantuono (2014) 156 on Virgil's use of *Mars* at *Aen*. 11.374–5 in metonymical and mythological senses.
[83] See Elliott (2014) 240–3 on Ennius's construction of space here as dominated by males such as Mars and Ilia's father Numitor.

cities. To such a point the mob of the human race has been reduced! We nations who are born around the whole world are able to fill neither walls nor fields with men. One city contains us. The seeds of Hesperia are tilled by a plowman in chains. The decaying home under an ancestral roof is about to fall—on nobody! We have brought Rome—occupied by no citizen of her own, but filled with the dregs of the world—to such a point of disaster that, in a body as large as this, civil war can no longer be waged. (7.397–407)

Matthew Leigh has expertly demonstrated Lucan's demolition in these and the preceding lines of Augustan myth-making by the likes of Virgil, Horace, and Ovid.[84] But, again, it is not just or even principally the Augustan story that is under attack: Lucan is setting the stakes higher, and given the contents of this passage, it seems important to understand the Ennian story of global Roman growth as a crucial anti-model here too. So, alongside the images of abandoned cities (7.399), walls, fields (7.401), and homes (7.403–4), the narrator keeps to the poem's globalizing reach, equating the victims of Pharsalia with the human race (7.399–400), and those born around the whole world (7.400). However, in a shrinking process that reverses the expansive movement so familiar from the outward march of the *Annales*, the global Roman population that Lucan's narrator imagines is now contained by one city (*urbs nos una capit*, 7.402). He then zooms in further still—microscopically—to the seeds of Hesperia (*Hesperiae segetes*, 7.403) that are now being tilled by a chained plowman. In Chapter 1, I considered Lucan's picture of "Hesperia, unplowed for many years" (1.28–9), and in Chapter 2 I looked at the wilting of the *flos Hesperiae* at 2.196. These earlier markers of reversing the Ennian story of *Hesperia's* growth (recall the programmatic *Ann.* 20) are strengthened in Book 7: if *Hesperia's* seeds require replanting, then the very *origins* of her story have been destroyed. Both the farms of Hesperia and the textual story of Hesperia are dried up, eradicated by Pharsalia/*Pharsalia*.

When we look at the narratorial statement at 7.387–459 as a whole, we see a systematic upheaval of the Roman universe, a universe whose component parts were assembled, ordered, and brought into Latin epic by Ennius in the *Annales*. The story of Rome's growth in time and space—together with the humans who executed that growth and the gods who oversaw it—is comprehensively annihilated, replaced by Lucan's radical rewrite. When reflecting on the great loss of life at the battle, the narrator had stated that,

---

[84] Leigh (1997) 87–91.

after Pharsalia, "the whole Latin name will be a story" (*omne Latinum | fabula nomen erit*, 7.391–2). With the old Roman story no longer accurate or *true*, it is this new story about Rome, *Pharsalia*, that will live on.[85]

3.8. The cast of characters wiped out

One of the most frequently quoted lines from the *Annales* in antiquity was *Ann*. 156: *moribus antiquis res stat Romana uirisque* ("The Roman state rests on its ancient morals and on its men"). The line takes much of its power from its inherent tautology: the ancient morals on which the Roman state relies are of course made manifest by the state's men.[86] The *uiri* and their shared moral code are what made the Rome of the *Annales* work—in perpetuity, as the present-tense *stat* neatly conveys. Augustine tells us that Cicero quotes the line in the (now largely lost) fifth book of his *De Republica*, writing that Ennius "seems to me to have spoken the line, with its brevity and its truth, as though from some oracle (*tamquam ex oraculo quodam*)."[87] Cicero identified a great truth in Ennius's assessment of Rome's reliance on her collective of men, and surviving fragments make it clear that the *Annales* indeed celebrate the *plurality* of men contributing to Rome's ongoing movement forward.

A fragment preserved by Gellius also speaks to the *Annales*' emphasis on the collective, shared execution of Roman expansion:

insece Musa manu Romanorum induperator
quod quisque in bello gessit cum rege Philippo.

Proceed to tell us, Muse, what each commander of the Romans achieved
in combat in the war with King Philip. (*Ann*. 322–3 [= Gell. 18.9.3–6])

The lines convey that a collaborative effort of multiple commanders, leading the collective *Romani*, contributed to the combat with and ultimate defeat of Philip V in the Second Macedonian War (200–197 BCE). The re-invocation

---

[85] In the Conclusion, I will return to the matter of how Lucan animates his story as one that lives on.
[86] Wallace-Hadrill (2008) 230 on this line: "The men made the *mores*, and the *mores* made the men."
[87] August. *Civ.* 2.21. The line is also quoted in *Hist. Aug., Avid. Cass.* 5.7. On the line's context, see Skutsch (1985) 317–18; and on its popularity, Elliott (2013) 41 and 131, and Goldschmidt (2013) 21, suggesting that it may have influenced a first-century BCE inscription (*CIL* 1.632 = Courtney (1995) 7).

of the Muse[88] indicates (as in the invocation before the catalog of ships at *Il.* 2.484–7) how many names will be recalled, and thus how many commanders will take part in this effort. Individual Romans do of course distinguish themselves throughout the epic, but as exemplary contributors to a greater collective.[89] In the adaptation of Homeric forms for his Roman narrative, then, Ennius transforms the individual warrior's *aristeia* that is so familiar from the *Iliad* into a fundamental part of a communal, national story, a transformation that Goldberg has called "the secret of Ennius' success."[90] In his portrait of Ennius in *Pro Archia* 22, Cicero explicitly views the glories of men he celebrated, such as Scipio Africanus, the elder Cato, the Maximi, Marcelli, and Fulvii, as bringing "common glory for all of us" (*communi omnium nostrum laude*). Each of Cicero's references—and most plainly in the plural list *omnes . . . illi Maximi, Marcelli, Fulvii*—also speaks to the sense of familial continuity that was a through line in the *Annales*. The forward march in time and space of the collective *populus Romanus* was conducted by leading *gentes*; their members made up a recurring cast, advancing over the centuries and into further reaches of imperial sway. As Ingo Gildenhard concisely puts it, "the *Annals* provided a unified vision of Roman history, combining the achievement of various families in one display."[91]

This emphasis on individual contributions to the collective under the Republic and on the continuity of *gentes* is not surprising to the student of Roman history who is familiar with the works of Polybius, Livy, and others, not to mention material evidence that tells similar stories. But Ennius's place in this tradition of Roman storytelling is paramount. Cicero's remarks in the *Pro Archia* attest to the *Annales*' staying power as a model for Romans' conception of collective civic contribution. To him, Ennius is the one who "produced these things" (*qui haec fecerat*, *Arch.* 22). And so as we look to Lucan's claims and aims in the *Pharsalia*, it is important to emphasize once again the primacy of Ennius's story of the Roman collective. The *Annales*, as Elliott puts it, "were the crucible in which the figures that were to become Rome's exemplary past were forged"; the stories of Republican heroes and of enduring families that would become familiar across literary genres at Rome

---

[88] Which Skutsch (1985) 498–9 places at the opening of *Ann.* 10.
[89] See, e.g., the Decii and their oath of *deuotio pro Romano populo* (*Ann.* 191–4); the self-sacrificial efforts of the military tribune (*Ann.* 391–8; with discussion in Chapter 2); and the consuls whose initiatives served as the engine for action across the *Ann.* (with my later discussion in this chapter).
[90] Goldberg (1995) 148. See also Dominik (1993) 49: "Instead of a personal hero [such as Achilles or Odysseus] Ennius seems to glorify a civilization and an ethos."
[91] Gildenhard (2007) 85. See too his discussion at (2003) 111–112.

"derive quite immediately from the *Annales*."[92] As with his transformation of the Homeric gods to fit the Roman story, Ennius drew from Homer the template of a genre hardwired for repetition and tradition[93] and adapted it to his Roman tale of collective civic advancement.

This whole story of communal Roman glory and progress is demolished in the *Pharsalia*. If Ennius's accomplishment was to redirect the *aristeia* of the individual from Homeric poetry toward Rome's sweeping collective advance, Lucan picks apart and closes off this entire narrative movement—and another crucial ideological element of the Latin epic norm is eliminated. At the beginning of the second major narratorial statement in Book 7 (7.617–46), the narrator states: "on the occasion of the death of the world, it is a shame to expend tears on the countless deaths, and to follow individual fates" (*inpendisse pudet lacrimas in funere mundi | mortibus innumeris, ac singula fata sequentem*, 7.617–18). As Leigh puts it, "this is not to be a poem of individual *aristeiai* . . . Pharsalus is a universal disaster"[94]—the old story of individuals contributing to a collective is imploded. Later in the book, Caesar will conspicuously play out the dishonoring of the communal Roman populace by gleefully withholding not just individual funeral rites but even a collective pyre (7.794–808).[95]

The narrator had conceptualized and broadened this point about Rome's collective death at Pharsalia amid the statement at 7.617–46:

                mors nulla querella
digna sua est, nullosque hominum lugere uacamus.
non istas habuit pugnae Pharsalia partes
quas aliae clades: illic per fata uirorum,
per populos hic Roma perit; quod militis illic,
mors hic gentis erat: sanguis ibi fluxit Achaeus,   635
Ponticus, Assyrius; cunctos haerere cruores
Romanus campisque uetat consistere torrens.
maius ab hac acie quam quod sua saecula ferrent
uolnus habent populi; plus est quam uita salusque

---

[92] Elliott (2013) 232.
[93] So Hardie (1993) 89 on epic as "an ideal vehicle for the representation of [the] conception of the relation between individual and family."
[94] Leigh (1997) 78. See also Day (2013) 208–9 and Sklenář (2003) 23–58 on Lucan's replacement of traditional epic *aristeiai* with the self-destructive *aristeiai* of villains such as Curio, Vulteius, and Scaeva.
[95] See McClellan (2019) 152 on the dehumanizing of the collective here.

quod perit: in totum mundi prosternimur aeuum. 640
uincitur his gladiis omnis quae seruiet aetas.

No death is worthy of its own lament, and we have the room to mourn no individual men. Pharsalia did not play the same part in battle as other disasters: in those it was in the fates of individual men; here Rome dies by the death of nations. What was the death of a solider there was the death of a race here. In this place Achaean, Pontic, Assyrian blood flowed—and the torrent of Roman blood prevents it all from staying in the fields. From this battle populations have a greater wound than their own ages can bear. It is more than life and safety that die here: we are being laid low for all of the world's time. By these swords every age that will be enslaved is being conquered. (7.630–41)

The scale of the loss makes it impossible to recount the deaths of individual men (7.630–1); Rome's death at Pharsalia was a global event, involving entire nations (*per populos hic Roma perit*, 7.634). Though joined by blood from around the world, the torrent of Roman blood predominates (7.635–7). In an effort to define precisely who and what died (*quod perit*, 7.640) at Pharsalia, the narrator tautly figures the death of the Roman people in spatial and temporal dimensions: *in totum mundi prosternimur aeuum* (7.640).[96] This totalizing statement reinforces the declarations at 7.387–459: the destructive place and day of Pharsalia reaches back (recall *retro* at 7.426) as well as forward into the future, "for all of the world's time" (*in totum mundi . . . aeuum*). Use of the present tense (*perit, habent, perit* again, *prosternimur, uincitur*) underscores that the destructive reality of Pharsalia stretches to the Romans of Lucan's day and beyond, to be experienced by "every age that will be enslaved" (7.641). The first-person plural in *prosternimur*, which is picked up several times in the following lines,[97] communicates with vehement clarity that the slaughter at *Pharsalia* is communal—even omnitemporal and omnispatial.[98]

---

[96] Thus fulfilling Caesar's demand to his troops at 7.278: *primo ferri motu prosternite mundum*.
[97] *Gessimus* in 7.643, *teximus* in 7.644, and *in nostra ceruice* in 7.645.
[98] Day (2013) 209, commenting on 7.617–46: "this slaughter ensured the end of an entire order of existence . . . [and thus] the narrator's ability to identify actual Romans." See too Connolly (2016) 289 on the "horrible unity" of the dead captured in this passage.

The shared slaughter of *Pharsalia nostra* pointedly counters the communal heroism and advance initiated in Ennius's *poemata nostra* (*Ann.* 12; see my discussion in Chapter 1). And while the action of the *Annales* had driven assuredly forward in space and time, the *Pharsalia* is bidirectional in its destructive movement, eradicating Rome's past and future. The reversal of the epic story of Roman progress articulated in 7.387–459 and 7.617–46 plays out further in Lucan's treatment of particular individuals and families. Whereas Ennius had famously concretized and embodied Rome's forward movement through the depiction of exemplary Romans and long-serving *gentes*, Lucan is sure to include such figures and families among the slaughtered at Pharsalia.[99] In the thick of the battle itself, we read of the victims of Caesar's army:

caedunt Lepidos caeduntque Metellos
Coruinosque simul Torquataque nomina, rerum
saepe duces summosque hominum te, Magne, remoto.

They slaughter the Lepidi, and they slaughter the Metelli, along with the
Corvini at the same time as the names of the Torquati, and again and
again the leaders of the state and the loftiest of men, with you excepted,
Magnus. (7.583–5)

This statement is historically inaccurate; in fact, there was "a notable absence of patrician deaths"[100] at the battle. Rather, as in the *Annales* and numerous subsequent texts, these names are representative of a tradition, of *Roman tradition itself* moving forward in time and space. The plural form of each name captures the continuity of the families' contributions to that movement—a continuity now brutally cut down at Pharsalia (note the bludgeoning repetition *caedunt ... caeduntque*). Lucan reveals what he is up to here by including among the slaughtered "the names of the Torquati" (*Torquataque nomina*, 7.584). Again, we have no reason to think that any Torquati died at the battle. It is the use of the *names* of this old *gens*—along with the Lepidi, Metelli,

---

[99] See Hardie (1993) 90 ("Lucan's epic is obsessed with the theme of names that have come to lack substance") and 94 ("this is a war from which there will be no resurrection through the continuity of generations"), as well as Bexley (2014) 378–81.

[100] Roche (2009) 10, pointing to Cic. *Phil.* 2.71, Caes. *BC* 3.99, and App., *BCiv.* 2.82. See too Dilke (1960) 143; Roche (2019) 198; and Lebek (1976) 258 on Lucan's poetic liberties here. Domitius, treated at 7.597–616, is the only noble whose death at Pharsalia is recorded by historical sources.

Corvini, et al.—and what those names represent that are put to a brutal end at Pharsalia.

Lucan had incorporated this same conceit earlier in Book 7, in Pompey's pre-battle *cohortatio*:

> subiere pericula clari
> sponte uiri sacraque antiquus imagine miles.
> si Curios his fata darent reducesque Camillos
> temporibus Deciosque caput fatale uouentes,
> hinc starent.

Of their own accord distinguished men have entered upon these dangers, as well as ancient soldiers of sacred appearance. If the fates were to give back to these times the Curii and the reborn Camilli and the Decii, offering their heads in death, they would stand on this side. (7.356–60)

Pompey's claim that distinguished men (*clari ... uiri*) and, strikingly, ancient soldiers (*antiquus ... miles*) of sacred appearance were entering the battle on his side recalls Ennius's much-remembered statement about the ancient morals and men on which Rome's strength stands (*Ann.* 156: *moribus antiquis res stat Romana uirisque*). But Pompey's whole statement is a counterfactual, with the shaky subjunctive *starent* belying the sturdy *stat* of Ennius's celebrated formulation.[101] In any case, if the *fata*—that is, this story—were to bring them back to life, the Curii, Camilli, and Decii and the other ancient soldiers would be heading for slaughter on the losing side.

Lucan had wheeled out these same characters, for a similar effect, in the previous book. In a long speech foretelling the Pompeians' doom at Pharsalia (6.777–820), the clairvoyant corpse beckoned by Erictho describes the parallel civil war being waged among Roman shades in the Underworld (6.780–1). In one camp stand the blessed shades:

> tristis felicibus umbris
> uoltus erat: uidi Decios natumque patremque,   785
> lustrales bellis animas, flentemque Camillum
> et Curios, Sullam de te, Fortuna, querentem;
> deplorat Libycis perituram Scipio terris

---

[101] See similarly Mulhern (2020) 211.

infaustam subolem; maior Carthaginis hostis
non seruituri maeret Cato fata nepotis.   790

On the blessed shades there were grim expressions. I saw the Decii, both father and son, spirits that sacrificed themselves in war, as well as Camillus weeping and the Curii, and Sulla complaining about you, Fortune; Scipio laments that his unlucky offspring will die on Libyan land; a greater enemy of Carthage, Cato, weeps for the fate of his descendant who refuses to be a slave. (6.784–90)

The Decii, Camillus, and the Curii, joined here by the arch-patrician Sulla as well as Scipio and Cato, weep because they know the outcome.[102] Their long familial lines and the communal sacrifice to which they had committed—concisely captured in the ahistorical[103] but evocative plural *Curios* and the honorific characterization of the Decii (*Decios natumque patremque, | lustrales bellis animas*)—are meeting their end at Pharsalia and in the *Pharsalia*.

Readers have emphasized that the zombie's vision of Roman shades in strife in many ways inverts the Elysium that Anchises had shown Aeneas in *Aeneid* 6.[104] While Aeneas sees Rome's future in the Decii, Torquatus, and Camillus (6.824–5), to Lucan's corpse these same men are shades of her destroyed past. Many of Virgil's Underworld figures, together with some of the imagery and language in the passage, appear to be drawn from Ennius,[105] with Goldschmidt concluding that here Virgil is evoking the *Annales* as "the canonical epic repository of the exemplary Roman past"—only to reclaim that authority for himself.[106] When Lucan populates his Underworld with those same figures, it seems fair to conclude that he is evoking the *Annales* too. Put another way, wasn't conjuring up old Roman names in this way inherently "Ennian?" The Decii, the Torquati, Camillus, Curius, and the many

---

[102] See my discussion in Chapter 6 of how their weeping contributes to the poem's antiphony of lament.

[103] We know of only one celebrated Curius, Manius Curius Dentatus, consul in 290, 275, and 274 BCE.

[104] See Ahl (1976) 137–49 (143: "Once again Lucan is taking a Vergilian situation and altering the characters and outcome"); Johnson (1987) 21–33 (21: "a witty parody of *Aeneid* 6"); Hardie (1993) 76–7; and Fratantuono (2012) 250–62.

[105] See Hardie (1993) 103–5 and Goldschmidt (2013) 166–79. See, e.g., the figures familiar from the *Ann.* at *Aen.* 6.824–5: *quin Decios Drusosque procul saeuumque securi | aspice Torquatum et referentem signa Camillum.*

[106] Goldschmidt (2013) 179, writing also of a similar dynamic on Aeneas's shield at *Aen.* 8.642–70.

other Republican Romans they represent first enter the Roman story in the *Annales*.[107] Ennius, we recall from Cicero's characterization in *Arch.* 22, was the producer of this story. While it is true that Virgil includes many of these names in *Aeneid* 6 and 8, it is not accurate to say that his epic—with its focus on the continuity of one particular *gens* from Aeneas to Augustus—is a vessel of the collective Roman *Republican* story. That story was Ennius's, those men were Ennius's protagonists.

So the defeat and retrojection of these heroes into the lost past in *Pharsalia* 6—and then, as we have seen, in the conspicuously ahistorical placement of their names on the losing side in Book 7—seem to cue for the reader the end of the fabled continuity they represented, the closure of the storylines that were referenced in the *Aeneid* (and elsewhere) but that began with so much fanfare in the *Annales*. Pharsalia and the *Pharsalia* mark, in Hardie's words, "the end of success and succession."[108] At this battle and in this poem the chief part in the Roman story passes from Rome's communal *gentes* to one *gens*, indeed to one name. Gone is the evocative plurality of the Ennian Decii, Torquati, and the rest. It is the "line of the house of Caesar" (*Caesareaeque domus series*, 4.823)—the Caesar (that is, Nero) of the poem's opening address (1.41 and 1.59) being an extension of the Caesar of the ensuing narrative[109]—that now dominates.

3.9. The end of the consular year

Another victim of Caesar(ism) is the consulship and the continuance of the Roman story that it represented. When Caesar arrives in Rome in Book 3, the remaining senators gather and "the sacred seats did not shine with a consul" (3.105–6: *non consule sacrae | fulserunt sedes*). The empty chairs were moved out (3.107) and "Caesar was everything" (3.108: *omnia Caesar erat*). This passage strikingly visualizes the diminution of the office that Lucan demonstrates across the *Pharsalia*'s early books. In the opening scene, Lucan inaugurates January 49 not with the consuls, but with Caesar at the Rubicon addressing

---

[107] For the Decii, see *Ann.* 191–4; for the Torquati, *Ann.* 476 (with Skutsch [1985] 635–6); for Curius, *Ann.* 456; and for Camillus's role in the *Ann.*, see Skutsch (1985) 306 (on *Ann.* 154–5) and 314–15.

[108] Hardie (1993) 109, on the death of the Pompeian line in the *Ph.* as representative of a larger theme.

[109] Lucan also explicitly aligns Caesar with the Caesars at 3.168, in a passage I discuss in Chapter 4; and 7.695–6. Tracy (2011) 37 fittingly groups these three passages together.

"Jupiter Latiaris who resides on lofty Mount Alba" (1.198), thus bringing to mind the *feriae Latinae* traditionally overseen by each year's consuls—but not this year. The first mention of the consuls in the poem comes conspicuously on Caesar's terms, when he inveighs against the "togaed partisans" (1.312) of Pompey and singles out the consul Gaius Claudius Marcellus Maior as "loquacious Marcellus" (1.313: *Marcellusque loquax*). In the event, Marcellus neither takes any meaningful action nor actually says *anything* in the poem. An active if not leading figure in the accounts of the civil war by Caesar (*BC* 1.6, 1.14, 3.5), Cicero (*Att.* 7.15–18 and 20–1), Plutarch (*Pomp.* 58–9), and Appian (*BC* 2.33, 36–7, 39), the consul *Marcellus loquax* is made silent in the *Pharsalia*. The other consul for 49, Lucius Cornelius Lentulus Crus, is a major player in other accounts of the year (see Caesar, *BC* 1.1–1.5, 1.14, and 3.4; Appian *BC* 2.33 and 76) and gets significant attention in the *Pharsalia* too. But Lucan first gives him voice—and first gives his name—only at the very *end* of the year, right as 49 is turning to 48 in the opening scene of Book 5. In a grandiose speech to the senate (5.17–46), Lentulus talks of abiding consular and senatorial authority (5.44–5), but his chief act is to cede all military power to the private citizen Pompey (5.46–7).[110] Once Lucan turns the calendar to 48, one consul, Publius Servilius Vatia Isauricus (on whom see Plut., *Caes.* 37; App., *BC* 2.48; and Caesar, *BC* 3.1 and 3.21), is erased altogether; the other, Caesar, is all.

This narrative demonstration of the collapse of the consulship is joined by a number of pronouncements about what that collapse means. When at 5.381–402 Caesar attains the consulship for 48, he is already an all-powerful dictator, a position attained in the fall of 49 on the nomination of Marcus Lepidus (Caesar, *BC* 2.21 and Dio, 41.36.1). So there is irony in Lucan's designation of the consulship as the "highest office" (5.383: *summo . . . honori*), words that the poet splits in 5.383 with the word *dictator*, a gesture mirroring Caesar's rupture of the Republican system. In the next line, Lucan writes that Caesar "made the calendar happy by becoming consul" (5.384: *laetos fecit se consule fastos*); while the office of the consulship is now defunct, the calendar speciously preserves the custom of consular dating. Later he declares the outright death (*perit*,

---

[110] See Masters (1992) 99 and Bexley (2009) 463–4 on Lentulus's delusions of importance in this passage; and Ducos (2010) on the senate in the *Ph.* Lentulus returns in Book 8 for a long and ultimately destructive speech in which he encourages Pompey to sail to Egypt (8.331–453). In a poem that tracks the collapse of the consulship, it is fitting that Lucan introduces the speech by writing that Lentulus "offered words worthy of one who had just been consul" (8.330). See Fucecchi (2011) 244–6, on Lentulus's "republican voice" as "nothing more than a further instrument of hostile fate" (246).

5.397) of the consulship—perishing just like the Roman nobility (*perit*, 7.597) and Rome herself (*perit*, 7.634). The office and thus the calendar year that remain are forever disfigured, cut up into the monthly units of suffect consulships (5.399). In the statement on the consequences of Pharsalia at 7.387–459, the narrator again bemoans the loss of the consuls' erstwhile leadership (7.429–30) and, when remarking on the return of tyranny to Rome, asks, "Why did we live in times ruled by laws, or years that take their names from a consul?" (7.440–1: *quid tempora legum | egimus aut annos a consule nomen habentis?*). When focusing on the turn of the calendar in Book 5, Lucan calls 48 the *Pharsalicus annus* (5.391), concisely encapsulating the idea that one destructive day, rather than Rome's consuls and the traditions they represent, now defines and dominates the Roman unit of the year. The consular year—in a true sense, the Roman year itself[111]—is killed at Pharsalia.[112]

In her discussion of *Zeitstoff* in Latin epic, Anna Wolkenhauer emphasizes how unconventional Lucan's attention to features such as the calendar and the consular year is in the genre and compares his method with "the time-telling practices of historiography."[113] And while this focus distinguishes the *Pharsalia* from works such as the *Aeneid* and *Metamorphoses*, the year's consuls and so the year-to-year continuation of the consulship had been crucial in the march of the *Annales*. It is unclear whether Ennius employed consular dating in the way later authors of historiography did,[114] but we can confidently glean from surviving fragments that the *Annales* marked moments of the transfer of consular power and drew attention to the continuance of the office. *Annales* 324 (= Isid., *Orig.* 1.36.3: *Graecia Sulpicio sorti data, Gallia Cottae*) describes the provincial allotments to the consuls Publius Sulpicius Galba and Gaius Aurelius Cotta in 200 BCE, and so is revealing of the poem's attention to the passing of consular *imperium*. The introduction of the consuls for 204

---

[111] Feeney (2007) 171, in his discussion of consular dating: "the consuls *were* the particular year."
[112] Lucan carries his interest in the transformation of the calendar into Book 10, when Caesar says to the Egyptian priest Acoreus, "And *my* year will not be defeated by the calendar of [the fourth-century Greek astronomer] Eudoxus" (10.187: *nec meus Eudoxi uincetur fastibus annus*), a reference to his reforms of the calendar in 46–45 BCE, and so a way for Lucan to extend his story of Caesar's assault on the Roman year beyond the bounds of his narrative proper. On the exchange between Caesar and Acoreus, see Manolaraki (2013) 80–117 and Tracy (2014) 99–108.
[113] Wolkenhauer (2020) 236; see also 231 on Lucan's extraordinariness as a time-teller.
[114] See the cautious assessments by Gildenhard (2003) 97–102 and Elliott (2013) 52–8, in response to the argument by Beck and Walter (2001) 40–1 (which has many scholarly precedents) that the poem had an annalistic order based upon that of the pontifical *annales*.

BCE (*Ann.* 304–6 [= Cic., *Brut.* 58)]: *additur orator Cornelius suauiloquenti | ore Cethegus Marcus Tuditano collega | Marci filius*, "Added as a colleague to Tuditanus is the orator Marcus Cornelius Cethegus, son of Marcus, of sweet-sounding speech") conveys a sense of continuity in the consulship in two ways. While marking Cethegus's placement (*additur*) into the seat of consul and thus his replacement of another who had held the position, Ennius also notes that he is the "son of Marcus" (*Marci filius*), evoking the idea of continued contributions by the Cornelii Cethegi to Roman success.[115]

Fragments such as these demonstrate Ennius's attention to the perpetuation of the transfer of consular power, to the order of that year-to-year system. Alongside these important moments of hand-off, a number of fragments make it clear that, beginning with the outset of the Republic in Book 4, the *Annales* gave center stage to the consuls as the drivers of the epic's action. Surviving fragments highlight, for example, the steadfastness of Manius Curius Dentatus, consul in 290, 275, and 274 (*Ann.* 456); the brilliance of Quintus Fabius Maximus, consul in 233, 228, 215, 214, and 209 (*Ann.* 363–5);[116] the triumph earned by Marcus Livius Salvinator, consul in 207 (*Ann.* 299); the shrewdness of Sextus Aelius Paetus, consul in 198 (*Ann.* 329); and the successes of Marcus Fulvius Nobilior, consul in 189, in *Ann.* 15 (see Cic., *Prov. Cons.* 20 and *Arch.* 27). No fragments of crucial early figures (and consuls) such as Marcus Iunius Brutus and Publius Valerius Publicola survive, but it is safe to say that, from Book 4 onward, the consuls had collective top billing as the heroes of the *Annales*. As in the Republican system itself, in much of the *Annales* the consuls were undoubtedly the engines of action.

Scholars have argued for the seminal place of the *Annales* in all literature covering Roman history, not just later epic on Roman affairs but also annalistic historiography such as Livy's *History*.[117] The story of Rome's year-to-year march, with her annually altering consuls at the fore, may have been another landmark Ennian contribution. When Lucan's epic

---

[115] Gildenhard (2003) 99 describes the inclusion of *Marci filius* as "an assertion of genealogical continuity" (though nothing is known about the elder M. Cornelius Cethegus).

[116] See Sheets (1983) 27 and Gildenhard (2003) 106–7 on the potent uses of *nobis* and *nunc* in *Ann.* 363–5 to connect Fabius Maximus Cunctator to the Roman community of Ennius's day. See too Goldschmidt (2013) 155–6 on Ennius's Fabius as an exemplary figure.

[117] See Rüpke (2006) 508–10; Gildenhard (2003) and (2007); Beck (2007) 262–3; and Elliott (2013) 231–2, *pace* Frier (1979) and Rich (2011) 16–17.

revives an interest in the consulship and the consular year, only to show both demolished by the *Pharsalicus annus*, is this another plank in his program of closing the Ennian story?

Lucan's focus on the turn of the calendar and transformation of Rome at 5.381–402 may serve to showcase such a gesture of poetic closure. The occasion of Caesar's trip to Rome to secure supreme political standing leads the narrator to enumerate several devastating firsts: the consolidation of civil and military power in one individual (5.387–92); the onset of phony elections (5.392–4); the neglect of the reading of portents (5.395–6); the disempowerment (5.398), death (5.397), and disfigurement (5.398–9; see earlier discussion) of the consulship itself; and (here again) a Jupiter who looks on (*uidit*, 5.402) from Mount Alba (5.400) but offers no providence.[118] These historical firsts are also emphatically *poetic* firsts. When Lucan writes in 5.385–6 that this age "first (*primum*) produced all the voices (*omnis uoces*)" used mendaciously of autocrats, he also marks his own poem as the first to tell that story and record those voices. When he writes in 5.397–8 that "then for the first time" (*inde ... primum*) the consulship died, again his own primacy in narrating this seismic shift in the Roman story is underscored.[119] And let us recall that many of the constitutive elements of long-lasting Roman success recounted in 5.381–402— not just the continuity of the consulship, but the providence of Jupiter's *numen*, and the practice of augury to maintain a relationship with the gods—are also constitutive elements, or narrative building blocks, of the epic that initiated that story. Could Lucan bring forward and close off these hallmarks of the Roman story *without* evoking the poem that launched that story? When he decries the onset of indifference by "the divine power that presides over Ilian Alba" (5.400), this certainly calls to mind the Latin epic tradition that turned the Iliadic Zeus into Roman Jupiter—a tradition embraced by Virgil and others, to be sure, but forged by Ennius. His commentary on the now cynical use of the consular calendar (5.384), the disfiguring partition of the consular year into months (5.399), and, most powerfully, the Pharsalian day's possession of the Roman year (*Pharsalicus annus*, 5.391) also surely evokes—and abruptly thwarts—the stout, year-to-year march of the *Annales*.

---

[118] On Caesar's conquest of Jupiter here, see Fratantuono (2012) 194–5; and see Nix (2008) on Caesar's antagonism toward Jupiter across the poem.

[119] Cf. the similar metapoetic use of *tum primum* at 3.443, with my discussion in Chapter 2.

3.10. The closure of *annales*

In the preceding pages, I have explored how Lucan subverts, opposes, and closes off the Ennian master trope of Roman expansion in time and space, guided by her gods and executed by her collective of men. We have seen that Lucan picks apart and blows up these thematic and ideological elements of Latin epic—laying waste to the grand Latin epic story that Ennius had famously formalized. I want to conclude this chapter by suggesting that Lucan's polemical closure of this master trope also operates at the level of the poem's overall structure. Readers of the *Pharsalia* have proposed that Virgil's twelve-book epic provided a model for Lucan,[120] and others have looked to the episodic structure of Ovid's *Metamorphoses* as an influence on Lucan's arrangement of his narrative.[121] There is merit to both of these arguments, but I will suggest here that the forward-thrusting and to a great extent "year-centered" arrangement of the *Annales* also stands as an important structural model and anti-model—and may help us to understand the *Pharsalia*'s much disputed final lines.[122]

Lucan's contemporary Petronius, in what is most certainly a reference to the immediately popular *Pharsalia*,[123] has the character Eumolpus criticize epics about civil war that are too linear:

> non enim res gestae uersibus comprehendendae sunt, quod longe melius historici faciunt, sed per ambages deorumque ministeria et fabulosum sententiarum tormentum praecipitandus est liber spiritus, ut potius furentis animi uaticinatio appareat quam religiosae orationis sub testibus fides.

> For verse should not be used to recount events from history, which historians do far better. But—through twists and turns and the dealings of the gods and a fabulous anguish of expression—the free spirit of the poet

---

[120] With, e.g., the handling of the Underworld in Book 6 of each poem; and see the (influential) speculation by Ahl (1976) 324 that Lucan concluded Book 12 of the *Ph.* with the suicide of Cato, in response to Virgil's conclusion of *Aen.* 12 with Aeneas's murder of Turnus.

[121] Williams (1978) 246–50 compares Lucan's procession of "alien episodes" (247) across the poem with the structure of the *Met.* Quint (1993) 140 writes similarly that the *Ph.* "collapses into episodic fragmentation."

[122] See Elliott (2013) 298 for a cautious assessment of the ordering of the *Ann.* and 299–303 for the possible triadic structure of the poem's eighteen books (with Skutsch [1985] 5–6). The proems to Book 7 (*Ann.* 206–11) and Book 16 (*Ann.* 401–3) give some sense of Ennius's use of book-beginnings as demarcations.

[123] See Connors (1998) 100–16.

must rush, so that the poem resembles more the prophesying of a raging
soul than the accuracy of a statement made under oath before witnesses.
(*Satyr.* 118)

This critique of Lucan's poem, echoed centuries later in Voltaire's memorable put-down of Lucan as a "Gazetteer,"[124] overlooks or fails to understand the twists and turns of time (in, e.g., flashbacks, prophecies, and digressions) and the sophisticated, though of course unconventional, involvement of the neglectful gods. But Eumolpus is right in saying that the *Pharsalia* is structured and advances in a largely linear, annalistic fashion. The epic as we have it totals ten books: the narrative of Book 1 commences in January 49; the opening of Book 5 marks the passing of 49 to 48; and the remaining books cover the year 48. Book 10 closes just past the endpoint of Caesar's own *commentarii* on the civil war, with Caesar embroiled in battle against the party of Ptolemy in Alexandria. Caesar had arrived in Egypt in October 48 and, according to Appian (*BC* 2.90), does not exit for another nine months. The dating of the events during his time in Egypt is difficult, since neither Caesar in his account of this period at *BC* 3.106–12 nor the author of the *Alexandrian War*, which picks up where Caesar's writing ends, provides any dates. We are dependent in large part on the remarks by Cicero, who writes to Atticus on June 14, 47, that Caesar had not sent a letter to Rome since December 13, 48 (*Att.* 11.17a.3).[125] To those back in Rome such as Cicero, then, Caesar was in a sense "missing in action" in Egypt as the year 48 came to a close. This is precisely the condition of Lucan's Caesar at the end of Book 10, as he fights for the Egyptian island of Pharos and for his own survival (10.529–46).

The *Pharsalia*, then, covers the years 49 and 48 more or less in full, with a conspicuous year-break in Book 5. There is an orderly, essentially linear, year-based movement to the poem—which, however, comes to a surprising and messy halt. Book 10 and the poem break off at 10.546 while Caesar is still engaged in battle on the Heptastadion, the stretch of land connecting Pharos with Alexandria. At 10.543–4 he looks back and spots Scaeva, leading the narrator to recall, in the poem's final line and a half, the latter's exploits at Dyrrachium, "where he alone, with the walls opened, besieged Magnus as he trampled on the ramparts" (*ubi solus apertis | obsedit muris calcantem moenia*

---

[124] Voltaire (1727) 63: "the Frame of his Poem is dry and tedious, because he dares not deviate from the History.... Lucan with all the force of his Painting, with his Grandeur, with his Wit, with his political Notions, is but a declamatory Gazetteer."

[125] See Lord (1938) 21 on Cicero's difficulties corresponding with Caesar.

Magnum, 10.545–6). This ending is abrupt and jarring, and stopping here makes Book 10 a significantly shorter book than the nine preceding books. But while the *communis opinio* has long been that the poem is unfinished, a growing number of scholars argue for its completion as is.[126] There is, for example, the fact that the narrative of Lucan's poem as we have it concludes just past the endpoint of Caesar's *commentarii*. And the appearance of *Magnum* as the book's and poem's last word echoes the appearances of *Magnus* in the final lines of Books 2, 5, and 8. Further, just as Homer had given the last words of the *Iliad* to the dead Hector (Ἕκτορος ἱπποδάμοιο, 24.804) and Virgil had given the *Aeneid*'s last line to the dying Turnus (12.952), Lucan "seems to make a point of picking Pompey's name out of the blue"[127] and gives the last word to the poem's loser, to loss, to death.

In his extensive treatment of the ending, Masters discusses numerous details in the final twelve lines that may also stand as markers of closure, emphasizing that the boldness of this ending should be read as a marker of Lucan's ambition as an epic poet ("genre is not prescriptive; it is a challenge").[128] But he also argues for the impossibility of closure in a poem such as this, and so the necessity of endlessness: "the civil war can have no ending. Everything about the war and the poem is boundless, illimitable, infinite."[129] This argument about Lucan's self-presentation and the boundlessness of his poem is an important one, and one I will take up again in my Conclusion. But at the same time, Masters's point as it relates to the poem's narrative content (the civil war) requires reconsideration. We have seen that the *Pharsalia* details at great length—most fully at 5.381–402 and then in the crushing statements at 7.387–459 and 7.617–46[130]—the victory of Caesar and the devastating consequences of that victory. And while textual closure can be conceptualized in a number of ways,[131] one helpful way is to regard resolution of conflict as determinative. As the narratologist H. Porter Abbott puts it,

---

[126] See. e.g., Haffter (1957); Masters (1992) 216–59; Rossi (2005); Tracy (2011); Rimell (2015) 244–52; and McClellan (2019) 158 n. 176. Dinter (2012) 140–54 considers the issue from the perspective of responses to the ending by medieval readers. See Ahl (1976) 306–32 for the argument that the poem is incomplete and that Lucan had planned twelve books. Stover (2008) argues that Lucan's characterization of Cato in Books 2 and 9 points toward an endpoint with Cato's death at Thapsus in 46 BCE.

[127] Masters (1992) 258.

[128] Masters (1992) 250.

[129] Masters (1992) 251.

[130] Passages that Masters does not address. Dinter (2012) 148: "the real ending of the *Bellum Civile* would be found in the melee of the battle of Pharsalus."

[131] See Fowler (1997) 3 and his ensuing discussion, as well as Grewing, Acosta-Hughes, and Kirichenko (2013b) 1–11.

"When a narrative resolves a conflict, it achieves closure"[132]—whether that resolution is at the story's ending or not.

The conflict at the center of the *Pharsalia is* resolved: Caesar and Caesarism win. Rome and her story die. And this narrative development is matched at the end of Book 10 on the formal level. If the ending is jarring, messy, and comes abruptly soon in the book, this is because here the *form* of the Roman story, advancing from year to year, falls off, dissolves, lost and "missing in action" somewhere far away from Rome. Content and form trail off and end together. With the *Pharsalicus annus*—a year defeated and defined by a day—comes an end to the epic story of year-to-year Roman advance launched, codified, and given an ongoing vitality in the *Annales*. Ennius's epic had not only been formative and life-giving for future Roman epic and Latin literature more broadly, but also, prior to that, ever growing itself, with the poet continually adding content as Rome's story grew during his lifetime.[133] The *Annales* was an inherently open-ended Roman story, its threads and themes ready to be picked up and perpetuated. If Lucan's epic was to bring a harsh, halting end to that story of progress and growth and to the corresponding generative poetic trajectory,[134] then a harsh, halting end to his poem was in order. Here Derrida's conception of genre as ultimately a "formless form" fated for degenerescence may again be helpful: we might say that the abrupt, even violent break in the form of the *Pharsalia* at 10.546 signals the formlessness and dissolution toward which the epic genre was inevitably headed.[135]

In her study of the imagery of enclosure in early imperial literature, Victoria Rimell profitably considers how Lucan uses the final scene of Book 10 to entrap Caesar, who stands in "in the space of the confined mole" (*molis in exiguae spatio*, 10.534) on the Heptastadion, is "surrounded" (*cingitur*, 10.537), and pressed by tightly packed ships (*densae . . . classes*, 10.537).[136]

---

[132] Abbott (2002) 52, going on to write that "closure does not have to come at the end of a narrative." At 53–4, Abbott points to the work of Barthes (1970) on narrative codes. Per Barthes's proairetic code, which involves expectations and actions, the *Pharsalia* has closure. Per his hermeneutic code, which involves questions and answers, the *Pharsalia* answers some (such as "who won?") while leaving others ("what now for us defeated Romans and our story?") less certainly answered. In Chapter 6 and my Conclusion, I return to that latter question.

[133] See Skutsch (1985) 4–5 of Ennius's treatment of *bella recentia*.

[134] See my discussion in Chapter 2 of the contrasts between the groves in *Ph*. 3.440–5 and *Ann*. 175–9.

[135] Derrida (1980) 65, with my discussion at the outset of Chapter 2. See too the remark about the *Pharsalia*'s implosion of its own linearity by Henderson (1987) 136.

[136] Rimell (2015) 244–52. See also Tracy (2011) 47–53 on Caesar's "moment of inner frailty" (48) here, with a similar reading of the passage as offering "a measure of hope for successful resistance against the Caesars" (53).

The image seems to provide the reader with an alternative outcome to Caesarian success and, as Rimell suggests, to the direction of epic: "Hemmed in with Caesar inside Lucan's culminating enclosure, we imagine all the ways epic might open up, reboot and show us a way out."[137]

But is it too late? Has the Roman epic story lost its chance? Is the *Pharsalia* closing the door? Just prior in this concluding passage, Lucan wrote of Caesar's predicament on the Heptastadion:

> potuit discrimine summo
> Caesaris una dies in famam et saecula mitti.
>
> On that occasion of utmost crisis for Caesar, one day could have achieved glory for the ages. (10.532-3)

On several occasions Lucan states that not just years but ages (*saecula*) were wiped out by the day of Pharsalia (recall 1.73, 7.446, and 7.638). Here in this critical moment (*discrimine summo*) in the poem, he raises the possibility that this one day in Egypt could have changed everything, bringing a different outcome to the following ages (*saecula*) and changing the story (*fama*). It did not. And in any case, the damage at Pharsalia had already been made apparent, the finality of that day and its consequences already drummed over and over across the poem. The upshot of this passage is ultimately that there was and is no alternative outcome. The very act of raising the counterfactual at 10.532-3—fronted by the opening stroke of resignation in the perfect-tense *potuit* ("It could have been . . .")[138]—serves to underscore the non-occurrence of this outcome, and thus the fancy of the entrapment episode that follows and concludes the poem.[139]

In this chapter we have tracked Lucan's presentation of the *Pharsalia* at and indeed as the end of the Roman epic story, with an eye to Ennius's formative *Annales* as a necessary foil to Lucan's poetics of closure. Like Ennius's spatiotemporal sweep and Lucan's redirection and closure of that sweep,

---

[137] Rimell (2015) 252.

[138] *Pace* Tracy (2011) 47, who reads *potuit* as expressing "the real possibility" of Caesar's destruction.

[139] See similarly Lucan's frequent foreshadowing of the "avenging day" (7.782) of Caesar's assassination, March 15, 44 BCE, referred to at 2.283-4, 5.206-8, 7.451, 7.586-96, 8.609-10, 9.17-18, 10.340-2, and, just before these lines, at 10.528. The references have a cumulative effect, but through his continuous attention to the lasting impact of the victory at Pharsalia, Lucan makes it clear that Caesar's assassination could not undo what was done to Rome at Pharsalia.

our view here—across Roman time and space—has been broad. The next chapter, the last concentrating on Lucan's closure for the Latin epic tradition, will concentrate on a particular node on the continuum of Roman time, and a pivotal one for the rise of the epic genre at Rome. To that moment we turn now.

4
Lucan and the Closing of the Maritime Moment

Latin epic begins on the sea. More specifically, it begins with Roman expansion on the sea. Livius's *Odusia*, Naevius's *Bellum Punicum*, and Ennius's *Annales* each had a claim to primacy in the Latin epic tradition, and the matter of which epic merits the mantle of "first" would immediately become contentious and long debated.[1] But one thing these poems have in common is a close relationship with the sea: not only a thematic focus on the sea and the power and opportunities it offers, but also a provenance in a particular historical context. Each appears right as Rome is emerging as a maritime power; as Matthew Leigh has put it, "to a significant degree, the maritime moment and the epic moment are in fact one."[2] Leigh is one of several scholars who have underlined and examined the synchronicity of Rome's expansion on the Mediterranean and the development of Latin epic. While the fragmentary state of each of these early poems makes any comprehensive analysis impossible, recent readings have profitably considered how, for example, the seas that the hero of Livius's *Odusia* sails "are also the storm-tossed seas of the First Punic War";[3] how in the *Bellum Punicum*, written in the years following the First Punic War, "epic primacy and naval primacy allegorically coalesce";[4] and how, when Ennius composed the *Annales* in the years after Roman victory in the Second Punic War, "the moment was . . . ripe for the emergence of a new type of narrative about Rome, one that made the City the

---

[1] See my Introduction.
[2] Leigh (2010) 265, focusing on Livius and Naevius. See too Morford (1967) 22 ("It was the excitement of fresh explorations that had inspired Homer's treatment of the sea; something of the same dynamic influence gave the impulse to the early Roman poets, after the Punic wars and Rome's conquest of the sea"); and Goldberg (1995) 147, of Naevius and Ennius ("They created epic, at just the time Roman aristocrats began developing history, not simply to record and extoll but to understand the scope and meaning of the Roman achievement"); Giusti (2018) 208–11 argues that Virgil evokes the maritime moment of the First Punic War in *Aen.* 1.
[3] Leigh (2010) 273. See also Goldberg (1995) 50 ("The story he retold was of immediate interest to Romans of the later third century"); and Feeney (2016) 63–4.
[4] Biggs (2017) 352.

central node linking together the rest of the known world."[5] The launch of the epic genre at Rome coincides with—and narrates—the launch of Rome herself onto and across the Mediterranean.

The story of Rome's entrance onto the sea is also closely aligned with the story of her contest with Carthage for control of the Mediterranean. While Rome had engaged in maritime commerce and some naval activity, it was the dispute with Carthage over hegemony in Sicily in the 260s that not only set off their decades of war with one another, but also led directly to Rome's commitment to a full-sized fleet.[6] Rome's maritime story and Carthaginian story also launch together in early Latin epic. Naevius of course initiates epic about Roman affairs by narrating the first conflict with Carthage (264–241 BCE), and Ennius's *Annales* gives the backdrop of the years 264–218 BCE (Book 7) and then tells the story of the Second Punic War (218–202 BCE) in great fullness (Books 8–9).[7] To stretch out Leigh's formulation, Rome's maritime moment, Carthaginian moment, and epic moment are one and the same.[8]

Lucan's *Pharsalia* is similarly consumed with Rome's place on the sea, with extensive episodes of seafaring and sea battle appearing in Books 2, 3, 4, 5, 8, 9, and 10.[9] But these are episodes of shipwreck, shattered plans, and self-destruction on the seas. During his description in Book 1 of the terror that took hold of Rome before Caesar's arrival, Lucan compares citizens fleeing from the city to men jumping overboard during a storm at sea, when "every man makes a shipwreck for himself" (*naufragium sibi quisque facit*, 1.503). The

---

[5] Elliott (2013) 240.

[6] In 1.20 Polyb. explicitly identifies the First Punic War as the cause for Rome's development of a fleet. Walbank (1957) 75 writes: "The probability is that prior to the First Punic War there was no *permanent* fleet, and that ships were put in commission only when required." See the full-length study of Thiel (1954) and the reassessment by Harris (2017), who traces Roman development of ships back to 314 BCE.

[7] Elliott (2013) 298–302 offers, with caution, a table reconstructing the text, with Books 7–9 as a unit in the poem's triadic structure. See too her discussion at 60–71.

[8] So Feeney (2017) 308: "Latin epic in particular was centrally concerned with Carthage, and the successive literary treatments of the conflicts with Carthage generated a new kind of literary history at Rome." Goldschmidt (2013) 109 writes of the Punic Wars as a "moment in Roman collective consciousness, which, for [the *Aeneid*'s] first readers, would have been crucially bound up with the two earliest Roman historical epics" (109). In a fragment from the second c. BCE, the poet Porcius Licinus writes: *Poenico bello secundo Musa pinnato gradu | intulit se bellicosam in Romuli gentem feram* ("During the Second Punic War the Muse brought herself, full of war, on a winged course to the savage race of Romulus," fr. 1 Courtney = Aul. Gell. 17.21.44). Though the syntax of the line and the author or even poetic genre to which Porcius may be referring are unclear (see Skutsch [1985] 373 n. 4; Courtney [1993] 82–6; and Welsh [2011]), "one of the things the fragment neatly brings out is that early Roman poetry (symbolized in the *Musa bellicosa*) is anchored in Rome's wars with Carthage" (Goldschmidt [2013] 106).

[9] Saint-Denis (1935) 419–40 collects and categorizes references to the sea in the *Ph.*, concluding: "la mer de Lucain est grandiose et romantique" (439).

simile evokes the familiar allegory of the ship of state,[10] but in the books that follow, the vehicle of this simile spills—rather, gushes—over into the tenor of Lucan's narrative.[11] Roman loss on the seas carries across the poem, most often resembling the self-reflexive, self-destructive shipwreck that is pictured in this Book 1 simile. At the same time, the poem narrates the re-emergence and vengeance of Rome's chief maritime enemy, Carthage. If Rome's successful launch onto the sea and the defeat of her great naval rival had animated the works of Rome's foundational epics, then the *Pharsalia* tells the opposite story, the reversal of that story. If the maritime moment and the epic moment are one and the same, then the *Pharsalia* marks and narrates the moment of that story's crashing end. Readers of Lucan have noted how extraordinary his attention to the sea is,[12] and have also long dwelled on the poem's focus on Africa and the Carthaginian threat, with one ancient reader even seeming to give Lucan's poem the title *Punica*.[13] These points of focus on the sea and on Rome's great rival on the Mediterranean are not haphazard; they are, I will argue, a running, constitutive element of Lucan's project of bringing closure to the Latin epic story.

I will examine this poetic endeavor in a manner similar to that of the book as a whole, in a sense chronologically backwards. I will begin by tracing the more particular matter of the narrative arc of Hannibal's vengeance and the consequent undoing of Rome's victory over Carthage. Then I will move to the related but broader theme of Rome's crossing the sea over to Africa, and the reversal of past African landings that Lucan charts, before considering his inclusion in Book 3 of a full-scale—and fully self-destructive—naval battle. I will conclude with a look at prolonged passages in which Lucan visualizes the self-destruction and sinking of individual Roman ships. As I proceed,

---

[10] See Roche (2009) 310, with reference to Hor., *C.* 1.14, and the interpretation of Quint. at *Inst.* 8.6.44; as well as Taylor (2020) 92. In Chapter 5, I consider this and a similar simile at 7.123–7, describing Pompey on the morning of Pharsalia, as evocative of Odyssean themes.

[11] In a particularly bold stroke, Lucan even describes the Caesarian army that endures a flood in Spain with the image *iam naufraga campo | Caesaris arma natant* (4.87–8: "now Caesar's army was shipwrecked in the field and swimming").

[12] Particularly regarding the extensive naval battle in Book 3, an epic scene-type that Opelt (1957) has suggested Lucan invented. See further Hunink (1992) 200.

[13] The author of the preface to the second book of the *Disticha Catonis*, from the third or fourth century. See Connolly (2010), writing at 197: "it is . . . very possible that the author of the *Disticha*'s preface, like many others, simply thought of the poem as both Roman and Punic in subject matter." See also Leigh (2000) and Asso (2002) on the place of Africa in the poem; Manolaraki (2013) 45–117 on the Nile's strong presence and significance; and Tracy (2014) on Egypt as a place that can represent both utopia and dystopia. We may read Silius Italicus's commitment to writing an epic about Roman victory over Carthage as a response to Lucan's focus on Roman failure and loss in (and of) Africa. On Silius Italicus as a close reader of Lucan, see Marks (2009).

I will consider fragments from the *Odusia*, *Bellum Punicum*, and *Annales*, at times held up alongside passages in the *Pharsalia*. But on the whole, I will look at the early Latin epics in their capacity as code models for Lucan: the core constitutive element or master trope of early Latin epic that Lucan seeks to undo and reverse is that of Roman embrace of and advance on the sea.

I will also keep in mind that there existed in these early epics a keen sense of the precariousness of Rome's launch onto the sea. The limited evidence again prohibits any sweeping statements, but, in the case of the *Odusia*, the titular character's journey is of course famously perilous and uncertain. For example, in the longest fragment we have (fr. 18 Blänsdorf), Livius writes expansively when characterizing Odysseus's story as a violent contest between the sea and humanity (*namque nullum | peius macerat humanum quamde mare saeuum*, "for nothing weakens a human worse than the savage sea").[14] Leigh comments on these lines that Livius "adopts a distinctly more pathetic register" than that in the model passage at *Odyssey* 8.138–9; and he connects this heightened *pathos* with the Roman experience of Livius's time: "for those who have seen the cruel sea at first hand, the epic storm is more than just a stock trope of the poets."[15] Naevius's *Bellum Punicum* certainly featured the ups and downs of war, "victory being rolled out by turns" (*uicissatim uolui uictoriam*, fr. 41 Blänsdorf), and it seems to dwell on the fragile and inherently uncertain condition of the seafarer, both in the flashbacks to Aeneas's journey and in the narration of the First Punic War, which, as Polybius's account makes clear, included a devastating series of shipwrecks and losses on the sea. Scholars have proposed that Naevius's line *onerariae onustae stabant in flustris* ("the weighed down freight-ships were standing still in the calm," fr. 48 Blänsdorf) comes from his description of the Roman fleet just prior to the second disaster off Cape Camarina in 249, when a storm destroyed 103 of 105 warships in the fleet and all of its transports.[16] We will see that Ennius too included a number of passages focused on the perils of Rome's naval ventures.[17] The conquest of the sea was an inherently fluctuating and

---

[14] See Goldberg (1995) 70, noting how Livius expands the Homeric models into a more general statement.
[15] The first quotation of Leigh (2010) is from 275–6; the second from 276. Saint-Denis (1935) 38–9 also considers differences between fr. 18 (Blänsdorf) and *Od.* 8.138–9.
[16] See Cichorius (1922) 45–6, citing Diod. Sic. 24.1.9 and Polyb. 1.54.8; and Leigh (2010) 271 and 274–5. Polyb. 1.37.2 narrates the sinking of the fleet in this same spot in 255. Leigh connects the events from Aeneas's tale that Naevius narrated with those of the poet's main narrative: "What Aeneas endures in the archaeology, the men of Rome endure in the First Punic War" (275). Fragments 37 and 64 (Blänsdorf) also highlight Roman activity on the sea.
[17] Elliott (2014) 252 collects the seven fragments from the *Ann.* that describe naval exercises of any sort.

deadly struggle, and the precariousness that seems to have been present and pregnant in Latin epic's beginnings is seized and carried out to its disastrous outcome by Lucan. His embrace of the *mare saeuum* (so *Odusia* fr. 18 [Blänsdorf]) as a place to engage with early epic models is akin to the attraction we considered in Chapter 2 to scenes of violation and slaughter as *loci* for metapoetic assertions.

In identifying and going right to the scenes in the tradition's beginnings where the epic story's finality is already near, Lucan may thus be pointing to the precariousness of the epic enterprise, the fragility with which epic launched at Rome—and thus the imminence if not inevitability of its ultimate end. It is hard to overstate how bold the literary undertakings of Livius, Naevius, and Ennius were, each inventing Latin epic in distinct ways, testing the waters of meter in the imposition of the Saturnian on Homeric epic (Livius) and then the restoration of hexameter (Ennius), and creating a genre and an audience for that genre where they had not before existed.[18] In this precariousness, too, the epic and maritime moments align, and Lucan looks to what is inherently fragile and unsure and implodes it, the *Pharsalia*'s reversals of imperial success, its shipwrecks, and its crash landings speaking in a metapoetic way to the inescapable crash of the Latin epic project.

4.1. "There is a lot of Hannibal in that empty heart": Hannibal reanimated and the Roman story reversed

Later in this chapter, I will consider Ennius's narration of Rome's efforts on the uncertain seas in his telling of the Punic Wars. But the contingency in Ennius's text on which I will focus first—one that Lucan picks up in full force—is that of the existential threat that Hannibal represented for Rome. The story of the Carthaginian general's invasion of Italy and Latium was, to be sure, known to all Romans and recounted by numerous authors,[19] and it remained a subject for declamations in schools well into Lucan's lifetime.[20] But Ennius was the first to tell this story, and his sprawling

---

[18] See Feeney (2016) 4–8 and *passim* on the contingency of Latin literature's emergence; and McElduff (2013) 48–9 on the need for Livius to create a literary place and audience for epic at Rome, and 49–52 on his inventive choice of Saturnian meter.

[19] See Polyb. 3.92 and Livy, 26.7–11. And see O'Gorman (2004) on the power of "Carthage the undead city" (100) in Roman thought.

[20] See Sen., *Nat.* 3, *pref.* 6; and Juv. 10.164–7.

narrative[21] of that war—and of Hannibal leading his legions up to Rome's walls (*Ann.* 292: *ob Romam noctu legiones ducere coepit*)—would be long remembered. Over a century after the publication of the *Annales*, Lucretius evokes the "terrifying tumult" (*trepido . . . tumultu*, 3.384) of the Second Punic War with an echo of the *Annales*.[22] Cicero turns to "that greatest poet of ours" for a memorable anecdote about Hannibal (*Ann.* 234 = Cic., *Balb.* 51; see my later discussion), and, like Lucretius, recalls Ennius's harrowing picture of "Africa, rough land, trembling with terrible tumult" (*Africa terribili tremit horrida terra tumultu, Ann.* 309 = *De or.* 3.167). Cicero also quotes Ennius's description of the breakdown of civic stability and norms that occurs amid the terrors of war (*Ann.* 248–53 = Cic., *Mur.* 30), a passage that Gellius (20.10.3–5) places in Book 8, presumably amid the Hannibalic War. Nearly a century and a half after the *Annales*' publication, Propertius includes in his seven-line list of events from Ennius's poem a series of perilous episodes from the Second Punic War (3.3.6, 9–11).[23] The specter of the Carthaginian threat and especially of Hannibal was towering, and it would have a long afterlife in Roman culture and particularly in Roman epic, most notably in the *Aeneid* and Silius Italicus's *Punica*.[24] Nonetheless, it is clear that the first epic telling of that story of supreme danger kept a strong hold over readers and authors at Rome. Indeed, nearly 600 years after Ennius's death, Claudian would closely identify Roman victory over Hannibal with Ennius's own success, writing that "the laurel of Mars was a garland for the poet" (*sertum uati Martia laurus erat, Cons. Stil.* III.20).

In the *Annales*, of course, Rome defeats Hannibal by warding him off and in time bringing the battle back over the sea to Africa, to a victory at Zama in 202 under the leadership of Scipio Africanus. It is a story of the most frightening of obstacles overcome, of the Roman march across time and space imperilled but resilient and ultimately triumphant. This entire tale of Roman victory over Hannibal and Carthage is undone in Lucan's poem, as

---

[21] See Goldschmidt (2013) 131 on the Second Punic War as "the greatest of the wars narrated in the *Annales*." Feeney (1991) 127–8: "Ennius was presumably the first to cast the Hannibalic war as the struggle between Rome and Carthage for rule over the world."

[22] *Ann.* 309 = Cic., *De or.* 3.167. On Lucretius's adaptation of Ennius's narrative of that war, see Kenney (1971) on Lucr. 3.832–42; Feeney (1984) 181; Elliott (2013) 116; Goldschmidt (2013) 25–6; and Giusti (2018) 258–60.

[23] Goldschmidt (2013) 25 writes that Prop. 3.3.6–12 "suggests ways in which the poem could still be thought of in Augustan Rome as a repository of stories of early Rome, wars against the Greeks, and the Hannibalic War."

[24] See Giusti (2018) on the important place of Carthage in the *Aen.*

the existential danger of the Carthaginian threat is made real—its specter brought to life and to victory.

The vengeful re-emergence of Hannibal is introduced and developed right from the start of the *Pharsalia*. In the address to Nero at 1.33–66, as he outlines the events that led to the emperor's reign, Lucan introduces the theme in terms that are viscerally clear.[25] At 1.38–9 he writes: "Let Pharsalia fill its dread fields and let the shades of the Punic one be sated with blood" (*diros Pharsalia campos | inpleat et Poeni saturentur sanguine manes*). Hannibal, we learn, will be appeased; Carthage will emerge victorious in this poem. In the preceding lines, Lucan had written that Roman hands, not Pyrrhus or the Punic one, would be responsible for Rome's destruction (*non tu, Pyrrhe ferox, nec tantis cladibus auctor | Poenus erit*, 1.30–1; see Chapter 1). However, when the poem's action gets underway, it becomes immediately apparent that this division will not be so clear: a Roman character, Caesar, will take on the part of the avenging Carthaginian general. Earlier authors had pointed to parallels in the aggressive acts of these two, but Lucan transforms this connection into a reanimation of sorts, with his Caesar emerging as a Hannibal reborn and poised for revenge.[26]

This poetic agenda is launched when Lucan makes Caesar's crossing of the Alps the very first action of the poem's narrative: "Caesar had already conquered (*superauerat*) the chilly Alps in his march and had taken up (*ceperat*) in his mind huge undertakings and the war that was to come" (1.183–5). The pluperfect tense in *superauerat* and *ceperat* is significant: as the poem's action begins, Caesar has already accomplished Hannibal's most celebrated feat,[27] and has already planned the war that is to come (*bellum...futurum*). Lucan reinforces the image of Caesar as African invader by comparing him to a Libyan lion just as he transgresses the boundary of the Rubicon (1.205–12). Shortly afterward, as Caesar enters the northern Italian town of Ariminum, its fearful citizens recall a similar invasion by the "Mars of Libya" (*Martem*

---

[25] See Roche (2009) 7–10 on 1.33–63 as an "aetiology of autocracy."

[26] On Hannibal in the poem, see Ahl (1976) 107–12; Hunink (1992) 144–5; Roche (2009) 128; and Day (2013) 116–20. Cicero had drawn this comparison when asking Atticus about Caesar's aggression: *utrum de imperatore populi Romani an de Hannibale loquimur?* (*Att.* 7.11.1). At *Aen.* 6.830–1, Virgil had made a similar suggestion about Caesar's crossing of the Alps (see Reed [2007] 159–62). Giusti (2018) 227–8 considers how Virgil presents Turnus as a Hannibalic figure. That ancient readers were attentive to the Hannibalic qualities of Lucan's Caesar becomes clear in Silius Italicus's use of Lucan's language for Caesar to characterize Hannibal in victory, and then of Lucan's language for Pompey to cast the Carthaginian leader in defeat. See Marks (2009), 129 and 146–50.

[27] Day (2013) 120: "Caesar's actions out-sublime not only the Alps but the mountains' previous conqueror too."

150 THUNDER AND LAMENT

Libyes, 1.255). Then, in a speech to his assembled troops, Caesar himself makes the comparison explicit: "Rome would be struck by no greater tumult of war if the Punic Hannibal were crossing the Alps" (1.303–5: *non secus ingenti bellorum Roma tumultu | concutitur quam si Poenus transcenderet Alpes | Hannibal*). The name *Hannibal* had been withheld up to this point—and the dramatic delay is redoubled by the hyperbaton and enjambment in these lines—but any doubts about who will revive the Punic one and his Ennian *tumultus* (recall *Ann.* 309) are here set straight.[28]

In his speech on the horrors of Marius's and Sulla's reigns at 2.68–232, the old man casts Marius in the role of the Punic avenger. Of his refuge in Africa prior to his return to Rome, he says:

> nuda triumphati iacuit per regna Iugurthae
> et Poenos pressit cineres. solacia fati
> Carthago Mariusque tulit, pariterque iacentes
> ignouere deis.

> [Marius] lay hidden in the stripped realm of Jugurtha, whom he had paraded in triumph, and he pressed down on Punic ashes. Carthage and Marius took solace from this fate, and, both lying down, they forgave the gods. (2.90–3)

Marius is figured as taking power and rising from Punic ashes (*Poenos... cineres*). Whether a reference to *the* Punic's ashes or to the torched city's ashes, or both, Marius's imminent return to Rome from Africa and the ensuing slaughter will satisfy Carthage as much as it does him. The old man's speech as a whole, as I discussed in Chapter 2, mirrors and reinforces themes that run through the poem's main narrative, with Marius and Sulla operating as anticipatory doublets of Caesar and Pompey. The presentation of the vengeful Marius as emerging from Punic ashes thus keeps the Hannibalic typology fresh in readers' minds, with Caesar himself offstage—but lurking—for the first half of Book 2.[29]

In Book 3, Caesar at last makes his way to Rome, and Lucan depicts him as out to accomplish what the historical Hannibal did not: scaling Rome's walls

---

[28] See Ahl (1976) 107–8 on how condensed the references to Hannibal are in Book 1 (108: "Lucan clearly did not intend us to keep [Caesar and Hannibal] discrete in our minds").

[29] Caesar first appears in Book 2 at 2.439, resuming the march that Lucan had paused at 1.468. See Fantham (1992) 25 on this suspension of Caesar's action.

and sacking the city. The poet has Caesar speak directly to the city walls (*suae sic fatur moenia Romae*, 3.90), in a speech (3.91–7) that leads Roman citizens to respond with great terror:

> sic fatur et urbem
> attonitam terrore subit. namque ignibus atris
> creditur, ut captae, rapturus moenia Romae
> sparsurusque deos.

> So he speaks and enters a city struck by terror. For there is a belief that [Caesar] will lay waste to the walls of Rome with black fires, as though the city has been captured, and he will put the gods to flight. (3.97–100)

Like the Romans who expressed fears for the worst at the outset of Book 2 (2.16–233), the citizens here assume that Caesar will take the walls and burn the city down. But he does not. After a short stay, "once he left the walls of trembling Rome, he took his army and flew over the snow-capped Alps" (3.298–9: *ille ubi deseruit trepidantis moenia Romae | agmine nubiferam rapto super euolat Alpem*). Just like Hannibal, Lucan's Caesar threatens Rome's walls and fills the city with trembling, but does not go through with a sack of the city. Instead, he marches back up the Italian peninsula and over the Alps.

The close parallels that Lucan develops between Caesar and Hannibal in Books 1–3 set the stage for an important difference. Multiple sources report Caesar's looting of the state treasury in the Temple of Saturn and the tribune Metellus's efforts to stop him.[30] Lucan expands this episode into a transformational moment in the ascent of Caesar and Caesarism. The lengthy scene (3.112–68) concludes with the poet's enumeration of what exactly Caesar stole from the temple:

> tunc rupes Tarpeia sonat magnoque reclusas
> testatur stridore fores; tum conditus imo   155
> eruitur templo multis non tactus ab annis
> Romani census populi, quem Punica bella
> quem dederat Perses, quem uicti praeda Philippi,
> quod tibi, Roma, fuga Gallus trepidante reliquit,

---

[30] See (with Hunink [1992] 82 and 96–7) Caes., *BC* 1.33.3–4; Plin., *NH* 33.35–6; Plut., *Caes.* 35; Florus, *Epit.* 2.13.21; App., *BC* 2.41, and Oros. 6.15.5.

152 THUNDER AND LAMENT

> quo te Fabricius regi non uendidit auro, 160
> quidquid parcorum mores seruastis auorum,
> quod dites Asiae populi misere tributum
> uictorique dedit Minoia Creta Metello,
> quod Cato longinqua uexit super aequora Cypro.
> tunc Orientis opes captorumque ultima regum 165
> quae Pompeianis praelata est gaza triumphis
> egeritur; tristi spoliantur templa rapina,
> pauperiorque fuit tum primum Caesare Roma.

Then the Tarpeian rock roars as it witnesses the doors opened up with a great creaking. Then the wealth of the Roman people, which had been stored deep within the temple and untouched by many years, is raided. It was the wealth that the Punic wars and Perses had provided, along with the spoils of the defeat of Philip; that which the Gaul in his trembling flight left for you, Roma; and the gold that Fabricius did not trade to the king for you—whatever you, noble character of our frugal ancestors, saved up; whatever tribute the wealthy nations of Asia paid, and what Minoan Crete gave to victorious Metellus, what Cato bore over the seas from faraway Cyprus. Then the wealth of the East and the last treasure of the captured kings, which had been paraded in Pompey's triumphs, is brought out. The temples are robbed in an act of sorrowful theft, and then, for the first time, Rome was poorer than a Caesar. (3.154–68)

Lucan quantifies Caesar's theft of the treasury in terms of past Roman victories that led to the abundant wealth now being stolen.[31] Lines 157–67 move quickly across Roman space and time, spanning over 300 years and the breadth of the Roman world, from Africa to Gaul to the expanse of the East. The poet lists the wealth gained in the Punic Wars (3.157) and in victories over Perses and Philip V of Macedon in the years 168 and 197, respectively (3.158); the recovery of treasure from invading Gauls in 387–6 (3.159); the wealth preserved by the consul Fabricius, who refused to bribe Pyrrhus in 282 (3.160); the Pergamene king Attalus III's bequest to Rome in 133; and the wealth from conquests of Crete by Metellus Creticus in 69–67 (3.163),

---

[31] With dubious historical accuracy: the treasury had first been used in 209 BCE amid the Hannibalic threat, and so the inclusion of the recovery of treasure from the Gauls in 387–6 is inaccurate.

of Cyprus by Cato in 58 (3.164), and of numerous Eastern kingdoms by Pompey in the 60s (3.165–7). In a formulation that anticipates the more extensive meditation on the conquest of all those years of growth by one day (7.421–8),[32] Lucan presents the dramatic loss, in one moment and one place, of Roman gains over so many years and so many lands. The many years (*multis . . . annis*, 3.156) that had protected and compounded the wealth of the Roman people are here ended by Caesar.

Lucan thus presents the theft as tantamount to the retroactive loss of all of these victories and gains.[33] And the connection between Caesar and Hannibal that Lucan has developed so carefully up to this point leads us to understand the dynamics of the passage better. Like Hannibal, Caesar does not go through with the hellfire attack and sack of Rome that its citizens fear. Nevertheless, Lucan does figure the ransacking Caesar as undoing Rome's victories in the Punic Wars (3.157). If Lucan's Caesar is Hannibal reanimated, then this passage makes clear that this time around Hannibal *succeeds*, taking back from Rome the wealth—the victory—won in the Punic Wars. Significantly, however, Hannibal-as-Caesar gets *more*. The list begins with the Punic Wars, fronted in 3.157 to prioritize that victory: the *Romani populi* of the line's first half now give up the *Punica bella* introduced in the second half. But this plunderous victory in the Roman treasury is not limited to the recuperation of Carthaginian losses. It stretches across Roman space and time: Hannibal-as-Caesar takes it all. In her discussion of Carthage's place in the *Aeneid*, Giusti proposes that Virgil's epic seeks to make "Carthage Roman before Rome even existed" and so to accomplish "Carthage's obliteration from memory."[34] The reanimated Hannibal of the *Pharsalia* achieves the reversal of this trajectory, making Rome belong to Carthage.

While it is not my contention that the Hannibal-as-Caesar whom Lucan constructs in the *Pharsalia* is solely a response to the Hannibal of *Annales* 7–9, the presence of Ennius here in Lucan's Temple of Saturn is hard to miss, as the figuring of accumulated Roman wealth in 3.154–68 appears to engage closely with the master trope of Ennius's epic, the theme of Roman

---

[32] See my discussion in Chapter 3.
[33] Hunink (1992) 97: "He is not merely robbing a temple, but ravaging the history of Rome." Ahl (1976) 107 writes that Caesar, unlike earlier enemies of Rome, "will complete the task his predecessors were never able to accomplish"; but in his treatment of the Caesar-Hannibal union in the poem, Ahl does not consider Caesar's invasion of Italy and Rome. Rather, he speculates (at 109 and 112) that the moment of Hannibalic vengeance in the poem comes in Caesar's victory at Thapsus (near Zama), in planned but unfinished later books.
[34] Giusti (2018) 200.

expansion across time and space, over the years and the seas. The progression of Roman successes in 3.157–67, though not in systematic temporal order, has the arrangement of annalistic narrative, moving from more remote history (3.157–61) to more recent events (3.162–7).[35] The *Annales* had narrated this progress (and indeed many of the specific events included here)—and Lucan's Caesar undoes it all, all those many years (3.156) of consolidation of territory, wealth, and power.

Moreover, as opposed to the collective Roman march narrated in the *Annales*, all the movement in 3.154–68 heads toward one individual, the all-consuming Caesar of the passage's final line. And Lucan emphasizes how the loss is all happening at one time. He brings out this temporal convergence toward one critical event by using *tunc* (3.154), *tum* in contraposition to *multis non tactus ab annis* (3.155–6), and, in the episode's climactic line, *tum primum* (3.168).[36] The *Annales* had charted Rome's year-to-year expansion, a process shared by the individuals committed to the state's advance.[37] The ethos of collective Roman advance over time, so central to that epic, is halted at once in the *Pharsalia* by the takeover of one man. And if we are prepared to read this passage as capturing the abrupt end of Ennian advance, then the series of pointed adverbs *tunc . . . tum . . . tum primum* may double as a marker of Lucan's poetic achievement. While the *Annales* was the first epic to present that story of Roman progress and prosperity, the *Pharsalia* is the first—and only—to narrate its end.

In Chapter 3, I considered how Lucan, like Ennius, aligns Roman temporal and spatial expansion with divine providence, only to narrate the simultaneous collapse of both. So it is not surprising that he places Caesar's act of "ravaging the history of Rome"[38] not just in the Temple of Saturn but in its *aerarium sanctius*, the emergency chamber whose reserve had been "untouched by many years" (3.156). This detail is historically inaccurate: the *aerarium sanctius* was fed by a tax on manumissions, not by wealth from foreign conquests.[39] By inventively stocking this most sacred part of the temple

---

[35] Lebek (1976) 202–5 discusses this structural arrangement and its movement toward Caesar: "Die zeitlich Einengung auf die Gegenwart ist also verbunden mit einer Konzentration auf Caesars Wirkungsbereich" (204).

[36] Lebek (1976) 205 compares the temporal language here to that in the grove violation later in Book 3. Note esp. *numquam uiolatus ab aeuo* at 3.399 and *tum primum* at 3.443 (with my discussion in Chapter 2).

[37] See my discussion in Chapter 3.

[38] Hunink (1992) 97.

[39] See Hunink (1992) 96–7: "Lucan has invented these details, in order to lend pathos to the scene." See too Radicke (2004) 244. On the *aerarium*, see Burton (1996).

with the wealth representing Roman expansion, Lucan maximizes the poignancy of this loss, this reversal of Rome's divinely backed progress over the years.

Lucan follows the episode in the temple with a catalog of Pompey's vast forces from the East (3.169-295). Like the accumulated Roman wealth detailed at 3.155-68, these forces will all go to Caesar: "So that fortunate Caesar could take everything at once, Pharsalia extended the world to him, to be conquered at the same time" (3.296-7). When the Caesarian narrative resumes with the march to Massilia (3.300-74), Lucan keeps the parallels with Hannibal front and center. The people of Massilia meet Caesar (3.303-6), hold out olive branches (3.306), and plead for peace in a long speech (3.307-55). They draw a direct parallel with the people of Saguntum, a town that Hannibal had besieged in 219 on his march toward Italy, when stating: "For the sake of our freedom, the people of this town are not afraid to endure what Saguntum bore when besieged by that Punic god of war (*Poeno . . . Marte*)" (3.349-50). The Massilians view their opposition to Caesar as analogous with Saguntum's opposition to Hannibal. And so yet another perspective in the poem links and equates the two invaders.[40] Moreover, as in the momentous episode at the treasury earlier in the book, a significant reversal takes place. In the opening words of their speech, the Massilians declare to Caesar:

> semper in externis populo communia uestro
> Massiliam bellis testatur fata tulisse
> conprensa est Latiis quaecumque annalibus aetas.

> Every age that has been recounted in Latin *annales* bears witness to the fact that Massilia has always brought common cause to your people in foreign wars. (3.307-9)

The people of Massilia begin their plea for peace by holding up their long and beneficial allegiance to Rome, an allegiance that included support in the Hannibalic War.[41] But their decision to side with Rome now—that is, with the senatorial party—will be disastrous. This time the invading Hannibal-as-Caesar will prevail over Massilia.[42]

---

[40] So Rowland (1969) 206, connecting this passage with Caesar's statement at 1.305.
[41] Livy notes Massilia's allegiance to Rome against Hannibal at, e.g., 21.20.8, 21.25.1, and 22.19.5. See DeWitt (1940) on the alliance, with discussion of Massilia's resistance to Carthage in the Second Punic War at 605 and 613.
[42] See Rowland (1969) on Lucan's Massilia as "paradigmatic" (204) of Rome's fortunes in the poem.

The Massilians' lofty opening words also include a curious citation. They appeal to "every age that has been recounted in Latin *annales* (*Latiis . . . annalibus*)" (3.309), a surprising reference from the Greek-speaking townspeople. The phrase *Latiis annalibus* is conspicuous, marking Lucan's only use of a form of *annalis*. It may refer in a general sense to "history," as some translators have seemingly understood it;[43] or perhaps it is a peculiarly informed reference by the Massilians to the *Annales Maximi* maintained by Rome's pontifex maximus. Virgil also uses a form of *annalis* exactly once, at *Aeneid* 1.373, to characterize Aeneas's recap of his adventures (*annalis nostrorum . . . laborum*) to the disguised Venus. Goldschmidt has described the Virgilian phrase as a "metaliterary nod to Ennius' title" and Giusti has suggested that it points toward the *Aeneid*'s engagement with Ennius's treatment of Carthage in the *Annales*.[44] Is Lucan's gesture in 3.309 similar to Virgil's in *Aeneid* 1? Is he encouraging the reader to recall the first epic telling of Massilian allegiance to Rome and resistance to Hannibal?[45] The reference to *Latiae annales* (or *Latiae Annales*), at a location that was a flashpoint in the contest between Rome and Carthage, surely catches the reader's eye. And if Lucan is evoking Ennius's epic, then the reversal of Massilian/Roman success into Hannibalic/Caesarian success in the action of this passage is accompanied by a suggestion of poetic reversal. Lucan's story of the defeat of Massilia by the forces of Hannibal-as-Caesar emerges as a reversal of Ennius's story of Massilian and Roman victory.

Furthermore, there is again a conspicuous amplification in the Hannibal whom Lucan has reanimated in the person of Caesar. We know of no effort by the historical Hannibal to lay waste to Massilia, despite its exceptional fealty to Rome during his march from Spain through Cisalpine Gaul.[46] The Hannibal-as-Caesar who comes to the city in the *Pharsalia* is not so mild, rejecting the Massilians' olive branches in a speech (3.358–72) crowned by the declaration, "You will pay the penalty for seeking peace" (*dabitis poenas pro pace petita*, 3.370). He then lays siege to the city, and his forces ultimately

---

[43] Duff (1928) 137 translates the line as "every age included in Italian history." Braund (1992) 50 translates *Latiae annales* as "Latian annals" and Fox (2012) 68 as "Latin annals."

[44] Goldschmidt (2013) 167, n. 77; and Giusti (2018) 226.

[45] No surviving fragments of the *Ann.* certainly refer to Massilia or its people. Skutsch (1985) 788 discounts the line attributed to Ennius in the *Explanationes in Donatum* 4.565 (*Massili portabant iuuenes ad litora tanas* = Spuria fr. 6) as spurious, due to its metrical problems and his conclusion that "bottles of Massilian wine . . . can have been of little concern to Ennius" (a matter on which other readers of Ennius might disagree).

[46] Livy (21.20.7–8) notes that the Massilians were the only Gauls who offered support to the Roman envoys urging Gallic councils to resist Hannibal's march.

defeat the Massilians in a decisive sea battle (3.509–762; see later in this chapter). Lucan's reanimated Hannibal once again gets more.

In the aftermath of Caesar's victory at Pharsalia, the poet draws out yet again the Hannibalic threads that I have considered here. Wading amid the corpses on the battlefield, Lucan's raging (*furens*, 7.797) Caesar decides to deny burial to his dead opponents. The poet writes:

> non illum Poenus humator
> consulis et Libyca succensae lampade Cannae   800
> compellunt hominum ritus ut seruet in hoste,
> sed meminit nondum satiata caedibus ira
> ciues esse suos.

The examples of the Punic one, who buried a consul, and of Cannae, lit up by a Libyan torch, do not compel [Caesar] to preserve the rites honored by men in the treatment of enemies. Rather, since his anger is not yet satisfied by slaughter, he keeps at the front of his mind that these are fellow citizens. (7.799–803)

Lucan creates the extraordinary fiction of Caesar recalling the *exemplum* of Hannibal's respect for Aemilius Paullus and the other Roman dead at Cannae[47] but being unmoved by it (*non . . . compellunt*). In Book 2, Lucan had crafted Roman soldiers longing for the days of Cannae (2.46), and earlier in Book 7, the narrator states that Pharsalia has replaced Cannae (and Allia) as the preeminent day of evil on the Roman calendar (7.408–9). The action at 7.799–803 confirms those fears. The enemy of Rome in the *Pharsalia*, this reanimated Hannibal, treats Rome and her citizens much more savagely than Hannibal himself had.

The motivation Lucan attributes to Caesar here deepens his depravity— and may serve to sharpen opposition to Ennius's Hannibal. Caesar actively calls to mind (*meminit*) that the dead are his fellow citizens (*ciues . . . suos*), and this motivates him to leave them unburied, since the act will feed his insatiable anger.[48] In his consideration of the fragments of the *Annales* that may relate to Cannae, Skutsch concludes that "the death of Paullus . . . must

---

[47] See Livy, 22.52.6, Val. Max. 5.1 *ext.* 6, and Sil. 10.547–77, on the burial rites Hannibal grants to the consul Aemilius Paullus.
[48] Lanzarone (2016) 499 writes of the "stravolgimento paradossale" of the thought imputed to Caesar here.

have been told by Ennius."[49] While it is not possible to know how Ennius depicted Hannibal in that scene, the one surviving fragment of the *Annales* containing Hannibal speaking may shed light on his appearance at *Pharsalia* 7.799–803. In a discussion of whether to grant citizenship to allies during war, Cicero quotes the following from an exhortation by Hannibal in the *Annales*: *hostem qui feriet + erit [inquit] mi + Carthaginiensis | quisquis erit, cuiatis siet* (Cic., *Balb.* 51 = *Ann.* 234–5). The text is corrupt at a few points, but commentators agree on a translation such as, "whoever strikes the enemy will be a Carthaginian to me—whoever he is, and wherever he is from." Ennius's Hannibal, then, offered Cicero a model of the merits of opening up citizenship.[50] In *Pharsalia* 7, Lucan follows an explicit contrast between Hannibal and Caesar (7.799–801) with a focus on the latter's irreverence for the concept of citizenship (7.802–3)—which itself stands in stark opposition to the credo Ennius attributes to Hannibal.[51] While the historical Caesar had famously expanded citizenship, Lucan imagines just the opposite. He makes Caesar a destroyer of citizens, one who watches them rot—and all in pointed contrast with what Hannibal had done at Cannae. The upshot of this moment is that it adds to the sense of total victory by the avenging, now degenerated, winner-take-all Hannibal-as-Caesar of the *Pharsalia*. While the *Annales* had initiated and codified the story of Rome's defeat of Hannibal, Lucan's epic swiftly and stunningly undoes that story, reanimating and granting Ennius's great villain complete and merciless victory over Rome.

The final reference to Hannibal in the poem comes when Pompey, desperate after the defeat at Pharsalia, raises the possibility of seeking aid from the Numidian king Juba (8.283–8). He quickly dismisses the idea, stating that this distant relative of the Carthaginian general "is a threat to Hesperia, and there is a lot of Hannibal in that empty heart" (*inminet Hesperiae, multusque in pectore uano est | Hannibal*, 8.285–6). Pompey may be right that Juba, though he had helped Varus defeat Curio's Caesarian forces (4.666–787), is not a trustworthy ally. But the choice of words Lucan gives to him shows just how out of touch Pompey is, just how much he has missed over the prior seven books. The characterization he uses of Juba—that "he is a threat to Hesperia, and there is a lot of Hannibal in that empty heart"—in fact perfectly describes the character of Caesar whom Lucan has depicted over the

---

[49] Skutsch (1985) 449–50.
[50] Elliott (2013) 166.
[51] Roche (2019) 144 compares Caesar's twisting of the concept of citizenship at 7.319 (*ciuis qui fugerit esto*) with *Ann.* 234–5.

preceding books. It is Caesar who not only threatens but makes good on his threats of conquering Hesperia; it is Caesar whose empty heart has been occupied by the spirit of Hannibal. It is Lucan's story of Caesar that revives and reverses the old Ennian story of the defeat of Hannibal.

4.2. "Well-known spots" revisited and reversed

A concurrent and equally cataclysmic arc of Roman reversal runs through Books 4 and 9, where Lucan crafts the failures of Curio and Cato in Africa into stories of the undoing of Roman maritime reach and prowess. As Italy and Rome on one side of the Mediterranean are lost to Hannibal in the person of Caesar, earlier Roman successes in expeditions to Africa are dashed and undone in Curio's and Cato's ventures there.

Let us recall that Naevius's *Bellum Punicum* and Ennius's *Annales* both narrated Rome's launch across the Mediterranean. From surviving fragments we can determine that each poem zeroed in on primal moments of launch, contact, and conflict. The *Bellum Punicum*, covering the first conflict with Carthage and the corresponding debut of Rome's fleet, naturally had an authoritative claim to the narration of this "first-ness."[52] Though Cicero (*Brut.* 76) tells us that the *Annales* did not treat the First Punic War with narrative fullness,[53] Ennius does seem to give close attention to the war's beginnings (*Ann.* 216–19) and in particular the emerging Roman navy's exercises (*Ann.* 218–19). In a fragment that editors have placed in Book 9 at the time of Rome's successful direction of the Hannibalic War across the sea, Ennius writes artfully of the Straits of Gibraltar: *Europam Libyamque rapax ubi diuidit unda* ("where the rapacious sea divides Europe and Libya," *Ann.* 302 = Cic., *Tusc.* 1.45 and *Nat. D.* 3.24).[54] The *Annales* charted this uncertain and perilous crossing into the land described elsewhere as "Africa, rough land, trembling with terrible tumult" (*Africa terribili tremit horrida terra tumultu, Ann.* 309 = Cic., *De or.* 3.167). Integral to Ennius's narrative was, to be sure, the figure of Scipio Africanus, who crossed over the sea and defeated

---

[52] It is significant that at the outset of the poem (and the war) Rome must employ an army for its mission to Sicily: *Manius Valerius | consul partem exerciti in expeditionem | ducit* (fr. 3 Blänsdorf = fr. 1 Mariotti), a fragment that may stand at the beginning of a progression of Roman naval development across the poem. See further Biggs (2017) 360.

[53] See *Ann.* 206–7, with Skutsch (1985) 366–71 and Elliott (2013) 60–1.

[54] Giusti (2018) 62: "Ennius' Libya apparently usurps the role of Europe's antagonist which we would more normally expect to be played by Asia."

160 THUNDER AND LAMENT

Hannibal at Zama. Though no surviving fragments of the *Annales* make specific mention of him, Cicero speaks in the *Pro Archia* (22) of the personal closeness between the general and the poet and of the belief that a marble image of Ennius was included on the Tomb of the Scipios.[55] Moreover, the surviving fragments of Ennius's *Scipio* (fr. 29–34 Courtney) make clear the work's laudatory quality.[56] Scipio the sea-crosser and conqueror of Africa was surely a central figure in the *Annales*.

The Roman launches overseas in the *Bellum Punicum* and *Annales*, though bold and uncertain enterprises, are ultimately successful: the Rome of Naevius's and Ennius's poems wins, *Africa horrida terra* is defeated. When Caesar's ally Curio and, later, Cato retrace these expeditions to Africa in the *Pharsalia*, the outcome is just the opposite. And these episodes of reversal include cues toward landings on African terrain in earlier Latin epic. The passages have the quality of palimpsests, with the narratives of successful Roman arrivals made to lie beneath—be replaced by—Lucan's tales of faltering and failed landings. The fundamental precariousness and fragility, indeed erasability, of those earlier maritime and poetic ventures are realized in the *Pharsalia*'s disastrous reversals in these palimpsestic geographical and textual spots.

The first of these comes at the outset of Lucan's African narrative in Book 4. Curio's arrival marks the poem's arrival in Africa as a plane of action, and here Lucan introduces much of the thematic and textual ground that he will explore in the *Pharsalia*'s African passages:

... rates audax Lilybaeo litore soluit
Curio, nec forti uelis Aquilone recepto
inter semirutas magnae Carthaginis arces   585
et Clipeam tenuit stationis litora notae,
primaque castra locat cano procul aequore, qua se
Bagrada lentus agit siccae sulcator harenae.

Bold Curio released his ships from the shore of Lilybaeum and, after taking a gentle gust of the North Wind in his sails, took the shores of a well-known spot between the half-destroyed towers of great Carthage and Clipea. And he placed his first camp far from the

---

[55] See the caution of Goldberg (1995) 16–18 on this story and its significance.
[56] And see Claudian's picture of Scipio and Enn. walking side by side in *Cons. Stil.* III.

hoary sea, where the slow Bagrada carries itself and furrows the dry sand. (4.583–8)

Lucan flags the location of Curio's landing on the shore as a "well-known spot" (*stationis . . . notae*), and the details in the surrounding lines point to the famous Roman landing here by Scipio Africanus in 204 BCE, en route to his victory that ended the Second Punic War. Unlike in other accounts of this campaign, Lucan specifies that Curio had set out from Lilybaeum (4.583), the port from which Scipio had sailed in Livy's account (29.24).[57] He then sets up camp along the Bagrada River, where Scipio had encamped in advance of his victory at Zama. The assortment of details Lucan chooses to include—or invent—make it unmissable that Curio, bold (*audax*, 4.583) just like Scipio before him, has arrived at the entry point and foothold for that most renowned of Roman adventurers to Africa.

At this moment of narrative touchdown in Africa, the description of this location as "the shores of a well-known spot" (*stationis litora notae*) also cues the reader to recall the noted (*notae*) literary texture of this entry point.[58] Scholars have concentrated on possible engagement with the *Aeneid* in the ensuing narrative, with the argument that "Curio's arrival in Africa [is] intended in part as a deflation of Aeneas's arrival on the same shores."[59] But in light of the explicit evocations of Scipio's landing, we must also consider that Lucan is directing us to the epic that first told not just Aeneas's but also Scipio's African story.[60] Further reminiscences of Scipio come soon afterward, when a local inhabitant, identified only as a *rudis incola* (4.592), responds to Curio's questions about the area. He is presented as "teaching things learned over many generations" (*cognita per multos docuit . . . patres*, 4.592), and most of his speech is an artful, allusive account of Hercules's

---

[57] So Asso (2010) 216–17, concluding: "Whether or not Curio actually sailed from Lilybaeum, L. may have chosen to name Lilybaeum because it evokes all these campaigns" (217). See also Radicke (2004) 300–3 on Lucan's creativity with historical material here.

[58] See Harrison (2017) 241 (on Hor., *C.* 2.20.13) on how *notus* "can refer to fame in poetry."

[59] Sklenář (2003) 41. See also see Thompson and Bruère (1970); Ahl (1976) 94 ("Curio as a *reductio ad absurdum* of Aeneas") and Hardie (2012) 192; as well as Asso (2010) 281–2 and Fratantuono (2012) 171 on Curio's loss as appeasement to Virgil's Dido.

[60] And there is the possibility that reference to the Bagrada here evokes still another textual layer in this spot: Naevius's account of Regulus's mission to Africa during the First Punic War, which included his defeat of an enormous snake along the Bagrada. On the episode see (with Asso [2011] 218) Tubero fr. 8 (Peter) = Gell. 7.3; Livy, *Epit.* 18; Val. Max. 1.8 ext. 19; Plin. *NH* 8.37; and Sil. 6.140–205. For speculation on Naevius's treatment of Regulus, see Bleckmann (1998). Like Curio and Cato (who has a Regulan contest with snakes; see Ahl [1976] 271), Regulus does not make it back from Africa, but his mission ultimately serves Rome and her victory in the war.

162 THUNDER AND LAMENT

defeat there of the Earth-born beast Antaeus (4.593–655)—revealing that this "crude local" is quite the learned storyteller and, like the old man of Book 2, something of an embedded doublet for Lucan himself.[61] After relaying what "the guardian of the old past, age that is full of fame" (*aeui ueteris custos, famosa uetustas*, 4.654) has handed down about Antaeus and Hercules, he concludes his response to Curio by highlighting what he believes to be the even greater achievement—and greater name—of Scipio:

>   sed maiora dedit cognomina collibus istis
>   Poenum qui Latiis reuocauit ab arcibus hostem,
>   Scipio; nam sedes Libyca tellure potito
>   haec fuit. en, ueteris cernis uestigia ualli.
>   Romana hos primum tenuit uictoria campos
>
>   But the one who called back his Punic enemy from the citadels of Latium, Scipio, gave a greater name to these hills. For this was his home settlement when he took possession of Libyan land. Look, you can see the traces of the old fort. These are the fields that Roman victory first held. (4.656–60)

The "greater name" to which the local refers is the *Castra Cornelia* that Scipio set up here,[62] a name that replaced the designation "the realm of Antaeus" (*Antaei regna*, 4.590) and at the same time marked Scipio's feat here as greater than Hercules's. In this turn from the story of Hercules and Antaeus to Scipio, R. Sklenář sees an instance of *aemulatio* with Virgil, as "Lucan's historical subject matter wins out over Vergil's mythic themes."[63] But the abrupt turn to Scipio in the learned local's report of *fama* from the past (recall 4.654) surely must direct the reader to another conveyor of *fama*. With the command, "Look, you can see the traces of the old fortification" (*en, ueteris cernis uestigia ualli*), he points to the physical traces of Scipio's old camp but also nudges the reader to look closely (*en . . . cernis*) for traces of the old, foundational story of Scipio's ventures there. The word *uestigia*, evoking the image of footprints

---

[61] Sklenář (2003) 39: "This *rudis incola* is a *doctus poeta*, with all the requisite Alexandrian credentials; the ending of his story must therefore be regarded as something carefully contrived." See too Keith (2000) 55 on this "internal narrator." On the speech's allusive engagement with the Hercules tale at *Aen.* 8.184–275, see Thompson and Bruère (1970) and Ahl (1976) 91–9.
[62] On the echo of Scipio's second cognomen *Maior* in *maiora*, see Keith (2000) 55 and Asso (2010) 246.
[63] Sklenář (2003) 39.

left behind, can serve as a marker of poetic memory,[64] and a metapoetic use here would be in keeping with the erudite and "carefully contrived"[65] character of the local's speech. The traces of Scipio's old African story would of course be found in the *Annales*, and in the next line, the last of the speech, the *incola* underlines what he wants the reader to see in those *uestigia*: "these are the fields that Roman victory first held" (4.660: *Romana hos primum tenuit uictoria campos*). Looking through this textual ground will uncover traces of Roman "first-ness," of the beginnings of prosperous Roman ventures.

This passage on Scipio's famed African first leads us to think back and interrogate the "first camp" (*primaque castra*, 4.587) that Curio set up upon arrival. What kind of Roman first will this be for Curio and other Romans landing here in Africa, and how will their firsts stack up against Scipio's? Further: how will Lucan's telling of Roman landings in Africa interact with the first epic landings here? By leading the reader to this "famed spot" (*stationis . . . notae*) in Latin epic and to the old traces (*uestigia*) here, Lucan raises the stakes for what is to come on this fraught textual ground.

Mention of Scipio's past successes leads Curio to be "overjoyed, as though the good fortune of the place (*fortuna locorum*) would wage the wars for him and keep for him the fates of leaders of old (*ducum . . . fata priorum*)" (4.661–2). He believes that this territory (*loci*) will treat him as it had Scipio, and on a metapoetic level he seems to flag that the passages (*loci*) in Lucan's African narrative will play out just as past epic did for Scipio (note the near gloss of the genre in the phrase *ducum . . . fata priorum*).[66] But there have already been omens of a far different outcome for Curio. For one, the benefits to Curio of a "Roman victory," like the one remembered at 4.660, are not at all clear in this civil war.[67] Moreover, the very inclusion of the toponym *Antaei regna* (4.590) leaves open the possibility of a return to perilous pre-Cornelian times,[68] when "colonizers of the Libyan fields died; those driven there by the sea died" (4.605–6: *periere coloni | aruorum Libyae, pereunt quos appulit aequor*). Indeed this outcome—far from the *ducum fata priorum*—is the one that befalls Curio and the Romans who crossed the sea with him from

---

[64] See the similar use of *uestigia* at 9.965, in the manifestly metapoetic context of Caesar's visit to Troy at 9.961–99 (with my discussion in Chapter 1). See too Fitzgerald (2016) 6 on *uestigia* at Virg., *Ecl.* 2.12.

[65] Sklenář (2003) 39.

[66] For *locus* as a metapoetic term, see Hinds (1998) 5–6 on Ov., *Met.* 3.499–501; and Westerhold (2013) on Ov., *Am.* 3.1.1–6.

[67] Asso (2010) 247: "This closing remark deceives Curio into believing that *Romana uictoria* is a good omen for himself." See too Narducci (2002) 170–1 and Hardie (2012) 194–5.

[68] See Asso (2002).

Lilybaeum. In the battle narrative of 4.666–787, Juba's cavalry ultimately outmaneuvers, encircles, and crushes Curio's army. At the moment of defeat, "an army of such great size is packed into a small circle" (4.777: *acies tantae paruum spissantur in orbem*). The phrase *paruum . . . in orbem* compels us to think of the condensing of worldwide Roman might, now shrunken[69] and scaled down into a "little world." The moment mirrors the wholesale loss of global might to Caesar's reanimated Hannibal at the treasury (3.154–68), but now that loss is happening on African ground.

In the ensuing lines, Lucan makes this dynamic of the contraction of Roman might on African soil explicit, when connecting Curio's defeat with the broader theme of Punic vengeance:

excitet inuisas dirae Carthaginis umbras
inferiis Fortuna nouis, ferat ista cruentus
Hannibal et Poeni tam dira piacula manes.   790
Romanam, superi, Libyca tellure ruinam
Pompeio prodesse nefas uotisque senatus.
Africa nos potius uincat sibi.

Let Fortune stir up the hated shades of dread Carthage for these new offerings. Let bloodied Hannibal and the Punic ghosts take in these dread expiations. Gods, it was unspeakable that Roman destruction on Libyan land benefited Pompey and the prayers of the senate. It would have been better for Africa to defeat us for herself. (4.788–93)

The Caesarian Curio's loss in Africa to the allied forces of Pompey and Juba marks another victory over Rome for Hannibal, to go with the conquest of Rome that Caesar wins for him. Scholars have (again) focused on this passage's ties with Virgil's epic, viewing Curio's defeat as the long-awaited fulfillment of Dido's curse in *Aeneid* 4.[70] But we have seen that the reversal that Lucan charts here is specifically of Scipio's victory. Earlier the *incola* described the location of Curio's arrival as Scipio's "home settlement when he took possession of Libyan land" (4.658–9: *nam sedes Libyca tellure potito* | *haec fuit*). At the episode's conclusion, Lucan marks the Roman loss that occurred in Libya with the same phrase, in the same metrical

---

[69] See Rimell (2015) 240–52 on images of confinement and shrinkage in the *Ph*.
[70] See n. 59 in this chapter.

position: *Romanam, superi, <u>Libyca tellure ruinam</u>* (4.791).[71] Scipio's landing and subsequent gains (*potito*) in Libya—and the "half-ruin" (recall *semirutas* at 4.585) of the Carthaginian citadel—are replaced by Curio's landing and the subsequent Roman destruction (*ruinam*) in the same spot. And again, a statement about poetics operates in conjunction with the statement about Roman loss and destruction. The marker of this story as *nefas* (4.792)—one that the poet should not tell but does—compels us to think about Lucan's choices as a storyteller. He has chosen to emphasize Roman loss on the spot of Scipio's landing, a site well known both in history and in Latin epic. Scipio's—and the genre's—arrival in the *Annales* caused Africa to tremble (*Ann.* 309) and be defeated by Rome. Here now in the *Pharsalia* it is Rome that is ruined (*Romanam . . . ruinam*, 4.791) in that spot; here now Africa—working again through Rome's own self-destructive forces—does not cower but conquers (*Africa nos . . . uincat*, 4.793) Rome and her story.

To return to the dynamic of primacy in Africa, Curio's establishment of a first camp (*primaque castra*, 4.587) and then the self-destructive defeat his army suffers undo the primal Roman victory by Scipio that the *incola* had held up so prominently (4.660: *Romana hos primum tenuit uictoria campos*). At the same time, that well-known literary locale, rich with traces of old epic tales, has a new poetic fortification on it. This landing place for what was surely a central episode of foundational Roman victory in Ennius's epic is transformed by Lucan—now for the first time—into a place of Roman shrinkage and loss. If, as Feeney has put it, "Latin epic . . . was centrally concerned with Carthage,"[72] here now the genre heads to a fitting place to die. In the closing passage of Book 4, the narrator concisely captures the metapoetics of the *Pharsalia* when saying to the fallen Curio, "You lie dead before dreadful Pharsalia brings the leaders together" (*ante iaces quam dira duces Pharsalia confert*, 4.803). While Curio does not make it to the destructive time and place (or the central poetic panel) of *dira Pharsalia*, the African narrative of Book 4 tells much the same story. It is fitting that just previously, when hailing Carthage's vengeance in Curio's defeat, Lucan had given the same epithet to Carthage: *dirae Carthaginis* (4.788). Within and in conjunction with his *dira Pharsalia*, Lucan's story of *dira Carthago* renders an end to Roman victory and the poetic medium that accompanied it.

---

[71] These are the only two passages where Lucan modifies *tellus* with *Libycus*. Silius Italicus is the one other author to do so (3.40 and 10.124).
[72] Feeney (2017) 308.

4.3. Lamenting the loss in Libya

The narrator's exploration of the significance of Curio's life and death in Book 4's final lines is a freewheeling passage with apostrophes to Curio himself (4.799–804 and 809–13) and the parties' leaders (4.805–6; see Chapter 3), as well as a biting epigram for the fallen Roman at the book's close (4.814–24). The pair of apostrophes to Curio contain many of the hallmarks of lament, and, when looked at together, read as a *goos* of sorts for the dead youth. Like mourners in conventional *gooi*, the narrator reproaches Curio in a series of rhetorical questions (4.799–802), but also praises his laudable deeds (4.811–13: *at tibi nos . . . | digna damus, iuuenis, meritae praeconia uitae*, "But to you we grant, young man, due praise for the commendable part of your life") and so consciously perpetuates his *fama* (4.812).[73] The juxtaposition of first- and second-person deictics (*tibi nos*) that is characteristic of *gooi* heightens the emotional register, as does the direct address to Curio's "noble corpse" (*nobile corpus*, 7.809) as Libyan birds feed on it. Ritual lament was delivered over the corpse of the dead, and if the *Pharsalia* as a whole functions as a lament over Rome's once great but now self-destroyed corpse—an argument I will develop in Chapter 6—the narrator's lament over the corpse of Curio, the once admirable but corrupted and now self-destructive Roman nobleman, stands as a fitting representation in miniature of the poem itself.

Perhaps the most powerful expression of lament for the Roman reversal and ruin in Libya comes in Book 6, by two characters from Rome's—and Roman epic's—glorious past. Recounting for Sextus Pompey the "mournful look on the blessed shades" (*tristis felicibus umbris | uultus*, 6.784–5) in the Underworld, the corpse evoked by Erictho recalls: "Scipio laments that his unlucky offspring will die on Libyan land; a greater enemy of Carthage, Cato weeps for the fate of his progeny who refuses to be a slave" (6.788–90: *deplorat Libycis perituram Scipio terris | infaustam subolem; maior Carthaginis hostis | non seruituri maeret Cato fata nepotis*). While pointing to the eventual deaths of their descendants Scipio Metellus and Cato in Africa in 46 BCE, the image also stunningly inserts the original conqueror of Africa himself and the paradigmatic enemy of Carthage himself into the poem's antiphony of lamenting voices. Whereas the arc of African victory over Rome running through the poem showcases violent ends in both narrative content and epic

---

[73] See Hardie (2012) 196. See the Introduction and Chapter 6 on conventions of the *goos*.

poetics, this detail of Scipio Africanus and the elder Cato—heroes of Ennius's epic[74]—now weeping in despair lends a complementary voice of lament for those ends. Put another way, the scope and scale of the reversal of the Roman story in Africa can only be fully and rightly captured if met by lamenting voices: the narrator's own in the climactic conclusion to Book 4, and two books later, keeping the arc of Libyan loss on the reader's mind, the wailing voices of the most storied enemies of Carthage.

4.4. Epic's crash landing in Libya

As crushing and complete as Carthage's victories are in the series of passages we have considered, there is still more to Lucan's story of Roman loss in Libya. The greater part of Book 9 focuses on the naval journey of Cato's Republican forces from Greece to Libya, and then their torturous march across the African sands. Here I will focus on Lucan's presentation in the first part of the book of the dissolution and eventual crash landing of the Roman fleet in the African Syrtes, an episode that complements and reinforces his narrative of the undoing of Roman sway on the sea, the undoing of the maritime moment. The poetic choices in this episode also speak to the crash of the genre that launched on the seas, and may point back to a moment of perilous but foundational struggle on the seas in Naevius's *Bellum Punicum*.

Leading up to the crash of Cato's fleet at 9.319–47, Lucan draws repeated attention to its disintegration in the aftermath of Pharsalia. This fleet, which Lucan had built up in the grandiose catalog at 3.169–295 as surpassing the fleets of Cyrus and Agamemnon (3.287), is now "scattered across the sea" (9.16) and in a fragmentary state as Cato takes control:

Corcyrae secreta petit ac mille carinis
abstulit Emathiae secum fragmenta ruinae.
quis ratibus tantis fugientia crederet ire
agmina? quis pelagus uictas artasse carinas?   35

[Cato] sought the seclusion of Corcyra and took away with him, in a thousand ships, the fragments of Emathia's destruction. Who would believe

---

[74] See Skutsch (1985) 642–3, building off Cic. *Arch.* 22, on books where Cato may have been prominently featured.

that an army in flight was traveling in so many ships? Who would believe that a conquered fleet could have closed off the sea? (9.32–5)

The Roman fleet remains vast (*mille carinis*), but after Pharsalia it contains just *fragmenta*, and its size now serves only to compress, choke, or close off (*artasse*) the sea—two images that bring with them complementary metapoetic resonances. Andrew Zissos has argued that Lucan's contemporary Martial uses the word *fragmentum* in *Epigram* 7.19 as "something on the order of a literary-critical term" to characterize the small-scale genre of epigram as "emerg[ing] from the wreckage of epic."[75] I want to propose that *fragmenta* operates similarly in 9.33, marking the first stage of the process that Zissos explores, the wreckage of epic.[76] Launched on the sea and grown into a sprawling enterprise, Latin epic is, like the fleet here in *Pharsalia* 9, now being broken into pieces. Emathia's/the *Pharsalia*'s destruction (9.33) lays waste to the fleet and to the genre that told its story. And when we consider that *arto* can mean "cut down" (*OLD* 7a) or "cut short" (*OLD* 7b), the language in 9.34–5 seems to continue the thought expressed in 9.33. Just as the defeated and broken fleet has closed off (*artasse*) the sea, so the broken pieces of epic now close off any further passage.

As the fleet moves around the eastern Mediterranean (9.36–50), it is slowed by its size but also something much weightier: "those ships were carrying lamentation and the beating of breasts and ills that provoked tears even from stern Cato" (9.49–50: *illae puppes luctus planctusque ferebant | et mala uel duri lacrimas motura Catonis*). Lucan makes the fleet quite literally a vehicle of lament. As in so many of the poem's scenes—beginning with the appearance of Roma herself at the Rubicon—this representation of Roman greatness is under attack while simultaneously lamenting that attack, functioning as both victim and mourner. Soon after this fraught image, Cornelia delivers a long speech of lament (9.55–108; see further in Chapter 6) in which she recalls Pompey's misplaced confidence that "any Pompey who takes to the waves will find fleets for him" (9.93–4).[77] She sees the situation more clearly, and after her speech she retreats into a ship where

---

[75] Zissos (2004) 418 and 419, arguing that Mart. takes particular aim at Val. Flac., *Argon.* (represented as a *ratis*).

[76] It may be significant that, after Plin. *NH* (14 times) and Celsus, *Med.* (12), each in scientific contexts, no author uses *fragmentum* more times than Lucan, the poet of demolition and ending. See also 3.686 (again of shattered ships), 6.193 (of the shattered pieces of Scaeva's helmet; see Chapter 2), 6.536 (of the pieces going into Erictho's unholy pyre), and 8.755 (see later discussion in this chapter).

[77] A vain hope echoed by the younger Magnus at 9.148–94.

>   caput ferali obduxit amictu
> decreuitque pati tenebras puppisque cauernis
> delituit, saeuumque arte conplexa dolorem
> perfruitur lacrimis et amat pro coniuge luctum.

She covered her head in a funereal veil and decided to endure the darkness
and hid in the hollows of the ship. And, tightly embracing her savage
grief, she thoroughly enjoys her tears and loves lament for her husband.
(9.109–12)

The image of Cornelia choosing the "hollows of the ship" for her act of lamentation reinforces those at 9.32–5 and then 9.49–50: this fleet is a carrier of things that mark *ends*, both the broken pieces of ruin and the tears and lament that accompany that ruin. The adverb *arte*, like the related form *artasse* at 9.35, underscores the tightening and thus closing inherent in this act of lamentation.

The fleet nevertheless sails on—but not for long. Kept from Cyrene, Cato resolves to head toward Juba's kingdom in western Africa (9.300–1)—but the journey is promptly cut short by the Syrtes, the gulfs along the northern coast of Africa containing a series of treacherous sandbanks.[78] A number of authors (Strabo, 17.3.20; Mela, 1.7; Plutarch, *Cato Minor* 56) mention the incident on the Syrtes and Cato's subsequent march in Africa, with varying degrees of sensationalism. Lucan crafts the episode with unrivaled fullness. A digression on the formation of the Syrtes (9.303–18) sets the stage for the storm that halts the fleet there (9.319–47). The greater part of the fleet survives and makes it to Lake Tritonis (9.345–7), but no further: "And so, driven from this area and cast out by the Syrtes, the fleet did not touch the Garamantian [= Libyan] waves again" (9.368–9: *his igitur depulsa locis eiectaque classis | Syrtibus haud ultra Garamantidas attigit undas*).[79] From this point onward, Cato is a "wanderer of the sands" (*hareniuagum*, 9.941), as the army proceeds only on foot.[80] This episode thus marks the last action of the fleet in the poem, and here again we may see metapoetic connotations. Earlier I argued that *loci* at 4.661 points to Curio's arrival on both physical

---

[78] See Quinn (2011) on the Syrtes in ancient thought; and Taylor (2020) on Lucan's explanations of the Syrtes at 9.303–18.
[79] I follow the manuscript tradition in printing *his . . . locis* instead of *hos . . . locos*, proposed by Housman (1926) and accepted by Shackleton Bailey (1988).
[80] See further on Cato's journey in Chapter 5.

and literary ground. When Lucan describes Cato's fleet as *his . . . depulsa locis* ("driven out from this area"), he may also be marking the expulsion of the Roman fleet from the long familiar pages of Latin epic.

During the storm Lucan details what happened to the ships that had removed their masts (9.331), in a striking image representative of the stopping of the fleet as a whole:

> has uada destituunt, atque interrupta profundo 335
> terra ferit puppes, dubioque obnoxia fato
> pars sedet una ratis, pars altera pendet in undis.
> tum magis inpactis breuius mare terraque saepe
> obuia consurgens: quamuis elisus ab Austro,
> saepe tamen cumulos fluctus non uincit harenae. 340
> eminet in tergo pelagi procul omnibus aruis
> inuiolatus aqua sicci iam pulueris agger.

The shallows strand these ships, and the land, interrupted by the deep sea, strikes them; relying on uncertain fate, one part of a ship sits on ground, while the other part hangs in the waves. Then, as the ships are struck more, the sea becomes smaller and the land rises up and frequently meets them. Though pushed by the South Wind, waves nevertheless do not conquer the banks of sand. Rising up on the surface of the sea, far from all land, is a mass of already dry dust, untainted by water. (9.335–42)

In a slow-motion sequence, the ships are struck by the land (9.335–6), then occupy both land and sea simultaneously (9.337), and finally are met by the surging land (9.338–9), which, by the end of the passage, has risen up free of water (9.342).[81] The ships are halted, with nowhere to go. Even in the middle of the sea, far from any land (9.341), there is no more sea for them to sail.

The historical event of Cato's landing in Africa along the Syrtes, we see, provided a perfect opportunity for Lucan to picture the halting of Roman naval sway. Leigh has described this episode on the Syrtes as "a characteristically epic accretion" and compares the experience of the Argonauts in Book 4 of Apollonius of Rhodes's *Argonautica*.[82] We might also think of the storm in *Aeneid* 1, when "the East wind drives three ships from the deep into the

---

[81] Seewald (2008) 199–200 discusses the artistry of the topothesia in 9.341–2.
[82] Leigh (2000) 97. See too Seo (2011) 88–9.

shallows and the Syrtes" (*Aen.* 1.110–11), with Aeneas's fleet ending up on the African coast.[83]

It is also reasonable to surmise that the Syrtes played a pivotal part in the story of Roman conquest of Africa and the seas in the earliest Latin epic about Roman affairs. The scant surviving fragments of the *Bellum Punicum* contain no reference to the Syrtes, but we can gather a sense of their outsized importance in the First Punic War from Polybius. In his account of the year 253, eleven years into the conflict, he describes the launch of the entire fleet (1.39.1) on a mission to Libya. Upon arriving in the region of the Syrtes (1.39.2), the fleet, unfamiliar with the area, hits sandbanks and gets stuck as the tide moves out (1.39.3)—ending up in a nearly impossible impasse (εἰς πᾶσαν ἦλθον ἀπορίαν, 1.39.4). The fleet does escape, but in a hasty manner, as in flight (1.39.5), and on their incautious return to Italy a storm destroys 150 ships.[84] The result of this fiasco is that Rome decides to abandon its fleet altogether (1.39.7). The failed expedition to the coast of Libya resulted in nothing less than Rome giving up on the sea!

However, after two years Rome decides to rebuild a fleet and enroll sailors to man it (1.39.14–15). The rebuilt fleet will of course be critical to her ultimate victory in the First Punic War. And so the story of the grounding on the Syrtes and subsequent grounding of the fleet as a whole is one of Roman error and struggle—but a struggle that is part of a larger story of ultimate success on the seas. To return to Naevius: we know from fragments of the *Bellum Punicum* that the poem portrayed moments of prosperity and plunder (see fr. 37) but also of peril and precariousness on the seas. There is the image of "weighed down freight-ships standing still in the calm" (*onerariae onustae stabant in flustris,* fr. 48 Blänsdorf) that scholars have proposed describes a moment of calm before a storm,[85] along with the description of sailors sweating as they steer toward a collision with the enemy: "That they may be able to clash their bronze ship [against the foe], they who cross the clear sea, sweating as they sit" (<*ut*> *conferre queant ratem aeratam* | *qui per liquidum mare sudantes* | *eunt atque sedentes,* fr. 64 Blänsdorf = Varro, *ling. Lat.* 7.23).[86] Though this fragment cannot be placed in the *Bellum Punicum* with certainty,

---

[83] Note that Mynors (1969) 106 prints *syrtis* (for the common noun "sandbanks"), while Geymonat (2008) 179 prints the place name *Syrtis*. Virgil unambiguously mentions the "unwelcoming Syrtis" (*inhospita Syrtis*) at *Aen.* 4.41.
[84] Walbank (1957) 100 accepts the number 150 and estimates that this disaster reduced the fleet to a total of c. 70 ships.
[85] See earlier discussion in this chapter.
[86] See Kent (1936) 76 on the difficulties in this fragment.

it surely reflects Naevius's portrayal of the anxious maritime experience. The episode at the Syrtes in 253 and its aftermath were in a sense emblematic of Rome's story on the seas: it is a devastating setback and a major challenge to Rome's naval growth, but one that does not ultimately halt her advance. Given the paucity of surviving fragments from the *Bellum Punicum*, caution is necessary. But it is hard to imagine that Naevius did not make the crash on the Syrtes, the catastrophic flight back to Italy and decision to ground the fleet, and, to be sure, Rome's ultimate recovery from that setback a centerpiece to his epic about the First Punic War.

The crash in *Pharsalia* 9 has no recovery; the Roman fleet that smashes into the Syrtes does not, in the poem as we have it, return to Rome. Later in the book the narrator apotheosizes Cato (9.593–604) and figures his march through the Syrtes and the Libyan desert as a triumph (*per Syrtes Libyaeque extrema triumphum*, 9.598)—but this is of course a *moral* triumph.[87] Cato will not return from Africa. The Roman fleet—as he knew it, as Rome knew it—will not come back. And that *story* will not be told again.[88] As we recall from the fraught phrase *his . . . depulsa locis* (9.368), not only is the fleet pushed out from the physical location of the sea, but its story is pushed out from the *loci* of epic narrative. With the halting of the fleet, the genre that narrated its launch also hits its end.

4.5. "Rostra roaring at rostra" in Lucan's epic naval battle

Earlier in this chapter I considered how Lucan presents Caesar's decision to go to war with Massilia as a meaningful departure from Hannibal's policy of avoidance of that Gallic city. The contest that Lucan goes on to narrate begins with the Massilians fending off the Caesarians' siege (3.453–508) but then centers on an extended naval battle off the Massilian coast (3.509–762). In his own account of these events, Caesar writes of two naval contests outside Massilia (*BC* 1.36 and 56–58; 2.3–7), but Lucan conflates these for a sprawling scene of clash and slaughter on the seas. Significantly, there are no models in surviving epic for Lucan's naval battle.[89] The closest parallel may

---

[87] See Ahl (1976) 278 and D'Alessandro Behr (2007) 128–31 on Cato's moral victory in the poem.

[88] See too Taylor (2020) on the "arresting of narrative progress" (93) on the Syrtes in Lucan's telling, but also for the suggestion that the explanations for the Syrtes in 9.303–18 point toward narrative openness.

[89] See Opelt (1957); Hunink (1992) 200–1 (citing Naevius and Ennius as possible models for Lucan); and Fratantuono (2012) 117 (marking a contrast with the *Aen.* in particular). Lost epics such as Cornelius Severus's *Bellum Siculum* and Rabirius's *Bellum Actiacum* most certainly included naval

be the depiction of the Battle of Actium on Aeneas's shield at *Aeneid* 8.671–713, a passage that is much shorter and less concerned with naval action per se. Given the subject matter of the *Bellum Punicum* and *Annales*, we can be confident that Naevius and Ennius included extended treatment of grand naval battles. By including a scene of this sort in his epic—and stretching it out over 250 lines—Lucan may be evoking what had been a set piece in the earliest epics about Roman affairs.

The absence of more fragments or testimonia about Naevius's depiction of naval activity in the First Punic War makes it difficult to draw further conclusions about Lucan's engagement with him at Massilia, but connections with—and inversions of—Ennius in this passage are clear. Early in the episode we encounter what appears to be an anchoring allusion to the *Annales*, in the initial approaches of the Massilian and Caesarian ships:

> ut tantum medii fuerat maris, utraque classis
> quod semel excussis posset transcurrere tonsis,
> innumerae uasto miscentur in aethere uoces, 540
> remorumque sonus premitur clamore, nec ullae
> audiri potuere tubae. tum caerula uerrunt
> atque in transtra cadunt et remis pectora pulsant.
> ut primum rostris crepuerunt obuia rostra,
> in puppem rediere rates. 545

> When there was only so much of the sea between them that each ship
> could cover it with a thrust of the oars, countless voices are mixed together
> in the vast sky, and the sound of the rowing is overwhelmed by shouting,
> and the war-horns could not be heard. Then they sweep the deep blue
> and fall into their benches and pound their chests with their oars. When
> rostra facing rostra roared at each other, the ships backed up to the fleet.
> (3.538–45)

Here at this moment of first contact between the warring fleets, Lucan zeroes in on the clamor at sea (3.540–2) and then the rowers' exertions (3.542–3). Conte has argued that in the vivid imagery of 3.543 (*atque in transtra cadunt et remis pectora pulsant*) lies "un altro caso di flagrante imitazione enniana

---

battles too. Silius Italicus's depiction of a naval battle at Syracuse in Book 14 may have been modeled on Lucan's at Massilia (Marks [2010] 144).

in Lucano."[90] The fragment that Conte has in mind is *Annales* 218 (= Fest. 488), which Festus preserves and places in Book 7 of Ennius's epic. It appears to come from a speech of instructions delivered to oarsmen: *poste recumbite pectora pellite tonsis* ("Lean back and pound your chests with your oars"). Festus's identification of Book 7 has led editors to place the fragment amid Ennius's treatment of the launch of the Roman fleet in the early years of the First Punic War (pointing enticingly at a possible Naevian provenance).[91] In the same passage, Festus quotes the hexameter *pone petunt, exim referunt ad pectora tonsas* (*Ann.* 219: "They strive back, and then pull the oars back to their chests"), a line that may be from the same Ennian passage. Whatever the fragments' relative placement, their existence reflects Ennius's interest in capturing visceral images of oarsmen at work. In the passage from *Pharsalia* 3, Conte notes a number of parallels with *Ann.* 218: Lucan's *pectora pulsant* in 3.543 echoes Ennius's *pectora pellite*, both in diction and in the use of characteristically Ennian alliteration;[92] and, though Lucan writes *remis* in 3.543, he had used the more poetic synonym *tonsis* just a few lines earlier, at 5.539, in the same metrical position as Ennius had in *Ann.* 218. More broadly, Conte notes, Lucan will go on to relate that the Caesarian ships succeed in converting the contest into a sort of stationary land battle (3.556–75), just as the Romans famously did at the early Battle of Mylae (260 BCE; see Polyb. 1.22) and at other sea battles in the First Punic War.

To Conte's observations about 3.543, I will add that Lucan's word choices in the preceding line, earlier in the same sentence, are also conspicuous and possibly Ennian. The phrase *caerula uerrunt* ("they sweep the deep blue," 3.542) marks Lucan's only use of the verb *uerro* and one of only two times in the poem he includes the color blue (the other being 2.220). Earlier epic (Cat. 64.7; Virgil, *Aen.* 3.208 and 4.583) had used this same collocation of *uerro* and *caerula*, and the model for each instance appears to be *Annales* 377–8: <u>uerrunt</u> *extemplo placidum mare: marmore flauo* | <u>caeruleum</u> *spumat*

---

[90] Conte (1988) 28. Skutsch (1985) 391–2 is more cautious, writing of the correspondence in the expression *remis pectora pulsant* that "a certain similarity of phrasing in such contexts is inevitable" (391). Hunink (1992) 214 n. 2 takes a middle ground: "Lucan's expression is surely not everyday Latin. It must be understood within the Roman epic tradition starting with Ennius."

[91] See Skutsch (1985) 390, of 218 and 219 together: "The occasion probably were [sic] the exercises preceding the launching of the first Roman fleet in 260 BC."

[92] Hunink (1992) 214 cites a number of passages with periphrases for rowing, but the only other passage I have found predating Lucan and including the image of oars striking chests is Ov., *Met.* 11.461–2 (*reducunt . . . ad fortia pectora remos*). After Lucan see Val. Flacc. 1.369 (*tum ualida Clymenus percusso pectore tonsa*), Stat., *Theb.* 5.375 (*remique cadunt in pectus inanes*), and Sil. 11.489 (*adductis percussa ad pectora tonsis*). Lucan writes *pectora pulsant* again at 7.128, of hearts beating chests in the run-up to Pharsalia.

sale conferta rate pulsum ("At once they sweep the peaceful sea; with yellow marble the deep blue salt foams, struck by the gathered fleet").[93] Gellius quotes these lines and places them in *Annales* 14. And so this image of a fleet sweeping across the sea and picking up speed would have described Roman naval exploits in the early second century; Skutsch proposes Ennius's account of Roman naval victories over Antiochus III's Seleucid fleet in 191 or 190.[94]

The full sentence in *Pharsalia* 3.542–3, then, may include adaptations of two images that appear to originate in Ennius's maritime narrative. Whether the reader recalls particular Ennian scenes on the sea or his naval language more generally, the effect of the evocation is to recall the driving advance of the Roman fleet in the *Annales*—and perhaps Naevius's sweating oarsmen too (recall fr. 64). As the ships sweep across the sea and their rowers exert themselves at Lucan's Massilia, the memory of the emerging, expanding, and in time triumphant ships of early Latin epic enters the reader's mind.

But there is of course a crucial difference in the nature of the naval combat at Lucan's Massilia. While Lucan emphasizes the Greek ethnicity of the Massilians on several occasions (e.g., 3.516, 3.526, and 3.553), at the same time he confounds any certainty about which side represents Rome. We have seen that it is Caesar who has just completed a Hannibalic invasion of Italy, and the Massilians who have taken cause with Rome's senatorial forces. In the final lines of the episode, Lucan depicts lamenting Massilian widows, finding only disfigured bodies on the shore, embracing Roman corpses (3.758–9)—a scene that neatly captures the terrific emotional confusion of this and any civil-war battle.[95] This dynamic is also explicit in the initial clash on the seas, where, as the battleships engage, "rostra facing rostra roared at each other" (*rostris crepuerunt obuia rostra*, 3.544). By picturing clashing *rostra* and employing a verb commonly used of competing human voices (*crepo*), Lucan recalls the obstreperous debates among Roman speakers at the rostra in the Forum. The image also anticipates the unforgettable episode in the coming narrative when two clashing ships simultaneously pierce a soldier with their *rostra* (3.652–61), a characteristically Lucanian snapshot of Roman internecine slaughter.

---

[93] Hunink (1992) 213: "a conventional phrase," but "[t]he underlying model is Enn. *Ann.* 377–8." See too Horsfall (2006) 180.
[94] Skutsch (1985) 542–3.
[95] Rowland (1969) 208: "Roman corpses have now become Massilian corpses, and whether the headless body is Roman or Massilian is irrelevant." Hunink (1992) 212 appears to miss the effect: "Somewhat surprisingly, the poet pays relatively little attention to the difference between the contesting parties." See further discussion later in the chapter.

The succinct description at 3.544 (*rostris crepuerunt obuia rostra*) also picks up on the theme of "spears threatening spears" (*pila minantia pilis*, 1.6) that Lucan introduced in his proem. As with *pila* there, here he pits characteristically Roman images (*rostra*) against one another; and, as with the descriptor *minantia*, the warring Roman hallmarks are personified, taunting one another (*crepuerunt*) in internecine animus. Let us recall from Chapter 1 that the *Commenta Bernensia* identified the Ennian line *pila retunduntur uenientibus obuia pilis* (*Ann.* 582) as the model for the programmatic image in 1.6. A line that had characterized Roman war with enemies in the *Annales*, I argued there, is redirected inward, transformed into a powerful marker of Lucan's story of Roman self-destruction. At 3.544 he perpetuates the piercing image from 1.6 to the seas at Massilia, perhaps again evoking the Ennian model.[96]

When we look at 3.542–4 together, what comes into view is a taut cluster of Ennian language:

> tum **caerula uerrunt**
> atque in transtra cadunt et **remis pectora pulsant.**
> ut primum **rostris crepuerunt obuia rostra,**
> in puppem rediere rates.

> They sweep the deep blue, and they fall into their banks and pound their chests with their oars. As soon as rostra facing rostra roared at each other, the ships headed back astern.

The presence of each Ennian correspondence in the cluster strengthens the case for the others. Whether or not Lucan is pointing the reader to a particular episode in the *Annales*, it appears that he is using this moment at Massilia of ships embarking on the seas to draw yet another sharp line between Ennius's (and possibly Naevius's) epic and his own—that is, to pinpoint the movement from the adventuresome beginning of the Latin epic story to its self-defeating end in the *Pharsalia*. As in the confrontation of *pila minantia pilis* on the fields, now Roman *rostra*—and the genre recording their roar—advance only inward toward self-destruction.

The movement in the cluster at 3.542–4 is representative of the passage as a whole. The fighting at Massilia begins with the Caesarians' display of

---

[96] Hunink (1992) 214 compares the three passages.

a hallmark of Roman success in the First Punic War, the use of the *corvus* (see 3.574) to create a sort of battlefield on the waters (3.556–75). But very soon Lucan's narrative becomes a string of varied and gruesome death scenes on the water (3.583–751), an exposition of "many dazzling displays of different deaths on the sea" (*multaque ponto* | . . . *uarii miracula fati*, 3.633–4). Over these nearly 170 lines of maritime slaughter, the dying warriors are given individual *aristeiai*, but they are of the self-destructive, pointless kind: "warriors find glory in meeting death rather than inflicting it upon others."[97] The whole episode stands as an inversion of the type of collective, forward-moving, successful advance on the seas that characterized maritime movement at the launch of Latin epic.

The scene at Massilia and Book 3 as a whole end with acknowledgment of victory for Decimus Brutus and the Caesarians (3.761–2). But what stays with the reader is the immediately preceding vignette of the response by Massilian wives, mothers, and fathers to the bloody battle:

> quis in urbe parentum
> fletus erat, quanti matrum per litora planctus!
> coniunx saepe sui confusis uoltibus unda
> credidit ora uiri Romanum amplexa cadauer,
> accensisque rogis miseri de corpore trunco   760
> certauere patres.

> What weeping from the parents there was in the city! What great lamentation from mothers along the shores! Since faces had been mangled by the sea, often a wife—believing she saw the face of her husband—embraced a Roman corpse, and amid lit pyres grieving fathers fought over a headless body. (3.756–61)

The gutting violence of the episode necessitates an expression of lament from kin, and for the process a Roman corpse (3.759) is accordingly drawn out, just as Curio's will be at the conclusion of the following book. Mourners of the war-dead get the last word at Massilia, and, with their tears and wailing, bring the closure of lament to the events there. Lucan takes the reader of epic onto the seas for a proper naval battle, thus restaging the naval contests that

---

[97] Hunink (1992) 201. Bartsch (1997) 16–17 describes the battle as "another prolonged metamorphosis of bodies into fragments."

were certainly prominent in and even constitutive of early Latin epic. But his story of that battle emerges as another venue for thematic and textual self-destructiveness and the gesture of lamentation that must accompany it.

4.6. "Fama spoke of no ship with a greater voice": The final sinking of the Roman ship

The planes of narrative and poetic action examined in this chapter have been broad: Lucan's telling of Hannibalic victory in Italy, his tale of the relanding in Africa and undoing of Roman success there, and the Ennian sweep of ships and thrust of *rostra* back into one another at Massilia. In this final section I will move from the crashes and crash landings of the Roman fleet to zoom in on Lucan's related focus on the wreckage and sinking of individual ships. In these focused moments, I will argue, Lucan brings to repose the stories of enterprising individual ships that had populated early Latin epic.

The solitary ship as a symbol of survival and promise sails into the Roman reader's view in the very first epic in Latin, Livius's *Odusia*. Odysseus's ship in Homer's model poem offered both Livius and his readers a perfect vehicle for exploring the themes of adventure, hardship through precarious circumstances, and ultimately survival. More immediately, as I discussed at the outset of this chapter, the ship venturing on the Mediterranean in the *Odusia* neatly paralleled the ships of Rome's own venturing and expanding fleet. Aeneas sailed these seas, too, and Servius Danielis writes that Naevius's epic included the "strange detail" (*nouam rem*) of the hero embarking at Troy in a single ship (*unam nauem*; fr. 7 Blänsdorf = Serv. Dan. on *Aen.* 1.170). Thomas Biggs relates this detail to the project of the *Bellum Punicum* as a whole, proposing that "the epic ship of Aeneas sets sail as a symbol of Rome's first fleet."[98] And then there is the solitary ship that Ennius pictures in a fragment that Priscian (2.485) places in *Annales* 7, the book that included select events from the First Punic War. The fragment reads: *urserat huc nauim conpulsam fluctibus pontus* (*Ann.* 217: "The sea had pushed to this place the ship, driven by the waves"). Editors have suggested that this line describes the Romans' chance discovery of an abandoned Carthaginian warship in the year 261,[99] an

---

[98] Biggs (2017) 353, continuing: "In fact, within the extant fragments of the poem that depict Roman naval activity we can perhaps still perceive the glimmer of the ship's progression from that moment in the proto-Roman past, to the narrative present of Roman fleets at war with Carthage." See too Leigh (2010) 274.

[99] Skutsch (1985) 388–9, building on a reading first made by Müller (1884) (*non uidi*).

episode that Polybius makes central to his story of Rome's rise as a sea power, writing that the Romans built their entire fleet on the model of that ship (Polyb. 1.20.15). It is impossible to say whether there is any historical accuracy to this story,[100] but if scholars are right that *Ann.* 217 refers to the same ship, then it appears that Ennius too presented Rome's fortunes on the sea as originating with the story of a single ship.

The emergence, progression through uncertainty, and promise of these symbolic individual ships from early Latin epic come to a crashing halt in the *Pharsalia*'s images of solitary ships as sites of sinking and self-destruction. Perhaps the most famous single ship in the poem is the meager Egyptian skiff that acts as the stage for Pompey's death at sea in Book 8, a setting and a scene of humiliation for the once great naval captain that Lucan appears to draw from Caesar's own account (*BC* 3.104.3) and expand into a grandiose poetic exercise in diminishment.[101] Later in Book 8, Lucan pictures the makeshift bier that Cordus constructs for Pompey as built from the "fragments of a shattered ship" (*lacerae fragmenta carinae*, 8.755), another image that poignantly captures the fall of this erstwhile master of the seas—the marker of his loss, and so of the Roman loss that Lucan has Pompey's death represent, being a pitiful splintered ship. Here too, as in the tableau of the fragmentary fleet at 9.32–5, *fragmenta* may carry metapoetic force: Latin epic poetry's age-old monument to Roman sway on the sea is briskly reduced to a pile of combustible fragments.

Amid the sea battle at Massilia in Book 3 comes an elaborate picture of solitary, lonely death at sea. In a series of strung-together individual deaths,[102] Lucan details the varied ends of Catus (3.585–91), Telo (3.592–9), and Gyraeus (3.600–2), before highlighting the increasingly limbless, dying exploits of an unnamed Massilian twin (3.601–25). This man's death is strung together, through a lunging leap (3.625–6), with the individual death not of another warrior, but of a Roman ship:

strage uirum cumulata ratis multoque cruore
plena per obliquum crebros latus accipit ictus
et, postquam ruptis pelagus conpagibus hausit,
ad summos repleta foros descendit in undas   630

[100] See the cautious assessment of Walbank (1957) 75.
[101] See Joseph (2017b) 299–300. Lucan highlights the smallness of Pompey's ship at 8.541, 8.562, 8.565, and 8.624.
[102] Hunink (1992) 250 compares this "chain fight" with *Il.* 13.576–672 and 14.440–507.

uicinum inuoluens contorto uertice pontum.
aequora discedunt mersa diducta carina
inque locum puppis cecidit mare.

Piled up with the carnage of men, and full of much gore, the ship takes frequent blows on its side and, after the sea has broken and consumed its parts, it descends, full to the top of its decks, into the waves, as it draws in the nearby sea in a twisted eddy. With the ship sunk, the water that had been submerged parts, and the sea falls into the place where the ship had been. (3.627–33)

Lucan follows these lines with the observation that there were "many marvelous deaths" on that day (3.633–4), and soon moves on to another individual's dying day (3.635–45). But the death at 3.627–33 is not like the others. Though he describes corpses on the ship's deck (3.627), here the ship has agency in receiving (*accipit*, 3.628) blows, in its consumption (*hausit*, 3.629) of water into its cracking core, and then in its dying descent (*descendit*, 3.630) into the waves. Like other civil warriors in Lucan's poem, the ship participates in its own destruction,[103] actively consuming the sea that, in its many forms (*pelagus, undas, pontum, aequora, mare* all appear here) overwhelms it. The vessel is soon out of sight, sent under in the swift ablative absolute *diducta carina* (3.632), and conclusively replaced, in the final word of the vignette, by the victorious sea (*mare*)—an almost too neat symbol of Rome's loss of power over the sea.

The lonely death of this ship at Massilia is still on the reader's mind when Lucan stages a second solitary naval death scene in the next book, in his account of the collective suicide of the Caesarian general Vulteius and his men on a raft in the Adriatic Sea (4.402–581). Whereas the poet figures the sea battle of Massilia as a display of Roman self-destruction, this episode is literally that—an iconic moment of willful self-slaughter. The basics of the historical event, which is noted by Livy and Florus, are as follows: a raft of fleeing Caesarian auxiliaries from the Gallic town of Opitergium is outmaneuvered and roped to the Illyrian cliffs by Pompeian forces; after a day of battle, the men choose not to surrender but to commit mass suicide.[104] In Lucan's

---

[103] See my discussion in Chapter 2 of Marius Gratidianus's self-sacrificial death at 2.173–93.
[104] See Livy, *Per.* 110.10–15 and Flor. 2.13.33, as well as Quint. 3.8.23 and 3.8.30, citing the *exemplum* of the Opitergini in a section on *suasoriae*. Leigh (2007) 492 argues that Lucan is the source for Florus's episode.

hands, the story stretches to 180 lines, transformed into a "micro-image of the larger conflict."[105] It is a spectacular event, with the raft acting as "a central stage, viewable from land and sea"[106] by both internal audiences and later external readers. In his consideration of the passage as a *mise en abyme* for the work as a whole, Martin Dinter considers the metapoetic diction Lucan uses of the raft, which is characterized as a "new trick" (*noua furta*, 4.416) and built "not in the customary way" (*neque . . . de more*, 4.417); rather, the Caesarians "weave together firm planks on an unfamiliar tract, so it can bear great weight" (4.418–19: *firma gerendis | molibus insolito contexunt robora ductu*). Three times in these lines the poet marks the raft as something new or extraordinary, and, as Dinter discusses, the words *furtum, moles, contexo, robor*, and *ductus* are all used elsewhere of literary production: "The raft's building process thus brims with metaliterary vocabulary suggestive of the composition of a work of literature."[107] In short, Lucan highlights the extraordinariness not only of the events on this vessel, but also of his textual presentation of it, as a novel and landmark literary effort.

This one-of-a-kind, miraculous (see *praebet miracula* at 4.425) feat of engineering and literary artistry offers a one-off setting for the suicide, which commences with Vulteius's own blow at 4.540–1 and concludes with the following climactic lines:

>   cum sorte cruenta
> fratribus incurrunt fratres natusque parenti,
> haud trepidante tamen toto cum pondere dextra
> exegere enses. pietas ferientibus una   565
> non repetisse fuit. iam latis uiscera lapsa
> semianimes traxere foris multumque cruorem
> infudere mari. despectam cernere lucem
> uictoresque suos uoltu spectare superbo
> et mortem sentire iuuat. iam strage cruenta   570
> conspicitur cumulata ratis, bustisque remittunt
> corpora uictores, ducibus mirantibus ulli

---

[105] Dinter (2012) 128, amid his discussion at 127–38. See too Saylor (1990); Leigh (1997) 259–64; and Sklenář (2003) 26–34.

[106] Asso (2011) 193. Leigh (1997) 259–61 emphasizes the theatricality of the passage and compares it with a *naumachia*.

[107] Dinter (2012) 134, pointing at 133–4 to OLD references (*furtum* (OLD 1c), *moles* (OLD 6), and *contexo* (OLD 1 and 2); and to the uses of *ductus* at Quint. 4.2.53 and in the *Epitaphium Lucani* (5.74.3). See too Masters (1992) 27 on *robur*.

esse ducem tanti. nullam maiore locuta est
ore ratem totum discurrens fama per orbem.

Although, because of their blood lot, brothers clashed with brothers and a son with his father, nevertheless they drove their swords with all their weight, and no hand trembled. The one gesture of piety for those delivering the blow was not to strike twice. Now, as the half-dead dragged their spilling guts onto the broad gangways, they poured much blood into the sea. It is pleasing for them to see the light that they have scorned, to look at the victors with a haughty glance, and to feel death. Now the boat is seen piled high with bloody carnage, and the [Pompeian] victors send the corpses into the pyre, as their leaders marvel that a leader could be so highly regarded by anyone. Fama, running about through the whole world, spoke of no ship with a greater voice. (4.562–74)

The suicidal ship in the Adriatic is paradigmatic of the larger war, even containing the convention of brothers killing brothers and a son killing his father (4.563). Like the war and the poem as a whole, this raft is piled high with carnage (*iam strage cruenta | conspicitur cumulata ratis*, 4.570–1), a clear echo of the solitary boat at Massilia (*strage uirum cumulata ratis*, 3.627). This parallel compels us to read these two deaths together, twin icons of the swift sinking of the Roman ship. And whereas the ship at Massilia actively directs its own plunge (recall the verbs in 3.628–30), here the half-dead (*semianimes*, 4.567) sailors take agency, dragging their own guts onto the gangways (*uiscera . . . traxere foris*, 4.566–7)—so in a sense *sharing* the gory process of dying with the ship—and, in an arresting image, actively pouring their own blood into the sea (*multumque cruorem | infudere mari*, 4.567–8)!

This willful offering to the sea of their blood, their life source, reads as a concise expression of the complete loss of Roman power over the sea. At the end of Book 2, Caesar had attempted to blockade Pompey by filling up the bay at Brundisium with mounds of earth, an effort to conquer the sea that fails, as "the voracious sea eats up all the rocks" (*omnia pontus | haurit saxa uorax*, 2.663–4).[108] The image at 4.567–8 thus complements and expands upon the one at Brundisium: while there the sea had eaten up and thus

---

[108] Lucan's personification and empowerment of the sea in Book 2 contrasts with Caesar's more clinical presentation of the attempted breakwater at *BC* 1.25–7. See Masters (1992) 32.

dismissed Caesar's attempt at mastery, here on the Adriatic the sea receives the gushes of blood marking the culmination of its victory over Rome.

This self-destructive moment on Vulteius's raft offers a key for understanding many of the threads in the *Pharsalia* that I have explored in this chapter. Lucan places the episode immediately before Curio's arrival on the shores of Libya and the beginning of the poem's African narrative (4.581– 9; see earlier discussion). The placement appears to reflect the historical sequence of events in the spring and summer of 49 BCE,[109] but in Lucan's telling the juxtaposition also reads as ominous. Curio's and, later, Cato's maritime ventures to Africa were doomed from the start; their seafaring stories were certain to end in wreckage and the loss of Roman lifeblood.

I have argued here that Lucan narrates not just the moments marking the inverse of the Roman maritime moment, but also the end of that story, the story of Rome's bold exploration and conquest of the Mediterranean that was begun in the works of Livius, Naevius, and Ennius. In this light it is significant that Lucan writes of the sinking ship in Book 4 that "*fama*, running about through the whole world, spoke of no ship with a greater voice" (*nullam maiore locuta est | ore ratem totum discurrens fama per orbem*, 4.573– 4, fulfilling Vulteius's wish for *fama* at 4.509). The appearance in this moment of *fama* leads the reader to think of the episode in the arc of epic, the genre that, from its Homeric beginnings, traffics in what is said and heard about the past, in *kleos* or *fama*. Scholars have proposed that Lucan is holding his famed boat up against the Argo celebrated in epics such as Apollonius's and Varro of Atax's *Argonautica*.[110] But we must also keep in view the *Odusia*, *Bellum Punicum*, and *Annales*, the pioneering epics that launched the genre at Rome with stories of ships: first solitary ships, then the growth of those ships through peril and perseverance—and the existential transmarine threat of Carthage—into a sprawling imperial fleet. With the *Pharsalia* this all halts. Roman epic's story on the seas—the *fama* that will now be spread around the whole world (4.573–4) —becomes one not of exploration and expansion, but of wreckage, self-sinking, and blood poured into the sea. The

---

[109] See the sequencing at Livy, *Epit.* 110; and, after Lucan, Flor. 2.13.30–34, Dio Cass. 41.40–42, and Oros. 6.15.8–9. App., *BC* 2.44–7, narrates the landing in Africa prior to mentioning the episode in the Adriatic. See further Avery (1993), proposing that Caesar treated the mass suicide in a lost section of his *BC*.

[110] See Asso (2010) 212 and Dinter (2012) 128. Murray (2011) considers the significance of Lucan's three explicit references to the Argo at 2.709–25, 3.190–8, and 6.395–401, arguing that Lucan prioritizes the version of Ap. Rhod., who (unlike Varro) does not regard the Argo as the first ship. See too Biggs (2019) 981 on Lucan's "agonistic relationship" with these two authors.

184   THUNDER AND LAMENT

Roman maritime story, together with the genre that had boldly launched and long told that story, is now crashed, sunk, lost, ended.

When we recall that the earliest epics had reflected the precariousness of both maritime and epic enterprises—the possibility that these "free-floating"[111] and daring imperial and poetic projects could end at any moment—perhaps we can identify another gesture of closure in the final lines of Book 10, to go with those I considered in Chapter 3. As Caesar is preparing to move his war with Ptolemy onto the sea (*dum parat in uacuas Martem transferre carinas*, 10.535), he is trapped, with "no path to safety, in flight or by force, and scarcely any hope even for an honorable death" (*uia nulla salutis, | non fuga, non uirtus; uix spes quoque mortis honestae*, 10.538–9).[112] Doomed to be defeated (*uincendus*, 10.541), he is "left hanging, seized by the destiny of this spot" (*captus sorte loci pendet*, 10.542). In this snapshot that Lucan has so carefully crafted, right at the poem's precipice, Caesar's condition reflects that of the *Pharsalia*—and now epic itself: at last cut off, kept from another foray onto the seas, captured hanging in a perilous passage of text (*loci*).

---

[111] So McElduff (2013) 52.

[112] See Tracy (2011) 47 on "Caesar's sudden, overwhelming peril and his proximity to total disaster," and Rimell (2015) 247–52 on the language of enclosure here (with my discussion in Chapter 3).

5
The *Pharsalia* and the Loss of *Nostos*

In the previous chapter I proposed that the sinking of solitary ships in the *Pharsalia* is emblematic of the ending of the Latin epic story of Rome's ascent and sway on the sea, as the individual ships that accompanied the launch of Latin epic in the poems of Ennius, Naevius, and Livius are met by the shattered and shipwrecked vessels of the *Pharsalia*. In this chapter I to a great extent stay on the sea, or, rather, on the process of departure and return via the sea, as I address the *Pharsalia*'s persistent and (again) polemical engagement with the *Odyssey*. As the argument of this book moves chronologically backward through the foundational works of Latin and Greek epic, this chapter is thus in many ways a "prequel" to Chapter 4, with some of the same maritime movement covered, though with a fundamentally distinct thematic focus.

Odyssean themes were as old as Latin epic itself, beginning of course with Livius's launch of the genre in his *Odusia*. The hero's tale would remain popular in Roman culture for centuries and find an extraordinary range of adaptations in Roman literature,[1] as Odysseus *polutropos* had a "quintessential adaptability" and "was, in short, good to think with."[2] Writing his epic three centuries after the pioneering endeavor of the *Odusia*, Lucan picks up this attraction to the story of Odysseus, but engages with it in a wholly different manner from that of Livius and later Latin authors: through systematic negation and undoing. Readers of the *Pharsalia* have been keen to observe parallels and reversals of elements of the *Iliad*—and Lucan's involvement of one of the master tropes in that epic, lament, will be the focus of the next chapter. Here I will argue that the story of Odysseus holds a similarly important place for Lucan's project of closing the epic genre. Odysseus's tale is a story of *nostos*, of, as A. B. Lord put it in his comparative study of return poetry, the sequence of absence, devastation, and return.[3] The war at Troy leads

---

[1] See Farrell (2006) on Roman cultural affinity to Odysseus.
[2] Johnston (2019) 212, in a chapter on the reception of the *Od*. by Greek writers living under the principate.
[3] See Lord (1960) *passim* and the expansion of this schema by Foley (1990) 362 to absence, devastation, return, retribution, and wedding. See too Bakker (2013) 13–35. Alden (2017) 16–75 discusses the *Od*.'s many para-narratives of return.

to Odysseus's absence from Ithaca and his wife Penelope; ten years of warfare and ten more of wandering and loss on the seas constitute the devastation he experiences; then his ultimate arrival in Ithaca and reunion with Penelope mark his return. To be sure, there are openings in the *Odyssey*, in both the hero's arc beyond Book 24 and the poem's structure.[4] Lucan, I will argue, takes the element of *aporia* that complicates and enriches the *Odyssey*'s story of *nostos* and blows it wide open. His heroes (Cato, Pompey, Caesar, and the *populus Romanus*) are persistently and conspicuously denied the type of *nostos* that Odysseus achieved.

In his discussion of the richness of the theme of *nostos* in the *Odyssey*, Egbert Bakker closely connects Odysseus's achievement in the poem with that of Homer himself, writing that "hero and poet negotiate the accomplishment of a *nostos* that is their common goal."[5] Lucan accomplishes the opposite end. The denial of *nostos* in his poem, recurring in varied but related forms for each of his chief characters, constitutes a denial and in turn an ending of the poetic tradition of *nostos* poetry. And so the correspondence of content and poetics that I have explored in previous chapters thus operates in Lucan's treatment of *nostos* too. A fundamental difference here is that Lucan's gesture of ending the Odyssean epic tradition is done, paradoxically, through the opening up of the closure that is central to a successful *nostos*. In this regard we might say that his polemic with the Odyssean *nostos* plays off what Don Fowler called the dialectic between closure and aperture.[6] On one level, Lucan the epic poet is himself "returning home" to address and incorporate this master-trope of *nostos* that was codified by Homer.[7] But at the same time, he completes and concludes the arc of *nostos*-poetry through the very inverse of reaching "home," by narratively opening up the sense of completeness and fulfillment that are inherent in the concept of *nostos*.

Another factor that may have made the story of Odysseus's journey home appealing to Lucan is that the hero's *nostos* is achieved, ultimately, through an act of civil warfare, the killing of the suitors. Odysseus's slaughter of his fellow Ithacans in Book 22 precedes his reunion with Penelope in Book 23: it is a crucial step in the completion of the *nostos*. What is more, Book 24 narrates the

---

[4] See Goldhill (1991) 22–4; Silk (2004) 43–4; Graziosi and Haubold (2005) 146–7; and Christensen (2018); and further discussion later in this chapter.
[5] Bakker (2013) 20. See too Goldhill (1991) 1–68 on the sympathy of poet and hero in the *Od.*; and Bonifazi (2009) on the etymology, cognates, and range of meanings of *nostos*.
[6] See Fowler (1989) 79 and (1997) 4–5.
[7] See Biggs and Blum (2019b) 7 on how "Homer becomes 'home'—a point of departure to which later authors, implicitly or explicitly, return in a sort of literary *nostos*."

mourning in the city over this slaughter (24.412–20), a call for revenge by the Ithacan elder Eupeithes (426–37), and then further bloodshed of Odysseus's Ithacan rivals (522–7).[8] In the final lines of the poem, Athena and Zeus quash the civil combat, and the goddess brokers a lasting peace (528–48). Odysseus, who himself has been assured a peaceful death in a prosperous Ithaca (11.121–33 = 23.268–80[9]), thus accomplishes victory in civil war *and* a secure *nostos*—the one indeed contributing to the other. In this regard the civil conflict in Ithaca stands as another challenge to Odysseus's *nostos*, but one that is overcome by the hero and the gods seeking resolution. In the *Pharsalia*, lacking the providence of gods such as Homer's Zeus and Athena, such an outcome is not achievable. While there are victories and victors in Lucan's poem, there are, pointedly, no *nostoi* of the sort that Homer's poem achieves.

As I pursue this argument in the coming pages, the place of Homer's epic as an anti-model will be paramount. But I also want to propose, in a more speculative way, that Livius's *Odusia* stands alongside the Homeric poem as a foil for Lucan in his opening up and consequent closing of the theme of *nostos*. Livius's bold permutations of Homer's *Mousa* to the Latin *Camena* (fr. 1 Blänsdorf), of Homer's Zeus to *pater noster* (fr. 2 Blänsdorf), of the hexameter to the Saturnian meter, and so on, marked the birth of the genre in Latin.[10] And we get a sense of Livius's process of adapting the Odyssean theme of *nostos* and its challenges from a fragment preserved by Festus: *partim errant, nequinont Graeciam redire* ("while some wander about, others are unable to return to Greece," fr. 11 Blänsdorf = Fest. 160 L).[11] The transformational poetic endeavor of the *Odusia* stood as a "significant cultural break"; the traveling, publicly singing (so Suet., *Gramm*. 1), pioneering epicist Livius achieved the status of an "indispensable power broker."[12] Though Ennius's own firsts would allow him to supplant Livius in a number of ways,[13] and critics of his style as primitive abounded, the primary place of Livius's efforts was long remembered (see Cicero, *Brutus* 72, and Horace, *Epist*. 2.1.62). And so when Lucan affects an unraveling and thus a closure of *nostos* poetry, the act—I want to suggest here—engages with both Homer's *Odyssey*

---

[8] De Jong (2001) 582 (on *Od*. 24.412–548) identifies earlier passages that anticipate the vengeance the suitors' families will seek.
[9] Considered later in this chapter alongside Pompey's imagined return home.
[10] See Goldberg (1995) 64–73 on Livius' adaptations of Homeric passages.
[11] Which editors have compared with *Od*. 4.495 (πολλοὶ μὲν γὰρ τῶν γε δάμεν, πολλοὶ δὲ λίποντο).
[12] Quotations from Kahane (2013) 44 and Feeney (2016) 67, respectively. See too McElduff (2013) 43–55 on Livius's principal place; and Suerbaum (1992) 168–73 on the possible length of the *Odusia*.
[13] See the Introduction.

and the poem that brought Odysseus's tale into the Latin language and set off Latin epic.

Let us recall from Chapter 1 that in his proem Lucan marks the central hero of his story, the Roman people (*populum*, 1.2), as *conuersum* (1.3), an evocation and inversion of Homer's epithet for his hero, *polutropos*, as well as Livius's self-referential translation of that epithet, *uersutum* (fr. 1 Blänsdorf). In the final section of this chapter I will focus on Lucan's presentation of the Roman people as absent from home and devastated, but without hope for the return that came to complete Odysseus's story. But first I will consider the comparable journeys of the poem's three most prominent characters: Cato, Pompey, and Caesar. Their stories of absence, devastation, and failure to return operate in Lucan's epic as, to employ a term from Maureen Alden's study of the *Odyssey*, para-narratives of Rome's lost *nostos*.[14] In the *Pharsalia* each of these heroes, like the Roman people as a whole, conspicuously fails to get home. Correspondingly, Lucan underscores how each fails to achieve a proper reunion with his spouse. Each story is crafted as a journey without return, recovery, and renewal. Scholars have fruitfully discussed the movement of the poem's center from West to East, from Rome to Pharsalia in Books 6–7, then to Egypt in Books 8–10, and even back to Troy in Book 9,[15] and analysis of this movement as a reversal of the East-to-West progression of the *Aeneid* has been profitable.[16] But the centrifugal movement of the *Pharsalia*'s characters, together with the poem's concentration on the failure of its characters to achieve homecoming and reunion, responds most meaningfully to the Odyssean model.[17] As Lucan crafts a poem to reverse, negate, and close the epic tradition, the undoing of the Odyssean master-trope of the fulfillment of *nostos* is a key part of this agenda.

5.1. Cato *hareniuagus*

The journey by Cato and his army across the Syrtes and then the neighboring sands of Africa runs over some 650 lines in Book 9 (9.294–949). It

---

[14] Alden (2017).
[15] See Rossi (2000); Bexley (2009); Myers (2011); and Pogorzelski (2011).
[16] Rossi (2000).
[17] Dinter (2013) 7 briefly though perceptively writes that the "'Iliadic' first part of Lucan's epic full of battle and warfare is then followed by books featuring an 'Odyssean' lack of orientation and closure (a reverse of the *Aeneid*'s pattern of Homeric influence)." This chapter extends such a reading of an Odyssean thread across the poem.

is a torturous affair, marked by the wreck and abandonment of their fleet,[18] a series of gruesome deaths during their march, and toil through extreme conditions for all involved. The exhausting prolongment of the journey in Lucan's telling[19] is programmatic: with this extended episode of wandering, the poet is to a great extent defining his Cato. At the end of the journey, Lucan invents and applies to Cato the epithet *hareniuagus*, "wanderer of the sands" (9.941). The use of this word—which appears nowhere else in Latin literature—puts special emphasis on Cato's identity as a wandering one. Earlier in the passage, when apostrophizing Cato and proposing his deification (9.593–604), the narrator had also focused on his achievements as a wanderer, when stating, "I would prefer to conduct this triumph (*hunc... triumphum*) through the Syrtes and the extreme conditions of Libya rather than ascend the Capitol three times in Pompey's chariot, or break Jugurtha's neck" (6.598–600). The march through Libya—*this* triumph—is Cato's shining accomplishment, a distinction, the narrator claims, surpassing the military triumphs others had earned.[20]

Like Odysseus, then, Lucan's Cato endures and is even defined by a perilous journey away from home—by, in Lord's terms, absence and the consequent devastation. In his dialogue *De Constantia Sapientis*, Seneca had explicitly compared Cato with Ulixes (as well as Hercules), each being in his terms a "model of the wise man" (*exemplar sapientis uiri*, Constant. 2.2.1).[21] So the comparison was certainly a familiar one when Lucan wrote his epic. And Marion Lausberg has noted a number of particular parallels between the journeys of Odysseus and Cato that Lucan appears to have crafted into Book 9.[22] Each journey begins with a military venture against a coastal city (that of the Cicones at *Od.* 9.39–61; and Cyrene at *Ph.* 9.297–99) and, immediately afterward, a storm at sea strikes (*Od.* 9.67–75; *Ph.* 9.319–44). In each narrative the survivors of the storm end up in a land of temptation, an opportunity for reprieve from their suffering: Odysseus and his companions

---

[18] See my discussion in Chapter 4.
[19] Contrast the more measured account by Plut. *Cat. Min.* 56. Strabo (17.3.20) writes that the march took thirty days and emphasizes the challenges brought on by the deep sand and heat. On these different accounts see Quinn (2011) 12.
[20] So Tracy (2011) 46: "Significantly, it is not the suicide, but the desert march, that Lucan exalts as the pinnacle of Cato's achievements at 9.593-604." See too D'Alessandro Behr (2007) 14 on Lucan's minimizing of the importance of historical triumph here.
[21] Cf. (with Lausberg [1985] 1600) Hor., *Epist.* 1.2.17–22, on Ulixes as exemplar of *uirtus* and *patientia*.
[22] Lausberg (1985) 1601–2. Seewald (2008) 186–9 compares the storm at sea at 9.319–47 in more general ways with passages in earlier authors.

in the land of the Lotus-eaters (*Od.* 9.82–104), Cato's army at the Lake of Triton (*Ph.* 9.347–54). This lake neighbors the River Lethon and its drafts of forgetfulness (9.355–6), as well as the Garden of the Hesperides, which had grown the famed apples taken by Hercules. And so Lucan, self-consciously indulging in the insertion of these mythical locales (9.359–60), chooses to place his wandering protagonist in a situation where, like Odysseus, he must confront temptation. Like the Greek hero, he is able to resist these diversions and proceed with his journey.[23] A final parallel that Lausberg draws is the focus on the heroes' relationships with their companions.[24] Odysseus, as Homer's proem places right up front (*Od.* 1.5–9), fails to secure the *nostos* of any of his companions, the last of whom succumb to the temptation of eating Helios's cattle and are punished with death at sea (*Od.* 12.260–419). Cato loses many of his men along the way, too, most famously in the series of attacks by a motley crew of poisonous snakes at 9.700–899.[25]

These numerous parallels suggest that Lucan drew his Cato *hareniuagus* as an Odyssean figure. But these significant points of narrative and thematic contact also lead us to see a stark line of contrast: Cato does not make it home. Odysseus's tale is completed by his return to Ithaca, the retribution he wins against his enemies the suitors, and a series of reunions, most importantly, and climactically, with Penelope. Cato's story in the *Pharsalia* ends not at home, but rather in the very locale that came to define his journey: the Libyan desert, where he is held still, indeed canonized (9.593–604) in a state of absence from home, still beset by perpetual devastation, with no return home in reach.

It is of course a fact of history that Cato does not leave Africa. After settling in Utica, his forces are defeated by Caesar's at the nearby Battle of Thapsus in 46 BCE, and he commits suicide soon afterward. But how Lucan chooses to close Cato's story is striking. In what are the final lines of the *Pharsalia*'s Catonian narrative, the poet writes of the end of his trek in Africa and his emergence out of the desert:

---

[23] Ahl (1976) 261 makes this comparison. See too Seo (2011) 218.
[24] Von Albrecht (1970) 275 and Lausberg (1985) 1602 also suggest that Cato's suppression of a mutiny at *Ph.* 9.217–93 is modeled on Odysseus's similar effort at *Il.* 2.155–210.
[25] In light of the deaths in *Ph.* 9, Lausberg (1985) 1602 overstates the contrast between Odysseus's failure and Cato's success as protector of his men. Seo (2011) is more on target, writing of the "collateral damage wreaked in Cato's Stoic odyssey" (220) and that "like Hercules or Odysseus, Cato's superiority is proved at the expense of others' suffering and death" (221). Seewald (2008) 225 sees in Cato's transparency with his companions at 9.388–9 a pointed contrast with Odysseus's famed duplicity.

THE *PHARSALIA* AND THE LOSS OF *NOSTOS*   191

> hoc igitur tandem leuior Romana iuuentus
> auxilio late squalentibus errat in aruis.
> bis positis Phoebe flammis, bis luce recepta   940
> uidit hareniuagum surgens fugiensque Catonem.
> iamque illi magis atque magis durescere puluis
> coepit et in terram Libye spissata redire,
> iamque procul rarae nemorum se tollere frondes,
> surgere congesto non culta mapalia culmo.   945
> quanta dedit miseris melioris gaudia terrae
> cum primum saeuos contra uidere leones!
> proxima Leptis erat, cuius statione quieta
> exegere hiemem nimbis flammisque carentem.

And so the Roman troops, alleviated at last by the aid [of the Psylli], wander far and wide in the rough fields. Twice Phoebe put out her flames and twice took up light again, as, rising and setting, she observed Cato the wanderer of the sands. And now beneath him the dust began to harden more and more, and thick Libya began to return to the condition of earth. And now, far off, here and there the leaves of groves began to rise, and uncultivated huts arose on piled up straw. What joys over this better land did it give the pitiful men, when for the first time they saw savage lions facing them! Leptis was closest, and in a quiet settlement there they spent a winter without storm clouds or the flames of heat. (*Ph.* 9.938–49)

As the wandering far and wide (*late . . . errat*, 9.939) of Cato's army comes to an end, Lucan captures his emergence out of the desert to *terra firma* in a peculiar way. At the critical moment of touchdown, he gives agency not to his hero but to the Libyan earth, whose dust hardens for Cato (9.942–3). Then, at the end of a narrative that has characterized Cato as a wandering Odyssean figure, it is notable when in 9.943 Lucan marks a return (*redire*)—but it is a return not of this "wanderer of the sands," but of the earth, to its more solid state (*in terram Libye spissata redire*). Rather than Cato returning anywhere, the Libyan land actively meets him and becomes his place of settlement. In the ensuing lines Lucan describes the joy of Cato's men as they at last encounter signs of life—however meager (the huts in 9.945) or terrifying (the lions in 9.947); they have at last reached "better land" (9.946). So there is a sort of restoration here, but the quiet dwelling they take up (*statione quieta*, 9.947) will not be just for the winter; this will be their last. This moment of arrival and "homecoming" in Libya, then, is conspicuous for what it is not, for the failure of return that it marks.

5.2. Cato at home and the preclusion of *nostos*

The conclusion of Cato's journey with an arrival far afield in Libya marks his story as pointedly un-Odyssean. But to fully appreciate the inversion of *nostos* in Cato's arc in the *Pharsalia*, we must look to how Lucan chooses to begin his story. He first introduces Cato into the poem's action in Book 2, in his home, where his nephew Brutus seeks him out (2.238: *atria cognati pulsat non ampla Catonis*, "[Brutus] knocks at the humble home of his kinsman Cato"). In a lengthy speech (2.242–84), Brutus asks his uncle about his plans for the civil war and proposes that "you alone would be better off partaking in peaceful leisure, without taking up arms" (2.266–7: *melius tranquilla sine armis | otia solus ages*). In his response (2.286–323), Cato rejects this suggestion—"Should I alone partake in leisure?" (2.295: *otia solus agam?*)—and vows to "stand in the center and take on the blows from the whole war" (2.311).[26]

No other source has a scene of this sort between Cato and Brutus. Lucan appears to have crafted it and, in doing so, he may well have had Homeric model passages in mind. Lausberg has compared their conversation with the one between Hector and Paris at *Iliad* 6.321–41, another exchange of speeches, in a domestic setting, that results in the elder individual convincing the younger of the need to fight.[27] The setup of the passage also resembles the Homeric type-scene of a recruiting mission for an upcoming expedition.[28] There is one conspicuous reference to this type-scene in the *Odyssey*. At 24.114–19 the shade of Agamemnon describes the trip he and Menelaus took to Ithaca to recruit Odysseus, who, we learn, resisted their recruiting efforts. Odysseus's reluctance to head off for the war appears in multiple sources, and so was clearly a well-known episode in the tradition.[29] To return to the scene in *Pharsalia* 2, Lucan stages a comparable setup, with one

---

[26] See Stover (2008) and Seo (2011) 201–4 on how this conversation is reflective of broader themes in the poem.

[27] Lausberg (1985) 1598, followed by Fantham (1992) 123 and Seo (2011) 201. Lausberg notes how both Paris and Brutus go on to murder their cause's great enemy (Achilles and Caesar, respectively).

[28] See, with Ebbott (2014), *Il.* 4.372–81, 9.338, 11.765–70, and 17.215–24, as well as the references to Hera (4.27–8) and Athena (11.714–17) gathering Greeks for the war.

[29] Ebbott (2014) 328.

major figure visiting the home of another in advance of an imminent war. But the scene at Cato's home reads as an inversion of the Homeric type-scene and the episode of the recruitment of Odysseus in particular. In *Pharsalia* 2, Brutus comes to *discourage* Cato from fighting. Contrary to the resistant Odysseus, Cato rejects Brutus's suggestion and resolves straightway to fight. So Lucan chooses to begin Cato's story with him pointedly rejecting the leisure of home (recall *otia* at 2.267 and 2.295) and heading off to war: from the get-go, Lucan's Cato—unlike the Odysseus who had resisted departure and begins his story absent and longing for home—is on the move *from* home.

This impression of a reversal of Odysseus's story is enhanced in the next sequence in Book 2. There is another knock on the door of Cato's house (2.327: *pulsatae sonuere fores*), this time from Marcia, coming from the funeral of her husband Hortensius. As Lucan goes on to explain (2.327–33), she had been married to Cato before divorcing him and marrying Hortensius Now, with Hortensius dead, she is returning to this "better man" (2.329). And so Cato's story, like Odysseus's, also involves a reunion of husband and wife[30]—but one, again, with meaningful differences. In her discussion of the role of Penelope in the *Odyssey*, Sheila Murnaghan brings out how "Odysseus' marriage is at once the most crucial and the most vulnerable of the relationships that allow him to recover his former position."[31] Put another way, for the *nostos* to be complete, Odysseus and Penelope—through her steadfastness and thwarting of the suitors—must both participate.[32] It is notable that Ovid had understood Homer's epic in this way, asking during his defense of the *Ars Amatoria* in *Tristia* 2, "What is the *Odyssey* except the story of a woman, while her husband is away, being pursued by many suitors for the sake of love?" (2.375–6). To the reader, writer, and defender of love poetry Ovid, Penelope and her commitment to a reunion were more central to the *Odyssey* than the titular hero and his efforts.

The reunion of Penelope and Odysseus, and thus the accomplishment of the *nostos*, takes place around the set piece of the marriage-bed he had fixed in place in their bedroom long ago. The greater part of *Odyssey* 23 (23.166–349) occurs here, and knowledge of the marriage-bed is indeed Odysseus's final test: after Penelope suggests that it be moved out of the bedroom to

---

[30] As Lausberg (1985) 1600 notes in brief.
[31] Murnaghan (1987) 122, amid her broader discussion at 118–47. See too Nagy (1979) 38–9 and Goldhill (1991) 97–9.
[32] Murnaghan (1987) 124: "Penelope's steadfastness becomes a more prominent element in Odysseus' success than his own." See too Baragwanath (2019) 120–2 on Penelope's "existential" presence in the *Od*. Stat. gives Od. the (rebuking?) epithet *tardus* at *Silv.* 2.6.57, 2.7.48, and 5.3.148; cf. 2.1.118.

accommodate him (23.174–80), Odysseus angrily responds that it cannot be moved by a mortal, which he knows because he himself had crafted it (23.183–204). This response at last satisfies Penelope (23.205–8); and so we see that "the bed functions as a token between them ... [and] derives its value as a token entirely from the meaning it has for both of them."[33] The reunion of Odysseus and Penelope and in turn the fulfillment of his *nostos* is then formalized physically when they "come in joy to the appointed place (θεσμὸν) of their old bed" (23.296) and "the two of them delight in pleasant lovemaking" (23.300). The word θεσμός ("appointed place") in 23.296 underscores that, here in the couple's bedroom, the *nostos*—the story of the *Odyssey*—is to a great extent accomplished. Indeed, several Alexandrian scholars regarded 23.296 as the *telos* and thus the rightful endpoint of the poem.[34]

The reunion of Cato and Marcia in *Pharsalia* 2 evokes the famous model of Odysseus and Penelope, but with key differences. First of all, this reunion of long separated spouses will not last. While Marcia asks to accompany Cato on his upcoming journey, this does not happen. He will soon depart for Greece, never to return, while Marcia remains in Italy (so too Plut., *Cat. Min.* 52). Lucan brings out the starkness of their split here—and thus how fleeting the reunion is—by never again in the poem referring to Marcia. While Odysseus, as he explains to Penelope at *Od.* 23.264–84, will have to follow Tiresias's instructions and head out once more after their reunion, he will return again to Ithaca, to die "with his people living happily around him" (23.283–4). There will be no such return for Cato, no lasting reunion with Marcia.

There is also the more particular matter of the marriage-bed in each poem. While the bed of Odysseus and Penelope emerges as the pivotal site of their renewed trust and, subsequently, of the consummation of their physical reunion, Lucan also dwells on the symbol of the bed as a token of sorts, but with a striking inversion of the Odyssean model. After introducing Marcia as one who "as a young woman had been joined to the bed (*toris*) of a better man" (2.329), the poet gives her a speech (2.338–49) in which she outlines the purpose of her return to Cato:

uisceribus lassis partuque exhausta reuertor
iam nulli tradenda uiro. da foedera prisci
inlibata tori, da tantum nomen inane

---

[33] Murnaghan (1987) 141. So too Heubeck (1992) 333 (on 23.182–204) and de Jong (2001) 556.
[34] See de Jong (2001) 561–2 and Christensen (2018) 142.

conubii; liceat tumulo scripsisse: "Catonis
Marcia" . . .

Exhausted in my tired insides and from childbirth, I return, to be handed over now to no other husband. Grant me the bonds of our old bed—without consummation; grant me only the hollow name of marriage. Let them write on my tomb "Marcia, wife of Cato." (2.340–44)

As in *Odyssey* 23, here there is a return (note Marcia's pointed *reuertor*) and restoration of the "bonds of the old bed" (*foedera prisci* | . . . *tori*), but these bonds are now devoid of physical consummation (*inlibata*).[35] Lucan follows Marcia's speech with an extended description of the marriage rite itself, detailing at length all of the nuptial conventions that are *missing* (2.350–71).[36] Mention of the omission of the customary garlands, torches, veil, and ornamental marriage-bed (*torus*, 2.357) leads into the poet's focus on the absence of sex itself from the marriage. In a close echo of Marcia's own phrasing at 2.341–2, Lucan writes that "the bonds of their old bed (*foedera prisci* | . . . *tori*) were not attempted: [Cato's] strength resisted even lawful love" (2.379–81), a line underscoring the reunited Cato's and Marcia's rejection of the marriage-bed and pointing to something fundamentally fruitless about Cato's imminent venture and arc in the poem going forward.

In his discussion of the "ascetic and sexless" reunion of Cato and Marcia, Ahl argues that the passage "stands in obvious contrast to the parting of Aeneas and Creusa in *Aeneid* 2," in that Virgil's hero, unlike Lucan's, leaves his old wife behind and goes on to a new marriage and a new land in Italy.[37] But Lucan's repeated focus in this episode on their restored but now sexless marriage-bed invites us more particularly to read the passage alongside the essential but very different place of the marriage-bed in Odysseus's and Penelope's reunion. Like the famously resolute Homeric couple, Marcia and Cato mirror one another in numerous characteristics, but their complementarity centers around fruitlessness, dissolution, and devastation.[38] We saw earlier that Cato's Libyan journey in Book 9 traces Odysseus's in a number

---

[35] See Fantham (1992) 142–3 on the translation of *inlibata* as "without consummation."
[36] See Ahl (1976) 248–9; Fantham (1992) 144–5; Panoussi (2007) 120–4; Mulhern (2017) 445–8; and Fertik (2018) 462–4 on the "anti-wedding" here. In his account of the remarriage at *Cat. Min.* 52, Plut. does not address the wedding ceremony or the couple's sexual practices, an absence pointing to Lucan's hand in crafting the whole episode.
[37] Ahl (1976) 249 and 251.
[38] See Panoussi (2007) 123–4.

of ways, and that Lucan crafts Cato's arc from Books 2 to 9, beginning within the walls of his home and ending in indefinite absence abroad, as a reversal of the Odyssean model. Cato's story in the *Pharsalia* is anti-Odyssean from the start, and the foregrounding of the fleeting marital reunion with Marcia and their sexless marriage-bed underlines this contrast. If Odysseus's and Penelope's reunion in their marriage-bed in *Odyssey* 23 marks the completion of that poem's *nostos* narrative, then the reunion and conspicuous rejection of their old marriage-bed by Cato and Marcia conveys at once that an Odyssean *nostos* is unachievable for Cato. His journey—which will end in absence and death abroad—is marked from the outset as un-Odyssean, his *nostos* unattainable even before he has left home.

5.3. Pompey *discedens*

Immediately after the anti-wedding of Cato and Marcia, Lucan pick ups his narrative of Pompey's movements, with the segue "meanwhile, Magnus, departing (*discedens*) with his fearful army, took hold of the Campanian walls of the Dardanian settler"[39] (2.392-3). Fantham remarks that the choice of *discedens* to modify Pompey is "surprising" and that in his edition Luck preferred the reading *descendens* suggested by the corrector of the manuscript G.[40] But as the author of the *Commenta Bernensia* explained,[41] *discedens* picks up on the scene of mass flight from Rome that is lavishly told at 1.486-522, a passage concluding with the detail of Pompey himself on the run (*Pompeio fugiente*, 1.522). Ahl reads the focus here on Pompey's retreat as a marker of contrast with Cato's resolve,[42] but we also see here a line of continuity between Cato and Pompey: both are headed out of Italy, on similar journeys of devastation, never to return.

We read similar characterizations of Pompey across the poem. After his victory at Dyrrachium, Lucan has him declare: "I shall never, on the model of Caesar, return myself to my fatherland, and Rome will never see me return—unless I have put down my army" (6.319-21: '*numquam me Caesaris*' inquit | '*exemplo reddam patriae, numquamque uidebit* | *me nisi dimisso redeuntem milite Roma*'). While the character intends the remark as an assertion of his

---

[39] Capys, the Trojan exile said to have founded Capua.
[40] Fantham (1992) 156, citing Luck's 1985 edition.
[41] *Commenta ad* 2.392 reads: DISCEDENS *ab urbe*.
[42] Ahl (1976) 250.

refusal to threaten Rome with his army, and thus of his patriotic integrity, the reader sees the ironic foreboding in these words, enhanced by the anaphoric *numquam ... reddam, numquam ... redeuntem*. Later, prior to his doomed venture to Egypt, Lucan packs similar irony into Pompey's instruction to the astrologer on his ship to "leave behind Hesperia on the water and in the heavens" (8.189, *Hesperiam pelago caeloque relinquas*). Soon afterward, Lentulus gets to the heart of the matter when asking Pompey, of his plan to consult the Parthians, "Why must you be a deserter of the world?" (8.335: *quid transfuga mundi?*).

Pompey *discedens* is ever adrift and ever moving away from home in the *Pharsalia*, from Rome to Brundisium to Epirus to Thessaly to Lesbos and at last to Egypt. And while scholars have regularly read his journey eastward as a core component of the poem's anti-*Aeneid* design,[43] Lucan at the same time conspicuously casts Pompey's arc as a reversal of the Odyssean *nostos*. In his discussion of Pompey's indecisiveness, Ahl contrasts him with the resourceful Odysseus *polumechanos*.[44] But the connection with Homer's hero is more precise, in that the contrasts hinge on the fulcrum of *nostos*/anti-*nostos*, and at the same time expansive, in that this depiction of Pompey's anti-*nostos* runs across the poem. At a critical moment in the epic, on the morning of the Battle of Pharsalia in Book 7, Lucan appears to underscore this contrast with Odysseus. After Pompey delivers a characteristically uninspiring exhortation to his troops, Lucan writes:

>   sic fatur et arma
> permittit populis frenosque furentibus ira
> laxat et ut uictus uiolento nauita Coro   125
> dat regimen uentis ignauumque arte relicta
> puppis onus trahitur.

> So he speaks and entrusts arms to the nations, and loosens the reins on those raging with anger; and, just like a sailor overcome by the violent Northwest Wind, he gives his control over to the winds and, once he has abandoned his skill, is pulled around, just an idle burden on his ship. (7.123–7).

While much of the poem follows Pompey's drift on the seas, here even his actions as a commander on land are figured as those of a feckless sailor, one

---

[43] Henderson (1987) 149; Fantham (1992) 220–1; Leigh (1997) 149–50; Rossi (2000); Fratantuono (2012) 85–6.
[44] Ahl (1976) 153.

willing to abandon his craft (*arte relicta*) and be pulled around (*trahitur*). And this sailor, unlike the archetypal mariner from Homer's epic, will not ultimately overcome the waves that beset him and make it home.[45]

Just as he had opened Cato's story of centripedal movement within his home, Lucan begins the arc of anti-*nostos* for Pompey by putting great emphasis on the moment of departure from his homeland. In a passage that stretches across the close of Book 2 and the opening of Book 3, the poet zooms in on the general's farewell to Italy. As his fleet pulls away from Brundisium in Book 2's final lines, the narrator addresses Pompey:

> cum coniuge pulsus
> et natis totosque trahens in bella penates
> uadis adhuc ingens populis comitantibus exul.
> quaeritur indignae sedes longinqua ruinae.

> Driven off with your wife and children, and dragging your whole household with you into war, you venture out, still huge, with nations attending you—an exile. What is desired now is a faraway seat for your undeserved destruction. (2.728–31)

Lucan depicts Pompey as not just leaving home, but taking with him all that constitutes home—his wife, sons, and *penates*.[46] And he imagines the journey as a search for a new physical site (*sedes*) for his home, one that is far away (*longinqua*) and a seat of destruction (*ruinae*). The hallmarks of a *nostos* are all here, but dislocated, sent away with Pompey *from* his home to a far-off place of devastation. This conceit sets up the paradox that, for Pompey, a homecoming to Italy is not even possible: his home leaves with him.

Keeping his focus on this moment as Book 3 begins, Lucan writes that, while all of the sailors on Pompey's ship look ahead (*omnis in Ionios spectabat nauita fluctus*, 3.3), their leader keeps his eyes on Italy:

> solus ab Hesperia non flexit lumina terra
> Magnus, dum patrios portus, dum litora numquam   5

---

[45] And in this way Pompey has more in common with the feckless Latinus of *Aen.* 7.585–600, who figures his failure as a shipwreck (7.594).

[46] Leigh (1997) 150 fittingly compares *Aen.* 3.11–12 (*feror exsul in altum | cum sociis natoque penatibus et magnis dis*), though the inclusion at *Ph.* 2.728 of Pompey's spouse is important for the motif of anti-*nostos*.

ad uisus reditura suos tectumque cacumen
nubibus et dubios cernit uanescere montis.

Magnus alone did not move his eyes from the Hesperian land, until he realized that his fatherland's harbors, the shores that would never return to his sight, the hilltop covered by clouds, and uncertain mountains were vanishing. (3.4–7)

A fabulously indecisive character across the poem, here, in the resoluteness expressed by *solus . . . non flexit lumina* (3.4), Pompey exhibits great fixity of focus. Just as the hero of the *Odyssey* time and again demonstrates his resolve to return to Ithaca,[47] Lucan's Pompey shows a similar resolve in his concentration on his homeland. And in each tale, the leader's focus is highlighted by a contrast with his travel companions: Odysseus's crew had been famously distracted and self-destructive,[48] and here each of Pompey's sailors (*omnis nauita,* 3.3) looks away from Italy.[49] But a crucial difference lies in the fact that Pompey's resolute concentration on home comes as he is moving away from it, indeed at the very moment he is leaving his fatherland's harbors for good. Lucan demarcates and widens the distance between Pompey and his home by making the shores of Italy themselves actively participate in the dissolution of *nostos*: just as Pompey will never return to them (recall 6.319–21), they will never return to him (*litora numquam | ad uisus reditura suos,* 3.5–6).

5.4. The disunion of Pompey and Cornelia

Readers of the *Pharsalia* have observed similarities between the story of Pompey and Cornelia and that of Homer's Hector and Andromache;[50] and the poignant episodes of farewell in Books 5 and 8 certainly echo the famous final conversation between the Trojan couple in *Iliad* 6. But when we recall, with Murnaghan, that the Odyssean *nostos* is an achievement shared by husband and wife, then Lucan's extended concentration on

---

[47] See, as a sort of summary of Odysseus's acts of determination, the description of what he recounts to Penelope at *Od.* 23.306–41.
[48] Most consequentially when they eat Helios's cattle at *Od.* 12.352–398, resulting in Zeus's lethal punishment of them at 12.403–19.
[49] Morford (1967) 80 notes the symbolism of the contrast.
[50] See Leigh (1997) 113; Hutchinson (2013) 331; and Christophorou (2017) 368–72.

the rupture of Pompey's and Cornelia's union reads—like that of Cato and Marcia—as an inversion of that Homeric motif. The saga of these doomed lovers undoubtedly appeared in early sources, and we read many details of their encounters in Plutarch's *Life of Pompey* (especially at 74–5 and 78–9). But Lucan elevates Cornelia, the most fully developed female character in the *Pharsalia*, to the level of full participation in Pompey's story. Bruère discusses this emphasis and notes connections with Ovidian heroines at a few critical moments,[51] but when we look at Cornelia's participation in the epic as a whole, she emerges most meaningfully as a Penelope figure—but one marked by repeated failure to accomplish a lasting reunion.

The parting of Pompey and Cornelia along the Egyptian shore in Book 8 was surely included in earlier sources, as it is at Plutarch, *Pompey* 78–9. But Lucan chooses to narrate a moment of grandiose marital departure and disunion not once but twice, preempting the farewell in Book 8 with an extended description in Book 5 of their farewell at Lesbos, Cornelia's retreat during the war with Caesar (5.723–815). After Pompey explains his reasoning for placing Cornelia there (5.739–59), she delivers an impassioned response (5.762–90) that figures their parting as a split (5.765: *careo dimissa marito*, "sent off by him, I lose my spouse") and as a rupture of their marriage bonds (5.766: *rumpamus foedera taedae*). Significantly, as Lucan hints at 5.734–8 and 5.749–50 and then makes clear at 5.791, the entire conversation takes place in their bed, a staging detail that recalls Odysseus's and Penelope's extended bedroom conversation in *Odyssey* 23. Again, as in his treatment of Cato's and Marcia's ill-fated reunion, the poet concentrates almost obsessively on this token of their marriage-bond,[52] with the final image of Book 5 a close-up of Cornelia's "widowed bed" (*uiduo ... lecto*, 5.806):

>   nudumque marito
> non haerente latus. somno quam saepe grauata
> deceptis uacuum manibus conplexa cubile est
> atque oblita fugae quaesiuit nocte maritum!   810
> nam quamuis flamma tacitas urente medullas
> non iuuat in toto corpus iactare cubili:

---

[51] Bruère (1951b), focusing on parallels with Ovid's Alcyone and Ariadne. On their relationship in the poem, see too Narducci (2002) 294–8 and McCune (2014), comparing lovers in Latin elegy.

[52] Fratantuono (2012) 215: "Lucan crafts a sad ring, as the news of the dismissal is first given in bed, and the sequence ends with Cornelia in her new bed, alone."

seruatur pars illa tori. caruisse timebat
Pompeio; sed non superi tam laeta parabant:
instabat, miserae Magnum quae redderet, hora.   815

With her spouse no longer clinging to her, her side was now bare. How often did she, weighed down by sleep, embrace the empty bed with deceived hands and, forgetful of his flight, look for her husband in the night. For, though the flame of love is burning up her quiet marrow within, she does not want to throw her body across the whole bed: his part of the bed is preserved. She feared that she had lost Pompey. But the gods were not preparing such happy news: the hour was pressing on that would return Magnus to her, wretched. (5.807–15)

The picture of Pompey clinging (*marito . . . haerente*, 5.807–8) to Cornelia's side, coming soon after the characterization of her as the "faithful companion of Magnus" (*fida comes Magni*, 5.804), underlines the sense of the two of them as a pair, co-participants in the poem's action.

But then there is the repeated focus in 5.806 (*uiduo lecto*), 5.807–8 (*nudum latus*), 5.809 (*uaccum cubile*), and 5.811–12 on Pompey's physical absence from their marriage-bed, which is imagined as partitioned (5.813) and so in a sense cut up by his absence.[53] A contrast with the climactic reunion of Penelope and Odysseus on their deeply rooted, nearly immovable (*Od.* 23.184–94) marriage-bed emerges clearly. Nevertheless, the story of Lucan's lovers is not over: there *will* be a return and a reunion; the hour is coming that will bring a return (*redderet*, 5.815) for Pompey and Cornelia.

The reunion that comes, after the crushing defeat at Pharsalia, is of course dour and doomed once again. Pompey returns to Cornelia on Lesbos and will soon declare: "here has been my sacred home and my dear *penates*; here has been my Rome" (8.132–3: *hic sacra domus carique penates, | hic mihi Roma fuit*), a jarring[54] line that underscores not just the drift away from Rome that has come to define Pompey in the poem, but also the wholesale dislocation of his home that Lucan had cued in the final lines of Book 2 (2.728–31). Prior to this statement, Cornelia had met Pompey's embrace (8.66–70) and words of encouragement (8.72–85) with a speech of despair

---

[53] See McCune (2014) 188 on the image of the empty bed, drawing an analogy with the abandoned lover of elegy.
[54] See Fratantuono (2012) 318; and Mulhern (2017) 438–45 on Cornelia's emergence in the poem as the equivalent of "home" for Pompey.

(8.88–105) that Lucan again colors with the imagery of their marriage-bed. She begins by expressing the wish that she "had entered the marriage-bed of hated Caesar" (*o utinam in thalamos inuisi Caesaris issem*, 8.88), so that Caesar could suffer the misfortune that unions with her seem to bring.[55] After addressing Pompey as "undeserving of [her] marriage-bed" (*o thalamis indigne meis*, 8.95), she then bids the ghost of Pompey's deceased wife Julia to "avenge our bed, and come here and exact punishment from us" (*nostros ulta toros, ades huc atque exige poenas*, 8.103).[56] The *thalamus* of Cornelia, it is clear, brings with it not reunion but division and devastation. While the metonymy of both *thalamus* (OLD 2b) and *torus* (OLD 5b) for "marriage" is common, Cornelia's fixation here on the image of her calamitous marriage-bed seems to hearken back to the focus on that bed and its abandonment at the close of Book 5, and thus to develop further the strong counterpoint with the Odyssean narrative of reunion around Penelope's and Odysseus's marriage-bed.

In her final speech in the poem (9.55–108), a lament for her now dead husband that I will consider more fully in the next chapter, Cornelia picks up on the imagery of their marriage-bed one last time. Indignant that she could not participate in burial rites, she regrets that she was unable to "lie with her husband" (*incubuisse uiro*, 9.57). This is Cornelia's final wish, and indeed her wish throughout the poem. Lucan thus emphasizes one last time their failure to lie together in a lasting reunion and so to accomplish an Odyssean *nostos*. In the previous book, in Cornelia's final words to Pompey as she watches him board the fatal Egyptian skiff, Lucan had in fact made her comment on the recurrence of this theme when pleading:

> quo sine me crudelis abis? iterumne relinquor
> Thessalicis summota malis? numquam omine laeto
> distrahimur miseri.

> Where are you going off to without me, cruel one? Am I being left behind
> again, after being dispatched from the evils in Thessaly? Never under
> a happy omen are we, miserable ones, pulled apart from each other.
> (8.584–6)

---

[55] Before Pompey, Cornelia had been married to Publius Crassus, who died at Carrhae in 53 BCE.
[56] Drawing on the image that Julia's ghost had herself used when speaking to Pompey at 3.21: *fortuna est mutata toris*. ("Your fortune has changed with your bed"). Note, with Keith (2000) 87–8 and 127 and Chiu (2010), that Lucan also develops Julia as a destructive force.

The most recent commentator on Book 8 regarded Cornelia's words here as hyperbolic,[57] but his observation misses the point. This couple is defined across the poem by their shared failure to achieve a lasting reunion, by being ever pulled apart (*distrahimur*). It is fitting that, after her lament in Book 9, Lucan chooses to depict Cornelia at sea but "unbothered by the waves and the East wind that roars in the rigging" (9.113-14), praying for the elements that frightened the sailors (9.115); indeed, "ready for death, she lay there and favored the gusts of wind" (*conposita in mortem iacuit fauitque procellis*, 9.116). While Homer had underscored the mirroring of Penelope and Odysseus by comparing her, at the climactic moment of their reunion, with a shipwrecked sailor who at last reaches land (*Od.* 23.233-40),[58] in this culminating image Lucan aligns Cornelia and Pompey in their devastation at sea and failure to accomplish *nostos*. This is the state—of loss and death (note *conposita in mortem iacuit*[59])—in which this couple will at last be able to lie together.

5.5. Pompey's loss of homecoming

During his marriage-bed reunion with Penelope in *Odyssey* 23, Odysseus informs her of Tiresias's prophecy that another journey still awaits him (23.268-80 = 11.121-33); and so there is a "a momentary flash of an anti-*Odyssey*,"[60] of the possibility that his return will be denied. But Tiresias had assured Odysseus—as he later relays to Penelope—that he will have a peaceful death at home:

πᾶσι μάλ' ἐξείης. θάνατος δέ τοι ἐξ ἁλὸς αὐτῷ
ἀβληχρὸς μάλα τοῖος ἐλεύσεται, ὅς κέ σε πέφνῃ
γήρᾳ ὕπο λιπαρῷ ἀρημένον· ἀμφὶ δὲ λαοὶ
ὄλβιοι ἔσσονται. τὰ δέ τοι νημερτέα εἴρω.'

And death shall come to you yourself away from the sea, the gentlest imaginable, that shall lay you low when you are overcome with sleek old age,

---

[57] Mayer (1981) 154 (on 8.585): "like Miss Joliffe in Meade Faulkner's *The Nebuly Coat*, Cornelia 'falls into a common hyperbole in qualifying an isolated action as a habit.'"

[58] De Jong (2001) 559: "the effect is a merging of the experiences of man and wife."

[59] *Iaceo* is commonly used of lying defeated (*OLD* 5a; see 7.115 and 7.845) or dead (*OLD* 6; see 4.394 and 4.803).

[60] Segal (1992) 20. See too Roberts (1997) 252-3 on this episode as "aftermath."

and your people shall be dwelling in prosperity around you. This is the truth that I tell you. (*Od.* 11.134–7 [= 23.281–4]; trans. by A. T. Murray; rev. by G. E. Dimock)

This passage, while affirming the lastingness of Odysseus's *nostos*, also underscores another fundamental component of it, to go with his reunion with Penelope: the company and prosperity of his people at death. Michael von Albrecht has considered this passage alongside Lucan's epic, noting the contrast between Odysseus's return home and gentle death and Pompey's flight from home and violent death.[61] In light of the prolonged emphasis Lucan puts on Pompey's failure to enjoy the company and love of his people at death, further consideration of this Odyssean contrast is fitting.

The spotlight on the Roman people's absence from Pompey's death comes in two prominent passages that in a sense frame the two-book saga of his defeat at Pharsalia and demise in Egypt. The first is the picture of Pompey's dream, on the night before the battle, of entering his theater in Rome to the applause of the throng inside. It is clear that this story appeared in a source, as its inclusion at, e.g., Plutarch, *Pompey* 68.2 and Florus 2.13.45 seems to demonstrate.[62] But Lucan develops the episode with great fullness (7.7–44), and with particular attention to the prominence of the Roman people in Pompey's dream. He had introduced the man's attachment to the people of Rome in his initial character sketch in Book 1,[63] where we read that Pompey, "a seeker of fame, gave much to the mob, was wholly driven by popular breezes, and took joy in the applause within his theater" (1.131–3). In Book 7 the dreaming general "seemed to see in the seating of Pompey's Theater an uncountable image of the Roman people" (7.9–10). When considering possible meanings of the dream, the narrator proposes that "Fortune gave Rome to you in this way since you would be forbidden to see (*cernere*) your fatherland home again" (7.23–4). Pompey will be denied the sight of his "fatherland home" (*patrias . . . sedes*)—the extended gaze granted him at the outset of Book 3 (recall *non flexit lumina* and *cernit* at 3.4 and 3.7) will indeed be his last. But at 7.29–39 the poet incorporates an extended counterfactual in which Pompey returns to Rome before death and is greeted by the

---

[61] von Albrecht (1970) 308.
[62] Lanzarone (2016) 79 and Roche (2019) 60. And note (with n. 104 in Chapter 4) that Lucan may have been an important source for Florus.
[63] Ahl (1976) 178 connects the two passages. See too Roche (2009) 183 and Lanzarone (2016) 83. Leigh (1997) 114: "Lucan's Pompey is a showman, never happier than when amidst the adoring audience of his own theatre at Rome."

Roman people in a proper farewell. Lucan animates the Roman populace by picturing it as a collective entity (*tua Roma*, 7.29;[64] *patriae*, 7.30; and then as the subject, *illa*, in the poignant reference to their prayers at 7.34-6); and also through the individualized images of a young man, an old man, a child, and a crowd of weeping women (7.37-9). The description in 7.32 of the love that Rome and Pompey might have shared on that occasion (<u>*extremum* tanti *fructum* raperetis *amoris*</u>) is identical to the phrasing used of the love he and Cornelia shared and had to cut off (<u>*extremusque perit tam longi fructus amoris*</u>, 5.794).[65] The echo compels us to read together these two losses of reunion—with one's spouse and one's people—that are both fundamental to an Odyssean homecoming; the two losses thematically compound one another, reinforcing the sense of the deprivation of *nostos* from Pompey.

The second of the two passages underlining Pompey's failure to reunite with his people comes at the very end of Book 8, in the narrator's reflection on the meagerness of Pompey's Egyptian grave (8.823-72). Part of his address focuses on the wish that Pompey's ashes might be returned to Rome:

tu quoque, cum saeuo dederis iam templa tyranno,
nondum Pompei cineres, o Roma, petisti;
exul adhuc iacet umbra ducis.

You too, Roma, though you have already given temples to the savage tyrant,
have not yet sought out Pompey's ashes. The leader's shade still lies adrift.
(8.835-7)

As often in the poem, here the narrator takes the perspective of the Rome of Lucan's lifetime, after Caesar's victory and apotheosis. He decries the fact that Pompey is still being buffeted about (*exul adhuc*, 8.837), still a *transfuga mundi*, still Pompey *discedens*, still away from home in perpetual absence and devastation. He soon pivots to address Pompey's ghost and proposes that perhaps, at a time when Rome is in need of relief from a disaster, "by the plan and order of the gods, you will cross over to your city, Magnus, (*in urbem, | Magne, tuam*) and the high priest will take your ashes" (8.849-50). The characterization of Rome as "your city" emphasizes again, as in the phrase *tua*

---

[64] Lanzarone (2016) 113 writes that the expression *tua Roma* "sintetizza l'attaccamento di Roma a Pompeo."
[65] Ahl (1976) 180-1.

206 THUNDER AND LAMENT

Roma at 7.29,[66] the personal, affectionate relationship between Pompey and his homeland. But like the dream at the opening of Book 7, this prayer gets at the abiding failure of Pompey to achieve a *nostos*; a rightful and rite-ful return to the company of his people is still due. At the outset of Book 9, Lucan does grant Pompey a sort of spiritual homecoming, as his shade, after further leaping (*prosiluit*, 9.3) and flying (*uolitauit*, 9.16) about, settles (*sedit*, 9.18) in the breast of Brutus and establishes itself (*posuit se*, 9.18) in Cato's heart. But there is an impermanence to this arrival, too, an opening foreclosing any sense of abiding *nostos*: beyond the ultimate failure of Cato and Brutus to fend off Caesarism, Pompey's spirit, we had learned at 8.835–7, will continue to lack the peaceful repose—for himself and his people—that Tiresias promises Odysseus, remaining ever adrift, *exul adhuc*.

5.6. Caesar against "home"

The stories of Cato and Pompey, both in history and in the *Pharsalia*, come to an end abroad, with the men never returning to their homelands. The story of the historical Caesar of course does not conclude away from home: as Lucan repeatedly reminds the reader,[67] Caesar's end comes in his assassination in the heart of Rome, at a meeting of the Senate. But his arc in the *Pharsalia* has perhaps the clearest makings of an anti-Odyssean narrative, as a lasting return to his homeland is conspicuously denied in several ways, while at the same time the character of Caesar realizes a spirit of both anti-"home" and anti-*nostos*. Put another way, both the movement of the poem and Caesar himself assert opposition to any sense of homecoming and return.

The poem's very first episode draws attention to Caesar's status as a problematic figure of return, as he arrives in Italy after nine years of wanderlust and conquest in Gaul—but with the personification of his homeland, the *patriae trepidantis imago* (1.186) striving to thwart that return. In Chapter 1, I considered how this passage marks Lucan's trampling of the Homeric-Ennian-Virgilian epic tradition; and here he also introduces the theme of Caesar's pursuit/attack of his homeland, of a return home that is disruptive and destructive. Here we may see a particular point where Lucan takes an opening from the *Odyssey*—the return of Odysseus that is personally restorative but

---

[66] Mayer (1981) 188 compares the two phrases.
[67] See 2.283–4, 5.206–8, 7.451, 7.586–96, 7.782, 8.609–10, 9.17–18, 10.340–2, and 10.528.

also leads to a spell of vicious civil war—and expands it to stretch across his story. Over the ensuing three books, Caesar makes it down the peninsula and ultimately to Rome itself. In a pointed contrast with Pompey's pained farewell to his fatherland's harbors (*patrios portus*, 3.5) earlier in Book 3, Caesar successfully reaches/attacks the fatherland's homes (*tecta petit patriae*, 3.73).[68] He will proceed to take possession of the Senate and treasury (3.97–168) and in Book 5 makes a second victorious return/attack of the city (*petit trepidam . . . Romam*, 5.381) to shore up his strength and the pillars of Caesarism (5.381–402).

So Caesar's arc in the poem begins with return from absence and then devastation *of* home. But the exploration of Caesar as an anti-Odyssean figure then plays out in wildly different ways over the remainder of the poem. When the *Pharsalia* closes, he, like Cato and Pompey, is far afield, off in Egypt, trapped with no *nostos* in sight. I will return to Caesar's settlement in Egypt in Book 10, but first we must consider his third and final attempt to get home, his effort to contact Antony's delaying troops in Italy by crossing over the Adriatic from Illyria in a small boat (5.476–702). A number of sources mention a mission of this sort,[69] but Lucan expands it into a characteristically over-the-top episode, focusing first on Caesar's escape from his camp and strong-arm recruitment of the skipper Amyclas (5.504–93), then on the vast storm that strikes the boat (5.593–653), next on Caesar's speech of bravado during the storm (5.654–671) and the boat's safe landing—not in Italy, but back in Illyria (5.672–7)—and finally on the reaction of Caesar's companions to the venture (5.678–702).

In his detailed treatment of this passage, Mark Morford discusses the number and complexity of literary models that went into Lucan's development of the storm scene.[70] Morford begins by observing that "[s]torms are part of the furniture of Epic" and that "Homer's storms provided the elements of all that followed."[71] The Homeric passage that seemed to exert the greatest influence on later storm scenes is the description in *Odyssey* 5 of the storm sent by Poseidon during Odysseus's passage from Calypso's island to the land

---

[68] See Hunink (1992) 67 on the language of attack here.

[69] Val. Max. 9.8.2; Suet., *Caes.* 58; Plut., *Caes.* 38; App. *BC* 2.56–8; and Cass. Dio 41.46. See Matthews (2008) 307–14, a compendium of the details in each source, as well as Morford (1967) 37, suggesting that Livy is the original source, and Barratt (1979) 156.

[70] Morford (1967) 20–36 on the literary background for storm scenes in the *Ph.*; and 37–44 on 5.504–677 in particular. See too Day (2013) 143–56, arguing that Lucan's storm "outdoes its epic models" (146).

[71] Morford (1967) 20.

of the Phaeacians. Here Homer pictures the four cardinal winds (the North, South, East, and West) blowing together to roll a wave toward Odysseus's raft (*Od.* 5.295–6);[72] and the inclusion of named, often personified winds becomes commonplace in later literary accounts of storms, with the elder Pliny identifying Homer as the source for the ancients' understanding of the four winds (*NH* 2.119). During the storm on the Adriatic that strikes Caesar, Lucan stretches the four winds' activity across fifteen lines (5.598–612), each wind bringing with it the sea from its region of the globe.[73]

Another clear point of contact with *Odyssey* 5 comes in the speech Caesar gives at the height of the storm at 5.654–71. At *Od.* 5.299–312, Homer's hero, mid-storm and certain of a death at sea, decries his failure to reach his fatherland (5.301) and then counts as "three and four times blessed" (5.306) the Greeks who died at Troy and received proper funeral rites and the accompanying *kleos* (5.306–11). This is a definitive moment in the *Odyssey*, one Virgil would conspicuously emulate in the opening episode of the *Aeneid* (*Aen.* 1.94–101) during the storm along the African coast set off by Juno. When Lucan's Caesar is similarly tossed at sea and considers whether "the glory of my death has been given to the sea, and I am being kept from [death in] wars" (5.656–7: *si gloria leti | est pelago donata mei bellisque negamur*), the reader certainly recalls Aeneas's speech in his perilous passage to Italy. And while readers of *Pharsalia* 5 have concentrated on counterpoints with Aeneas's speech and situation,[74] a number of important details in Lucan's passage connect it more closely with the Homeric model lying behind the Virgilian one.[75] First, Homer's and Lucan's heroes both face the storm as isolated figures, Odysseus alone on his raft and Caesar in a tiny boat accompanied only by Amyclas (in contrast with Aeneas, who is leading a fleet of Trojan refugees). Both characters are in fact pointedly separated from their companions: Odysseus has already lost his men at sea, and we will read after the storm that Caesar's troops thought he had abandoned them (see.

---

[72] *Od.* 5.295–6: σὺν δ' Εὖρός τε Νότος τ' ἔπεσον Ζέφυρός τε δυσαὴς | καὶ Βορέης αἰθρηγενέτης, μέγα κῦμα κυλίνδων.

[73] See Morford (1967) 40–2, who notes that Lucan's passage is closest to the description at Sen., *Ag.* 474–90. Matthews (2008) 315 regards Lucan's as a "fairly conventional battle of the winds."

[74] Quint (1993) 137–8; Fratantuono (2012) 201–2; and Day (2013) 152. Fratantuono (2012) 202–3 proposes that evocations of the storm that kills Ceyx and keeps him from home in Ov., *Met.* 11.474–572, and of the subsequent failure of Priam's son Aesacus to reach Hesperia (*Met.* 11.749–95), enhance the sense that "Caesar will fail in his attempt to reinvent the settlement of the *Aeneid*" (203).

[75] See Matthews (2008) 225–7 and 244; and Hutchinson (2013) 330–1, writing, "Aeneas' speech at Virg. *Aen.* 1.94–101 is clearly connected; but the intertextuality gains more force from setting that speech in its Homeric tradition."

5.682–99, esp. 5.683 and 5.688[76]). In his speech during the storm, Lucan's Caesar, like Odysseus (*Od.* 5.303–4) but unlike Aeneas, blames the gods for the storm (5.654–5 and 658–9).[77] And the longing for a proper burial that Odysseus (*Od.* 5.311), though not Aeneas, voices is matched but inverted by Caesar's exclamation "As for me, o gods above—I have no need for a funeral... I can do without a grave and pyre" (5.668–70).

In the following line, the final line of his speech, Caesar qualifies his dismissiveness of burial with the proviso "as long as I am always feared and expected by every land" (5.671: *dum metuar semper terraque exspecter ab omni*). Lucan's Caesar embraces death at sea and the possibility that, with his fate unknown to others, he could live on as a haunting figure always and everywhere. Ahl contrasts Odysseus's and Aeneas's anxiety about an unheroic death with the "perverse kind of immortality in death" that Lucan's Caesar anticipates in a death at sea.[78] But another critical counterpoint, and particularly with the Odyssean passage, lies in Caesar's rejection of the very notion that a return home is important. Whereas Odysseus had expressed the specific fear (δείδω, *Od.* 5.300) that he would fill up with woes "before he reached his fatherland" (*Od.* 5.301), Caesar asserts that he is fearless (*intrepidus*, 5.658[79]) and will accept any death the gods give him (5.658), making no mention of reaching home. Far from being afraid, he imagines himself as a *source* of fear, eternally haunting every land (recall *semper terraque exspecter ab omni*, 5.671). Lucan's Caesar—so different from the Odysseus of *Odyssey* 5 and the many epic heirs to his lot—would be happy to remain forever anticipated, forever out in the world, forever not-home.

5.7. Caesar the homewrecker

The motif in this scene of the self-satisfied Caesar as a figure of anti-*nostos* may be enhanced by a curious inclusion at the outset of the passage. When describing Caesar's recruitment of the skipper Amyclas, Lucan dwells

---

[76] With Pitcher (2008).

[77] Even though, as Ahl (1976) 208 discusses, the narrator makes no mention of divine causation for the storm.

[78] Ahl (1976) 208. So too Matthews (2008) 225 and McClellan (2019) 143, contrasting also the wishes for burial by Achilles at *Il.* 21.273–82 and Ceyx and his crew at Ov., *Met.* 11.539–42 and 564–5. On Caesar's bold statements here, see also Morford (1967) 44; Dinter (2012) 85–6; and Day (2013) 152–6.

[79] Matthews (2008) 232 notes the contrast.

extensively on the man's humble seaside home. At 5.515–18 we read of its safety (*secura . . . domus*, 5.515–16) and quaint makeshift construction out of various maritime materials, and at 5.526–31 of Amyclas's safety from the cares of war (*securus belli*, 5.526[80]). The narrator then apostrophizes his carefree life and the simplicity of his meager dwelling (5.527–8: *o uitae tuta facultas | pauperis angustique lares!*), to be contrasted with the temples and city walls that would surely fear a knock from Caesar (5.528–31). Morford has read the passage as providing "an opportunity for Lucan to slip in a *locus communis* on the virtues of the simple life,"[81] but there is much more going on here. Just after his initial description of the humble abode, Lucan writes:

> haec Caesar bis terque manu quassantia tectum
> limina commouit. molli consurgit Amyclas
> quem dabat alga toro. "quisnam mea naufragus" inquit
> "tecta petit, aut quem nostrae fortuna coegit
> auxilium sperare casae?"

> This threshold Caesar shook with his hand two and three times—a move that shattered the roof. Amyclas got up from the soft bed that seaweed was providing him and said, "Who is this shipwrecked man pursuing/ attacking my home? Or whom has fortune led to hope for assistance from my hut?" (5.519–23)

Immediately following the picturesque description of Amyclas's abode comes an attack on that home. The verb Lucan uses for Caesar's first action is the violent *commoueo* and then, for what happens to the hut's roof, a form of *quasso*, which he uses elsewhere only of destruction in war.[82] Amyclas immediately identifies this aggressive act for what it is, asking who is "pursuing/ attacking" his home (*mea . . . tecta petit*), a phrase that echoes and builds upon the use of these same words for Caesar's arrival at (attack on) Rome at 3.73 (*tecta petit patriae*). Even this quaint, isolated home will not be safe from the brutal incursions of Caesar's war. The entire conceit of the scene inverts the peaceful meeting in *Odyssey* 14 between Odysseus and Eumaeus

---

[80] Fratantuono (2012) 198 notes this repetition.
[81] Morford (1967) 38. See too Fratantuono (2012) 198. On the encounter with Amyclas, see also Tracy (2016) 235–8 and Seidman (2017) 75–82.
[82] See 6.22 and 10.479, as well as *quassabile* at 6.136.

at the swineherd's similarly humble hut (see esp. 14.48–52), a passage that marks the hero's arrival and is crucial to his *nostos*. The episode of violent wreckage at Amyclas's hut operates in the opposite way, anticipating the disdain for the very idea of *nostos* that Caesar will articulate during the storm at 5.654–71, establishing him as a destroyer of homes and "home," as a literal homewrecker.

5.8. Caesar's un-Odyssean landing

This depiction at the beginning of the episode of Caesar as a figure of anti-*nostos* is powerfully underscored at the conclusion of the storm scene. His escape from the storm and his landing in many ways recall but reverse the sequence in *Odyssey* 5, where Homer's hero makes it out of the storm and onto land, here not Ithaca but Scheria, a necessary stop on his way home (as Zeus states at 5.34–5); from there the Phaeacians will escort him home (13.78–125).[83] The passage begins when Odysseus's speech is interrupted by a great wave, which shatters his mast and sail, reducing his boat to a raft, and sends him adrift (5.313–18). The hero's landing then stretches out in painful fashion, with seventy lines passing between his first sight of land and the kiss he eventually plants on the earth (5.392–463). The cragginess of the shore (5.405) makes landing difficult, with the result that a wave strikes him against the rocks and sends him back out to sea again (5.424–35); he is saved only by the intervention of Athena, who leads him along the shore to the mouth of a river (5.436–44). We find many of these details echoed, condensed, and countered in Caesar's moment of landing. For starters, just like Odysseus, Caesar has his speech interrupted by a wave:

> haec fatum decumus, dictu mirabile, fluctus
> inualida cum puppe leuat, nec rursus ab alto
> aggere deiecit pelagi sed pertulit unda
> scruposisque angusta uacant ubi litora saxis
> inposuit terrae. pariter tot regna, tot urbes
> fortunamque suam tacta tellure recepit.

---

[83] See Loney (2019) on the important part of *pompē* (the "conveyance" by others, notably the Phaeacians) in the story of the *Od*.

As he said these things, a tenth wave—marvelous to tell—lifted him up, along with his shoddy boat, and it did not throw him back again from a high mound of sea; but a wave brought him out to where a narrow stretch of shore is free of craggy rocks, and placed him on land. As he touched the earth, at once he got back so many kingdoms, so many cities, and his own fortune. (5.672–7)

Here the great wave does not sink Caesar and shatter his boat, as it did to Odysseus, but rather lifts (*leuat*, 5.673) them both to shore. And he is pointedly *not* thrown out to sea again (*nec rursus ab alto | aggere deiecit pelagi*, 5.673–4), as Odysseus had been, but instead the wave escorts (*pertulit*, 5.674) him and places him on land (*inposuit terrae*, 5.676), on a stretch of shore that is specified as free of the craggy rocks (*scruposisque . . . uacant ubi litora saxis*, 5.675) that had beleaguered Odysseus. The counterpoints are striking, and the succinctness of the description itself marks a sharp contrast with the torturous 150-line affair that Homer's hero endures.

So Lucan's Caesar does not struggle in the paradigmatic Odyssean way; he is made to conspicuously avoid the travails and devastation of an Odysseus. And perhaps this contrast prepares the reader for a more fundamental and more significant distinction. While Odysseus's struggle ultimately lands him at a critical place for his *nostos*, with the Phaeacians who will assist his homecoming, Caesar gets . . . nowhere. The ambiguity of *inposuit terrae* (5.676) leaves the reader in suspense—the author of the *Commenta Bernensia* felt the need to gloss this line with *unde nauigauerat*—but we soon learn (5.678–9) that the spot of his landing is back in Illyria, not Italy.[84] Caesar does not make it home.

Furthermore, if reading this passage as a sort of inverse of the storm scene in *Odyssey* 5, then the wording of the scene's conclusion may be important. When Lucan writes, "as he touched the earth, at once he got back so many kingdoms, so many cities (*tot regna, tot urbes*), and his own fortune" (5.676–7), we may again think of Homer's hero. The *Odyssey*'s proem introduces him as "many-turned" (πολύτροπον, 1.1), one who was "driven off in many ways" (πολλὰ | πλάγχθη, 1.2), "saw the cities and learned the thoughts of many men" (πολλῶν δ' ἀνθρώπων ἴδεν ἄστεα καὶ νόον ἔγνω, 1.3) and "at sea suffered many pains in his heart" (πολλὰ δ' ὅ γ' ἐν πόντῳ πάθεν ἄλγεα

---

[84] See Pitcher (2008) and Fratantuono (2012) 208 ("The audience would do well to imagine that this is an Italian landing, but Lucan soon reveals the trick").

ὃν κατὰ θυμόν, 1.4). Odysseus is definitively the man of many travels and travails;[85] and here, at 5.676-7, Lucan characterizes Caesar in a similar way as one who had entered, acquired, and now retains many kingdoms and cities, with the anaphora of *tot regna, tot urbes* emphasizing the scope of his wanderings, just as the repeated use of πολ- and πολλ- does in *Odyssey* 1.1-4 and beyond.[86] Is this echo—like those at Catullus, 101.1, and then Virgil, *Aeneid* 6.692-3[87]—another way in which Lucan invites comparison with Homer's celebrated "man of many"? It would be a fitting spot to do so, right at the moment when he is underscoring a fundamental disjunction between his hero and Odysseus. Though Caesar regains his many kingdoms and cities, in this poem that blows up notions of *nostos* he does not regain his homeland.

5.9. Caesar at home in Egypt?

Lucan's depiction of Caesar as a figure of anti-*nostos* extends into the characterization of him as another who, like Cato and Pompey but in distinct ways, fails at achieving an Odyssean domestic reunion. The fact that Lucan never depicts or even names Caesar's wife Calpurnia is notable in this regard, if not itself extraordinary: though she married him in 59 BCE and survived his death in 44, Calpurnia is not mentioned in Caesar's own *commentarii*, while Plutarch, Suetonius, and Appian note the marriage and mention her again only in the period around the assassination.[88] Perhaps more significant is the context of Lucan's one reference to that marriage: during his stay in Egypt with Cleopatra in Book 10. The inclusion of Caesar's relationship with the Egyptian queen is, again, far from unique,[89] but what catches our attention is how frequently, across Book 10, Lucan depicts Caesar as at *home* in Egypt, at home with the Egyptian dynast. Soon after introducing Cleopatra (10.56), he pictures Caesar in

---

[85] See also Odysseus's self-introduction at *Od.* 16.205-6. De Jong (2001) 396 notes the many times that Odysseus self-identifies as the man of many sufferings; see too Goldhill (1991) 3-4.

[86] *Tot . . . tot* is a favorite anaphora of Lucan's, especially in his characterization of Caesar's domination. Note, e.g., the descriptions of the city walls and citadels that gave in to Caesar at 2.653-4 (*tot moenia . . . tot . . . arces*) and of the many deaths and crimes that Thessaly witnessed at 7.848-9 (*tot mortibus . . . tot scelerum fatis*).

[87] Cat 101.1: *multas per gentes et multa per aequora uectus*; *Aen.* 6.692: *quas . . . terras et quanta per aequora uectum*. See Conte (1986 [1974]) 32-7.

[88] On the marriage, see Plut., *Caes.* 14.7; Suet., *Caes.* 21.1; and App., *BC* 2.14. On her dreams about the assassination, see Plut., *Caes.* 63-4; Suet., *Caes* 81.3; and App., *BC* 2.115.

[89] See, e.g., Plut., *Caes.* 49; Suet., *Caes.* 35 and 52; App., *BC* 2.84 and 90; and Cass. Dio 42.34-44.

bed with her (10.68–9), leading him to condemn Caesar for "mixing with warfare an unlawful marriage-bed and offspring not from his spouse" (10.75–6: *miscuit armis | inlicitosque toros et non ex coniuge partus*). This is the lone reference to Calpurnia, as the non-mother of the child Caesar fathers with Cleopatra. While Cato and Marcia resumed the bonds of their old bed, but without consummation (*foedera prisci | inlibata tori*, 2.341–2), Caesar's inversion of a proper marriage-bed comes in its illegality (*inlicitosque toros*, 10.76).[90]

And there are additional signs that Egypt has become home for Caesar. Lucan describes at length his un-Roman comfort at the luxurious feast spread for him (10.136–71), an event Caesar conspicuously aims to prolong with conversation (10.172–4). Later, when narrating the battle between Caesar and the forces led by Pothinus (10.434–546), Lucan stages the first part of the contest deep within the palace in Alexandria, where he describes Caesar as searching for the safety of home:

> ceu puer inbellis uel captis femina muris,
> quaerit tuta domus; spem uitae in limine clauso
> ponit, et incerto lustrat uagus atria cursu
>
> Like a defenseless boy or a woman when her city's walls have been captured, he seeks the safe parts of the home. He places his hope for survival in an enclosed doorway, and he courses the hallways, wandering around on an uncertain path. (10.458–60)

While recalling the panic in the Trojan palace in *Aeneid* 2,[91] the image of Caesar wandering (*uagus*) and seeking the comfort of home (*quaerit tuta domus*) unmistakably evokes the Odyssean arc. Just previously in this passage he had described Caesar as being "attacked by weapons, deep within the household (*intraque penates*)" (10.453–4), and soon writes that "now weapons are crashing against the home and shattering the household" (10.479: *inque domum iam tela cadunt quassantque penates*), and then that

---

[90] See Keith (2000) 89 on Cleopatra as a seducing Fury (so 10.59); Caston (2011) 147–50 comparing her with a ruthless elegiac lover; and Mulhern (2017) 450–4 on Caesar's dissociation from Rome through his association with Cleopatra.

[91] See *Aen.* 2.483 (*apparet domus intus et atria longa patescunt*) and esp. 2.528 (*uacua atria lustrat*) of Polites, a moment that Lucan had also recalled when depicting the defeated and adrift Pompey at 8.62 (*lustrat uacuas ... harenas*). See Narducci (2002) 295.

"the young troops, devoid of a plan, split up and circle the vast household (*uastos . . . penates*)" (10.482–3). It is striking that, three times in quick succession, Lucan uses this term for the old Latin household deities (*OLD* 1), and, by metonymy, for one's home more generally (*OLD* 3 and 4) to describe an attack on Caesar's residence—in Egypt. The notion of what is home, of where this Roman's penates reside, has been turned upside down.[92] Just as for the adrift Pompey who comes to see his home and penates in Lesbos (recall 8.132: *hic sacra domus carique penates*), for the wandering Caesar "home" itself has transformed.

For the final lines of the poem, the fighting moves out of the palace, and Caesar is pressed hard on the narrow mole connecting Alexandria with the promontory Pharos. Rimell has considered how Lucan packs these final lines with the language of entrapment, and so thematically and textually encloses Caesar.[93] The result, Rimell argues, is that the poem as we have it concludes in a state of both enclosure and charged possibility.[94] It is also important to consider *where* Lucan has chosen to enclose and in a sense "freeze-frame" Caesar. The location has unmistakably Odyssean associations. When he introduces Pharos, he writes that it "once stood as an island in the middle of the sea, at the time of the prophet Proteus; but now it is right next to the walls of Alexandria" (10.509–11). It is hard not to recall the *locus classicus* for the figure of Proteus, *Odyssey* 4.333–592. There Menelaus recounts to Telemachus that, during his own difficult journey home from Troy, he had been stranded on Pharos for twenty days before meeting with the prophetic, shape-shifting god in a nearby cave. There Proteus had told Menelaus of many of the Greek heroes' arduous and sometimes deadly journeys home.

That Lucan is evoking the Odyssean passage seems clear from the parallels in diction and structure between Lucan's statement introducing Pharos and Homer's introduction of the island in *Odyssey* 4:

Od. 4.354: νῆσος ἔπειτά τις ἔστι πολυκλύστῳ ἐνὶ πόντῳ
and then there is an island in the many-waved sea

---

[92] Fratantuono (2012) 424 draws a contrast with Aeneas's transfer of the Trojan Penates to Rome: "Caesar's Penates should be in Rome, in his home; he has left that home behind."
[93] Rimell (2015) 244–52.
[94] Rimell (2015) 252. See also my discussion in Chapter 3.

Ph. 10.509–10:   insula quondam
in medio stetit illa mari sub tempore uatis
Proteos, at nunc est Pellaeis proxima muris

it once stood as that famous island in the middle of the sea at the time of
the prophet Proteus; but now it is right next to the walls of Alexandria.

Note the correspondences in the prepositional phrases that set the scene
(πολυκλύστῳ ἐνὶ πόντῳ and *in medio . . . mari*) and the subjects (νῆσός τις
and *insula illa*), but with a progression from the indefinite τις ("a") to the demonstrative *illa* ("that famous"), a progression underscored by the temporal movement from *quondam* and *sub tempore uatis Proteos* to *nunc*. Pointing to the poetry of Proteus (*uatis Proteos*) and by extension Homer, Lucan, like Virgil before him,[95] returns to and traverses that now-famous epic ground. And again a contrast emerges. In the *Odyssey*, Menelaus of course tells his tale after escaping Proteus's lair and returning home to Sparta (see *Od*. 4.585–6 of the arrival). The Caesar of *Pharsalia* 10 revisits that spot of abandonment and struggle—but of ultimate escape and return for Menelaus—and he is entrapped there. This is the condition in which Lucan freezes him at the end of the poem: absent from home, suffering the devastation of the military conflict in Egypt, with "no pathway to safety, no means of escape, and no strength" (10.538–9: *uia nulla salutis, | non fuga, non uirtus*), no return home in view.

5.10. *Populus Romanus conuersus*

In his study of the significance of the Egyptian episode in Lucan's poem, Jonathan Tracy emphasizes the continuities in Caesar's ravenous character from earlier books into Book 10.[96] I have aimed to demonstrate that a similar continuity of thematic focus on the rejection of "home" and *nostos* carries across the poem and into Book 10. The Caesar at home away from Rome and then in peril at the geographical and textual *locus* of Pharos, with no way out, is an extension of the Caesar who is denied—and himself denies the

---

[95] See Thomas (1988a, vol. 2) 217 and Gale (2003) 335–6 on the *uates* Proteus in *G*. 4.
[96] Tracy (2014) 123–6 (126: "he continues to propagate the moral chaos that underlies the conflict").

significance of—a return to Italy in the elaborate set piece of Book 5. Lucan's Caesar, as subject and object, is a sort of embodiment of the poem's rejection of *nostos*. While Roma in Book 1 had failed in her efforts to repel his homecoming, the poem succeeds.

Caesar's arc of anti-*nostos*, though implosively destructive in unique ways, operates in conjunction with Cato's and Pompey's narratives of absence, devastation, and failure to return. David Quint has identified part of this design, writing that the *Pharsalia* "shows the victorious Caesar, as well as the defeated Pompey, cast in the role of a helpless romance wanderer."[97] But he applies too narrow an understanding of "romance narrative" when characterizing Caesar's battle with the storm and repulsion from Italy as "a separate episode" among the "purple passages that are to be admired for their own sake, rather than for their connection to a continuous narrative."[98] I hope this chapter has shown that there *is* a continuity and kinship in the arcs of the poem's three most developed characters, around the trope of anti-*nostos*. And this motif comes out in the words and actions of other characters, too. For example, when the Senate meets in Epirus at the outset of Book 5, the consuls call together "the senators who are wandering about for the tasks of war" (*uagos belli per munia patres*, 5.8), an image that leaves the reader wondering whether these wanderers will ever return home. Lucan then plays up the sense of absence from their true home by writing that "a foreign and filthy home took in Rome's leaders" (*peregrina ac sordida sedes | Romanos cepit proceres*, 5.9–10). The consul Lentulus's efforts to convince the adrift senators not to think about "how far we sit from our homes" (*quamque procul tectis . . . sedeamus*, 5.19) fall flat,[99] and most of these men indeed never make it home. Later, one of the Cilican troops fighting for the senatorial cause beseeches Cato after the death of Pompey, "Allow me to return to my fatherland penates, my abandoned home, and my sweet children" (*patrios permitte penates | desertamque domum dulcesque reuisere natos*, 9.230–1). Like others fighting for Rome in the poem, this cohort of Cilican soldiers—soon headed for a crash landing and loss in Libya—will not get home.[100]

At the same time, Lucan dwells on the inversion of *nostos* for the Roman people as a collective entity. When we recall that the first character Lucan

---

[97] Quint (1993) 139–40.
[98] Quint (1993) 140.
[99] See Masters (1992) 99; Bexley (2009) 463–4; and Mulhern (2020) 211 on the delusions of Lentulus's speech; and Ducos (2010) on Lucan's depiction of the Senate across the poem.
[100] See Fertik (2018) 465–6 on the Cilicans' loss of hearth and family here.

introduces in the proem—the poem's main character—is the Roman people (*populum*, 1.2), then the other trajectories of anti-*nostos* that we have considered in this chapter come to read as what Alden in her study of the *Odyssey* has called "para-narratives," storylines that are "set beside" the main narrative, resemble it, and shed light on it.[101] So, just as recurring references to the *nostoi* (successful or not) of Agamemnon, Oilean Ajax, Menelaus, and others inform our understanding of Odysseus's *nostos*, the loss of *nostos* in Lucan's poem for Cato, Pompey, Caesar, and others speaks to the greater matter of the absence, devastation, and failure to return of the Roman people.

Let us recall Lucan's characterization of the *populus* in his proem with the epithet *conuersum* (1.3), which translates but also emphatically turns in on itself Odysseus's definitive epithet *polutropos*, and which Livius had translated to *uersutum* for his *Odusia*. The turn of the Roman people in Lucan's poem is a turn away, outward—to twists, turns, and ventures that recall those of Odysseus—but simultaneously a turn inward toward self-destruction (*in sua . . . uiscera*, 1.3). Later in Book 1, Lucan emphasizes the sense that the story of the Roman people is one of anti-*nostos*, and with a marked anti-Odyssean bent, during his description of the panic at Rome and flight from the city when word of Caesar's arrival had spread (1.466–522). In an image that anticipates the senators' settlement in a foreign home at 5.9–10, Lucan writes that "the senate house and the senators themselves leapt from its foundation / their seats" (*sed curia et ipsi | sedibus exiluere patres*, 1.487–8). The syntax of the sentence compels us to envision not just individual senators but the *curia* itself jumping up from what was home (*sedibus*). Next to exit the city is the larger populace, whose homes are not burning or crumbling, even though the people's actions would make you think so.[102] Lucan captures the scene of mass exodus with a simile that is programmatic for much that will follow in the poem:

>   sic turba per urbem   495
> . . .
> inconsulta ruit. qualis, cum turbidus Auster
> reppulit a Libycis inmensum Syrtibus aequor
> fractaque ueliferi sonuerunt pondera mali,   500

---

[101] Alden (2017) 1, in her introduction of terms at 1–8.
[102] 1.493–5: *credas aut tecta nefandas | corripuisse faces aut iam quatiente ruina | nutantes pendere domos*. See Joseph (2020) 36–7.

desilit in fluctus deserta puppe magister
nauitaque et nondum sparsa conpage carinae
naufragium sibi quisque facit, sic urbe relicta
in bellum fugitur.

So the mob rushes through the city unadvisedly. Just as when the rough
South wind has driven the immeasurable sea from the Libyan Syrtes,
and the weight of the sail-bearing mast has been cracked and resounds,
and the captain deserts the ship and leaps into the waves, and, though
the core of the ship is not yet shattered, each sailor makes a shipwreck
for himself—in this way the city is abandoned and there is a flight to war.
(1.498–504)

So the people of Rome, here a rash mob (*turba ... inconsulta*), are compared with sailors on a storm-struck ship. The ship is still intact (*nondum sparsa conpage carinae*, 1.502), but rather than endure the storm, the captain hops off (1.501) and each sailor "makes a shipwreck for himself" (*naufragium sibi ... facit*, 1.503). This journey does not end in a safe return to land or even in just a shipwreck, but in a self-reflexive, self-destructive shipwreck, in a collective turned violently against itself, an image complementing the one in the proem of a *populum ... in sua ... conuersum uiscera* (1.2–3). Paul Roche compares this simile with the allegory of the ship of state that goes back to at least Alcaeus.[103] At the same time the image of a storm-tossed captain and his companions surely recalls the archetypal contests with the animated winds that Odysseus and his men endured. Homer's hero of course loses his companions, but survives the winds' assault with resolve, a paradigm dashed in *Ph*. 1.498–504, where Lucan emphasizes the self-destructive defeatism and wreckage of crew and captain alike. And while the vehicle of this simile speaks to the poem's trope of anti-*nostos*, the succinct tenor (*sic urbe relicta | in bellum fugitur*, 1.503–4) is just as programmatic of the ensuing story of absence, (self-)devastation, and failure to return. The Roman people abandon home (*urbe relicta*) and are in flight (*fugitur*), but it is a flight *toward* war. The striking paradox[104] concisely captures the poem's reversal of the Odyssean arc away from devastation and toward home.

---

[103] Roche (2009) 310, also comparing *Aen*. 1.81–123, though not its Homeric model.
[104] See Henderson (1987) 136; Roche (2009) 312; and Taylor (2020) 92.

As though to concretize the theme of the abandonment of home, Lucan focuses not only on those who leave Rome and their sustained absences, but also on individual homes that are destroyed or abandoned. He thus in a sense presents both perspectives—subject along with object—on this story of the loss of home and homecoming. Earlier we considered the close-up in Book 5 of Caesar shattering Amyclas's quaint home and the staging of the conspicuously un-Odyssean reunion of Cato and Marcia in the former's home in Book 2. This theme of broken and lost homes had been introduced in the narrator's initial address to Rome's citizens (1.8–32), where he describes the current condition of Italy that resulted from the civil wars:

> at nunc semirutis pendent quod moenia tectis
> urbibus Italiae lapsisque ingentia muris
> saxa iacent nulloque domus custode tenentur
> rarus et antiquis habitator in urbibus errat, . . .

> But now, as the city walls hang low beside half-destroyed homes in
> Italy's cities, and huge stones from fallen walls lie dead, and homes are
> maintained by no keeper, and in old cities the rare inhabitant wanders
> about . . . (1.24–8)

Alongside the image of sagging, dilapidated city walls (*pendent . . . moenia*), Lucan offers three different but complementary images of Roman homelessness: first half-destroyed homes (*semirutis . . . tectis*); then homes that are presumably intact but taken care of by no one (*nulloque domus custode tenentur*); and, most strikingly, the rare inhabitant (*rarus . . . habitator*) who does not in fact dwell anywhere but instead wanders about (*errat*).[105] Devastation, absence, and the failure to return are tautly captured in this pitiful panorama at the poem's outset.

Lucan found the imagery of homelessness in this programmatic passage gripping enough that he would revisit it in the long statement on the consequences of Pharsalia in Book 7. In an effort to convey the extent of the human loss that day, he again pictures the pair of the crumbling house and absent inhabitant:

---

[105] The rarity of the individual dweller is reinforced by the rarity of the word choice. As Roche (2009) 125 notes (writing, "there may be further point to the term"), this is the first appearance of *habitator* in Latin poetry. Statius found the collocation *rarus . . . habitator* to be memorable, using it at *Theb.* 4.150.

> stat tectis putris auitis
> in nullos ruitura domus nulloque frequentem
> ciue suo Romam sed mundi faece repletam
> cladis eo dedimus, ne tanto in corpore bellum
> iam possit ciuile geri.
>
> The decaying home under an ancestral roof is about to fall—on nobody.
> We have brought Rome—occupied by no citizen of her own, but filled
> with the dregs of the world—to such a point of disaster that, in a body as
> large as this, civil war can no longer be waged. (7.403–7)

The image here is more succinct and starker, as now the abandoned home falls, illogically, on an absent person. And in the use of a derivative of *ruo*, we may observe a devolution from the "half-destroyed homes" (*semirutis . . . tectis*, 1.24) of the earlier image to the fully destroyed and falling (*ruitura*) home here. Lucan then zooms out from the image of the individual abandoned home to Rome itself, now "occupied by not one citizen of her own" (*nulloque frequentem | ciue suo*), a condition of devastation and abiding absence that makes *bellum ciuile*, war among citizens, impossible in his time (7.406–7).

Ahl has read these images of post-Pharsalian devastation together with the picture of the Trojan wasteland at 9.961–99, arguing that the Trojan-Roman story comes full circle when Caesar, the descendant of Aeneas, returns to the foundational site of loss and destruction for their race.[106] But there is more: identifying the convolution of the Odyssean arc of absence, devastation, and return that runs through this nexus of passages helps us to understand their interplay more fully. Lucan has made Troy *and* Rome, each a place of "home" and of potential return for the Roman people, a site of devastation. Put another way, the arc of the *populus Romanus* in the long view is revealed to be a movement from devastation to more devastation, the one at the hands of the Achaeans, the other by their own hands. The consequence is that each home is now lost, and a sense of doubly felt Roman homelessness arises.

Furthermore, the picture of defeated and decrepit Troy in Book 9 puts into relief the fact that the abandonment and devastation of Rome in the *Pharsalia* has been self-enacted: this time Roma—a place and a people, a spatial and societal entity—abandons and destroys itself. The apostrophes that the narrator delivers to Roma across the poem bear this out: Roma is

---

[106] Ahl (1976) 214–22. See too Johnson (1987) 120 ("It is desolation and squalor that win out").

both deserted in this civil war (1.519–20: *tu tantum audito bellorum nomine, Roma, | desereris*, "you, Rome, when just the name of war was heard, are deserted"), and also the *cause* of the war and ensuing devastation (see the addresses 1.21–3 and 1.84–5).[107] We note again that the adjective attached to the *populus* at 2.116, *degener*, meaning "departing from or *abandoning* its own kind," joins *conuersus* to form a pair of perfectly evocative epithets for the Roman people of this poem.

The opening up and resultant undoing of the Odyssean master-trope of *nostos* is key in Lucan's effort to close off the epic project initiated by the Smyrnaean *uates*. If in the *Odyssey* "hero and poet negotiate the accomplishment of a *nostos* that is their common goal,"[108] then the poet of the *Pharsalia* accomplishes an analogous but inverse goal, as the sequences of departure, absence, devastation, and failure to return played out by the poem's characters reflect Lucan's own act of opening up and abandoning the theme of *nostos* that is so fundamental to his "home" genre of epic. This gesture of closure thus comes, as we have seen, through a sweeping agenda of poetic aperture, as Lucan pulls apart generic openings, pursuing in full the uncertainties and possibilities for the failure to return and reunite that are already present and pliant in the master-trope of *nostos*.

Moreoever, if Lucan is also evoking this theme as explored in Livius's pioneering *Odusia*, then he is ending the arc of poetic *nostos* in another way, undoing the successful, indeed momentous, arrival of Odysseus's tale into a new home in Latin epic. While Livius had, like Odysseus himself, improbably accomplished this epic feat—showing subsequent authors the passageways toward many more returns of epic themes into Latin verse—Lucan renders that project, like his characters, scattered and homeless. In this light we might revisit again the evocation at 1.2–3, with the phrase *populum ... conuersum*, of not just the Homeric *Odyssey*'s proem but also Livius' opening line *uirum mihi, Camena, insece uersutum* (fr. 1). When we consider these two proems alongside each other, the omission of Camena strikes as just as significant as the omission of the Homeric Muse (see Chapter 1). The Roman water divinity Camena had represented the specifically Roman setting for Livius' poetic career, arriving in the *Odusia*'s opening line as a source of continued inspiration for the epic genre in its new home along the Tiber.[109] Lucan

---

[107] 1.21–3: *tum, si tantus amor belli tibi, Roma, nefandi, | totum sub Latias leges cum miseris orbem, | in te uerte manus*. 1.84–5: *tu causa malorum | facta tribus dominis communis, Roma*. On 1.519–20 Roche (2009) 317 writes: "this civil war is desertion and abandonment on both sides."

[108] Bakker (2013) 20.

[109] See Goldberg (1995) 64 and Feeney (2016) 54–5.

makes Camena and the processes of poetic settlement and continuation that she represented[110] for Livius and his successors absent from the *Pharsalia*.

There is more to Lucan's closure of fundamental Homeric themes. In my final chapter I will turn to the incorporation and sweeping expansion in the *Pharsalia* of the elements of the intrinsically Homeric mode of lament. Here too, we will see, an opening up of the Homeric model is crucial to Lucan's claims of closure.

---

[110] On Camena, the plural *Camenae*, and their long literary afterlife, see Hardie (2016).

6
Epic's Last Lament

After focusing in the previous chapter on the failure of Lucan's characters and of Rome herself to return home, I want to open this chapter by looking at a successful return home that the poet puts right at the center of his epic. When giving the geological origin story for the site of Pharsalia in Book 6, Lucan writes that, after Mount Ossa was split in two, "then Pharsalos, the kingdom of watery Achilles, rose up—better if it had remained beneath the Emathian waves" (6.349–51: *melius mansura sub undis | Emathis aequorei regnum Pharsalos Achillis | eminet*). This is the poem's one direct reference to Achilles, and by bringing the story of epic back to the birthplace of the *Iliad*'s hero and staging his cataclysmic battle there, Lucan marks Pharsalia/the *Pharsalia*'s clinching containment of the epic story, which returns home for a violent end.[1] The gesture of generic return, succinctly captured in the juxtaposition *Pharsalos Achillis*, at the same time centers Lucan's poem around the grief that is constitutive of the character Achilles and the *Iliad* as a whole.[2] Scholars understand the hero's name to be derived from *akhos* and *laos* and thus to mean "grief of the fighting-people."[3] In the poem and in later literature, Achilles is, as Nagy has put it, "like the very essence of grief . . . the man of constant sorrow."[4] Further, his grief spreads to the people (*laos*) in his world, his enemies the Trojans and his Achaean allies alike.

The character Achilles is emblematic of the poem he inhabits, an embodiment of the grief that accompanies bloodshed across the poem. So when Lucan conspicuously stages his work of *Todesdichtung* at the birthplace of

---

[1] See my discussion in Chapter 1.
[2] The epithet *aequorei* evokes Achilles's mother, the water nymph Thetis (see Cat. 64.15: *aequoreae Nereides*; cf. Prop. 1.17.25 and 3.7.67), and so it may reinforce connections with lament, as a significant part of Thetis's identity in the *Il.* is as a lamenter of Achilles's imminent doom (see *Il.* 1.414–18 and 18.52–64; cf. 18.428–61). I thank David J. Wright *per litteras* for discussion of Thetis (suggesting the translation "watery and weepy" for *aequorei* here).
[3] See Palmer (1963) 79 and Nagy (1979) 69–83 and (1994), responding to an alternative etymology by Holland (1993).
[4] Nagy (1979) 78 and 81. See too Dué (2019) on Achilles's lament for Patroclus at *Il.* 19.315–37 and his possession of both the greatest *kleos* and the most profound *akhos*. On the reception of the sorrow of Achilles in Latin, see Boyd (2017) 103–4 on Ov. *Her.* 3.113–14; and see Dué (2002) 91–113 on the reception of Thetis's lament in Propertius's elegies.

Achilles, it is not just that he is bringing epic full circle, back to "the home city of the protagonist of the first epic of all."[5] He is also highlighting the genre's aboriginal identity as a poetry of sorrow, of grief spread to the people—of war, death, and the lament that always attends it. The inextricability of war and grief lies at the foundational, tectonic base of *Pharsalos Achillis* and of the *Pharsalia*. In previous chapters I have identified numerous episodes in which Lucan brings voices or expressions of lament to the fore, alongside the acts of transgression and violence that have been my focus. We have heard, for example, Roma weep for herself as Caesar storms past the Rubicon (1.185-90), the old man's speech about Roman self-slaughter that Lucan characterizes as a lament (2.68-232), the parents and widows mourning after the maritime massacre at Massilia (3.756-61), the lamentation over Curio's corpse at 4.799-815, the weeping shades of Camillus, Scipio, and Cato (6.784-90), to go with images such as the toppling, wailing trees at 3.443-4, the "grief-bearing" sun that rises over Pharsalia at 7.1-6, and the Roman fleet freighted with lamentation at 9.49-50. These descriptions of acts of lament are accompanied by the pervasive use of the thematic and stylistic features of speeches of lament, as introduced into epic in the Homeric poems. Lucan, we will explore in greater depth in this chapter, expands the antiphony of lament beyond his characters to the narrator and even the poem's post-Pharsalian readers, in this way polemically centering and completing the tradition of the epic song of sorrow begun by Homer.

6.1. The features of lament in Homeric poetry

Before examining the dynamic range of lamenting voices in the *Pharsalia*, I want to follow up on my remarks in the Introduction about the core elements of lament in epic by taking fuller stock of its foundations in Homer and characteristic features. Homer refers to two types, both sung over the body of the deceased[6]: the *threnos*, a formal dirge performed by a professional singer; and the *goos*, an informal lament sung by family members and others close to the dead (see the distinctions at *Il*. 24.719-22, with my discussion later in this chapter, as well as *Od*. 24.58-62). We hear no *threnoi* in the *Iliad* or *Odyssey*, but there are twelve *gooi* in the *Iliad*: three anticipatory laments (for Menelaus, Hector, and Achilles), and nine laments following the

---

[5] Masters (1992) 158.
[6] Alexiou (1974) 4-6 discusses the setting of laments around in the corpse of the deceased.

deaths of Patroclus, given three in Books 18 and 19, and Hector, given six in Books 22 and 24.[7] The laments thus occur predominantly in the second half of the poem, and the poem closes with the series of laments for Hector by Andromache, Hecuba, and Helen at the end of Book 24. As Tsagalis puts it, "It seems that when the lament is over, it is time for the poem to end."[8]

The form of these speeches was not restrictive; the *goos* was "from Homer onwards highly individualized."[9] But consideration of the twelve *gooi* in the *Iliad* reveals a number of recurring features.[10] Central to many of them is the exploration, in content and style, of two fundamental tensions: between praise and reproach and between distance/antithesis and closeness/similarity.[11] **Praise** of the deceased is commonly conveyed in an opening address, often with a laudatory descriptor, such as a superlative form. The content of this opening address can be reinforced by a tripartite structure, with the address followed by a central narrative and then a renewed address (thus showing a ring-composition). **Reproach** of the deceased—and the resistance to the pursuit of glory through war that this gesture articulates (see further discussion in the following)—comes in strong words of criticism and the common use of repeated questions addressed to the deceased. The theme of **distance** is frequently explored in contrasts in time between the past and present, often marked by adverbs indicating "then" and "now"; contrasts in space, with a focus on the distance between the place of death and the homeland of the deceased; contrasts in the current conditions of the mourner and deceased; and contrasts between the deceased and other dead, with an emphasis on the exceptionality of the present loss and thus of the present grief. The theme of **closeness** comes out in the articulation of the common fate of the mourner and deceased, often with a death wish by the mourner; and in self-reproach similar to the reproach for the dead. A stylistic manifestation of

---

[7] The *gooi* are at 4.155–82 (Agamemnon for Menelaus); 6.407–39 (Andromache for Hector); 18.52–64 (Thetis for Achilles); 18.324–42 (Achilles for Patroclus); 19.287–300 (Briseis for Patroclus); 19.315–37 (Achilles for Patroclus); 22.416–28 (Priam for Hector); 22.431–6 (Hecuba for Hector); 22.477–514 (Andromache for Hector); 24.725–45 (Andromache for Hector); 24.748–59 (Hecuba for Hector); and 24.762–75 (Helen for Hector). Tsagalis (2004) 51 includes a table of conventional elements in each of these *gooi*.

[8] Tsagalis (2004) 2. See too Flatt (2017) (building on Brooks's (1984) treatment of narrative desire) on lament as a consummation or *telos* for the narrator and audience of the Homeric poems, arguing that counterfactuals of mourning "prolong narrative desire until it can be satisfied through fully realized ritual laments later in the poems" (389).

[9] Alexiou (1974) 103. See also Tsagalis (2004) 15.

[10] The features highlighted here are discussed by Alexiou (1974), esp. 132–3 and 161–81, and in the analysis of the *gooi* in the *Il.* by Tsagalis (2004).

[11] Tsagalis (2004) 168: "mourners in their γόοι for heroes constantly emphasize a tension between distance and closeness, encounter and separation, past and future."

the tensions inherent in you/me, there/here, then/now, dead/alive is the use and frequent juxtaposition of first- and second-person verbs and deictics, underscoring both contrasts and the intimate proximity of the mourner and deceased.

It is also important to highlight again the antiphonal quality of Homeric lament, which "was always in some sense collective, and never an exclusively solo performance."[12] This element is apparent in the climactic exchange of laments over the corpse of Hector in *Iliad* 24, where professional singers perform *threnoi* (ἀοιδοὺς | θρήνων, 24.720–1), to which Andromache, Hecuba, and Helen respond (ἐπὶ... στενάχοντο, 24.722) with their *gooi*;[13] and also in the exchange of laments for Patroclus by Briseis and other captive women in Book 19 and the interchange of laments by Priam, Hecuba, and Andromache for Hector in Book 22. Tsagalis emphasizes the important point that "the antiphonal element refers not only to the external reenactment of the funeral laments, but also to the responsive nature of the themes"[14] that mourners emphasize. Put another way, continuity of theme across antiphonal laments was another characteristic feature.

6.2. The epic cry of the *goos* echoes on

As Alexiou's study shows, common features of lament come to carry across genres and across time in Greek culture. Roman culture had its own customs of mourning, namely the practice of a *laudatio funebris* performed by men, along with a *nenia* sung by professional female mourners (*praeficae*).[15] But in the continuum of the epic genre from Greek into Latin, much Latin epic takes up the conventions of the *goos* from Homeric poetry in a fairly straightforward manner, with the set-pieces of speeches of lament over the deceased becoming common.[16] For example, in the *Aeneid* the mother of Euryalus laments her dead son (9.481–97), Evander laments his son Pallas (11.152–81), and Juturna offers an anticipatory lament for her brother

---

[12] Alexiou (1974) 134, in her chapter on "antiphonal structure and antithetical thought" (131–60).
[13] See Dué (2002) 71–3 and Perkell (2008) on the antiphony of laments by Andromache, Hecuba, and Helen.
[14] Tsagalis (2004) 49. See too Dué (2002).
[15] See Habinek (2005) 234–53; Dutsch (2008); and Richlin (2014) 267–88.
[16] Fantham (1999) 222: "the cultural preeminence of Homer has ensured that aspects of the great laments of the *Iliad* are reproduced in Roman literature and developed by each successive composer of Roman epic."

Turnus (12.872–84), all speeches that include many of the hallmarks of *gooi* in the *Iliad*.[17] Ovid's *Metamorphoses* also includes laments with conventional features by, for example, Inachus for Io (1.651–63) and Hecuba for Polyxena (13.494–532).[18] This is not to say that Virgil and Ovid do not innovate in their adaptations of the *goos*, but an embrace of the conventions of Homeric *gooi* is clear. One notable development among Homer's Roman successors—and one we will see Lucan advance *ad extremum*—was toward the inclusion of laments spoken by a collective entity. After the final *goos* of the *Iliad*, performed by Helen for Hector, Homer had written that the *demos* respond with their own wailing (24.776).[19] The communal song of sorrow suggested here gains a fuller voice in Latin epic as early as Ennius's *Annales*, where the Roman *populus*, singing "together, among one another" (*simul inter | sese*, *Ann.* 105–6) lament Romulus;[20] and later in, for example, the moments of communal mourning that Virgil pictures at 4.666–7, 5.613–15, and 12.604–11.

A fundamental feature of lament in epic that had remained fairly consistent from Homer into the Latin tradition was its capacity to represent the marginalized place of epic's female characters. A distinction by gender was never clear-cut: male characters in epic had long participated in the practice, from Achilles, the man of sorrow himself, and several others in the *Iliad* to Evander in *Aeneid* 11 and Inachus in *Metamorphoses* 1. But the mode has historical origins in the practices of women;[21] and from the *Iliad* onward the lamenting voices of women are typically the strongest in their opposition to epic's dominant voice, in this way both prominent in their poems but also occupying places of resistance, on the margins of the action. Note once again the powerfully placed closing antiphony of Trojan women at the end of *Iliad* 24, as well as the pronounced but at the same time marginal *gooi* by the likes of Euryalus's mother in *Aeneid* 9 and the Hecuba of *Metamorphoses*

---

[17] See Hardie (1994) 161–2; Perkell (1997); and Seider (2013) 140–54 on these passages.

[18] On these laments, see Curtis (2017) and Westerhold (2011), respectively.

[19] See Dué (2002) 81 on the significance of this detail, pointing to the assessment by Greene (1999) 195 that lamentation serves to create "a hallowed communion" between the epic and the audience.

[20] *Ann.* 105–9. Cic. *Rep.* 1.64 preserves the fragment and attributes it to the *populus*. See Fantham (1999) 222–3 on the innovative use of the collective here. For another possible Ennian example, see *Ann.* 498 (*flentes, plorantes, lacrimantes, obstestantes*), with Skutsch (1985) 655 on possible placement. While it is difficult to draw many conclusions about lament in the *Ann.*, Ennius's familiarity with its conventions can be seen in the fourteen-line fragment of a lament for Troy from his *Andromacha Aechmalotis* (*FRL* fr. 23 = Cic. *Tusc.* 3.19.44), on which see Jeppesen (2016) 143–4.

[21] See Alexiou (1974) and the essays in Suter (2008a), incl. Suter (2008b), arguing that the gendered quality of lament is less clear in Greek tragedy.

13.[22] These laments, while serving as vehicles of praise and *kleos/fama* for the dead, at the same time threaten to destabilize the drive in the epics toward glory in warfare.

6.3. Lucan's Cornelia in the lament tradition

We see, then, that "by Lucan's day, the cultural authority of the Homeric epics had lent these laments a 'canonical' status—whether for emulation, transgression, or problematization."[23] And indeed Lucan's understanding of the elements of the Homeric *goos*—as well as its capacity to express the marginalized and resistant perspective of female characters—is clear. The character in the *Pharsalia* with the most prevalent voice of lament, and whose speeches (at 5.762–90, 8.88–105, 8.639–61, and 9.55–101) most clearly demonstrate Lucan's close familiarity with the *goos*, is Cornelia.[24] In Chapter 5, I explored Lucan's focus on the inability of Cornelia and Pompey to reunite, proposing that in this regard she stands in contrast with Homer's Penelope. Cornelia also emerges as something of a parallel figure to Andromache, the wife of Hector who occupied a place that was the inverse of Penelope's, as the lamenting widow-to-be and widow par excellence. Like Andromache, Cornelia performs a surrogate funerary rite for her absent husband,[25] and her four speeches to and about Pompey share a number of similarities with Andromache's three laments for Hector.[26] In this section I will consider in brief Cornelia's speeches within the *goos* tradition—thus establishing Lucan's familiarity with the form and its effects—before turning in the next section to the manifold ways he opens up not just Cornelia's lament, but the expression of the mode more generally.

Cornelia's first speech in the poem, to Pompey at 5.762–90, on the surface addresses only their imminent separation, but it also reads as an anticipatory lament similar to Andromache's to Hector at *Iliad* 6.407–39. Alison Keith

---

[22] On the lament and separation of Euryalus's mother as a threat to the Trojan cause, see Nugent (1992) 271–3 and (1999) 54–8 (noting contrasts with the lament of the empowered Evander in *Aen.* 11) and Keith (2016) 170–3. See Westerhold (2011) 306 on Hecuba's lament in *Met.* 13 as a destabilizing threat.

[23] Keith (2008) 254 n. 16.

[24] See Keith (2008) 236–45 and 248–9 on Cornelia's four speeches of lament and their articulation of the female perspective in the poem.

[25] McClellan (2019) 135, comparing 9.174–9 with *Il.* 22.508–15 and passages from Latin epic, writing: "Lucan will also no doubt have in mind Andromache's substitute funeral for Hector."

[26] Noted by Hutchinson (2013) 331 and McClellan (2019) 136.

observes that her swoon at 5.759-60 "evokes the long epic tradition of female lament"[27] and so in a sense marks what follows as a *goos*. The speech itself expresses both antitheses and commonalities between mourner and (soon to be) deceased, alternating complaints about the distance that will separate the two (5.762-5 and 5.771-2) with expressions of the common fate they are doomed to share (5.769-70 and 5.773-4). Moreover, while Cornelia twice addresses him with the honorific *Magne* (5.763 and 767), the series of urgent questions at 5.767-72 and her reproaches in the vocatives *saeue* at 5.770 and *crudelis* at 5.777 are in keeping with the oppositional stance that is characteristic of the medium.

Cornelia's speech to Pompey at 8.88-105, with its "pervasive self-reproaches and expressions of desire for death," also reads as an anticipatory lament,[28] setting up the speeches at the moment of Pompey's death in Book 8 and after his death in Book 9. Her speech at 8.639-61, delivered from her ship just as the fatal blow is being delivered on the Egyptian skiff, opens with many of the hallmarks of the *goos*:

> o coniunx, ego te scelerata peremi:
> letiferae tibi causa morae fuit auia Lesbos,
> et prior in Nili peruenit litora Caesar.

> O husband, I—guilty one—have destroyed you! Remote Lesbos was the cause of the delay that brought your death, and Caesar reached the shores of the Nile before you. (8.639-41)

An opening address (*o coniunx*) is followed immediately by juxtaposed first- and second-person pronouns, which together visualize the union and closeness of mourner and deceased. The next two words (*scelerata peremi*) introduce the theme of self-reproach, as Cornelia blames herself for Pompey's death. Self-reproach and the corresponding desire for a common fate with Pompey in death carry through the remainder of the speech: Cornelia wishes that Pompey's killer "would see *my* [fallen] head. I am not free of blame for these wars" (*meum uideat caput. haud ego culpa | libera bellorum*, 8.647-8); and later she resumes her death wish, this time directing the reproach at Pompey:

---

[27] Keith (2008) 236, pointing to *Il.* 22.447-8, *Aen.* 9.473-6, and *Met.* 11.416-20.
[28] See Keith (2008) 240-1; the quotation is from 240.

> hoc merui, coniunx, in tuta puppe relinqui?
> perfide, parcebas? te fata extrema petente
> uita digna fui? moriar, nec munere regis.

> Is this what I have earned, husband, to be left behind in this safe ship?
> Faithless one, were you sparing me? While you sought your final fate, was
> I worthy of life? Let me die! And not by the gift of the king. (8.651–3)

The force of her reproach and demand for a common fate with Pompey is conveyed by the conventional device of a battery of questions to the deceased.[29] After still further elaboration of her death wish (8.654–8), Cornelia concludes the lament by exclaiming:

> uiuis adhuc, coniunx, et iam Cornelia non est
> iuris, Magne, sui: prohibent accersere mortem;
> seruor uictori.

> You are still living, husband, but now Cornelia is not under her own law,
> Magnus. They forbid me to summon death. I am being saved for the
> victor. (8.659–61)

After dwelling for much of the speech on her desire to share Pompey's fate, Cornelia concludes with the realization of their inescapable separation. The fundamental contrasts between mourner and deceased ultimately outweigh the commonalities, a point reinforced by the speech's conventional tripartite structure.[30] We see that Cornelia opens (8.639–41) and closes (8.659–61) her speech with addresses to her *coniunx*, and the speech's central narrative concentrates on her sense of responsibility for his death and demand for a shared fate. But this focus on commonalities is inverted in the focus on difference and disparity in the renewed address that concludes the speech: Cornelia concludes by underscoring her feeling of abandonment, isolation, and looming danger. The movement from opening address through narrative to renewed address recalls the tripartite structure and progression of the *gooi* delivered by Andromache, Hecuba, and Helen over Hector's corpse in *Iliad*

---

[29] See Keith (2008) 244 on the effect of this series of questions.
[30] See Tsagalis (2004) 168 on thematic interplay between introductory and closing addresses in Homeric *gooi*.

24,[31] while also sharing with those speeches an emphasis on the mourner's ultimate sense of abandonment and marginalization.

With the flames from Pompey's makeshift pyre in sight (9.54), Cornelia delivers her final speech at 9.55–108, her most "proper" lament in the poem.[32] As in her earlier speeches, she reproaches herself (9.55, 9.71, and 9.103–4) and issues a series of six impassioned questions (9.66–72) about her miserable lot. She marks pointed contrasts between Pompey's past successes and current condition (9.80–2), as well as a spatial contrast when emphasizing numerous times the remote location of his death (9.58, 9.63, 9.74, and 9.82). Cornelia concludes with an extended focus on a conventional theme that recurred across her speeches: her wish to share a common fate with Pompey in death (9.101–8).

The speeches of Cornelia, then, demonstrate Lucan's dexterity with the conventions of the *goos* and understanding of its customary place in epic narrative. The "central role of Cornelia in the commemoration of Pompey,"[33] as a primary conveyer of praise, is clear. At the same time the continuity of focus across her four speeches on (self-) reproach and the wish for a common fate in death brings the conventionally female voice of opposition to the fore, loudly pushing back—in a manner similar to Homer's Andromache and women in later epic—with a gloomy fatalism at Pompey's efforts for glory in war.

6.4. Antiphonal lament in the *Pharsalia*

The extended crafting of Cornelia as a mourner who both praises and reproaches the deceased is thus in keeping with the expectations of epic. But I want to focus now on an element of her speeches that is at once conventional and, in Lucan's hands, boldly original: the placement of her laments—and the tension of the laudatory and the oppositional that they contain—within a broad, multivocal antiphony. The context of Cornelia's lament at 9.55–108 demonstrates this well. We recall from Chapter 4 that, just prior to this speech, Lucan had described the ships transporting the Pompeian forces as "carrying lamentation and the beating of breasts and ills that provoked

---

[31] See Tsagalis (2004) 46–7.
[32] See Keith (2008) 248 on some of the conventional features in this "lament proper."
[33] Keith (2008) 253, writing also that Lucan's Cornelia "affirms the power of women's lamentation in ancient Rome."

tears even from stern Cato" (*luctus planctusque ferebant | et mala uel duri lacrimas motura Catonis*, (9.49–50), an image that locates Cornelia's speech among a plurality of lamenting voices. But after the lament she decides to "endure darkness" (*pati tenebras*, 9.110) and withdraws into the hollows of her ship to partake in individual tears and lamentation for her husband (*perfruitur lacrimis et amat pro coniuge luctum*, 9.112), a scene that relegates her emotions to a private setting and seems, as Keith has written, to respect "the gendered separation of lamenting women from . . . public gatherings" that was familiar from earlier epic such as the *Aeneid*.[34]

However, following an account of the deliberations of Pompey's sons (9.117–66), Lucan includes a striking resumption of Cornelia's exercise of lament:

interea totis audito funere Magni
litoribus sonuit percussus planctibus aether,
exemploque carens et nulli cognitus aeuo
luctus erat, mortem populos deflere potentis.
sed magis, ut uisa est lacrimis exhausta, solutas
in uoltus effusa comas, Cornelia puppe
egrediens, rursus geminato uerbere plangunt.

Meanwhile, once the death of Magnus was reported, on all shores the ether, struck with the beating of breasts, resounded. This was lamentation that lacked precedent and was known to no age—that nations would weep for the death of a powerful man. But when Cornelia, stepping down from the ship and having poured her loosened hair across her face, seemed to be drained of tears, they redoubled their beatings again and struck their breasts even more. (9.167–73)

The lamentation for Pompey that had been cordoned off and limited to the grieving widow Cornelia just a few lines earlier erupts on "all shores" (*totis . . . litoribus*), with the ether itself resounding (*sonuit . . . aether*). The opening up of her hidden, domestic exercise of grief into an expansive antiphony thus counters the paradigm of earlier epic, as in *Aeneid* 9, where the lament of Euryalus's mother (9.481–97) leads to a brief expression of communal grief (9.498–9), before a group of Trojan men "grab hold of her" and

---

[34] Keith (2008) 249, comparing the separation of lamenting women in *Aen.* 5 and 9.

"put her back inside" (*corripiunt ... sub tecta reponunt*, 9.502).[35] Lucan goes on to write that the lament across the shores is unprecedented (*exemploque carens*) in that so many nations (*populos*) are weeping for one man.[36] The statement reads as both wildly hyperbolic and boldly metapoetic: Lucan is opening up the process of lament, pointedly redirecting it here from the private and particularly female setting to a scale of collective expression that lacks precedent in the epic tradition. When we read that "no age" (*nulli aeuo*) had known lamentation like this before, we think of the one other time in the poem when Lucan uses this expression, later in Book 9 when positioning his *Pharsalia* alongside the epics of Homer, Ennius, Virgil, and Ovid, and concluding with the assertion that "we will be condemned to darkness by no age" (*a nullo ... aeuo*, 9.986).[37] Both statements are audacious poetic assertions, claiming to supplant rival texts, with a scope stretching both backward and forward in time.

When bringing Cornelia back into his narrative here, Lucan specifically marks the nations' lament as antiphonal: those on the shorelines see that she is exhausted from her own lamentations (*ut uisa est lacrimis exhausta*, 9.171) and as a result pick up where she left off, in fact redoubling their expressions of grief (*rursus geminato uerbere plangunt*, 9.173). When Cornelia proceeds to perform funerary rites (9.174–9), others along the whole shore (*toto litore*, 9.180) respond in kind, now extending the duty to the war-dead more generally (9.181), a process that Lucan compares with the farming practice of burning soil to ensure new growth (9.182–5).[38] The interchange between Cornelia and the mourners along the coast recalls the passing of lament from singer to singer at *Iliad* 24.720–75 and then to the *demos* at 24.776 (ἐπὶ δ' ἔστενε δῆμος ἀπείρων, "and the countless throng lamented in response"). But what is a hemistich in Homer expands into a dynamic exchange between Cornelia and the *populi* across the shores—an episode of broad antiphonal lament that, as Lucan himself asserts, has no precedent. And while Latin epic predecessors such as Ennius and Virgil had depicted collective expressions of lamentation, Lucan's placement of communal lament within an antiphony opens up the process further, as the expression of praise but also mournful

---

[35] I thank Aaron Seider for pointing out this contrast.
[36] Keith (2008) seems to circumscribe the participation in the lamentation too narrowly when reading *populos* to refer only to socially inferior soldiers along the shore, concluding that this scene "illustrates both the gender and the class lines of lamentation" (250–1).
[37] See my discussion in Chapter 1.
[38] See Thorne (2011) 379 on the imagery of renewal in this simile.

resistance that Cornelia has voiced over much of the poem now spreads and grows among the far-flung *populi*.

This reading of the interchange between Cornelia and the *populi* in Book 9 help us to identity and appreciate the dynamics of antiphonal lament in other passages in the poem. A prominent example is the tableau of anticipatory mourning in Rome at the outset of Book 2 (2.16–233). Lucan includes three speeches here and characterizes each—by a grieving matron (2.38–42), a group of war-ready men (2.45–63), and the long-winded old man (2.67–232)—as an expression of lament.[39] And he seems to capture the echoing, compounding, antiphonal effects of the lamentation when writing after the matron's speech: "With these goads grief itself moves itself" (*his se stimulis dolor ipse lacessit*, 2.42). While the sequence of lamentation in Book 9 moves from collective mourning (9.49–50) to Cornelia's lament (9.55–108) and then to an even more expansive communal expression (9.167–73), in Book 2 the antiphony exchanges from an individual to a collective group and then to another individual. On their own these speeches lack the hallmarks of formal lament that Cornelia's speeches include. But when looked at together, operating in antiphony, they exhibit many of the crucial elements of the mode, though with a self-directed twist that befits the Romans' condition in this civil war. For example, the wailing matron addresses not the deceased per se but the other pitiable Roman matrons (*o miserae . . . matres*, 2.38). The men echo her and begin with the similarly reflexive address of *o miserae sortis* (2.45: "o you/us of a miserable lot!"). They go on to emphasize, in a way characteristic of *gooi*, the stark contrast between their present destiny to fight a civil war and the past lot of their ancestors who fought in the Punic Wars (2.45–6); and they ultimately extend to the gods a collective Roman death wish, a fate preferable to the pain of one side living and the other dying (2.56–60). The old man's speech is predicated entirely on comparisons and contrasts with the past: the self-destructive conflict between Caesar and Pompey recalls the one between Marius and Sulla but is doomed to bring more serious ills (*grauiora*, 2.225) and greater destruction of the human race (*humani generis maiore . . . damno*, 2.226; see Chapter 2).

A still bolder addition to the *Pharsalia*'s antiphony comes in the report from the Underworld by the corpse of a Roman soldier that Erictho

---

[39] The first speech is manifestly an expression of grief (note, e.g., *nunc flere potestas* at 2.40), and Lucan designates the men's collective speech twice with the word *querellas* (2.44 and 2.63), the same word used of Cornelia's laments at 5.761 and 8.87; and the old man's speech with the verb *flebat* at 2.233 (as I discussed in Chapter 2).

reanimates in Book 6. Let us recall from Chapter 4 that there we hear, in succession, Camillus weeping (*flentemque Camillum*, 6.786), Sulla offering reproach (*Sullam ... querentem*, 6.787), Scipio lamenting (*deplorat ... Scipio*, 6.788), and Cato grieving (*maeret Cato*, 6.790). Even Rome's dead contribute to the communal process of lament in this poem, offering personal testimony to the contrast between Rome's glorious past and grim present. Significantly, though Lucan gives each figure a distinct verb of lamentation, he introduces them as a collective, sharing one mournful face (*tristis felicibus umbris | uultus*, 6.784–5), an image underscoring their identity as a community of mourners. Further still, the corpse himself, a walking, talking manifestation of Rome's self-destructive end, is soaked with tears (*fletu manante*, 6.776) as he relays the report.

6.5. The inclusion of the narrator in the antiphony of lament for Pompey

Antiphonal lament in the *Pharsalia*, then, echoes and grows among both individuals, as Homer had depicted it, and groups, as Lucan moves the process of lament away from the margins of his epic, involving not just the Andromache-figure Cornelia but entire communities of lamenters, male and female, living and dead, in exchange with one another. In what follows I want to explore Lucan's expansion of that antiphony still further—to the character of the narrator himself. In her analysis of the *gooi* in *Iliad* 24, Christine Perkell writes that, in speeches of lament, "meaning is a function of, for example, who laments, who is being lamented, the specific content of the lament, and where it occurs in the text."[40] We will see in this section that Lucan meaningfully crafts his narrator as a lamenter, employing many of the mode's hallmarks and participating dynamically in the antiphony of mourning for Pompey. Here again there is precedent in epic as early as the Homeric poems, in, for example, the narrator's series of apostrophes to Melanippus after his death (*Il.* 15.582–4) and Patroclus in *Iliad* 16, the book of his death (16.19, 16.584, 16.744, 16.754, 16.812, and 16.843). And while apostrophes such as these may hint at a connection with lament,[41] we will see in the coming pages

---

[40] Perkell (2008) 108.
[41] See Dué (2020), as well as Graziosi (2013) 19–20 on the address to Melanippus; with the caution of Morrison (2007) 92 ("Homeric apostrophe to characters is ... remarkably free of emotional content"). And see my broader discussion later in this chapter.

that Lucan equips his narrator with the full register of thematic and stylistic effects familiar from the Homeric *goos*.

The lamentation over Pompey's corpse in the final tableau of Book 8 (8.712–872) demonstrates well Lucan's involvement of the narrator in the process of lament. For the act of burial and obsequies, the poet invents the Roman quaestor Cordus, who disposes of the body in a "ritually correct"[42] way and delivers three speeches (8.729–42, 8.746–51, and 8.759–75) over the corpse. Conventional elements of lament appear in each of the speeches,[43] and most of all in the last of them, which opens with a praising address to the deceased, enhanced by a superlative form: *o maxime . . . ductor et Hesperii maiestas nominis una* (8.759–60: "O greatest leader and sole glory of the Hesperian name"). The appeals to Pompey's greatness here (*maxime*, *maiestas*) are met and balanced in the closing address with the vocative *Magne* (8.775). A number of contrasts run through the speech, notably between the burial that Pompey deserved and the "sadder pyre" (*tristior iste rogus*, 8.762) that he is receiving, and in the distance between this remote site in Egypt and Pompey's home in Hesperia, where Cordus hopes his ashes may return (8.768–70).[44]

Whereas Plutarch (*Pomp.* 80) describes two individuals burying Pompey's body, the freedman Philippus and an old soldier, Lucan chooses the solitary figure of Cordus—a choice that surely generates pathos[45] but also makes way for the participation of the narrator in the process. After Cordus's third speech, he lights the pyre but soon puts it out and retreats (8.775–80), prompting the narrator to address him as a "fool" (*demens*, 8.781) and command him to "go" (*i*, 8.784) and demand Pompey's head (*posce caput*, 8.785) for burial. Cordus is seemingly roused by the narrator's orders to recover the unburned bones, bury them, and put up a stone as tombstone (8.785–93). Then, over twenty-one lines (8.795–815), the narrator makes an extended address to Cordus's "rash right hand" (*temeraria dextra*, 8.795), and in so doing fills in some of the praise that is missing from Pompey's meager tomb and from Cordus's earlier laments. For example, at 8.798–802 he includes the conventional element of a contrast with other deceased figures: if after death Hercules and Bacchus won domain over all of Oeta and Nysa, respectively,

---

[42] Keith (2008) 247. See Day (2013) 221–8 on this episode as a manifestation of the sublime.
[43] See Keith (2008) 245–8.
[44] Note esp. the contrast captured in the juxtaposition *in Hesperiam, non hac in sede* (8.768).
[45] So Keith (2008) 248. On the creation of Cordus, see Brennan (1969), proposing a nod to the famously pro-Republican historian Cremutius Cordus (Tac., *Ann.* 4.34–5); Mayer (1981) 171; and Fertik (2018) 466–8.

then Pompey's spirit merits possession of all of the Roman Empire. Then at 8.806–13 the narrator uses a series of imperatives (*adde, adde, adde* at 8.807, 8.808, and 8.811) to instruct Cordus's hand about which past glories should be added to Pompey's tomb.[46] The statement "If you think the stone is worthy of his sacred name, then add his great deeds and the greatest commemorations of his achievements" (*quod si tam sacro dignaris nomine saxum, | adde actus tantos monimentaque maxima rerum,* 8.806–7) creates the conceit that the narrator had heard Cordus address Magnus as *maxime ductor* (8.759) and is now responding that the lament requires more details about the man's greatness. The narrator's last order to Cordus is "Say (*dic*) that after war he always sought out the toga of the citizen, and that, after leading three processions, he was content to give back many triumphs to his fatherland" (8.813–15). The content of this command builds on what Cordus himself said in his first speech, that Pompey's greatness does not require an elaborate funeral procession that would relive his old triumphs (*ueteres . . . triumphos,* 8.733). The narrator thus echoes Cordus and reinforces his praise of Pompey's humility in success. And the verb used for this final command, *dic,* is frequently used of the act of singing.[47] Cordus and the narrator, we see, are engaging in complementary *song* over the corpse of the deceased Pompey.

Mayer sees in this burial scene a pointed contrast with burial scenes in the *Iliad*, writing: "The feeble flame is so unlike the pyre of Patroclus, at which victims were offered. In fine, the expectation of a reader who is acquainted with traditional epic accounts is baulked at every point, and his pity should be awakened by the sense of contrast."[48] But if the scene here evokes by contrast the grand burials of the final books of the *Iliad* and later epic, then it is another departure from epic precedent here that is more striking, and more significant for our understanding of Lucan's poetic aims. Of the narrator's interactions with Cordus over the corpse in Book 8, Mayer writes: "Lucan's hectoring rebuke to Cordus is unlike anything in previous epics."[49] This is true: nowhere before in epic do we read a narrator so intimately engaged with a character's actions, here attending to a dead hero's corpse and participating—I hope I have shown—in antiphonal lament. Let us recall Tsagalis's assessment that "the antiphonal element refers not only to the external

---

[46] Even if the task is impossible, as the question in 8.816 reveals: *quis capit haec tumulus* ("What tomb can capture all these things?").

[47] See, e.g., Catull. 61.39; Virg., *Aen.* 7.41–2; Hor. *Carm.* 1.12.13 and 25, 3.4.1, and 4.9.21; Ov. *Met* 1.1, and *OLD* 7b. Note also that Erictho directs the vatic corpse with *dic* at 6.762.

[48] Mayer (1981) 169.

[49] Mayer (1981) 178.

reenactment of the funeral laments, but also to the responsive nature of the themes."[50] Cordus's and the narrator's words operate in precisely this way, syntactically engaged through the apostrophes and imperatives that the narrator issues, but also complementing one another thematically. It is noteworthy that Statius's Calliope singles out this very passage as a demonstration of "Lucan the lamenter," when writing to him, "You will dutifully lament the crime of Palusian Canopus and give Pompey a tomb higher than bloody Pharos" (*Silv.* 2.7.70–2). Statius understood the persona of the narrator as "dutifully lamenting" (*deflebis pius*), as closely and seriously engaged in the poem's antiphony.

The interchange between Cordus and the narrator is, to be sure, "unlike anything in previous epics." But if we understand it as participation in antiphonal lament, then we can also begin to make better sense of the narrator's address to Pompey during his flight from Pharsalia to Larisa in Book 7. At this point, Pompey's fate is decided: he is now *infelix* (7.648 and 7.673) and even sees himself dying with the other corpses on the battlefield he has just fled (*ac se tam multo pereuntem sanguine uidit*, 7.653). And I want to propose that the narrator's engagement with Pompey at 7.680–727 reads as an anticipatory lament, containing as it does many of the mode's hallmarks.[51] The passage begins (7.680–2) and ends (7.726–7) with addresses to Magnus;[52] and like Cordus in his opening address at 8.759, in 7.681 the narrator plays on the name *Magnus* in referring to his greatness (*maiestate*). Throughout this set of lines, the narrator directs imperatives (*fuge*, 689; *respice*, 700; *prohibe*, 706; *ueta* and *remitte*, 707; *aspice*, 709 and 710; *elige*, 711) as well as other second-person verb forms (*aspicis*, 683; *fueris*, 689; *potes*, 718) at his addressee. Emphatic second-person pronouns and possessive adjectives appear nine times across these lines, and in the center of the passage the narrator directs two questions at Pompey (7.698–702).

Accompanying these stylistic hallmarks of a speech of lament are many of the themes common to the mode. At 7.686–9 and 7.718 the narrator explores the contrast between Pompey's more esteemed past and his doomed present.[53] In the first of these passages he includes customary markers of temporal antithesis with *iam* (686), *nunc* (687), *nunc* (689)—topped off with

---

[50] Tsagalis (2004) 49.
[51] See Seo (2011) 213–14 for the comparable argument that the narrator's apostrophe to Pompey here begins to prepare him for his Stoic death in Book 8.
[52] Who is also addressed at 7.691.
[53] See Day (2013) 218 on Lucan's focus here on how Pompey's "former life is lost forever."

the statement "What you *were, now* you may know" (*quid fueris, nunc scire licet*, 7.689). He also deploys the conventional contrast of the addressee with other figures, in this case Caesar, whose criminality, the narrator asserts in a separate address, Pompey does not match (7.699–706 and 7.721–3). He also unleashes biting reproach at his addressee, when noting that Pompey's flight left the senate to fight for itself (7.696–7).[54] Perhaps the most distinctive and striking element in the narrator's lament for Pompey here is his expression of the common fate they share:

> ceu flebilis Africa damnis
> et ceu Munda nocens Pharioque a gurgite clades
> sic et Thessalicae post te pars maxima pugnae
> non iam Pompei nomen populare per orbem
> nec studium belli, sed par quod semper habemus,
> libertas et Caesar, erit.

> Like Africa, lamentable for its losses, and like destructive Munda and the disaster by the Egyptian waters, so too after you the greatest stake in the Thessalian battle will no longer be the name of Pompey that is popular throughout the world, nor the passion for war, but rather the pair that we always have, freedom and Caesar. (7.691–6)

The narrator directly ties his own struggle as a Roman living under the Caesars with Pompey's fight at Pharsalia and the efforts of those at later defeats in Africa, Munda in Spain, and Egypt. The narrator and Pompey, speaker and addressee, mourner and deceased are closely aligned in the lot that they—united in the *habemus* of 7.695—share.[55] Like Cornelia in her series of speeches, the narrator forges an intimate connection with Pompey through his words, decries his fall from past glory, celebrates and rebukes him all at once—and is ultimately resigned to accept his common fate with the fallen hero.

---

[54] Leigh (1997) 156 describes the narrator's condemnation in 7.697 (*ostendit moriens sibi se pugnasse senatus*) as "sibilant in its scorn." See also Rolim de Moura (2010) 85–6 on the elements of criticism of Pompey that run across the narrator's words in this passage.

[55] D'Alessandro Behr (2007) 86 also notes the commonality between narrator and addressee brought out here: "In this apostrophe, and also later when he will describe Pompey's death (*BC* 8.595–636), the narrator shares his sorrow, highlights the horrific cruelty of his enemies, and stimulates the reader to be sympathetic with him." See too Thorne (2011) 378.

A striking feature of this passage is that the narrator discusses the process of lament when addressing Pompey, and in fact *discourages* it. The initial address at 7.680–2 begins with the approving observation that there was no groaning or tears (*non gemitus, non fletus erat*, 7.680) after Pharsalia from Pompey, only a respectful sorrow befitting his grandeur. Later the narrator attempts to make the case that Pompey should have no regrets, that "to prevail was worse" (*uincere peius erat*, 7.706); and so orders him to "prevent laments from resounding, forbid the people to weep, stop tears and mourning" (*prohibe lamenta sonare, | flere ueta populos, lacrimas luctusque remitte*, 7.706–7). It is a typically Lucanian paradox that, in the midst of this passage containing many of the formal features of lament, the mourner himself, the narrator, shuns the very process of lament. But the upshot is that the reader is compelled to think more about lament and its efficacy, and then to see that the prohibitions of lament at 7.706–7 gain no traction. Rather, the people of Larisa weep (*flentes*, 7.715) as they see the fleeing Pompey, whom "groans and tears follow" (*gemitus lacrimaeque sequuntur*, 7.724). Just as the mourning words of Cordus and the narrator complement and respond to one another in Book 8, here too at Pharsalia there is an antiphony of lament. The forceful imperatives at 7.706–7 about preventing the people's lament for Pompey, we realize, in fact just serve to build up tension for the release of their laments. The narrator's own words of anticipatory lament for Pompey have, it appears, actually had the effect of *generating* the lament from the people that comes at 7.724–5.

There is one final episode of lament for Pompey—or rather, feigned lament—that I think complements my argument for an antiphony among the *Pharsalia*'s characters and narrator. Book 9 closes with Caesar's arrival on Egyptian waters, where an agent of King Ptolemy (probably Pothinus) hands the head of Pompey to Caesar (9.1010–63), who then delivers a lengthy speech (9.1064–1104). And so the setting, with the remains of the deceased before him, is just right for a speech of lament. But it is no such thing. Caesar spends much of the speech berating the agent (addressed at 1064) and Ptolemy himself (addressed at 1076) for stealing the opportunity of pardoning his rival, a gesture that he calls "the one reward of civil war" (*unica belli | praemia ciuilis*, 9.1066–7). When he finally does address Pompey with his final words (9.1098–1104), Caesar focuses again on the greater legitimacy that a living Pompey would have brought him (9.1102–4). The last word of the speech is, fittingly, *mihi*.

What marks Caesar's speech as especially out of tune, however, is the response to it in the ensuing lines:

> nec talia fatus
> inuenit fletus comitem nec turba querenti   1105
> credidit: abscondunt gemitus et pectora laeta
> fronte tegunt, hilaresque nefas spectare cruentum,
> o bona libertas, cum Caesar lugeat, audent.

> After saying such things, he found no companion for his weeping, and the crowd did not believe the grieving man. They hid their groans and concealed their feelings with a happy front; and, while Caesar laments, they dare—o dear freedom!—to look happily at the bloody crime. (9.1104–8)

Caesar's speech over the remains of Pompey is met by the *absence* of antiphony. There is no "companion for his weeping" (*fletus comitem*) nor a collective response from the crowd (*turba*), such as those we read of after Cornelia's lament in Book 9 and the narrator's anticipatory lament in Book 7. With these details, Lucan flags the *expectation* for antiphonal lament, while at the same time underscoring that it is missing. Those in Caesar's company fear showing their true feelings about Pompey and so in fact conceal their grief (*abscondunt gemitus*).[56] Since Caesar's "lament" is patently disingenuous, it is not met by the antiphony that would attend proper lament.

Furthermore, just as the narrator had engaged in antiphony with other mourners for Pompey earlier in the poem, here too he is intimately involved, but this time inserting himself to reject Caesar's speech and discard it as a specious gesture of mourning. When Caesar first receives the dead man's head, we read that he "poured out tears that did not fall naturally, and released groans from a happy heart" (*lacrimas non sponte cadentis | effudit gemitusque expressit pectore laeto*, 9.1038–9) and so "with nothing other than tears is he able to conceal his heart's obvious joys" (9.1040–1).[57] The narrator then turns to address Caesar in an apostrophe running for sixteen lines (9.1047–62),[58] in which he badgers him with a series of questions (9.1048–51), dwells on the betrayal of his ties of kinship with Pompey (9.1048–9, 1054–5, and 1057–8,

---

[56] See Ormand (1994) 54 on the "complete convolutions of narrative" in this passage.
[57] Tracy (2014) 141 discusses Lucan's presentation of Caesar here as "an artful deceiver."
[58] McRoberts (2005) 46–8 treats Lucan's "skillful use of apostrophe" (47) in this address to Caesar.

capped with the vocative *perfide* in 1061), and explicitly identifies the fraudulence of his tears: "Whatever impulse drove you to weep, it was far removed from true piety" (9.1055–6). This address leads immediately into Caesar's own speech of non-lament and then the silence from those around him, the three gestures working together to expose the absence of lament. So here before the head of Pompey, Lucan points to all of the contextual elements of antiphonal, collective lament, only—on this occasion, with Caesar as prospective mourner—to pointedly omit them. The result is that, coming as it does after Cornelia, Cordus, throngs of *populi*, and the narrator himself have all voiced laments for the dead leader, the passage serves to amplify, through the careful depiction of its converse, the antiphony for Pompey resounding across the poem. What also becomes clear is that, while the interchange of lament in the *Pharsalia* is radically expansive—bursting open conventional barriers of gender and diegetic barriers separating character and narrator—there is no place in that antiphony for the vicar of Caesarism himself.

6.6. The *Pharsalia* as a lament

I hope to have brought out how Lucan's narrator enters into the process of lament for Pompey, employing the hallmarks of the *goos* as he intimately engages with both the dying/deceased hero and the poem's mourning characters. And while his gestures recall the *gooi* of epic narrative, could we also read his participation in the poem's mourning as a sort of *threnos*? Let us recall that at *Iliad* 24.720–2 Homer refers to the leaders of the dirge as singers (ἀοιδοὺς) who perform a song of lamentation (στονόεσσαν ἀοιδὴν). Given that the Homeric poems withhold these *threnoi* from us—leaving them just out of the performance and just off the page—here may lie another way in which Lucan outstrips the Smyrnaean bard. To the extent that we can align the poet Lucan with the narrator of his poem—and, given the many first-person references to the present day,[59] I think it is inescapable—then perhaps it is right to read the narrator's repeated engagements in the antiphony of lament as manifestations of the aoidic song of the *threnos*. This, we read, is what it looks like for a poet to deliver a lament. Here at last in the *Pharsalia* is what a *threnos* in epic looks like.

---

[59] See later discussion in this chapter.

To this end, I now want to extend our understanding of the narrator as a participant in lament beyond the passages addressing Pompey to our reading of the poem as a whole. For the engaged, indeed intrusive narrator we have tracked in this chapter makes himself famously present throughout the poem; the metalepsis of the narrator's incursions into the story is an abiding feature of the *Pharsalia*.[60] We observe this most notably in his frequent use of the first-person plural, often in the present tense,[61] and in his even more frequent deployment of apostrophe. Narratorial use of apostrophe was not at all alien to the epic genre: there are, for example, 30 such uses in the *Iliad* and 15 in the *Odyssey* (14 of them to the swineherd Eumaeus); 54 in the *Aeneid*; and 99 in the *Metamorphoses*.[62] Lucan goes to the next level. By Francesca D'Alessandro Behr's count in her book-length study of this trope in the poem, there are at least 197 apostrophes in the *Pharsalia*.[63] And the quantitative metrics do not tell the whole story. In his study of narrators in early Greek poetry, Andrew Morrison writes that "the narrators of both the *Iliad* and the *Odyssey* do not foreground themselves—they do not use their narratorial personas as a principal method of structuring their epics, nor are the epics about them. The narrators are there, of course, but they are self-effacing."[64] Such a characterization is more or less accurate for the narrators of prior Latin epic too; their intrusions—such as the Virgilian narrator's entrances to apostrophize the deceased Caieta at 7.1–4 and Nisus and Euyalus at 9.446–9[65]—are powerful, but extraordinary. This is not the case for Lucan's narrator: in many ways this epic *is* "about him." If Homer, Virgil, and others had shown some of the possibilities of an epic narrator interacting directly with the dead, Lucan opens that engagement up into a sweeping program. The elaborate apostrophes in passages displaying what I have identified as antiphonal lament are examples

---

[60] On Lucan's intrusive narrator, see Seitz (1965); Masters (1992) 88–90; Radicke (2004) 511–19; Rolim de Moura (2010) (on metalepsis at 89); Pandey (2014); and Roche (2019) 23; and Kimmerle (2015) 147–267 on Lucan's narrator as unreliable.

[61] See Leigh (1997) 79–80 and Fratantuono (2012) 141–2.

[62] So McRoberts (2005) 15–16, with an appendix at 219–34 that catalogs all of these examples, as well as 91 examples from Statius's *Theb*.

[63] D'Alessandro Behr (2007) 7. McRoberts (2005) 15–16, using a more limited definition, counts 155 examples in the *Ph*. On Lucan's use of the trope, see too Leigh (1997) 307–10; Narducci (2002) 88–92; Faber (2005); Asso (2008) and (2010) 29–30; and Roche (2019) 23–4.

[64] Morrison (2007) 46, while pointing to the seminal narratological work of de Jong (1987) and (2001): "De Jong, of course, has clearly demonstrated that the Homeric narrator is an ever-present controlling force in the narrative of the *Iliad*." See also Scodel (2006); Graziosi (2013), identifying elements of the Homeric narrator's presence in the action; and Dué (2020), proposing a connection between Homeric apostrophes and the lament tradition. Seitz (1965) and Lausberg (1985) 1571–2 draw pointed contrasts between the Homeric narrator and Lucan's narrator.

[65] See Block (1982) and Seider (2013) 137–54.

of the narrator inserting himself in the action—but this engaged, intimate mode carries across the poem.

The narrator's use of apostrophe may well be what led Quintilian to characterize Lucan as "burning and stirred up" (*ardens et concitatus*, 10.1.90).[66] And modern readers of the epic have long been puzzled or even perturbed by the pervasiveness of the trope. In his introduction to Haskins's 1887 text and commentary on the poem, Heitland wrote of apostrophes in the *Pharsalia* that "their effect on the poem as a whole is bad" and "destructive."[67] Nearly a century later, Roland Mayer would judge similarly that apostrophe is "a figure he overworks" and that "Lucan, it is obvious, did not see that over-use of such an emotional device was 'counter-productive' and leads to frigidity."[68] So great was J. D. Duff's discomfort with the device that, in his 1928 Loeb translation of the poem, he converts most of the narrator's apostrophes and the accompanying second-person verb forms into third-person narrative. In justifying this decision, Duff writes that "[i]n Latin apostrophe is often a metrical device, and often a meaningless convention."[69]

Readers of the *Pharsalia* in recent years have been less quick to disregard the narrator's uses of apostrophe as meaningless. Charles Martindale identified it as "sort-of a master-trope within the *Pharsalia*" that helps to create a textual "theatre for himself and his interlocutors"; and Leigh as something that is "deadly serious" in the poem, in that Lucan "truly is talking to his characters, does have a special relationship with the world of his verse, and, like it or not, this is part of his message communicated."[70] In her extensive treatment of the issue, D'Alessandro Behr aims to understand the narrator's use of apostrophes as a "cognitively useful Stoic trope."[71] Lucan incorporates them, she argues, to break the action and thus the *enargeia* of

---

[66] Mayer (1981) 16: "Surely it was this very fault which led Quintilian to describe Lucan as 'ardens et concitatus.'" See Faber (2005) 334–5 on how Lucan may have honed his use of apostrophe in the declamatory schools.

[67] Heitland (1887) lxxi. But see also Maes (2013) 408 on Scaliger's approval in the sixteenth century of the intrusive authorial voice as a moralizing force.

[68] Mayer (1981) 15.

[69] Duff (1928) viii. Though he does not state as much directly, the narrator's pervasive use of apostrophe was perhaps another factor (see p. 32, n. 37) leading Duff to conclude that "[n]o reasonable judgment can rank Lucan among the world's great epic poets" (xii).

[70] Martindale (1993) 67–8 and Leigh (1997) 310 (who at 39–40 writes of the political seriousness of the poem). See too Johnson (1987) 185 ("through apostrophe the dead is made present; it is a form of ventriloquism"); Henderson (1987) 135 on Lucan's way of "putting you, his readers, into the frame with incessant apostrophe"; and Rolim de Moura (2010) 72: "Interpreting the narrator's relationship with the characters as one implying dialogue does justice to the apostrophe as a figure not to be dismissed as empty *cacoethes*."

[71] D'Alessandro Behr (2007) 8, with the heart of this argument coming at 76–112.

the poem, with the result that readers may gain a pedagogically healthy detachment from its events. While (as we shall see) I have reservations about this larger argument about the reader's detachment by way of apostrophe, D'Alessandro Behr makes an important observation about the connection between many of the poem's apostrophes and *grief*. She writes that "[i]n a poem that is about the losers, grief cannot get in the way of representation, nor can lamentation be contained. In fact, it occupies many of the narrator's apostrophes . . . apostrophes that have the flavor of lamentations."[72]

This, I think, is a productive way to make sense of the abundance of apostrophes in the poem, of what we might call the "apostrophic position" that the narrator assumes for so much of the *Pharsalia*. Not every apostrophe, to be sure, initiates a speech of lament, as those I considered earlier do. Most of them do not.[73] But could the narrator's extensive and, yes, "deadly serious" embrace of this trope—and, correspondingly, his discursive relationship with the poem's characters—be a function of the status of the poem itself as a grand lament? Might we understand the narrator's seemingly frenetic impulses toward these plaintive insertions as part of a larger expression of agitation and mourning?[74] Scholars have compared the narrator's personal engagement with the poem's action, through apostrophe as well as his first-personal insertions, with the involvement of the chorus in the events of tragic drama.[75] I am suggesting that an explanation for the engaged, impassioned narrator of the *Pharsalia* lies closer to home, in the mode of lament that is constitutive of epic. In his consideration of the place of apostrophe in the poem, Asso aptly writes that "Rome receives Lucan's extended address in the form of an epic, and thus the entire poem can be read as an apostrophe to Rome, a forceful lament for lost Republican liberty."[76] Asso puts forward this clarifying suggestion but does not pursue it further; there is much more to say on the matter. In a similar way, scholars have identified apostrophe's potential as a structural and closural device in the *Pharsalia*, with attention to particular bookends.[77] I am proposing a broader understanding of

---

[72] D'Alessandro Behr (2007) 31.

[73] Geographical locations, mythical figures, and abstractions are also apostrophized in the poem. See, e.g., the apostrophes to the Cinga River (4.21), Luxuria (4.373–4), the Nile (5.712), Inachus (6.361–6), Thessaly (7.847–72), and Egypt (8.823–34).

[74] We might compare the distinction between "full" and "reduced" lament in Greek tragedy discussed by Suter (2003) 3–4, summarizing the work of Wright (1986). See too Bakewell (2016) 113–16.

[75] See Perutelli (2004) 97 and Ambühl (2015) 266 (on *petimus* at 7.803, discussed later in this chapter).

[76] Asso (2008) 164, limiting his focus to the apostrophe to Roma at 1.84–5.

[77] Faber (2005) 337–8 and Roche (2019) 24.

apostrophe's place in the makeup of the poem, grounded in the dynamics of lament.

After all, like any proper *goos* or *threnos*, this poem is sung over the corpse of the deceased, Rome. Lucan makes this clear right in his proem, when introducing his main character of "a powerful nation turned on its own innards with a victorious right hand" (*populumque potentem | in sua uictrici conuersum uiscera dextra*, 1.2–3).[78] Gutted insides, to go with severed heads, freestanding torsos, dismembered limbs, and every combination thereof fill the pages of the poem, and recent scholarship has focused on this ubiquity of corpses in the *Pharsalia*.[79] When we begin to understand the poem itself as a lament, its seemingly endless rollout of dead Romans comes to be appreciated not as superfluous or baroque but as *necessary*. A lament must be sung over the dead.

I will repeat that it would be incorrect to argue that each individual apostrophe in the poem sets off a speech of lament. But it surely is significant that the very first apostrophe of the poem lends itself to such a reading. Let us recall from Chapter 1 that the narrator's address at 1.8–32 to Rome's citizens (*o ciues*, 1.8) and correspondingly Roma herself (*Roma*, 1.21) contains many of the hallmarks of lament, including questions directed at the deceased in 1.8 and 1.9–12 and ring-composition, with the theme of citizens' self-destruction bookending the address in 1.8 and 1.32. The conventional contrast between past glory and present woe, delineated by the common marker *at nunc* at 1.24, is joined by reproach of Rome for her "madness" (*furor*, 1.8) in slaughtering herself rather than fighting foreign enemies (1.8–23).[80] Toward the end of the passage, the narrator also includes the conventional comparison between the addressee and analogous figures, in this case between Rome and other attackers of Rome, Pyrrhus and Hannibal (1.30–1), who were unable to accomplish the destruction she wrought on herself.

This address of lament over the *uiscera* of Rome's citizens makes for a fitting entrée into the poem, preparing the reader for the expressions of lament that will carry across the work. And the tone of self-reflexive lament that characterizes the opening address—and is then embodied in Roma's gesture

---

[78] An image revisited amid the slaughter at Pharsalia at 7.490–1: *ensis | . . . dextras Romana in uiscera ducit*. See Mebane (2016) 192.

[79] See Most (1992); Bartsch (1997) 10–47; Thorne (2011); Dinter (2012); Mebane (2016); McClellan (2019) 115–69 and (2020); and Roche (2019) 25 (on Lucan's extraordinary use of the chilling prosaic noun *cadauer*).

[80] A point the lamenting Roman men raise at 2.47–56. McRoberts (2005) 37–8 highlights how frequently Lucan's apostrophes include elements of reproach and invective.

of self-lamentation at the Rubicon[81]—continues into each of the narrator's subsequent apostrophes of Roma. There are nine more over the course of the poem; and in all of them, she is called on as either the perpetrator or the victim of her own destruction and death. And while these passages do not rise to the level of speeches of lament per se, they draw on many of that mode's common elements, together hammering home the sense of plaintive mourning for Rome's fall. Later in the poem's prologue, the narrator fires reproach at Roma as the "cause of evils" in an apostrophe made more personal by an opening second-person singular pronoun (*tu causa malorum | ... Roma*, 1.84–5).[82] During the account of the city's abandonment, he again uses the pointed, intimate combination of a second-person singular pronoun and vocative when highlighting Roma's abandonment (1.519–20: *tu tantum audito bellorum nomine, Roma, | desereris*, "you, Rome, when the name of war was only heard, are deserted").[83] The description in Book 3 of all of the Roman treasure lost to Caesar is punctuated by a poignant address to Roma (*tibi, Roma*, 3.159); and in the next book, the narrator inserts a similar apostrophe when characterizing Curio's part in destroying Rome (*dum regnum te, Roma, facit*, 4.692).[84] In Book 6, after Pompey's failure to press his victory at Dyrrachium, the narrator dwells on the contrast between Rome's free past and functionally dead present under tyranny with another personalized address to "you, Roma" (*Roma ... tibi*, 6.302–3). He delivers another intimate but resentful reproach to Roma in Book 8, when stating, "you too (*tu quoque*), Roma, though you have already given temples to the cruel tyrant, have not yet asked for Pompey's ashes" (8.835–6). And in what is an otherwise celebratory passage of praise for Cato in Book 9, the narrator again addresses Roma as transformed by the subjection to tyranny and doomed—even if there is a chance that she can unyoke her neck and stand up straight again (*Roma ... | ... si steteris umquam ceruice soluta*, 9.602–3).

Not surprisingly, it is in the twin statements on the destructive consequences of Pharsalia in Book 7 when the narrator's addresses to Roma read most like expressions of lament. Consideration of how many nations and chiefs went off to die in the battle (7.417–18) provides him with the opportunity to contrast past imperial sway with present doom, saying to

---

[81] See my discussion in Chapter 1.
[82] See Asso (2008) 163–5.
[83] See my discussion in Chapter 5.
[84] Asso (2010) 261: "Here, the apostrophe to Roma brushes the passage with a tragic tinge of pathos."

Roma: "Through them [Fortune] may show to you while you crash, Roma, how great you are as you fall" (*per quos tibi, Roma, ruenti | ostendat quam magna cadas*, 7.418–19). The fall from past greatness (*magna*) to present woe is doubly emphasized in the synonymous *ruenti* and *cadas*. In another address to Roma a few lines later, the narrator takes up the death wish that is also common to the mode of lament:

> uellem populis incognita nostris.
> uolturis ut primum laeuo fundata uolatu
> Romulus infami conpleuit moenia luco,
> usque ad Thessalicas seruisses, Roma, ruinas
> de Brutis, Fortuna, queror. quid tempora legum
> egimus aut annos a consule nomen habentis?

> Would that [freedom] had never been known among our people! From the time when Romulus first founded the city walls after the flight of a vulture on the left and filled them with a disreputable grove all the way to the Thessalian destruction, you, Rome, should have been enslaved. Fortune, I have a complaint about the Bruti! Why did we live through those times under law or the years that take their names from a consul? (7.436–41)

The poignancy in the wish that Roma had never been free, indeed had never *lived*,[85] is enhanced by the very personal manner in which is it expressed, with an interplay between first- and second-person forms. The first-person singular verbs conveying his emotional pleas (*uellem* in 7.436, *queror* in 7.440), along with first-person plural forms to capture Romans' collective experience (*populis... nostris* in 7.436, *egimus* in 7.441), surround the second-person wish that holds the thought together: *seruisses, Roma* (7.439: "you should have been enslaved through it all, Rome"). As in a *goos*, here the dynamic between first- and second-person forms generates the sense of Roma and Rome's—that is, the Republic's—distance from the narrator, but also their closeness, how personally attached the mourner is to the deceased.[86]

---

[85] Cf. Tsagalis (2004) 42: "By employing this self-effacing unattainable wish, the mourner dies although still alive; he does not experience a physical death but dies *within the poetic reality of the performance*."

[86] So Tsagalis (2004) 43 on how death wishes in Homeric lament "show clear traces of a self-blaming tone that blots out the distinction between self and other and results in self-condemnation and guilt."

When the narrator addresses Roma for the third and final time in Book 7, he in fact seems to *shun* lament as a response to his narrative. The passage, one of the most arresting and most celebrated in the poem,[87] comes right as he looks to the middle of the fray, where Roman brothers and fathers fought (7.545–50). It reads:

> hanc fuge, mens, partem belli tenebrisque relinque,
> nullaque tantorum discat me uate malorum,
> quam multum bellis liceat ciuilibus, aetas.
> a potius pereant lacrimae pereantque querellae:
> quidquid in hac acie gessisti, Roma, tacebo.

> Flee this part of the war, mind, and leave it in the darkness! And may no age learn from me as poet of such great evils how much is allowed in civil war. Ah! Rather, let tears perish, and let laments perish: whatever you did on that battlefield, Roma, I'll stay silent about it. (7.552–6)

Again we see the narrator personally engaged with his addressee Roma, this time moving from a bravura apostrophe of his own mind in 7.552 to apostrophize Roma in 7.556, in each line pledging to be silent about the corpses before him, to not perform the duties of the *uates*. The implication is that the deadly feats of war and the process of lament are inextricably bound: if what occurs on the battlefield (*quidquid in hac acie gessisti*) is not retold, then *lacrimae* and *querellae* can be eschewed too.

But of course the narrator does not stay silent about the carnage before him. As Hardie puts it, "Lucan has already said too much and will go on to say more."[88] The gesture is familiar from the proem, where he had designated the *Pharsalia*'s contents as "our common unspeakable thing" (*commune nefas*, 1.6)—only to commence speaking about those contents.[89] This is a poem of war and death, this is *Todesdichtung*, this is epic; and, accordingly, tears and lamentation must exist in these pages too. As we have seen, the narrator's feint at 7.552-6 is matched by a similar gesture later in the book, when he orders Pompey to prohibit the people's laments (7.706–7), only to describe their

---

[87] On the passage's extraordinariness, see Johnson (1987) 98–100; Leigh (1997) 18–19 and 102–3; and Narducci (2002) 175.
[88] Hardie (2013a) 235.
[89] See the discussions of Lucan's focus on the paradox of *nefas* by O'Higgins (1988) 215–17; Feeney (1991) 276–83; and Day (2013) 88–9.

mourning for him shortly thereafter (7.715 and 724–5). In both instances the stunt of rejecting the process of lament only serves, as in a *recusatio*, to bring it closer, to compel the reader to listen for it.[90]

6.7. The common fate of the first-person plural and the power to weep

We are seeing that, just as the war of the *Pharsalia* will be catastrophic on a global, universal, finalizing scale, so too will its lament be louder, broader, grander, inclusive of more voices, complete. And so it may be best to understand the narrator's use of apostrophe not as a means of extradiegetic detachment from the narrative,[91] but rather as a function of the deeply personal position of a mourner, engaged in a prolonged lament for Rome. To take this further, we might make sense of the narrator's frequent use of the first-person plural in this same way. Previously I suggested that the narrator's repeated uses of the first- and second-person, not only in the longer narratorial laments but also in the mini-laments addressed to Roma, recall the singer of the *goos* deploying first- and second-person deictics to poignant effect. Looking more broadly at the narrator's positioning and tone in the poem as a whole, could we extend this connection with lament to his other uses of the first-person plural? Nicola Lanzarone writes of how remarkable it is for the narrator to participate in the narrated events of the *Pharsalia*, and thus to rupture the objectivity of the genre in a way that no epic predecessor had before.[92] Through these intrusions "the voice of the 'Neronian narrator,' that is of Lucan in his capacity as a man from the Neronian age, manifests itself" in the poem.[93] Since these narratorial entrances in the first-person plural emphasize that the dead at Pharsalia and the living under the principate share a common fate, might we understand these passages too as reflective of the poem's position of lament?

---

[90] *Pace* Leigh (1997) 18–19 and 102–3, reading the statement at 7.552–4 more at face value as a rejection of the role of the *uates*.

[91] As D'Alessandro Behr (2007) 105 proposes. See also Rolim de Moura (2010) and Pandey (2014) on the narrator's engagement.

[92] Lanzarone (2016) 146 (on 7.60). See too Lausberg (1985) 1571–2 and Narducci (2002) 94–104, arguing that Lucan includes a traditional "omniscient" narrator alongside the unconventional "Neronian" narrator.

[93] Lanzarone (2016) 436 (on 7.638–46): "si manifesta la voce del 'narratore neroniano,' cioè di Lucano in quanto uomo dell'età neroniana." McClellan (2020) 242 n. 4 helpfully addresses the identity of "Lucan-as-narrator."

It is again in the Book 7 statements about the consequences of Pharsalia where the narrator makes his strongest assertions in the first-person plural. At 7.630–1 he states that "no death is worthy of its own lament, and we have room to mourn no individual men" (*mors nulla querella | digna sua est, nullosque hominum lugere uacamus*). But what follows is a series of statements in the first-person plural containing two hallmarks of lament: reproach of the deceased and an assertion of the common fate of the mourner and deceased. The deceased is, as he had just asserted, not an individual, but a much larger collective:

                    plus est quam uita salusque
quod perit: in totum mundi prosternimur aeuum.
uincitur his gladiis omnis quae seruiet aetas.
proxima quid suboles aut quid meruere nepotes
in regnum nasci? pauide num gessimus arma
teximus aut iugulos? alieni poena timoris
in nostra ceruice sedet. post proelia natis
si dominum, Fortuna, dabas, et bella dedisses.

It is more than life and safety that are dying: we are being laid low for all of the world's time. Every age that will be enslaved is being defeated by these swords. Why do the next generation or why do their descendants deserve to be born into slavery? Surely *we* did not wage war in fear or cover our throats? The penalty for another's fear lies on our necks. If, Fortune, you gave a master to those born after the battles, then you also should have given them the wars. (7.639–46)

Hectoring and belittling the war-dead at Pharsalia for their cowardice (note especially *pauide* and *timoris*) in a biting rebuke, and then using the first-person plural to generate reproachful distance from those men ("Surely *we* did not wage war [*gessimus*] in fear or cover [*teximus*] our throats?"), the narrator also emphasizes the fate he and the other Romans making up the collective "we" *share* with them. At Pharsalia "*we* are being laid low" (*prosternimur*) and the punishment for cowardice "lies on our necks" (*in nostra ceruice*). As I addressed in Chapter 3, the death of Rome narrated in this poem is a communal one, stretching from Pharsalia to the mourning "we" of Lucan's own time;[94] and the

---

[94] See my discussion of 7.630–41 in Chapter 3, as well as Leigh (1997) 77–80 on these lines and how they express the "temporal universality of the battle" (79).

tension inherent in the first-person collective's fits of reproach and cries of commonality and even affection, while surely inconsistent,[95] are in keeping with the position of a mourner.

This use of the first-person plural to accentuate this common fate that crosses generations, elaborated with particular forcefulness at 7.639–46, surfaces at several other points in Book 7. As the two sides are gathering before battle, the narrator asks the gods, "When you decide to overturn all things, is it pleasing, o gods, to add guilt to our errors (*nostris erroribus*)?" (7.58–9). And just as Roman errors in general are made the responsibility of the first-person collective, so too is the particular crime of engaging in civil combat, as we read in the very next line: "We rush into disaster, and we demand weapons that will harm us" (*cladibus inruimus nocituraque poscimus arma*, 7.60). The narrator's address to Pompey at 7.205–13, much-discussed and debated over the years,[96] is not all that surprising when understood as another expression of the common fate shared by the Romans of 48 BCE and Lucan's time. Here the narrator states that readers of the poem will follow the fates at Pharsalia "as though they are still to come, not passed" (*ueluti uenientia fata | non transmissa*, 7.212–13) and "will long favor you, Magnus" (*adhuc tibi, Magne, fauebunt*, 7.213). The passage thus explicitly places the readers *there*, "rendered present at the battle."[97] Here and across this series of passages I have considered, the readers are united with the poem's characters in the unfolding of the common fate that Lucan calls "our toil" (*nostri . . . laboris*, 7.209), the struggle against Caesar(ism) that "we always have" (*semper habemus*, 7.695; see my earlier discussion).

After the battle, the collective "we" actively pursue burial for the dead at Pharsalia (*petimus non singula busta*, 7.803); and, fifty lines later, regret overturning those tombs (*omnia maiorum uertamus busta*, 7.855) when plowing the land and seeing sheep pull up "our bones" (*nostris ossibus*, 7.865) as they graze. In these acts of burial in 48 BCE (7.803) and their macabre rediscovery years later (7.855 and 7.865), the "we" of then and now, Pharsalia and the present day, merge, sharing this fate of self-destructive doom.[98]

---

[95] Kimmerle (2015) 165–7.

[96] See, e.g., Bartsch (1997) 81 ("a startling deviation from the epic norm . . . the narrator himself reenters the text"); Leigh (1997) 12–15; Fratantuono (2012) 279 ("one of his more extraordinary authorial interventions"); and Roche (2019) 114–16.

[97] Leigh (1997) 13. See too Ormand (1994) 42.

[98] See Sinclair (1995) 54 and Joseph (2019) 94–5 on Tacitus's similar use of an "associative" first-person plural to unite his narrator with other members of Roman society.

Lucan brings forward this expansive first-person plural again in the later books. At the outset of Book 9 he imagines the spirit of Pompey seeing "under how great a night lay | our day" (*quanta sub nocte iaceret | nostra dies*, 9.13–14). And when describing the Roman soldiers fighting the Egyptian army in Book 10, he asks, "Where does the miserable fate of our empire (*imperii . . . nostri*) *not* find civil wars?" (10.410–11). The statement "our Pharsalia will live on; we shall be condemned to darkness by no age" (*Pharsalia nostra | uiuet; a nullo tenebris damnabimur aeuo*) at 9.985–6 thus comes to us within this context, within a poem that persistently uses the first-person plural to conflate the Romans of 48 BCE with the Romans of Lucan's time.[99] *Nostra* in that phrase points most immediately to the addressee in 9.982, Caesar; but—given the emphatic leveraging of the first-person plural over the nine books leading up to this point—the plurality within *nostra* also contains a broader "we," the cross-generational first-person collective that suffers together the common fate of that battle's consequences. "Our Pharsalia" is the battle we suffer together and the song of sorrow we sing together—the *canimus* at 1.2 carrying through the poem. Whereas Cornelia, the representative in the poem of the conventional place of lament on the margins of epic, had withdrawn into darkness (*tenebras*, 9.110) to mourn earlier in the book, the collective Roman "we" that carries on the mourning process will never be forced into darkness (*tenebris*, 9.986). In this way the old conception of the Roman people as a plurality, though squashed at Pharsalia—the Ennian story of collective advance halted (see Chapter 3)—gains an opening for continued communal expression and identity.

It is important to note that there is explicit pushback within the poem against the prospect of communal lament under the conditions of imperial rule, as we read on several occasions of the *inability* to weep that will come with the victory of Caesarism. Let us recall that in the tableau of anticipatory mourning in Book 2, a Roman matron ominously states, "Now, while the fortune of the leaders is in the balance, we have the power to weep. Once one of them has won, we will have to rejoice" (*nunc flere potestas | dum pendet fortuna ducum: cum uicerit alter | gaudendum est*, 2.40–42).[100] She is right: after imagining the proper funeral for Pompey that Rome might

---

[99] On Lucan's merging of the temporal perspective of the characters in his poem and his contemporary audience, see Bartsch (1997) 101–30; Leigh (1997) 39; Narducci (2002) 95; Radicke (2004) 514–19; Faber (2005); Pandey (2014) 132–3; and McClellan (2019) 169.
[100] See Fratantuono (2012) 57 and Fertik (2018) 453–4 on the far-reaching implications here.

have conducted but of course did not (7.31-9), Lucan describes Romans concealing their weeping for Pompey while making offerings at Caesar's triumph (7.41-2), with the exclamation, "O wretched ones, whose sighs covered your grief, who did not lament you [Pompey] together in a full theater" (*o miseri, quorum gemitus texere dolorem, | qui te non pleno pariter planxere theatro*, 7.43-4). Earlier we considered the similar scene in Book 9 where the Romans attending Caesar when he receives Pompey's head "hide their groans and conceal what's in their hearts (*pectora . . . tegunt*) with a happy front; and, while Caesar laments, they dare—o dear freedom!—to look happily at the bloody crime" (9.1106-8). The apostrophe to "dear freedom" is one of despair: with Caesar's victory and with liberty lost, the freedom to weep openly is lost too. The predicament of these Roman mourners is akin to that of the captive women lamenting Patroclus in antiphony with Briseis in *Iliad* 19, as they "put forward the name of Patroclus, while each has her own sorrows" (Πάτροκλον πρόφασιν, σφῶν δ' αὐτῶν κήδε' ἑκάστη, *Il.* 19.302). Just as for enslaved captives in the *Iliad*, antiphonal lament in the time of the Caesars can have limits, be muted, halted.

However, if lament was made dangerous or even impossible by Caesar's and the Caesars' victory, the *Pharsalia* brings it back, enjoining readers to take part and sing along. The time-transcending "we" of Lucan's epic figures the Romans of his time as fighting alongside and dying with the Romans at Pharsalia, but at the same time it involves post-Pharsalian readers in the poem's process of lamentation, empowering them to participate in this song of sorrow.[101] In this light, it is fitting to think again about the dynamic possibilities in the name *Pharsalia nostra* held up at 9.985. Gérard Genette pointed us to understanding a paratextual element such as a work's title as a "threshold" of interpretation, capable of operating as "a 'vestibule' that offers the world at large the possibility of either stepping inside or turning back."[102] The name or *sphragis Pharsalia nostra*, while not positioned on the poem's physical periphery per se, comes to readers in the uniquely marked programmatic passage 9.980-6, and is thus capable of the "dynamic interplay"[103] of a paratext, opening up for them the opportunity to engage with, fight alongside, and carry on the lamentation of Lucan and his characters.

---

[101] My argument thus complements but is more precise than the argument that "the poem itself constitutes the greatest triumph of memory" (Gowing [2005] 95); see similarly Thorne (2011).
[102] Genette (1997 [1987]) 1, quoted by Jansen (2014b) 7.
[103] Jansen (2014b) 2. Peirano (2014) reads authorial *sphragides* as paratexts.

6.8. The completion of the epic song of sorrow

Through the extension of the antiphony of lament to the narrator himself and Lucan's contemporaries living under the principate, the *Pharsalia* shows the medium of lament moving out of any marginal textual status it may have held in epic, reaching its full potential and full maturity. The *demos* to whom Homer's narrator had passed the song of sorrow in the final moments of the *Iliad* now takes it up in full. And at the same time, Lucan's epic offers a more expansive *object* of lament than Homeric poetry did or could. Indeed, the deceased in the *Pharsalia* is maximally large: it is the Rome that had accomplished global and universal dominion. This gesture, too, can be read as an expansion of a conceit that had been present in the genre's Homeric origins.

The story of the sack of the city of Troy and the accompanying lamentation lies always around the edges of the Homeric poems. There are frequent forebodings in the *Iliad*, as when Agamemnon and then Hector declare that "the day will come when holy Ilium will be destroyed, as well as Priam and the people of Priam of the ashen spear" (4.164–5 = 6.448–9). And at Hector's death we read that the hero's mother and father wail (22.405–8), and then:

> ἀμφὶ δὲ λαοὶ
> κωκυτῷ τ' εἴχοντο καὶ οἰμωγῇ κατὰ ἄστυ.
> τῷ δὲ μάλιστ' ἄρ' ἔην ἐναλίγκιον ὡς εἰ ἅπασα
> Ἴλιος ὀφρυόεσσα πυρὶ σμύχοιτο κατ' ἄκρης.

> Around them the people were taken by wailing and lamentation throughout the city; it was most like if all of ridged Ilium were burned up by fire, from its citadel. (*Il.* 22.408–11).

In describing the mournful response to the individual Hector's death, then, Homer looks ahead to the lament that will accompany the destruction of the city itself. The *Odyssey* then provides occasional glances backward, as in Demodocus's song about the wooden horse and the sack of Troy (*Od.* 8.499–520),[104] which tellingly evokes tears from the sacker himself, Odysseus, who is compared to a widow wailing during the capture of a city (*Od.* 8.521–31). These intimations of how lament for a city might sound

---

[104] See Alden (2017) 200–21 on the recurrence of the theme of the sack of Troy in Demodocus's songs.

are picked up in the laments for fallen cities that emerge in a number of genres.[105]

I want to propose that the absence from the Homeric poems of a full exploration of Troy's fall is met by two types of emulative response in the *Pharsalia*. For one, there is the polemical gesture that Lucan makes at 9.961–86: whereas Homer had only glanced forward and backward to fallen Troy, the *Pharsalia* looks right at it, giving us a burned-up (9.964), wall-less (9.965), uprooted (9.968), dried-out (9.974–5) Troy, whose ruins are in ruin (9.969), its story an afterthought, long past the point of lament.[106] Lucan's more significant and more sustained means of response to the *Iliad*'s omission of the fall of Ilium comes on a grander scale, in the *Pharsalia*'s realization of a lament for a fallen city. The picture of a collective city lament that was subordinated into a suggestive two-line simile at *Iliad* 22.410–11 is expanded by Lucan into a poem-length treatment. While such a lament is only imagined by Homer, the mourning people of Rome give it full voice in the antiphony of the *Pharsalia*. Now, just as Homer depicts Hector as doomed defender and symbol of the city of Troy, Lucan develops a close connection between the death of an individual defender (Pompey) and the city itself.[107] But he also speaks right to the city, right to *Roma*, leading a communal, antiphonal song of lament over her very guts, *sua uiscera*. Here, Lucan shows the reader of epic, is what a poem of lament for a city looks like.

The *Pharsalia*, then, closes the epic tradition of death-poetry by expanding, opening up, moving to the center, and in the process fully realizing the mode of lament introduced into epic in the *Iliad*—another gesture of aperture that serves to underpin claims of closure. Epic as a song of sorrow, a venue for antiphonal *gooi* and simultaneously capable of offering a grand *threnos*, achieves fullness in Lucan's poem. Moreover, if, with recent scholarship, we understand fully realized lament to mark the consummation of an epic poem in the Iliadic tradition,[108] then in this way, too, the limitless breadth and fullness of lament in the *Pharsalia* are fitting markers of the *telos* of the genre

---

[105] On the development of laments for cities in various genres, see the essays in Bachvarova, Dutsch, and Suter (2016). Alexiou (1974), in her discussion at 83–101, offers the proviso that city laments "do not belong essentially to the same group of ritual, functional songs as the laments for the dead" (83). See too her remarks at Alexiou (2016) xi.

[106] In this regard, Lucan also blows right by Virgil's account in *Aen.* 2 of Troy's fall and the attendant lamentation (2.486–90; note too that Aeneas relates the tale in tears, 2.6–12).

[107] McClellan (2019) 153, also drawing a comparison with Hector: "Lucan has cast Pompey as synecdoche for the destruction of the Republic, as the symbol of its fall." See too Day (2013) 225–33 and Mebane (2016) on the associations of Pompey with Rome in the poem.

[108] Greene (1999) 192 and Flatt (2017), with n. 8 in this chapter.

itself. In this light it is worth recalling from my Introduction that Statius, who would go on to fashion his own broad antiphony of lamenting characters in the *Thebaid*,[109] makes it clear in *Silvae* 2.7 that he understood this ambition of Lucan's to complete a crowning Calliopean song of lament.

6.9. "What you weep for is what you loved"

I want to close this chapter by looking at the significance in the *Pharsalia* of another integral element of lament: its function as a medium of praise. Let us recall from my earlier discussion the interconnectedness of lament and glory, how the former is a vehicle of the latter, how, in Murnaghan's words, "as a grieving response to the loss of an individual, lamentation is an urgent expression of that person's value, and so is a form of praise."[110] *Kleos* comes to Homeric heroes through the *gooi* that Homer interweaves into the narrative of the *Iliad*, and the recurrence of the mode and core themes of lament in the *Pharsalia* surely operates in this same way—a point seemingly missed by many readers of the poem. Henderson, for example, writes that the poem "is a lament, an epikedion, but the performative rhetoric of its structure of address and its narrated recitation of cycles of revenge and repetition poisons its delivery with self-loathing."[111] In his essay "Tears in Lucan," Paolo Asso writes in a similar way that "in the face of fate and civil war, only tears are appropriate" and that "Lucan reverses and thwarts the celebratory scope of the epic genre."[112] But in epic poetry the two—tears and celebration, lament and praise—are inextricably connected. This poem *does*, through the centering and predominance of the mode of lament, celebrate the greatness of Rome.

It is perhaps fitting that Lucan gives a clear articulation of this dynamic to a man named Magnus. After his fall from greatness at Pharsalia, when he is in essence a dead man walking, Lucan has the "Great One" reflect on the interconnectedness of death, lament, and praise when bidding Cornelia to

---

[109] See Fantham (1999) 226–32 and Augoustakis (2016), considering the uses of lament in the *Theb.* and Silius Italicus's *Pun.*
[110] Murnaghan (1999) 204.
[111] Henderson (1987) 149.
[112] Asso (2012) 170. See too Roche (2009) 97, of the proem: "We encounter in the first seven lines of Lucan an *Iliad* with no hero and no promise of glory." I also diverge from the assessment of Littlewood (2016) 159 that the *Ph.* is "an epic that mourns what it cannot praise: the death of the Roman Republic and the birth of autocracy."

save her tears for after his death (8.72–85). His words can read as dispassionate and even loveless,[113] but this may be because the speech so carefully outlines how grief and praise work together. After detailing the right time for lamentation ("To mourn your dead husband ought to be your last marker of fidelity," *ultima debet | esse fides lugere uirum*, 8.82–3), he concludes the speech by saying, "After the battles, Magnus is alive, though his good fortune has died. What you weep for is that which you loved" (*uiuit post proelia Magnus | sed fortuna perit. quod defles, illud amasti*, 8.84–5).[114] The implication is that Cornelia is weeping because it was Pompey's *fortuna*, his good fortune and prosperity, that she loved. It is a stinging remark, but the closing *sententia*—which would live on as a popular quotation for centuries[115]—also speaks to a greater truth. Love of something, be it of an individual, just that individual's success, or whatsoever else, is what generates tears. Lament is a means of praise, of expressing what you love. *Quod defles, illud amasti*.

We saw earlier in this chapter just how often the laments for Pompey celebrate his greatness, his *maiestas*; and Lucan compels the reader to think about it throughout the poem by using the name Magnus for him 192 times, in comparison with the 81 times he uses the name Pompeius,[116] while also frequently evoking this cognomen with cognates.[117] Denis Feeney has emphasized that Pompey's greatness comes most of all in his death.[118] To this point we must add that the poem's principal vehicle for capturing that greatness is the medium of lament. *Pace* Henderson and Asso, we should also understand the poem's broad exercise of lamentation for Rome as operating in the same way it does for Magnus. Time and again the *Pharsalia* highlights Roman greatness: in this story of Roman civil war "great things crash upon themselves" (*in se magna ruunt*, 1.81); Caesar knows well that it is a "great city" (*magnae . . . urbis*, 1.195) that he is invading; and "great names" (*magnis . . . nominibus*, 7.209–10) make up the dramatis personae. As the narrator puts it in a miniature expression of lament discussed earlier, the carnage

---

[113] Mayer (1981) 92 writes that Pompey's sentiments "illustrate the poet's concern for noble passion."

[114] Compare the narrator's similar words to Pompey at 7.723–7 (discussed earlier in this chapter) about the people's lamentation at Larisa as a sign of their love for him.

[115] See Sanford (1934) 4 on the quotations of the phrase by Peter of Cluny and John of Salisbury (both in the twelfth century).

[116] Roche (2019) 63.

[117] See Feeney (1986), writing at 239: "plays on the *cognomen* are elevated into something of considerable power, testifying to a consistent controlling design."

[118] Feeney (1986) 243: "Emancipating himself from the illusory greatness of his past, Pompeius achieves true greatness by and in death." At 242 he notes how the "shadow of a great name" (*magni nominis umbra*) introduced at 1.135 becomes a *tanta umbra* (9.2) after his death.

at Pharsalia Fortuna "shows you, Rome, while crashing, how great you are (*quam magna*) as you fall" (7.419). Of this line, Roche aptly writes: "*Fortuna's* purpose that Rome recognize her own magnificence as she collapses in the Roman casualties at Pharsalus is a goal that moves in step with Lucan's own poetic project."[119] This epic lament, this song of sorrow for Rome, is at the same time a testament to the greatness of the deceased.

In this same way we should read the *Pharsalia*, Lucan's *immensum opus* (1.68), as a work about the greatness of epic poetry, the "sacred and great work of bards" (*sacer et magnus uatum labor*, 9.980) hailed at the site of Troy. Masters has persuasively shown how the images of Caesar's destructiveness in the *Pharsalia* speak at the same time to Lucan's own destructive poetic bent.[120] And so when Lucan figures Caesar as a thunderbolt at 1.151–7, he also neatly captures his own thundering modus operandi: "With no material preventing its movement, [the bolt] brings great destruction far and wide when it crashes down and great destruction when it recoils" (1.155–7: *nullaque exire uetante | materia magnamque cadens magnamque reuertens | dat stragem late*). Like the thunderbolt bringing a great quantity of destruction (*magnam . . . magnam . . . stragem*), Caesar—in laying waste to Rome—brings destruction that is great. Lucan's poetics operate on the same course: the phrase *nullaque exire uetante | materia* speaks to the poet's pushing aside of other literary matter (*materia* OLD 7), but the devastation that he renders *from* that *materia* is, to be sure, great.

Lucan's use of lament makes the same metapoetic point, but on a grander scale. For much of this book I have traced how he reverses, inverts, pulls apart, defaces, sends crashing, and tears down the conventions and tropes established in the earliest Latin and Greek epic poems. But as he thunders, he laments. And any lament for the end of epic would be predicated on an understanding of the greatness of the genre. *Epos*, let us recall, was commonly understood as the most esteemed, loftiest, "greatest" genre in antiquity, with Calliope well established as the preeminent Muse.[121] The greatness of Homer in particular was axiomatic among Latin poets. Horace (*Sat.* 1.10.52) and Ovid (*Amores* 1.8.61) both apply the epithet *magnus* to him. Virgil boldly

---

[119] Roche (2019) 167. See too Day (2013) 219: "the greatness of the Republican past is sensed at the very moment of its loss." Day also draws a connection in this regard between Pompey and Rome: "As in Book 7 Rome's greatness manifested itself most fully amid the city's collapse (7.419), so it is only in death that the true stature of Pompey's sublime *nomen* emerges" (225).
[120] Masters (1992).
[121] See, e.g., Hes. *Theog.* 79–80 on Calliope's primacy, cited by Macrob. *In Somn.* 2.3.2. And see Arist. *Poet.* 1448b, 1451b, and frequently on Homer's supremacy.

claims at the outset of his Latin War to commence a "greater work" (*maius opus moueo*, 7.45), a polemical challenge, to be sure, to the supreme place of greatness held by the *Iliad*'s war narrative. Propertius wrote of Virgil's emerging effort for epic supremacy that "something greater than the *Iliad* is being born" (*nescio quid maius nascitur Iliade*, 2.34.66). Lucan's contemporary Quintilian is most explicit about the greatness of the genre, writing at *IO* 1.8.5 of the "loftiness of the heroic song" (*sublimitate heroi carminis*) and the "greatness of its material" (*magnitudine rerum*). Later he admires the "greatness [Homer] shows in one word" (*nam uerbo uno magnitudinem eius ostendit*, 8.3.84) and in Book 10 writes at length about Homer's grandeur and outsized place in the Greek and Roman tradition (10.1.46–51).[122]

The *Pharsalia* affirms this understanding of Homer and of the epic genre as a whole. Lucan sings a song that surpasses the epics of Homer. The gathered fleet of *magnus Homerus* was not as vast as Lucan's (3.286–7), nor was his lament as broad, centered, inclusive, and conclusive. But while completing and eclipsing the Homeric epic project, Lucan unmistakably *honors* it: let us recall that in the all-important statement at 9.980–6 he writes of the endurance of the "honors of the Smyrnaean poet" (*Zmyrnaei . . . uatis honores*, 9.984). Even as he contests and closes off Homer, he extends due *honor*—a word used often of proper burial rites.[123] By constructing his poem as a grand lament conferring praise, Lucan is certain not to withhold or diminish such honors. In executing and lamenting epic's end, the poet celebrates its greatness.

---

[122] See Hutchinson (1993) 8: "In Book X, sublimity or grandeur is thought to appear more naturally in some genres than in others. It belongs particularly in narrative epic, through subject-matter and style alike."

[123] See *Ph*. 8.773 and 9.62–3 (both times of the proper rites not given to Pompey), as well as Virg. *Aen* 11.52, Ov. *Fast*. 2.533, Mart. 1.116.1, Stat. *Theb*. 10.711, and Tac. *Agr*. 46.2.

Conclusion

Lucan and the Living Dead

In this study I have argued that Lucan fashions his *Pharsalia* as a work that closes off the epic tradition, with his poetics proceeding in step with his content of death and ends. In order to do this, he engages closely and polemically with the foundational elements and master tropes of the poems at the beginning of the tradition. While considering Livius Andronicus's *Odusia* and Naevius's *Bellum Punicum*, I have focused on Homer and the "Roman Homer" Ennius as Lucan's most significant early anti-models. As we saw in Chapter 1, this process of closural engagement is introduced in his proem and the epic's opening scene at the Rubicon, and also in his most explicit statement about his poetic aims, at 9.980–6. In Chapter 2, we looked at the *Pharsalia*'s inclusion of conventional scenes of violence that go back to Homer and Ennius, and at how Lucan redirects that violence back upon its actors. In the mutilation of Marius Gratidianus, the deforestation of the Massilian grove, and then the gory battlefield stand of Scaeva, the violence, while familiar to readers of epic, here is not externalized but self-destructive and self-ending.

The passages explored in Chapters 1 and 2 include allusions to early epic poets—often layered with one another, along with other important models such as Virgil and Ovid. I have maintained that these allusions "anchor" my arguments in the ensuing chapters for Lucan's engagement with epic mastertropes. In Chapter 3, I focused on the closure of the Roman story as introduced in the *Annales*. Ennius had to a great extent formed and canonized the story of Roman advance in space and time, with the support of the providential gods and executed by the collective *populus Romanus*. Lucan methodically and brutally undoes each of these components of the Ennian story: just as the place and day of Pharsalia brought death to Rome, the story of the *Pharsalia* brings an end to the Roman narrative launched in the *Annales*. We traced a corresponding poetic process in Chapter 4, with an eye to not only Ennius but also Naevius and Livius as foundational Roman epic models for

Lucan to invert and close. Building on scholarship on the synchronicity of Rome's emergence on the sea with the emergence of epic at Rome, I proposed that Lucan, with his persistent attention to shipwrecks, disastrous landings, and Roman loss of control of the Mediterranean, narrates the opposite of the maritime moment—something more like a crash landing for Rome on the seas and for the epic genre.

In Chapter 5, I considered the related matter of Lucan's attention to the loss of *nostos*, the theme lying at the core of both Homer's *Odyssey* and the very first work of Latin epic, the *Odusia*. We saw that the arcs of Cato, Pompey, and Caesar are all drawn with distinct anti-Odyssean elements, with Lucan underscoring the absence, devastation, and then failure of each to return home or reunite with their spouses. Each of these arcs, I argued, speaks to the larger theme of Rome's loss of "home" and to the corresponding undoing of *nostos*-poetry—with the opening up of the elements of a successful *nostos* here marking closure. In Chapter 6, I moved to argue that Lucan closes off the Homeric epic tradition in another way, through his expansion and indeed completion of the mode of lament that is so constitutive of the *Iliad* and subsequent epic. After establishing Lucan's close familiarity with the style and content of speeches of lament, I examined how the *Pharsalia* moves from the margins and opens up the antiphony of lament to include not only a range of characters, but also the narrator and even his readers living in post-Pharsalian Rome—another aperture that marks completion and closure. In this way the *Pharsalia* fully realizes epic's identity as a genre of grief and of the commemoration of great things that are lost. And in this way, too, Lucan's poem of historical and poetic ends is also about the greatness of what has ended.

With this argument for Lucan's ambitions of sweeping, multifaceted closure established, I want to conclude this study with further consideration of how the *Pharsalia* figures its own "life" and its own future. If Lucan has returned to epic's beginnings and closed off the genre, then what does that endeavor mean for the *Pharsalia* itself? If "our Pharsalia will live on" (*Pharsalia nostra | uiuet*, 9.985–6), but Pharsalia and the *Pharsalia* are emblematic of death and ends, how can this "death place/day" and "death text" live on?

Helpful here again is the writing of Don Fowler on the problems and possibilities of closure in Latin and Greek texts.[1] Just as his approach has aided particular arguments in previous chapters, his thoughts on closure may be

---

[1] Collected in Fowler (2000).

helpful as I try to close my broad argument about Lucanian closure of the epic tradition. In short, Fowler called attention to the difficulties that arise in defining textual closure, and to the many ways closure can be uneasy or false, frequently creating more opportunities for opening and outgrowth. Sensitivity to this dialectic between closure and aperture can help us to see broader strokes of the *Pharsalia*'s self-fashioning: while it is a song of ending, closing, and completing the epic genre, at the same time it preserves a particular kind of vital opening for the tradition. Because this death-text lives on (*uiuet*), the genre lives on, in the form of the poem that rendered that death. While ending and defining prior epic, the *Pharsalia contains* and carries on the tradition too.

In this light it is fitting to recall the numerous manifestations in the *Pharsalia* of the genre collapsing upon itself but still standing. In the poem's opening lines, Lucan makes clear that he will turn themes in both Ennius (recall his adaptation of *pila minantia pilis* in 1.6) and Homer (recall his direction of Homeric exculpation inward in 1.8) back onto themselves. The victims in Lucan's recurring images of violent redirection—Romans, Rome, the Roman story, the epic story—die, yet they still exist. The falling trees in the Massilian grove in Book 3 evoke the toppling trees from Ovid's, Virgil's, and Ennius's epics, but pointedly crash upon themselves and *stay upright*. An extraordinary, outsized case comes in the heroic stand of Scaeva, who evokes the defenses made by Virgil's Turnus, Ennius's tribune, and Homer's Ajax, but brashly arrogates all manner of violence onto himself—and keeps going. It is surely significant that the very last image of the *Pharsalia* is of Scaeva returning to Caesar's battle-lines, somehow still on his feet, undead. Lucan had written in Book 6 of the *fama* won by Scaeva (6.257), which here at the end of the poem becomes "everlasting fame" (*perpetuae . . . famae*, 10.544). The perpetual fame of this slaughtered but still standing inversion of epic precedent, this living dead thing, goes also to the textual living dead thing that contains Scaeva.[2] The closing image of Scaeva, the instrument and object of his own destruction, the human embodiment of epic violence directed inward, complements and is complemented by the abrupt, even violent break of the form of the text at 10.546 that we considered in Chapter 3. Like Scaeva, the *Pharsalia* itself demolishes the conventions of

---

[2] *Pace* Masters (1992) 257–8 (257: "Scaeva is, perplexingly, congratulated for having earned *perpetuae . . . famae*"), seemingly missing the metapoetic valence of the phrase and of Scaeva as a whole.

epic form—self-destructs—only to live on, to be read, condemned to darkness by no age.

Living dead things, then, fill and in a way come to define the pages of Lucan's living dead epic. This is perhaps no more apparent than in Lucan's inclusion of an actual talking corpse, the cadaver that Erictho brings to life in Book 6 to deliver a prophecy for Sextus Pompey and for Rome. Scholars have long understood the *Thessala uates* (6.651) Erictho, who could "fashion a song for new purposes" (*carmenque nouos fingebat in usus*, 6.577), as a doublet for Lucan.[3] But the corpse itself is equally revealing, and for different reasons. Andrew McClellan has profitably considered the broader interpretive significance of this zombie-like figure, reading his "bizarre continuation of life" as representative of the political condition of Rome under the principate: "If the principate is simply a 'revivified' *res publica libera*, as Augustus and later emperors claimed, then like the corpse-soldier it exists as a grotesque perversion of actual life, something caught between living and dying."[4] To McClellan's reading of the sociopolitical relevance of Lucan's animated corpse, I would add a corresponding metapoetic one: similar to the chopped down but still-standing trees in Book 3 and the slaughtered but undead Scaeva in Books 6 and 10, the talking corpse in Erictho's lair is a textual stand-in for Lucan's poem.

Like the text of the *Pharsalia*, the cadaver issues a song (6.777–820), marked as such when Erictho used the verb *canat* of his forthcoming speech (6.717). And like Lucan's epic, his prophetic song both resounds with the horrors of war and expresses lament for those horrors: as the prophecy begins, he is described as "the mournful cadaver, with tears dripping down" (*maestum fletu manante cadauer*, 6.776), and he keeps that mournful look through to the end of his speech (*maestus*, 6.821). Further, much of the content of the corpse's song convulses the Roman story begun by Ennius, with the fabled Republican heroes of old consigned to the roles of lamenting losers, their collective efforts now for nothing (6.784–90; see discussion in Chapters 3 and 6).

Most significantly for our purposes now, the cadaver is given the chance to *physically* live on. Conversing shades of the dead and visiting apparitions had been at home in epic since the Homeric poems; as we saw in Chapter 1, such apparitions in fact move about in Latin epic as interactive embodiments of

---

[3] See Johnson (1987) 18–33; O'Higgins (1988); Masters (1992) 179–215; and Dinter (2012) 68–75.
[4] McClellan (2019) 166 and 168.

the genre's traditions. What is fundamentally subversive and indeed defiant about Lucan's living dead thing—where it breaks the laws of epic—is that it appears *in the flesh*. The zombie-like figure in Book 6 is a physical instantiation of deathliness and of the subversion of epic tradition—just like the poem that contains him.

All of these images of living dead things—ended but open things—are representative of what the *Pharsalia* itself is. But in addition to these numerous avatars of living deadness that the poem showcases, there is the animation of Pharsalia as a character in her/its own right. The declaration *Pharsalia nostra | uiuet* is of course a flashpoint, but the process of giving life and agency to Pharsalia runs across the epic. Henderson and Masters revealed that there are interpretive possibilities in reading *Pharsalia nostra* also as *pars alia nostra* ("another part of ours"), suggesting that the Latin phrase within the Greek toponym exhibits "*Latinitas* conquer[ing] the 'Emathian' sign."[5] This reading is in keeping with the "implosiveness"[6] of Lucan's writing; but it also points, more broadly, to how the poet figures the *Pharsalia* as a personified entity, as a character taking on "another part" in his epic. And indeed Lucan appears to gloss *Pharsalia* in this way amid the slaughter in Book 7, when writing that "Pharsalia did not play the same part in battle as other disasters" (*non istas habuit pugnae Pharsalia partes | quas aliae clades*, 7.632–3). Battles, Lucan explains, can play parts; this battle—this story—has another, bigger, greater, more consequential part than others.

The animation of the battle and story of Pharsalia that comes out rather explicitly in 9.985–6 and 7.632–3 is also evident in the word's other appearances in the poem. While the scansion of *Pharsālia* limits its case usage in hexameter, it is nevertheless notable that Lucan chooses to use the word fourteen times in the nominative case, in the process granting it not just vitality but *agency*, engaged in and performing a number of actions.[7] So, the casting of Pharsalia as playing a part at 7.632–3 is reinforced in the statement about pre-battle portents that "if the human mind . . . had noted all of the new signs in heaven, Pharsalia could have been watched by the whole world (*spectari*

---

[5] Henderson (1987) 136, attributing this reading of a "catachretic appropriation" to Masters at 159 n. 105. See too Masters (1992) vii. I am thankful to Paul Roche for pointing me to this reading.
[6] Henderson (1987) 136.
[7] 1.38, 3.297, 4.803, 6.313, 7.61, 7.175, 7.204, 7.407, 7.632, 7.745, 7.781, 8.273, 9.232, and 9.985. The verbs expressing *Pharsalia*'s actions are, when looked at together, themselves revealing of her vitality and power: *impleat* (1.38), *praestitit* (3.297), *confert* (4.803), *exire . . . potuit* (6.313), *est* (7.61), *edere* (7.175), *spectari . . . potuit* (7.204), *habuit* (7.632), *fecit* (7.745), *uidit* (7.781), *sparsit* (8.273), and *uiuet* (9.986).

toto potuit Pharsalia mundo)" (7.202–4). Pharsalia/the *Pharsalia*, we see, is imagined as having the power to be watched (*spectari . . . potuit*), with the whole world as its audience.[8] In addition to being the willful, grandstanding object of the eyes of the world, the battle/story is also given the power to see (*Pharsalia uidit*, 7.781) the killing on the battlefield; to "offer the world" (*Pharsalia praestitit orbem*, 3.297) to Caesar; to "bring the leaders together" (*dira duces Pharsalia confert*, 4.803); and to exercise control over the war's resources (*fecit* at 7.745 and *sparsit* at 8.273, each time of *opes*). Together, the verbs create the picture of a place/time and a poem with great vitality and potency.

However, the most significant power of Pharsalia/the *Pharsalia* is as a *killer*, a bringer of death. The one appearance of *Pharsalia* in a case other than the nominative comes at 7.535, where the narrator addresses her in the vocative in a plea to curtail her slaughter:

> utinam, Pharsalia, campis
> sufficiat cruor iste tuis, quem barbara fundunt
> pectora; non alio mutentur sanguine fontes;
> hic numerus totos tibi uestiat ossibus agros.
> aut, si Romano compleri sanguine mauis,
> istis parce, precor.

Would that the blood that barbarian chests pour out would be enough for your fields, Pharsalia, that your springs would be soiled by no other blood, that *this* group would dress all of your fields with bones. Or, if you prefer to be filled up with Roman blood, then spare those ones, I beg you. (7.535–40)

Pharsalia is a bloodsucker, demanding the quenching (*sufficiat* in 7.535 and then *compleri* in 539) of its thirst for gore. Put another way, Pharsalia/the *Pharsalia* lives off the dead, killing and consuming the lifeblood of those—and those texts—it meets, only to live on itself. In the animation of *Pharsalia* in this passage, Lucan goes so far as to have her clothed, wearing the bones of the dead (*hic numerus totos tibi uestiat ossibus agros*).[9] From these details we

---

[8] Note also 9.232–3, where the character *Pharsalia*, whose animate qualities are well established by this point, is held up in parallel with another principal character, Pompey: *nam quis erit finis si nec Pharsalia pugnae / nec Pompeius erit?* ("For what will be the end of the fight if not Pharsalia, if not Pompey?").

[9] *Vestiat* here is conspicuous. Lucan uses the verb just one other time (10.119).

gain a particular and particularly ghoulish image of the living, killing place/time/character/story *Pharsalia*.

This series of passages later in the poem, and especially 7.535–40, helps us to better understand the first appearance of *Pharsalia*, at 1.38. During his facetious address to Nero, the narrator states that, if Pharsalia led to Nero's rule, then "the crimes themselves and the wrongs are worth it at this price. Let Pharsalia fill her dread fields" (*scelera ipsa nefasque | hac mercede placent; diros Pharsalia campos | impleat*, 1.37–9). Just as she was envisioned at 7.535–40 as taking lifeblood into her fields, here she actively fills up her fields; *impleat*, a verb commonly used of eating (*OLD* 3), fleshes out the personification that will be developed in grand fashion over the epic. Further, in a choice that keeps the scope of his story and poetic project open, Lucan omits reference to any specific means of filling up—allowing the reader to imagine, without limitation, the blood, bodies, and so much more that *Pharsalia* devours.

A chief victim of *Pharsalia*'s bloodsucking is, of course, Rome and the epic story of Rome. Lucan neatly captures this destructive act in Book 6. Just after the Battle of Dyrrachium, a missed opportunity for a Pompeian victory, the narrator exclaims in frustration:

> ultimus esse dies potuit tibi Roma malorum,
> exire e mediis potuit Pharsalia fatis.

> That could have been the last day for you, Rome—the last day of evils!
> Pharsalia could have vanished from the middle of your fates. (6.312–13).

Lucan pits *Pharsalia* in stark opposition to *Roma*, each poised in the fifth foot of its line. But the one will supplant the other; just as the word *Pharsalia* lies between *mediis* and *fatis* in 6.313, the Battle of Pharsalia at its consequences will remain forever enmeshed in Rome's fates, and Lucan's story of that battle will not exit from what is *said* about Rome.[10] The long afterlife of *Pharsalia* comes out again in the list of pre-battle portents "revealing future events" (*uenturos prodere casus*, 7.151) that Lucan includes at 7.151–204. He writes that many claimed to see disruptions of the physical terrain in Thessaly, including "Pharsalia emitting the nocturnal voices of war" (*edere nocturnas*

---

[10] See my discussion of *fatum* and *fari* in Chapter 3.

belli Pharsalia uoces, 7.175). While foreboding the war cries on the battlefield that day, the line also seems to portend the future utterances of the poem, the range of its "voices of war," its thunder and lament.[11] When we bear in mind that *edo* can mean to make known in words (*OLD* 7) and to publish (*OLD* 9), the line reads as a rather straightforward prediction of not just the battle's horrendous sounds, but the epic's afterlife as carrier of the gloomy words of war.

All of these evocative characterizations of Pharsalia/the *Pharsalia*, when looked at together, demonstrate what I think is Lucan's deliberate decision to give life to *Pharsalia*, both as a destructive place and time and as a story—his story, his poem. And each of them precedes Lucan's statement about poetic aims at 9.980–6 and the assertion *Pharsalia nostra | uiuet*. So when the reader comes to that passage and considers the poem's relationship with its epic models, *Pharsalia*'s identity as spectacular and powerful, a bloodsucker, a *killer* is well established. Indeed, when appearing in the context of the literary statement at 9.980–6, the poem *Pharsalia* emerges as the living dead thing that it is: a death text, capable of killing and closing off the epic tradition, but also poised to live on, perpetuating the genre it has ended and now contains, carrying with it the foundational themes launched in the epics of Homer, Livius, Naevius, and Ennius—but now subverted, collapsed, closed off, wholly transformed.

* * *

This study has focused on Lucan's poetics, in particular his self-fashioning in the epic tradition. But it has been impossible to read and analyze the *Pharsalia* without consideration of its historical content (Caesar's and Caesarism's victory) and historical context (the sociopolitical conditions that resulted from that victory). To end this book on poetic ends and death—and to pursue just a bit further the openings and life that may come out of them—I want to revisit in brief the relationship between Lucan's closural poetic agenda and the political/cultural setting for his writing. Fowler wrote that "to think of closure is to be forced to cross the

---

[11] In light of the close identification of *Pharsalia* with her fields (*campi*)—each given the epithet *dirus* (1.38 and 4.803)—we might also read the narrator's statement after the battle that "I would believe that the fields [of Pharsalia] groaned" (*ingemuisse putem campos*, 7.768) as another marker of Pharsalia/the *Pharsalia* as a singer of lament.

boundaries of the literary into wider cultural and political analysis,"[12] a point expanded on by Farouk Grewing, Benjamin Acosta-Hughes, and Alexander Kirichenko:

> If literature's metapoetic preoccupation with its own language turns out to encode some of the most fundamental concerns of its social context, if, in other words, self-reflexivity serves not so much to solidify the text's self-containment as to open it up to culture and politics at large, then, rather than a clear-cut semiotic dichotomy, form and content constitute an infinite continuum, which precludes the very possibility of final closure.[13]

Lucan's metapoetic positioning vis-à-vis his epic predecessors, while certainly self-reflexive, just as certainly speaks to the fundamental concerns of his social context, that is, cultural and political life under the rule of the Caesars. Realistic hopes of restoring the Republic were, to be sure, dashed by Lucan's time, and most of his contemporaries dodged the issue of the Republican past in their writing. Lucan, of course, does not.[14] As recent readers of the poem have emphasized, the *Pharsalia* captures the ongoing trauma of the loss to Caesarism a century earlier; it shows "the scar tissue of decades of Julio-Claudian rule."[15] Indeed, in this poem propping up Scaeva, Erictho's soldier-corpse, and numerous other haunting images of the living dead that showcase a self-destructive but still vibrant metatextuality, Lucan's readers may have seen the condition of their own society, the undead Republic of the Caesars.[16]

The expression of that condition is reflected in the closural poetic program I have explored in this study. A continuum from Lucan's multifaceted and multifront poetics of ending to his and his contemporaries' lived experiences is clear. When, for example, he positions the *Pharsalia* to close off the formative Ennian story of collective Roman advance through space and time, as

---

[12] Fowler (1997) 13.
[13] Grewing, Acosta-Hughes, and Kirichenko (2013b) 10.
[14] Gowing (2005) 68 ("the rich Neronian literary and artistic tradition dwells very little on that past") and 98 emphasizes this distinction. See too Thorne (2011) on Lucan's treatment of this "taboo" subject as "a shock to the Roman system" (364).
[15] Mulhern (2020) 215, writing also of how Lucan "emphasizes his own Julio-Claudian cage" (222). And see Walde (2011) and Thorne (2016) on markers of trauma in the poem; Fantham (2011) on Lucan's place in Neronian society, rivalry with Nero, and role in the Pisonian conspiracy. Kimmerle (2015), discussing the Neronian context at 268–302, expresses caution about our understanding of Lucan's politics. Rudich (1993) is an extensive assessment of political conditions under Nero.
[16] McClellan (2019) 167–9 and (2020) (241: "These living corpses function as visual analogues for Lucan's conception of an imperial slave-state").

well as the story of Roman maritime expansion codified in Livius's, Naevius's, and Ennius's epics, this gesture surely had meaning for Roman readers who knew that autocracy's rise had supplanted the communal ethic, who endured but understood the lie of the system of the principate. When Lucan constructs his poem in opposition to the *Odyssey* and *Odusia* as one of anti-*nostos*, of the undoing of return for his Roman characters and for Rome, this poetic act too speaks to a sense of longing under the early empire for return to a lost Roman past. When Lucan builds on the place of lament in Homeric poetry, moves it to the center of his poem, and so elevates his epic into a grand, expansive, communal lament, that endeavor also unmistakably reaches out to contemporary readers and asks them to join in the expression. These poetic ends carry over into a lived reality. When old, foundational epic modes and themes are inadequate for the times and no longer tell the right story, an end is needed—brought on by a new story, a new epic: *Pharsalia*.

Bibliography

Abbott, H. P. (2002). *The Cambridge Introduction to Narrative*. Cambridge.
Adams, J. N. (1980). "Anatomical Terminology in Latin Epic," *BICS* 27: 50–62.
Ahl, F. (1971). "Lucan's *De Incendio Urbis, Epistulae ex Campania* and Nero's Ban," *TAPA* 102: 1–27.
Ahl, F. (1976). *Lucan: An Introduction*. Ithaca, NY.
Alden, M. (2017). *Para-Narratives in the Odyssey: Stories in the Frame*. Oxford.
Alexis, F. (2013). "Lucan's BC and the Dynamics of the Epic Tradition," in G. Miles and M. Borg, eds., *Approaches to Genre in the Ancient World* (Cambridge), 79–99.
Alexiou, M. (1974). *The Ritual Lament in Greek Tradition*. Cambridge.
Alexiou, M. (2016). "Foreword," in Bachvarova, Dutsch, and Suter (2016), x–xiii.
Ambühl, A. (2010). "Lucan's 'Ilioupersis': Narrative Patterns from the Fall of Troy in Book 2 of the *Bellum civile*," in Hömke and Reitz (2010), 17–38.
Ambühl, A. (2015). *Krieg und Bürgerkrieg bei Lucan und in der Griechischen Literatur: Studien zu Rezeption der Attischen Tragödie und der hellenistischen Dichtung im "Bellum Civile."* Berlin.
Ambühl, A. (2016). "Thessaly as an Intertextual Landscape of Civil War in Latin Poetry," in J. McInerney and I. Sluiter, eds., *Valuing Landscape in Antiquity* (Leiden), 297–322.
Asso, P. (2002). "The Function of the Fight: Hercules and Antaeus in Lucan," *Vichiana* 4: 57–72.
Asso, P. (2008). "The Intrusive Trope: Apostrophe in Lucan," *MD* 61: 161–73.
Asso, P. (2010). *A Commentary on Lucan, "De Bello Civili" IV*. Berlin.
Asso, P. (2011). *Brill's Companion to Lucan*. Malden, MA.
Asso, P. (2012). "Tears in Lucan," in T. Baier, ed., *Götter und menschliche Willensfreiheit von Lucan bis Silius Italicus* (Munich), 159–70.
Augoustakis, A., ed. (2009a). *Brill's Companion to Silius Italicus*. Leiden.
Augoustakis, A. (2009b). "Silius Italicus, A Flavian Poet," in Augoustakis (2009a) 3–26.
Augoustakis, A. (2016). "Burial and Lament in Flavian Epic: Mothers, Fathers, Children," in N. Manioti, ed., *Family in Flavian Epic* (Leiden), 276–300.
Avery, H. (1993). "A Lost Episode in Caesar's *Civil War*," *Hermes* 121: 452–69.
Bachvarova, M., D. Dutsch, and A. Suter, eds. (2016). *The Fall of Cities in the Mediterranean. Commemoration in Literature, Folk-Song and Liturgy*. Cambridge.
Badian, E. (1972). "Ennius and His Friends," in O. Skutsch, ed., *Ennius: Sept exposés suivis de discussions* (Vandoeuvres and Geneva), 149–208.
Bakewell, G. (2016). "*Seven against Thebes*, City Laments, and Athenian History," in Bachvarova, Dutsch, and Suter (2016), 106–26.
Bakker, E. (2013). *The Meaning of Meat and the Structure of the Odyssey*. Cambridge.
Ballester, X. (1990). "La titulación de las obras en la literature romana," *Cuadernos de Filologia Clásica* 24: 135–56.
Baraz, Y., and C. Van den Berg (2013). "Intertextuality: Introduction," *AJP* 134: 1–8.

Barchiesi, A. (2015). *Homeric Effects in Vergil's Narrative*. Trans. by I. Marchesi and M. Fox of *La traccia del modello* (Pisa, 1984). Princeton, NJ.

Baragwanath, E. (2019). "Heroes and Homemakers in Xenophon," in Biggs and Blum (2019a), 108–29.

Barratt, P. (1979). *M. Annaei Lucani Belli Civilis liber V*. Amsterdam.

Barthes, R. (1970). *S/Z*. Paris.

Bartsch, S. (1997). *Ideology in Cold Blood: A Reading of Lucan's Civil War*. Cambridge, MA.

Beissinger, M., J. Tylus, and S. Wofford, eds. (1999). *Epic Traditions in the Contemporary World: The Poetics of Community*. Berkeley, CA.

Beck, H. (2007). "The Early Roman Tradition," in Marincola (2007), 259–65.

Beck, H., and U. Walter (2001). *Die frühen römischen Historiker*. Vol. 1. 2nd ed. Darmstadt.

Berno, F. R. (2019). "Apocalypses and the Sage: Different Endings of the World in Seneca," *Gerión* 37: 75–95.

Bernstein, N. (2011). "The Dead and Their Ghosts in Lucan's *Bellum Civile*: Lucan's Visions of History," in Asso (2011), 57–79.

Bexley, E. M. (2009). "Replacing Rome: Geographic and Political Centrality in Lucan's *Pharsalia*," *CP* 104: 459–75.

Bexley, E. M. (2014). "Lucan's Catalogues and the Landscape of War," in M. Skempis and I. Ziogas, eds., *Geography, Topography, Landscape: Configurations of Space in Greek and Roman Epic* (Berlin), 373–403.

Biggs, T. (2017). "*Primus Romanorum*: Origin Stories, Fictions of Primacy, and the First Punic War," *CP* 112: 350–67.

Biggs, T. (2019). "Varro of Atax in Lucan's Gallic Catalog," *Mnemosyne* 72: 973–93.

Biggs, T., and J. Blum, eds. (2019a). *The Epic Journey in Greek and Roman Literature* (Yale Classical Studies 39). Cambridge.

Biggs, T., and J. Blum, eds. (2019b). "Introduction," in Biggs and Blum (2019a), 1–8.

Blänsdorf, J., K. Büchner, and W. Morel, eds. (1995). *Fragmenta Poetarum Latinorum Epicorum et Lyricorum praeter Ennium et Lucilium*. Stuttgart and Leipzig.

Bleckmann, B. (1998). "Regulus bei Naevius: Zu frg. 50 und 51 Blänsdorf," *Philologus* 142: 61–70.

Block, E. (1982). "The Narrator Speaks: Apostrophe in Homer and Vergil," *TAPA* 112: 7–22.

Bonifazi, A. (2009). "Inquiring into *Nostos* and Its Cognates," *AJP* 130: 481–510.

Bowra, C. M. (1952). *Heroic Poetry*. London.

Boyd, B. W. (2017). *Ovid's Homer: Authority, Repetition, and Reception*. Oxford.

Braund, S. (1992). *Lucan, Civil War: A New Translation*. Oxford.

Breed, B., and A. Rossi, eds. (2006). *Ennius and the Invention of Roman Epic* = *Arethusa* 39.3. Baltimore, MD.

Brennan, D. B. (1969). "Cordus and the Burial of Pompey," *CP* 64: 103–4.

Brooks, P. (1984). *Reading for the Plot: Design and Intention in Narrative*. Oxford.

Bruère, R. T. (1951a). "Palaepharsalus, Pharsalus, and Pharsalia," *CP* 46: 111–15.

Bruère, R. T. (1951b). "Lucan's Cornelia, " *CP* 46: 221–36.

Buckley, E., and M. Dinter, eds. (2013). *A Companion to the Neronian Age*. Malden, MA.

Burton, G. P. (1996). "Aerarium," in S. Hornblower and A. Spawforth, eds., *The Oxford Classical Dictionary* (3rd edition, Oxford) 24–5.

Casali, S. (2006). "The Poet at War: Ennius on the field in Silius' *Punica*," in Breed and Rossi (2006), 569–93.

Casali, S. (2011). "The *Bellum Civile* as an anti-Aeneid," in Asso (2011), 81–109.

Caston, R. (2011). "Lucan's Elegiac Moments," in Asso (2011), 135–52.

Cè, M. (2021). "The *Ilias Latina* in the Context of Ancient Epitome Translation," in Maria J. Falcone and Christoph Schubert, eds., *Ilias Latina: Text, Interpretation, Reception* (Leiden), 39–66.
Chaudhuri, P. (2014). *The War with God: Theomachy in Roman Imperial Poetry*. Oxford.
Chiu, A. (2010). "The Importance of Being Julia: Civil War, Historical Revision and the Mutable Past in Lucan's *Pharsalia*," *CJ* 105: 343–60.
Christensen, J. (2018). "Human Cognition and Narrative Closure: The *Odyssey's* Open-End," in P. Meineck, ed., *The Routledge Handbook of Classics and Cognitive Theory* (London), 139–55.
Christophorou, I. (2010). "The Presence of Homer's Achilles in Lucan's Caesar," *Classica et Mediaevalia* 61: 177–91.
Christophorou, I. (2017). "Homeric Precedents in the Representation of Lucan's Pompey," *CW* 110: 351–72.
Cichorius, C. 1922. *Römische Studien*. Leipzig.
Closs, V. M. (2020). *While Rome Burned: Fire, Leadership, and Urban Disaster in the Roman Cultural Imagination*. Ann Arbor, MI.
Coffee, N. (2018). "An Agenda for the Study of Intertextuality," *TAPA* 148: 205–23.
Coffee, N., J. P. Koenig, S. Poornima, R. Ossewaarde, C. Forstall, and S. Jacobson (2012). "Intertextuality in the Digital Age," *TAPA* 142: 383–422.
Coleman, K. M. (1988). *Statius, Silvae IV*. Oxford.
Commager, H. S. (1981). "Fateful Words: Some Conversations in *Aeneid* 4," *Arethusa* 14: 101–14.
Connolly, J. (2016). "A Theory of Violence in Lucan's *Bellum Civile*," in P. Mitsis and I. Ziogas, eds., *Wordplay and Powerplay in Latin Poetry* (Berlin), 273–97.
Connolly, S. (2010). "Lucan's Punic War in the *Disticha Catonis*," *Classica et Mediaevalia* 61: 193–202.
Connors, C. (1992). "Cypresses in Virgil," *CJ* 88: 1–17.
Connors, C. (1998). *Petronius the Poet: Verse and Literary Tradition in the Satyricon*. Cambridge.
Consoli, M. (2014). *Quintus Ennius. Fortuna ed enigmi*. Lecce.
Conte, G. B. (1968). "La Guerra Civile nella Rievocazione del Populo: Lucano, II 67–233," *Maia* 20: 224–53.
Conte, G. B. (1970). "Ennio e Lucano," *Maia* 22: 132–8.
Conte, G. B. (1986 [1974]). *The Rhetoric of Imitation: Genre and Poetic Memory in Virgil and Other Latin Poets*. Trans. from the Italian by C. Segal. Ithaca, NY.
Conte, G. B. (1988). *La "guerra civile" di Lucano: Studi e prove di commento*. Urbino.
Courtney, E. (1993). *The Fragmentary Latin Poets*. Oxford.
Courtney, E. (1995). *Musa lapidaria*. Atlanta.
Curtis, L. (2017). "Ovid's Io and the Aetiology of Lament," *Phoenix* 71: 301–20.
D'Alessandro Behr, F. (2007). *Feeling History: Lucan, Stoicism, and the Poetics of Passion*. Columbus, OH.
D'Alessandro Behr, F. (2020). "Sage, Soldier, Politician, and Benefactor: Cato in Seneca and Lucan," in Zientek and Thorne (2020), 151–70.
Damon, C., and J. Farrell, eds. (2020). *Ennius' Annals: Poetry and History*. Cambridge.
Day, H. J. M. (2013). *Lucan and the Sublime: Power, Representation and Aesthetic Experience*. Cambridge.
De Jong, I. (1987). *Narrators and Focalizers: The Presentation of the Story in the Iliad*. Amsterdam.

De Jong, I. (2001). *A Narratological Commentary on the Odyssey*. Cambridge.
De Jong, I. (2012). Homer, *Iliad. Book XXII*. Cambridge.
Derrida, J. (1980). "The Law of Genre," trans. by A. Ronell, *Critical Inquiry* 7: 55–81.
Devillers, O., and S. Franchet d'Espèrey, eds. (2010). *Lucain en Débat: Rhétorique, poétique et histoire*. Paris.
DeWitt, N. J. (1940). "Massilia and Rome," *TAPA* 71: 605–15.
Diels, H. (1886). *Lucan und Seneca*. Berlin.
Dilke, O. (1960). *Lucan, De Bello Civili VII*. Bristol.
Dinter, M. (2012). *Anatomizing Civil War: Studies in Lucan's Epic Technique*. Ann Arbor, MI.
Dinter, M. (2013). "Introduction: The Neronian (Literary) 'Renaissance,'" in Buckley and Dinter (2013), 1–14.
Dominik, W. J. (1993). "From Greece to Rome: Ennius' *Annales*," in A. J. Boyle, ed., *Roman Epic* (London), 37–58.
Ducos, M. (2010). "Le Sénat dans l'epopée de Lucain," in Devillers and Franchet d'Espèrey (2010), 143–54.
Dué, C. (2002). *Homeric Variations on a Lament by Briseis*. Lanham, MD.
Dué, C. (2019). "Editor femina facti: What happens when women edit the *Iliad*?" *The Homer Multitext project blog* (http://www.homermultitext.org/commentary/2019-04-15-editor-femina-facti/).
Dué, C. (2020). "'The Best of the Achaeans Has Been Killed': An Introduction to *Iliad* 17," *The Homer Multitext project blog* (http://www.homermultitext.org/commentary/2020-02-17-iliad-17-intro/).
Duff, J. D. (1928). *Lucan, The Civil War I–X*. Cambridge, MA.
Durry, M., ed. (1970). *Lucain: Sept exposés suivis de discussions*. Geneva.
Dutsch, D. (2008). "Nenia: Gender, Genre, and Lament in Ancient Rome," in Suter (2008a), 258–79.
Ebbott, M. (2014). "Allies in Fame: Recruiting Warriors in the Theban and Trojan Epic Traditions," *Trends in Classics* 6: 319–35.
Edwards, M. (1991). *The Iliad: A Commentary*. Vol. 5: *Books 17–20*. Cambridge.
Elliott, J. (2013). *Ennius and the Architecture of the Annales*. Cambridge.
Elliott, J. (2014). "Space and Geography in Ennius' *Annales*," in M. Skempis and I. Ziogas, eds., *Geography, Topography, Landscape: Configurations of Space in Greek and Roman Epic* (Berlin), 223–64.
Esposito, P., and E. Ariemma, eds. (2004). *Lucano e la tradizione dell'epica Latina*. Naples.
Faber, R. (2005). "The Adaptation of Apostrophe in Lucan's *Bellum Civile*," in C. Deroux, ed., *Studies in Latin Literature and Roman History XII* (Brussels), 334–43.
Fantham, E. (1992). *Lucan, De Bello Civili, Book II*. Cambridge.
Fantham, E. (1999). "The Role of Lament in the Growth and Eclipse of Roman Epic," in Beissinger, Tylus, and Wofford (1999), 221–35.
Fantham, E. (2006). "'Dic si quid potes de Sexto Annali': The Literary Legacy of Ennius's Pyrrhic War," in Breed and Rossi (2006), 549–68.
Fantham, E. (2011). "A Controversial Life," in Asso (2011), 3–20.
Farrell, J. (1991). *Vergil's Georgics and the Traditions of Ancient Epic: The Art of Allusion in Literary History*. Oxford.
Farrell, J. (2005). "Intention and Intertext," *Phoenix* 59: 98–111.
Farrell, J. (2006). "Roman Homer," in Fowler (2006), 254–71.
Feeney, D. (1984). "The Reconciliations of Juno," *CQ* 34: 179–94.

BIBLIOGRAPHY 277

Feeney, D. (1986). "'Stat magni nominis umbra': Lucan on the Greatness of Pompeius Magnus," *CQ* 36: 239–43.

Feeney, D. (1991). *The Gods in Epic: Poets and Critics of the Classical Tradition.* Oxford.

Feeney, D. (2007). *Caesar's Calendar: Ancient Time and the Beginnings of History.* Berkeley, CA.

Feeney, D. (2016). *Beyond Greek: The Beginnings of Latin Literature.* Cambridge, MA.

Feeney, D. (2017). "Carthage and Rome: Introduction," *CP* 112: 301–11.

Fertik, H. (2018). "Obligation and Devotion: Creating a New Community in Lucan's *Bellum Civile*," *CP* 113: 449–71.

Fisher, J. (2012). "'Visus Homerus Adesse Poeta': The *Annals* of Quintus Ennius and the *Odyssey* of Homer," *CW* 106: 29–50.

Fisher, J. (2014). *The Annals of Quintus Ennius and the Italic Tradition.* Baltimore, MD.

Fitzgerald, W. (2016). "Resonance: The Sonic Environment of Vergil's *Eclogues*," *Dictynna* 13: 1–11.

Fitzgerald, W. and E. Spentzou, eds. (2016). *The Production of Space in Latin Literature.* Oxford.

Flatt, T. (2017). "Narrative Desire and the Limits of Lament in Homer," *CJ* 112: 385–404.

Fleischer, G. (1831). *Marci Annaei Lucani Pharsalia.* 3 vols. Leipzig.

Flores, E., P. Esposito, G. Jackson, and D. Tomasco, eds. (2002). *Quinto Ennio: Annali (Libri I–VIII).* Naples.

Foley, J. M. (1990). *Traditional Oral Epic: The Odyssey, Beowulf, and the Serbo-Croatian Return Song.* Berkeley, CA.

Fowler, D. (1989). "First Thoughts on Closure: Problems and Prospects," *MD* 22: 75–122.

Fowler, D. (1997). "Second Thoughts on Closure," in Roberts, Dunn, and Fowler (1997), 3–22.

Fowler, D. (2000). *Roman Constructions: Readings in Postmodern Latin.* Oxford.

Fowler, R., ed. (2006). *The Cambridge Companion to Homer.* Cambridge.

Fox, M., trans. (2012). *Lucan, Civil War.* New York.

Fratantuono, L. (2012). *Madness Unchained: A Reading of Lucan's Pharsalia.* Lexington, MD.

Fratantuono, L. (2014). "*Saevit medio in certamine*: Mars in the *Aeneid*," *Arctos* 48: 137–63.

Fratantuono, L., and A. Smith (2018). *Virgil, Aeneid 8: Text, Translation, and Commentary.* Leiden.

Freudenberg, K. (2018). "Donald Trump and Rome's Mad Emperors," *Common Dreams*, April 29, 2018. (https://www.commondreams.org/views/2018/04/29/donald-trump-and-romes-mad-emperors).

Frier, B. (1979). *Libri Annales Pontificum Maximorum: The Origins of the Annalistic Tradition.* Rome.

Fruyt, M. (1997). "Sémantique et syntaxe des titres en Latin," in J.-C. Fredouille et al., eds., *Titres et articulations du texte dans les œuvres antiques* (Paris), 9–34.

Fucecchi, M. (2011). "Partisans in Civil War," in Asso (2011), 237–56.

Gale, M. (2003). "Poetry and the Backward Glance in Virgil's *Georgics* and *Aeneid*," *TAPA* 133: 323–52.

Gale, M. and J. H. D. Scourfield, eds. (2018a). *Texts and Violence in the Roman World.* Cambridge.

Gale, M. and J. H. D. Scourfield. (2018b). "Introduction: Reading Roman Violence," in Gale and Scourfield (2018a), 1–43.

Genette, G. (1997 [1987]). *Paratexts: Thresholds of Interpretation.* Trans. by J. E. Lewin. Cambridge.

Geymonat, M. (2008). *P. Vergili Maronis Opera*. Rome.
Gildenhard, I. (2003). "The 'Annalist' before the Annalists: Ennius and his *Annales*," in U. Eigler, U. Gotter, N. Luraghi, and U. Walter, eds., *Formen römischer Geschichtsschreibung von den Anfängen bis Livius: Gattungen, Autoren, Kontexte* (Stuttgart), 93–114.
Gildenhard, I. (2007). "Virgil vs. Ennius or: The Undoing of the Annalist," in W. Fitzgerald and E. Gowers, eds., *Ennius Perennis: The Annals and Beyond* (Cambridge), 73–102.
Giusti, E. (2018). *Carthage in Virgil's Aeneid: Staging the Enemy under Augustus*. Cambridge.
Goldberg, S. (1995). *Epic in Republican Rome*. Oxford.
Goldberg, S. (2006). "Ennius after the Banquet," in Breed and Rossi (2006), 427–47.
Goldberg, S., and G. Manuwald, eds. (2018). *Fragmentary Republican Latin: Ennius*. 2 vols. Cambridge, MA.
Goldhill, S. (1991). *The Poet's Voice: Essays on Poetics and Greek Literature*. Cambridge.
Goldschmidt, N. (2013). *Shaggy Crowns: Ennius' Annales and Virgil's Aeneid*. Oxford.
Goldschmidt, N. (2019). *Afterlives of the Roman Poets: Biofiction and the Reception of Latin poetry*. Cambridge.
Goodyear, F. R. D. (1982). "Florus," in E. Kenney and W. Clausen, eds., *The Cambridge History of Classical Literature*, vol. 2 (Cambridge), 664–6.
Gorman, V. B. (2001). "Lucan's Epic *Aristeia*," *CJ* 96: 263–90.
Gotoff, H. (1971). *The Transmission of the Text of Lucan in the Ninth Century*. Cambridge, MA.
Gowing, A. (2005). *Empire and Memory: The Representation of the Roman Republic in Imperial Culture*. Cambridge.
Graziosi, B. (2013). "The Poet in the *Iliad*," in Marmodoro and Hill (2013), 9–38.
Graziosi, B., and J. Haubold (2005). *Homer: The Resonances of Epic*. London.
Green, C. M. C. (1991). "*Stimulos Dedit Aemula Virtus*: Lucan and Homer Reconsidered," *Phoenix* 45: 230–54.
Greene, T. M. (1999). "The Natural Tears of Epic," in Beissinger, Tylus, and Wofford (1999), 189–202.
Grewing, F., B. Acosta-Hughes, and A. Kirichenko, eds. (2013a). *The Door Ajar: False Closure in Greek and Roman Literature and Art*. Heidelberg.
Grewing, F., B. Acosta-Hughes, and A. Kirichenko. (2013b). "Introduction: Is This the End?" In Grewing, Acosta-Hughes, and Kirichenko (2013a), 1–16.
Griffin, J. (1980). *Homer on Life and Death*. Oxford.
Grimal, P. (1970). "Le poète et l'histoire," in Durry (1970), 51–117.
Habinek, T. (2005). *The World of Roman Song: From Ritualized Speech to Social Order*. Baltimore, MD.
Habinek, T. (2006). "The Wisdom of Ennius," in Breed and Rossi (2006), 471–88.
Haffter, H. (1957). "Dem schwanken Zünglein lauschend wachte Cäsar dort," *Museum Helveticum* 14: 118–26.
Hall, E. (2008). *The Return of Ulysses: A Cultural History of Homer's Odyssey*. Baltimore, MD.
Handley, E. W., ed. (1965). *The Dyskolos of Menander*. Cambridge, MA.
Hardie, A. (2016). "The Camenae in Cult, History, and Song," *CA* 35: 45–85.
Hardie, P. (1986). *Virgil's Aeneid: Cosmos and Imperium*. Oxford.
Hardie, P. (1993). *The Epic Successors of Virgil*. Cambridge.
Hardie, P. (1994). *Virgil, Aeneid Book IX*. Cambridge.
Hardie, P. (1997). "Closure in Latin Epic," in Roberts, Dunn, and Fowler (1997), 139–62.
Hardie, P. (2009). *Lucretian Receptions: History, The Sublime, Knowledge*. Cambridge.

Hardie, P. (2012). *Rumour and Renown: Representations of Fama in Western Literature.* Cambridge.
Hardie, P. (2013a). "Lucan's *Bellum Civile*," in Buckley and Dinter (2013), 225–40.
Hardie, P. (2013b). "Fame—the Last Word?" In Grewing, Acosta-Hughes, and Kirichenko (2013a), 309–23.
Hardie, P., and H. Moore, eds. (2010a). *Classical Literary Careers and Their Reception.* Cambridge.
Hardie, P., and H. Moore. (2010b). "Literary Careers: Classical Models and Their Receptions," in Hardie and Moore (2010a), 1–16.
Harris, W. V. (2017). "Rome at Sea: The Beginnings of Roman Naval Power," *Greece & Rome* 64: 14–26.
Harrison, S. J. (1991). *Virgil, Aeneid 10.* Oxford.
Harrison, S. J. (2017). *Horace, Odes Book II.* Cambridge.
Haskins, C. E., ed. (1887). *M. Annaei Lucani Pharsalia.* Edited with English notes. London.
Häußler, R. (1976–78). *Studien zum historischen Epos der Antike.* 2 vols. Heidelberg.
Heitland, W. E. (1887). "Introduction," in Haskins (1887), vii–cxxxi.
Henderson, J. (1987). "Lucan/The Word at War," *Ramus* 16: 122–64.
Heslin, P. J. (1997). "The Scansion of *Pharsalia* (Catullus 64.37; Statius, Achilleid 1.152; Calpurnius Siculus 4.101)," *CQ* 47: 588–93.
Heubeck, A. (1992). *A Commentary on Homer's Odyssey,* Vol. 3. Oxford.
Hinds, S. (1998). *Allusion and Intertext: Dynamics of Appropriation in Roman Poetry.* Cambridge.
Holland, G. B. (1993). "The Name of Achilles: A Revised Etymology," *Glotta* 71: 17–27.
Holst-Warhaft, G. (1992). *Dangerous Voices: Women's Laments and Greek Literature.* London.
Hömke, N. (2010), "Bit by Bit Towards Death: Lucan's Scaeva and the Aestheticization of Dying," in Hömke and Reitz (2010), 91–104.
Hömke, N., and C. Reitz, eds. (2010). *Lucan's "Bellum Civile": Between Epic Tradition and Aesthetic Innovation.* Berlin.
Horsfall, N. (1981). "Some Problems of Titulature in Roman Literary History," *BICS* 28: 103–14.
Horsfall, N. (2003). *Virgil: Aeneid 11: A Commentary.* Leiden.
Horsfall, N. (2006). *Virgil: Aeneid 3: A Commentary.* Leiden.
Housman, A. E, ed. (1926). *M. Annaei Lucani belli civilis libri decem.* Oxford.
Hübner, U. (1976). "Der Sonnenaufgang vor Pharsalus: Zu Lucan. 7, 1–3," *Philologus* 120: 107–16.
Hunink, V. (1992). *M. Annaeus Lucanus Bellum Civile Book III: A Commentary.* Amsterdam.
Hunter, R. (2018). *The Measure of Homer: The Ancient Reception of the Iliad and the Odyssey.* Cambridge.
Hutchinson, G. O. (1993). *Latin Literature from Seneca to Juvenal: A Critical Study.* Oxford.
Hutchinson, G. O. (2013). *Greek to Latin: Frameworks and Contexts for Intertextuality.* Oxford.
Ilberg, H. (1852). *Q. Ennii Annalium libri primi fragmanta emendate disposita illustrata.* Bonn.
Jansen, L., ed. (2014a). *The Roman Paratext: Frame, Text, Readers.* Cambridge.
Jansen, L. (2014b). "Introduction: Approaches to Roman Paratextuality," in Jansen (2014a), 1–18.

Jeppeson, S. (2016). "Lament for Fallen Cities in Early Roman Drama: Naevius, Ennius, and Plautus," in Bachvarova, Dutsch, and Suter (2016), 127–55.
Johnson, W. R. (1987). *Momentary Monsters: Lucan and His Heroes*. Ithaca, NY.
Johnston, A. (2019). "Odyssean Wanderings and Greek Responses to Roman Empire," in Biggs and Blum (2019a), 211–39.
Joseph, T. (2017a). "Pharsalia as Rome's 'Day of Doom' in Lucan," *AJP* 138: 107–41.
Joseph, T. (2017b). "Caesar in Vergil and Lucan," in L. Grillo and C. Krebs, eds., *A Companion to the Writings of Julius Caesar* (Cambridge), 289–303.
Joseph, T. (2019). "The Figure of the Eyewitness in Tacitus' *Histories*," *Latomus* 78: 68–101.
Joseph, T. (2020). "'One City Captures Us': Lucan's Inverted Roman Disaster Narrative," in V. Closs and E. Keitel, eds., *Urban Disasters in the Roman Imagination* (Berlin), 33–48.
Kahane, A. (2013). "The (Dis)continuity of Genre: A Comment on the Romans and the Greeks," in T. D. Papanghelis, S. J. Harrison, and S. Frangoulidis, eds., *Generic Interfaces in Latin Literature: Encounters, Interactions and Transformations* (Berlin), 35–54.
Kaufman, D. (2020). "Lucan's Cato and Popular (Mis)conceptions of Stoicism," in Zientek and Thorne (2020), 133–49.
Keith, A. (2000). *Engendering Rome: Woman in Latin Epic*. Cambridge.
Keith, A. (2008). "Lament in Lucan's *Bellum Civile*," in Suter (2008a), 233–57.
Keith, A. (2011). "Ovid in Lucan: The Poetics of Instability," in Asso (2011), 111–32.
Keith, A. (2016). "City Lament in Augustan Epic: Antitypes of Rome from Troy to Alba Longa," in Bachvarova, Dutsch, and Suter (2016), 156–82.
Keith, A., and J. Edmondson, eds. (2016). *Roman Literary Cultures: Domestic Politics, Revolutionary Poetics, Civic Spectacle*. Toronto.
Kenney, E. J. (1971). *Lucretius, De Rerum Natura Book III*. Cambridge.
Kent, R. G. (1936). "On the Text of Varro, *de Lingua Latina*," *TAPA* 67: 64–82.
Ker, J. (2009). *The Deaths of Seneca*. Oxford.
Kimmerle, N. (2015). *Lucan und der Prinzipat. Inkonsistenz und unzuverlässiges Erzählen im "Bellum Civile."* Berlin.
Kirk, G. S., ed. (1985). *The Iliad: A Commentary*. Vol. 1: *Books 1–4*. Cambridge.
König, F. (1970). "Mensch und Welt bei Lucan im Spiegel Bildhafter Darstellung," in W. Rutz, ed., *Lucan* (Darmstadt), 439–76.
Kucewicz, C. (2016). "Mutilation of the Dead and the Homeric Gods," *CQ* 66: 425–36.
Lamberton, R., and J. Keaney, eds. (1992). *Homer's Ancient Readers: The Hermeneutics of Greek Epic's Earliest Exegetes*. Princeton, NJ.
Lanzarone, N. (2016). *M. Annaei Lucani, Belli Civilis Liver VII*. Florence.
Lapidge, M. (1979). "Lucan's Imagery of Cosmic Dissolution," *Hermes* 107: 344–70.
Lausberg, M. (1985). "Lucan und Homer," *ANRW* II 32.3: 1565–1622.
Lebek, W. D. (1976). *Lucans Pharsalia: Dichtungsstruktur u. Zeitbezug*. Göttingen.
Leigh, M. (1997). *Lucan: Spectacle and Engagement*. Oxford.
Leigh, M. (2000). "Lucan and the Libyan Tale," *JRS* 90: 95–109.
Leigh, M. (2007). "History and Epic at Rome," in J. Marincola (ed.), *A Companion to Greek and Roman Historiography* (Malden, MA), 483–92.
Leigh, M. (2010). "Early Roman Epic and the Maritime Moment," *CP* 105: 265–80.
Littlewood, C. (2016). "Elegy and Epic in Lucan's *Bellum Civile*," in Keith and Edmondson (2016), 159–84.
Livingston, I. (2004). *A Linguistic Commentary on Livius Andronicus*. New York.
Loney, A. C. (2019). "Pompē in the *Odyssey*," in Biggs and Blum (2019a), 31–58.
Lord, A. B. (1960). *The Singer of Tales*. Cambridge, MA.

BIBLIOGRAPHY 281

Lord, L. E. (1938). "The Date of Julius Caesar's Departure from Alexandria," *JRS* 28: 19–40.
Lounsbury, R. C. (1975). "The Death of Domitius in the *Pharsalia*," *TAPA* 105: 209–12.
Luck, G. (1985). *Lukan, Der Bürgerkrieg.* Darmstadt.
Lyne, R. O. A. M. (1989). *Words and the Poet: Characteristic Techniques of Style in Vergil's Aeneid.* Oxford.
Maes, Y. (2013). "*Haec Monstra Edidit*: Translating Lucan in the Early Seventeenth Century," in Buckley and Dinter (2013), 405–24.
Maier, H. (2013). "Nero in Jewish and Christian Tradition from the First Century to the Reformation," in Buckley and Dinter (2013), 385–404.
Malik, S. (2020). *The Nero-Antichrist: Founding and Fashioning a Paradigm.* Cambridge.
Malamud, M. (1995). "Happy Birthday, Dead Lucan: (P)Raising the Dead in *Silvae* 2.7," *Ramus* 24: 1–30.
Manolaraki, E. (2013). *Noscendi Nilum Cupido: Imagining Egypt from Lucan to Philostratus.* Berlin.
Marincola, J., ed. (2007). *A Companion to Greek and Roman Historiography.* Malden, MA.
Mariotti, S. (1952). *Livio Andronico e la traduzione artistica: saggio critico ed edizione dei frammenti dell' Odyssea.* Milan.
Mariotti, S. (1955). *Il "Bellum Poenicum" e l'arte di Nevio: saggio con edizione dei frammenti del "Bellum Poenicum."* Rome.
Marks, R. (2009). "Silius and Lucan," in Augoustakis (2009a), 127–53.
Marmodoro, A., and J. Hill, eds. (2013). *The Author's Voice in Classical and Late Antiquity.* Cambridge.
Martindale, C. (1993). *Redeeming the Text: Latin Poetry and the Hermeneutics of Reception.* Cambridge.
Masters, J. (1992). *Poetry and Civil War in Lucan's "Bellum Civile."* Cambridge.
Matthews, M. (2008). *A Commentary on Lucan De Bello Civili, Book 5 lines 476–721.* Bern.
Mayer, R., ed. (1981). *Lucan: Civil War VIII.* Warminster.
Mayer, R. (1986). "Geography and Roman Poets," *Greece & Rome* 33: 47–54.
Mbembe, J.-A. (2003). "Necropolitics," trans. by L. Meintjes, *Public Culture* 15: 11–40.
McClellan, A. (2019). *Abused Bodies in Roman Epic.* Cambridge.
McClellan, A. (2020). "Lucan's Neronian *Res Publica Restituta*," in Zientek and Thorne (2020), 229–46.
McCune, B. C. (2014). "Lucan's *Militia Amoris*: Elegiac Expectations in the *Bellum Civile*," *CJ* 109: 171–98.
McElduff, S. (2013). *Roman Theories of Translation: Surpassing the Source.* New York.
McRoberts, S. (2005). *Lucan's War on Caesar.* Dissertation, University of Wisconsin-Madison.
Mebane, J. (2016). "Pompey's Head and the Body Politic in Lucan's *De bello civili*," *TAPA* 146: 191–215.
Meunier, N. (2012). "Ennius, les astres et les théories anciennes de la vision: À propos de *Sol albus*et *radiis icta lux* (v. 84–85 Sk)," *Revue de Philologue* 86: 101–21.
Morford, M. (1967). *The Poet Lucan: Studies in Rhetorical Epic.* New York.
Morrison, A. D. (2007). *The Narrator in Archaic Greek and Hellenistic Poetry.* Cambridge.
Most, G. W. (1992). "*Disiecti membra poeta*: The Rhetoric of Dismemberment in Neronian Poetry," in R. Hexter and D. Selden, eds., *Innovations of Antiquity* (New York), 391–419.
Mulhern, E. V. (2017). "Roma(na) Matrona," *CJ* 112: 432–59.
Mulhern, E. V. (2020). "Lucan's Nostalgia and the Infection of Memory," in Zientek and Thorne (2020), 209–27.
Müller, L. (1884). *Eine Einleitung in das Studium der römischen Poesie.* St. Petersburg.

Murgatroyd, T. (2013). "Petronius' *Satyrica*," in Buckley and Dinter (2013), 241–57.
Murnaghan, S. (1987). *Disguise and Recognition in the Odyssey*. Princeton, NJ.
Murnaghan, S. (1999). "The Poetics of Loss in Greek Epic," in Beissinger, Tylus, and Wofford (1999), 203–20.
Murray, J. (2004). "The Metamorphoses of Erysichthon: Callimachus, Apollonius, and Ovid," in M. Harder, R. Regtuit, and G. Wakker, eds., *Hellenistica Grongingana 7: Callimachus II* (Leuven), 207–42.
Murray, J. (2011). "Shipwrecked Argonauticas," in Asso (2011), 57–79.
Myers, M. Y. (2011). "Lucan's Poetic Geographies: Center and Periphery in Civil War Epic," in Asso (2011), 399–416.
Mynors, R. A. B. (1969). *P. Vergili Maronis Opera*. Oxford.
Nagy, G. (1979). *The Best of the Achaeans: Concepts of the Hero in Ancient Greek Poetry*. Baltimore, MD.
Nagy, G. (1994). "The Name of Achilles: Questions of Etymology and 'Folk-Etymology,'" *ICS* 19: 3–9.
Nagy, G. (2013). *The Ancient Greek Hero in 24 Hours*. Cambridge, MA.
Narducci, E. (1979). *La provvidenza crudele: Lucano e la distruzione dei miti augustei*. Pisa.
Narducci, E. (2002). *Lucano: Un' Epica contro L'impero*. Rome.
Nethercut, J. (2019). "History and Myth in Graeco-Roman Epic," in Reitz and Finkmann (2019), 193–211.
Nethercut, J. (2020). "How Ennian was Latin Epic between the *Annals* and Lucretius?" in Damon and Farrell (2020), 188–210.
Newlands, C. (2011a). *Statius, Silvae, Book II*. Cambridge.
Newlands, C. (2011b). "The First Biography of Lucan: Statius' *Silvae*," in Asso (2011), 433–51.
Newman, J. K. (1967). *The Concept of Vates in Augustan Poetry*. Brussels.
Nill, H.-P. (2018). *Gewalt und Unmaking in Lucans Bellum Civile*. Leiden.
Nix, S. A. (2008). "Caesar as Jupiter in Lucan's *Bellum Civile*," *CJ* 103: 281–94.
Norden, E. (1915). *Ennius und Vergilius*. Leipzig-Berlin.
Nugent, S. G. (1992). "Vergil's Voice of the Women in Aeneid V," *Arethusa* 25: 255–92.
Nugent, S. G. (1999). "The Women of the Aeneid: Vanishing Bodies, Lingering Voices," in C. Perkell, ed., *Reading Vergil's Aeneid: An Interpretive Guide* (Norman, OK), 251–70.
O'Gorman, E. (2004). "Cato the Elder and the Destruction of Carthage," *Helios* 31: 99–125.
O'Hara, J. (1990). *Death and the Optimistic Prophecy in Vergil's Aeneid*. Princeton.
O'Hara, J. (1996). *True Names: Vergil and the Alexandrian Tradition of Etymological Wordplay*. Ann Arbor, MI.
O'Hara, J. (2007). *Inconsistency in Roman Epic: Studies in Catullus, Lucretius, Vergil, Ovid and Lucan*. Cambridge.
O'Higgins, D. (1988). "Lucan as *Vates*," *CA* 7: 208–26.
Opelt, I. (1957). "Die Seeschlacht vor Massilia bei Lucan," *Hermes* 85 (1957): 435–45.
Ormand, K. (1994). "Lucan's Auctor Vix Fidelis," *CA* 13: 38–55.
Paleit, E. (2013). *War, Liberty, and Caesar: Responses to Lucan's Bellum Ciuile, ca. 1580–1650*. Oxford.
Palmer, L. R. (1963). *The Interpretation of Mycenaean Greek Texts*. Oxford.
Pandey, N. (2014). "Dilemma as a Tragic Figure of Thought in Lucan's *Bellum Ciuile*," *ICS* 39: 109–38.

Panoussi, V. (2007). "Threat and Hope: Women's Rituals and Civil War in Roman Epic," in M. Parca and A. Tzanetou, eds., *Finding Persephone: Women's Rituals in the Ancient Mediterranean* (Bloomington, IN), 114–34.
Peirano, I. (2013). "Ille ego qui quondam: On Authorial (An)onymity," in Marmodoro and Hill (2013), 251–86.
Peirano, I. (2014). "'Sealing' the Book: The *Sphragis* as Paratext," in Jansen (2014a), 224–42.
Perkell, C. (1997). "The Lament of Juturna: Pathos and Interpretation in the *Aeneid*," *TAPA* 127: 257–86.
Perkell, C. (2008), "Reading the Laments of *Iliad* 24," in Suter (2008a), 93–117.
Perutelli, A. (2004). "Dopo la battaglia: La poetica delle rovine in Lucano (con un'appendice su Tacito)," in Esposito and Ariemma (2004), 85–108.
Phillips, O. C. (1968). "Lucan's Grove," *CP* 63: 296–300.
Pitcher, L. (2008). "A Perfect Storm? Caesar and His Audiences at Lucan 5.504–702," *CQ* 58: 243–9.
Pogorzelski, R. J. (2011). "*Orbis Romanus*: Lucan and the Limits of the Roman World," *TAPA* 141: 143–70.
Prinzen, H. (1998). *Ennius im Urteil der Anitke*. Stuttgart.
Quinn, J. C. (2011). "The Syrtes between East and West," in A. Dowler and E. Galvin, eds., *Money, Trade and Trade Routes in Pre-Islamic North Africa* (London), 11–20.
Quint, D. (1993). *Epic and Empire: Politics and Generic Form from Virgil to Milton*. Princeton, NJ.
Radicke, J. (2004). *Lucans poetische Technik: Studien zum historischen Epos*. Leiden.
Rambaud, M. (1960). "L'opposition de Lucain au Bellum Civile de César," *L'Information Littéraire* 12: 155–62.
Rawson, E. (1987). "Sallust on the Eighties?" *CQ* 37: 163–80.
Reed, J. (2007). *Virgil's Gaze: Nation and Poetry in the Aeneid*. Cambridge.
Reed, J. (2011). "The *Bellum Civile* as a Roman Epic," in Asso (2011) 21–31.
Reinhardt, K. (1960). *Tradition und Geist: Gesammelte Essays zur Dichtung*. Göttingen.
Reitz, C., and S. Finkmann, eds. (2019). *Structures of Epic Poetry. Vol. I: Foundations.* Berlin.
Rich, J. (2011). "Structuring Roman History: The Consular Year and the Roman Historical Tradition," *Histos* 5: 1–43.
Richlin, A. (2014). *Arguments with Silence: Writing the History of Roman Women*. Ann Arbor, MI.
Rimell, V. (2015). *The Closure of Space in Roman Poetics: Empire's Inward Turn*. Cambridge.
Roberts, D. H. (1997). "Afterword: Ending and Aftermath, Ancient and Modern," in Roberts, Dunn, and Fowler (1997), 251–72.
Roberts, D. H., F. M. Dunn, and D. Fowler, eds. (1997). *Classical Closure: Reading the End in Greek and Latin Literature*. Princeton, NJ.
Roche, P. (2005). "Righting the Reader: Conflagration and Civil War in Lucan's *De Bello Civili*," *Scholia* 14: 52–71.
Roche, P. (2009). *De Bello Civili. Book 1/Lucan*. Oxford.
Roche, P. (2019). *Lucan, De Bello Ciuili, Book VII*. Cambridge.
Roche, P. (2020). "Imperial Ethics and the Individual in Lucan and Seneca's Letters," in Zientek and Thorne (2020), 17–31.
Rolim de Moura, A. (2010). "Lucan 7: Speeches at War," in Hömke and Reitz (2010), 71–90.

Rossi, A. (2000). "The *Aeneid* Revisited: The Journey of Pompey in Lucan's *Pharsalia*," *AJP* 121: 571–91.
Rossi, A. (2001). "Remapping the Past: Caesar's Tale of Troy (Lucan *BC* 9.964–999)," *Phoenix* 55: 313–26.
Rossi, A. (2004). *Contexts of War: Manipulation of Genre in Virgilian Battle Narrative*. Ann Arbor, MI.
Rossi, A. (2005). "Sine fine: Caesar's Journey to Egypt and the End of Lucan's *Bellum Civile*," in Walde (2005), 237–60.
Rowland, R. J. (1969). "The Significance of Massilia in Lucan," *Hermes* 97: 204–8.
Rudich, V. (1993). *Political Dissidence Under Nero: The Price of Dissimulation*. London.
Rüpke, J. (2006). "Ennius's Fasti in Fulvius's Temple: Greek Rationality and Roman Tradition," *Arethusa* 39: 489–512.
Rüpke, J. (2011). *The Roman Calendar from Numa to Constantine: Time, History, and the Fasti*. English translation by D. M. B. Richardson. Malden, MA.
Saint-Denis, E. de (1935). *Le rôle de la mer dans la poésie latine*. Lyon.
Sanford, E. M. (1934). "Quotations from Lucan in Mediaeval Latin Authors," *AJP* 55: 1–19.
Saylor, Charles (1990). "Lux Extrema: Lucan, *Pharsalia* 4.402–581," *TAPA* 120: 291–300.
Scodel, R. (2006). "The Story-teller and His Audience," in Fowler (2006), 45–55.
Seewald, M. (2008). *Studien zum 9. Buch von Lucans Bellum Civile. Mit ein Kommentar zu den Versen 1–733*. Berlin.
Segal, C. (1990). *Lucretius on Death and Anxiety*. Princeton, NJ.
Segal, C. (1992). "Bard and Audience in Homer," in Lamberton and Keaney (1992), 3–29.
Seider, A. (2013). *Memory in Vergil's Aeneid: Creating the Past*. Cambridge.
Seidman, J. (2017). "A Poetic Caesar in Lucan's *Pharsalia*," *CJ* 113: 72–95.
Seitz, K. (1965). "Der pathetische Erzahlstil Lucans," *Hermes* 93: 204–32.
Seo, J. M. (2011). "Lucan's Cato and the Poetics of Exemplarity," in Asso (2011), 199–221.
Serena, M. (2020). "World Geography, Roman History, and the Failure to Incorporate Parthia in Lucan's *Bellum Civile*," in Zientek and Thorne (2020), 111–30.
Shackleton Bailey, D. R. (1987). "Lucan Revisited," *PCPS* 33: 74–92.
Shackleton Bailey, D. R. (1988). *M. Annaei Lucani De bello ciuili libri x*. Leipzig.
Sheets, G. (1983). "Ennius Lyricus," *ICS* 8: 22–32.
Silk, M. (2004). "The *Odyssey* and Its Explorations," in R. Fowler, ed., *The Cambridge Companion to Homer* (Cambridge), 31–44.
Sinclair, P. (1995). *Tacitus the Sententious Historian: A Sociology of Rhetoric in Annales 1–6*. University Park, PA.
Sklenár, R. (2003). *The Taste for Nothingness: A Study of Virtus and Related Themes in Lucan's Bellum Civile*. Ann Arbor, MI.
Skutsch, O. (1968). *Studia Enniana*. London.
Skutsch, O. (1985). *The Annals of Quintus Ennius*. Oxford.
Spentzou, E. (2018). "Violence and Alienation in Lucan's *Pharsalia*: The Case of Caesar," in Gale and Scourfield (2018a), 246–68.
Stover, T. (2008). "Cato and the Intended Scope of Lucan's *Bellum Civile*," *CQ* 58: 571–80.
Stover, T. (2012). *Epic and Empire in Vespasianic Rome: A New Reading of Valerius Flaccus' Argonautica*. Oxford.
Suerbaum, W. (1992). "Zum Umfang der Bücher in der archaischen lateinischen Dichtung: Naevius, Ennius, Lukrez und Livius Andronicus auf Papyrus-Rollen," *ZPE* 92: 153–73.
Suter, A. (2003). "Lament in Euripides' *Trojan Women*," *Mnemosyne* 56: 1–28.

Suter, A., ed. (2008a). *Lament: Studies in the Ancient Mediterranean and Beyond*. Oxford.
Suter, A. (2008b). "Male Lament in Greek Tragedy," in Suter (2008a), 156–80.
Tarrant, R. J. (1983). "Lucan," in L. D. Reynolds, ed., *Texts and Transmission: A Survey of the Latin Classics* (Oxford), 215–18.
Tarrant, R. J. (2002). "Chaos in Ovid's *Metamorphoses* and its Neronian Influence," *Arethusa* 35: 349–60.
Tarrant, R. J. (2012). *Virgil, Aeneid, Book XII*. Cambridge.
Taylor, J. C. (2020). "Even Nature Nods: Lucan's Alternative Explanations of the Syrtes (9.303–18)," in Zientek and Thorne (2020), 91–109.
Tesoriero, C. (2005). "Trampling over Troy: Caesar, Virgil, Lucan," in Walde (2005), 202–15.
Thiel, J. (1954). *A History of Roman Sea-Power before the Second Punic War*. Amsterdam.
Thomas, R. F. (1986). "Virgil's *Georgics* and the Art of Reference," *HSCP* 90: 171–98.
Thomas, R. F. (1988a). *Virgil, Georgics*. 2 vols. Cambridge.
Thomas, R. F. (1988b). "Tree Violation and Ambivalence in Virgil," *TAPA* 118: 261–73.
Thomas, R. F. (2001). *Virgil and the Augustan Reception*. Cambridge.
Thomas, R. F. (2011). *Horace, Odes Book IV and Carmen Saeculare*. Cambridge.
Thompson, L., and R. T. Bruère (1970). "The Vergilian Background to Lucan's Fourth Book," *CP* 65: 167–72.
Thorne, M. (2011). "*Memoria Redux*: Memory in Lucan," in Asso (2011), 363–81.
Thorne, M. (2016). "Speaking the Unspeakable: Engaging Nefas in Lucan and Rwanda 1994," in A. Ambühl (ed.), *Krieg der Sinne—Die Sinne im Krieg. Kriegsdarstellungen im Spannungsfeld zwischen antiker und moderner Kultur* (= thersites 4; Berlin), 77–119.
Tipping, B. (2010). *Exemplary Epic: Silius Italicus' Punica*. Oxford.
Tolkiehn, J. (1991 [1900]). *Omero e la poesia latina*. Trans. from the German edition of 1900 and rev. by M. Scaffai. Bologna.
Tracy, J. (2011). "Internal Evidence for the Completeness of the *Bellum Civile*," in Asso (2011), 33–53.
Tracy, J. (2014). *Lucan's Egyptian Civil War*. Cambridge.
Tracy, J. (2016). "Knowledge, Power, and Republicanism in Lucan," in Keith and Edmondson (2016), 221–53.
Tsagalis, C. (2004). *Epic Grief: Personal Laments in Homer's Iliad*. Berlin.
Tucker, R. A. (1983). "Lucan and Phoebus," *Latomus* 42: 143–51.
Van Dam, H.-J. (1984). *P. Papinius Statius, Silvae, Book II, a Commentary*. Leiden.
Voltaire (1727). *An Essay Upon the Civil Wars of France: Extracted from Curious Manuscripts. And Also Upon the Epick Poetry of the European Nations, from Homer Down to Milton*. London.
Von Albrecht, M. (1970). "Der Dichter Lucan und die epische Tradition," in Durry (1970), 267–301.
Walbank, F. W. (1957). *A Historical Commentary on Polybius*. Vol. 1: *Commentary on Books I–VI*. Oxford.
Walde, C. (2011). "Lucan's *Bellum Civile*: A Specimen of a Roman 'Literature of Trauma,'" in Asso (2011), 283–302.
Walde, C., ed. (2005). *Lucan im 21. Jahrhundert*. Munich.
Wallace-Hadrill, A. (2008). *Rome's Cultural Revolution*. Cambridge.
Walters, B. (2013). "Reading Death and the Senses in Lucan and Lucretius," in S. Butler and A. Purves, eds., *Synaesthesia and the Ancient Senses* (Durham, NC), 115–25.

Welsh, J. (2011). "Accius, Porcius Licinus, and the Beginnings of Latin Literature," *JRS* 101: 31–50.
Werner, S. (1998). *The Transmission and Scholia of Lucan's Bellum Civile*. Hamburg.
Westerhold, J. (2011). "Hecuba and the Performance of Lament on the Epic Stage (Ovid, *Met.* 13, 399–575)," *Mouseion* 11: 295–315.
Westerhold, J. (2013). "Ovid's Epic Forest: A Note on *Amores* 3.1.1–6," *CQ* 63: 899–903.
Wheeler, S. (2002). "Lucan's Reception of Ovid's *Metamorphoses*," *Arethusa* 35: 361–80.
Wick, C. (2004). *Lucan, Bellum Civile. Liber IX*. Munich.
Willams, G. W. (1968). *Tradition and Originality in Roman Poetry*. Oxford.
Willams, G. W. (1978). *Change and Decline: Roman Literature in the Early Empire*. Berkeley, CA.
Wiseman, T. P. (2006). "Fauns, Prophets, and Ennius' *Annales*," in Breed and Rossi (2006), 513–29.
Wolkenhauer, A. (2020). "'Time as Such': Chronotopes and Periphrases of Time in Latin Epic," in C. Reitz and S. Finkmann, eds., *Structures of Epic Poetry*, Vol. II (Berlin), 215–42.
Woodman, A. J. (1983). *Velleius Paterculus: The Caesarian and Augustan Narrative (2.41–93)*. Cambridge.
Wray, D. (2007). "Wood: Statius's *Silvae* and the Poetics of Genius," *Arethusa* 40: 127–43.
Wright, E. (1986). *The Forms of Laments in Greek Tragedy*. Dissertation, University of Pennsylvania.
Zientek, L., and M. Thorne, eds. (2020). *Lucan's Imperial World: The Bellum Civile in Its Contemporary Contexts*. London.
Zissos, A. (2004). "Navigating Genres: Martial 7.19 and the *Argonautica* of Valerius Flaccus," *CJ* 99: 405–22.
Zissos, A. (2013). "Lucan and Caesar: Epic and *Commentarius*," in D. Papanghelis, S. J. Harrison, and S. Frangoulidis, eds., *Generic Interfaces in Latin Literature: Encounters, Interactions, and Transformations* (Berlin), 135–50.
Zwierlein, O. (1982). "Der Ruhm der Dichtung bei Ennius und seinen Nachfolgern," *Hermes* 110: 85–102.

Index of Passages Discussed

Appian
B Civ.
2.14: 213n88
2.33–9: 133
2.41: 151n30
2.48: 133
2.56–8: 207n69
2.76: 133
2.84: 213n89
2.90: 138, 213n89
2.115: 213n88

Aristotle
Poet.
1448b: 260n121
1451b: 260n121

Asconius
On Cicero's In Toga Candida
    75.5: 59

Caesar
BCiv.
1.1–5: 133
1.6: 133
1.14: 133
1.25–7: 182n108
1.33.3–4: 151n30
1.36: 172
1.56–8: 172
2.3–7: 172
2.21: 133
3.1: 133
3.4: 133
3.5: 133
3.21: 133
3.104.3: 179
3.106–12: 138

Cassius Dio
41.36.1: 133
41.46: 207n69
42.34–44: 213n89

Catullus
64.7: 174
64.15: 224n1
64.37: 33, n. 40
101.1: 213

Cicero
Arch.
22: 126, 132, 160, 167n74
27: 135

Att.
7.11.1: 149n26
7.15–18 and 20–1: 133
11.17a.3: 138

Balb.
51: 158

Brut.
76: 159

Div.
1.107: 97
1.114: 30

Fam.
10.31 [368].2: 12

Prov. cons.
20: 135

Claudian
Cons. Stil.
III.20: 148, 160n56

Commenta Bernensia
On *Ph.* 1.7: 36
On *Ph.* 2.392: 196
On *Ph.* 4.442: 82n93
On *Ph.* 5.676: 212

Diomedes
GL I, p. 484: 111

Ennius
Andromacha
FRL fr. 23: 228n20

288   INDEX OF PASSAGES DISCUSSED

Ennius (*cont.*)
Annales (Skutsch)
1: 45
3: 30
4: 24, 49, 92
12–13: 28–30, 106, 129
14–19: 24
20: 38–9, 50, 70, 124
34–50: 123
72–91: 97–101, 103–4
84–9: 110–11
94–5: 102–4
99–100: 123
105–6: 228
106–9: 101
156: 125, 130
175–9: 74–83
191–4: 126n89, 132n107
197: 40
205: 111n52
206–7: 30, 65
206–11: 137n122
209: 65
211–12: 65
216–19: 159
217: 178–9
218: 174
219: 174
220–1: 63
222: 63–6
223–6: 63, 64
234: 148
234–5: 158
258–60: 111–12
266: 90
292: 148
299: 135
302: 159
304–6: 134–5
308: 69–70
309: 148, 159, 165
322–3: 45, 125–6
324: 134
329: 135
333: 64
344–5: 24
348: 110–11
363–5: 135
377–8: 174–7

382–3: 111–13
389–90: 69–70
391–8: 86–94, 126n89
401–3: 137n122
404–5: 112n59
406: 111–12
415–16: 110
419: 110
420: 111
444: 119
456: 132n107, 135
476: 132n107
483–4: 61
494–5: 105, 111, 117
498: 228n20
518: 72
563: 70
571: 110–11
572: 110–11
582: 36–7, 64, 176
Spuria fr. 6: 156n45

Epigrammata
Fr. 46 (Courtney): 29

Scipio
Fr. 29–34 (Courtney): 160

Florus
2.9.26: 59
2.13.21: 151n30
2.13.33: 180
2.13.45: 204

Hesiod
Theog.
79–80: 260n121

Homer
Il.
1.1: 41
1.2–5: 44
1.8: 41, 46
1.348–427: 51–3
1.414–18: 224n2
2.155–210: 190n24
2.484–7: 126
4.164–5: 110, 256
6.321–41: 192
6.407–39: 229
6.448–9: 110, 256

8.31: 119
13.616–17: 61
15.582–4: 236
16.19: 236
16.102–11: 85–8, 93
16.584: 236
16.744: 236
16.754: 236
16.812: 236
16.843: 236
18.52–64: 224n2
18.239–40: 96
18.428–61: 224n2
19.302: 255
21.218–20: 58
21.235–8: 58
21.248–71: 51
21.377–84: 58
22.408–11: 256, 257
22.262–6: 50–1
23.114–22: 74–5, 79, 81
24.719–22: 225, 227, 243
24.720–75: 226–7, 231–2, 234
24.776: 228, 234, 256
24.804: 139

Od.
1.1: 42–3
1.1–4: 212–13
1.5–9: 44, 190
4.333–592: 215–16
4.495: 187n11
5.34–5: 211
5.295–6: 208
5.299–312: 208
5.313–18: 211
5.392–463: 211
8.29: 39
8.138–9: 146
8.499–531: 256
9.39–41: 189
9.67–75: 189
9.82–104: 189–90
11.121–33: 187, 203–4
12.260–419: 190
12.352–98: 199n48
12.403–19: 199n48
13.78–125: 211
14.48–52: 210–11

23.166–349: 193–4
23.184–94: 201
23.241–6: 96
23.264–84: 194
23.268–80: 187, 203–4
23.306–41: 199n47
24.58–62: 225
24.114–19: 192
24.412–20: 186–7
24.426–37: 186–7
24.522–48: 186–7

Horace
Epist.
1.2.17–22: 189n21
2.1.50: 4, 17
2.1.62: 187

Epod.
12.3: 65

Sat.
1.2.37: 105
1.10.52: 260

Jerome
Comm. on Micah 2.7.5: 17

Livius Andronicus
Odusia (Blänsdorf)
Fr. 1: 42–3, 187, 188, 222–3
Fr. 2: 187
Fr. 11: 187
Fr. 18: 146–7

Livy
21.20.7–8: 155n41, 156n46
21.25.1: 155n41
22.19.5: 155n41
22.52.6: 157n47
29.24: 161

Periochae
88: 59
110: 180

Lucan
1.1–7: 8, 35–46
1.1: 108, 116
1.2–3: 105, 188, 218, 219, 222–3, 247, 257
1.5: 107

Lucan (cont.)
1.6–7: 64, 71, 92, 176, 250, 264
1.8–32: 38–41, 247
1.8: 40, 41, 264
1.9–23: 37, 40, 108
1.15–18: 39
1.21–3: 222
1.24–32: 8, 38–41
1.24–8: 220
1.28–9: 38–9, 124
1.30–1: 149
1.37–9: 149, 268
1.41: 132
1.59: 132
1.63: 28
1.66: 9, 34
1.68: 260
1.69: 107n40
1.72–80: 8, 109
1.73: 141
1.81: 259
1.84–5: 222, 248
1.93–5: 104
1.128: 120
1.131–3: 204
1.135: 259n118
1.151–7: 14–15, 260
1.183–205: 47–53
1.183–5: 149
1.186: 206
1.195–6: 15, 259
1.198: 132–3
1.205–12: 149
1.224: 50
1.225: 51–2
1.255: 149–50
1.303–5: 150
1.312–13: 133
1.486–522: 196, 218
1.487–8: 218
1.498–504: 218–19
1.503: 144–5
1.519–20: 222, 248
1.522–695: 108
1.642–5: 120
2.1–2: 108, 120
2.4: 120
2.7–13: 120

2.16–66: 56, 73, 235
2.31–2: 83
2.40–42: 254
2.46: 157
2.47–56: 247n80
2.67–70: 56
2.68–232: 56–73, 225, 235
2.90–3: 150
2.107: 73
2.113–14: 58
2.116: 72, 122, 222
2.149–51: 56n8
2.160–73: 56n8
2.162–5: 56
2.167: 73
2.169–71: 62
2.173–85: 59–68
2.178: 62
2.187–90: 71–2
2.196–203: 68–71
2.196: 124
2.197: 73
2.198–201: 56n8
2.208: 62, 73
2.209–20: 58
2.223–32: 57
2.232–3: 73
2.238: 192
2.242–84: 192–3
2.286–323: 192–3
2.327–33: 193
2.329: 194
2.338–49: 194–5
2.341–2: 214
2.350–71: 195
2.379–81: 195
2.392–3: 196
2.663–4: 182
2.728–31: 198, 201
3.3–7: 198–9
3.5: 207
3.21: 202n56
3.73: 207, 211
3.90–100: 151
3.97–168: 207
3.105–8: 132
3.154–68: 108, 151–5, 164
3.159: 248

INDEX OF PASSAGES DISCUSSED 291

3.169-295: 155, 167
3.169: 108
3.286-7: 261
3.297: 108, 155, 267
3.298-9: 151
3.300-74: 155-7
3.394-452: 74-83
3.399: 154n36
3.443: 154n36
3.453-508: 172
3.509-762: 157, 172-7
3.538-45: 173-7
3.585-626: 179
3.627-33: 179-80, 182
3.612: 65
3.686: 168n76
3.756-61: 177, 225
3.761-2: 177
4.48-120: 8
4.87-8: 145n11
4.254-5: 120
4.402-581: 180-4
4.562-74: 182-4
4.583-8: 160-1
4.587: 163
4.590: 162-3
4.593-655: 161-2
4.605-6: 163
4.656-60: 162-3
4.661-2: 163
4.666-787: 158, 163-4
4.692: 248
4.777: 164
4.788-93: 164-5
4.799-824: 166
4.802: 103
4.803: 165, 267
4.803-6: 102-4
4.807-8: 120
4.823: 132
5.8-10: 217, 218
5.19: 217
5.17-46: 133
5.381-402: 8, 133-4, 136, 139, 207
5.476-702: 207-13
5.515-31: 210-11
5.598-612: 208
5.654-71: 208-9

5.672-7: 211-13
5.678-9: 212
5.734-59: 200
5.791: 200
5.762-90: 200, 229-30
5.794: 205
5.804: 201
5.806-15: 200-1
6.140-262: 84-94
6.176: 65
6.184-95: 84-94
6.193: 168n76
6.257: 264
6.302-3: 248
6.312-13: 268
6.319-21: 196-7, 199
6.333-412: 33, 108n44.
6.347-51: 33-4, 224-5
6.434-830: 64
6.536: 168n76
6.577: 265
6.651: 265
6.776: 236
6.777-820: 265-6
6.780-1: 130
6.784-90: 8, 130-1, 166-7, 235-6
7.1-6: 95-101, 103-4
7.7-44: 204-5, 254-5
7.58-9: 120, 253
7.60: 253
7.91-2: 109, 113
7.123-7: 197-8
7.131-3: 8, 110, 113
7.145: 110
7.151: 268
7.175: 268-9
7.182-3: 56n8
7.195: 109, 110
7.202-4: 266-7
7.205-13: 253
7.209-10: 259
7.214-17: 101
7.319: 158n51
7.356-60: 8, 130
7.387-459: 113-25, 129, 139
7.387-407: 114, 122-5
7.403-7: 220-1
7.407-27: 114-17

Lucan (cont.)
7.408–9: 157
7.417–19: 248–9
7.412–20: 56n8
7.421–8: 153
7.427: 101, 109
7.427–45: 117–18
7.429–30: 134
7.436–41: 249
7.440–1: 134
7.445–59: 8, 114, 117–21
7.446: 141
7.453–4: 56n8
7:419–36: 8, 108
7.419: 259–60
7.437–9: 104
7.490–1: 247n78
7.535–40: 267–8
7.545–556: 250
7.553: 28
7.583–5: 129–30
7.597: 134
7.617–46: 127, 139
7.617–18: 127
7.626–30: 56n8
7.630–41: 127–8
7.630–1: 252
7.632–3: 266
7.634: 8, 108, 134
7.638: 141
7.639–46: 252–3
7.648: 239
7.653: 239
7.673: 238
7.680–727: 239–41, 250–1
7.695: 253
7.723–7: 259n114
7.745: 267
7.762–3: 56n8
7.764–76: 64
7.768: 269n11
7.781: 267
7.789–803: 56n8
7.794–808: 127
7.797–803: 157–8
7.803: 253
7.829: 64
7.855: 253

7.862: 108, 122
7.865: 253
8.66–70: 201
8.72–85: 201, 258–9
8.88–105: 201–2, 230
8.132–3: 201, 215
8.189: 197
8.273: 267
8.283–8: 158–9
8.330–453: 133n110
8.335: 197
8.584–6: 202–3
8.639–61: 230–2
8.729–42: 237
8.733: 238
8.746–51: 237
8.755: 168n76, 179
8.759–75: 237, 239
8.775–80: 237
8.781–815: 237–8
8.835–7: 205–6, 248
9.2: 259n118
9.3–18: 206
9.13–14: 254
9.16: 167
9.32–5: 167–9, 179
9.36–50: 168–9
9.49–50: 225, 232–3
9.55–108: 168–9, 232
9.110–12: 233, 254
9.113–16: 203
9.167–73: 233–4
9.172–3: 83
9.217–93: 190n24
9.230–1: 217
9.232–3: 267n8
9.297–9: 189
9.300–1: 169
9.303–18: 169
9.319–47: 169–70, 189
9.335–42: 170
9.347–60: 189–90
9.368–9: 169, 172
9.593–604: 172, 189
9.602–3: 248
9.700–899: 190
9.938–49: 190–2
9.941: 169, 189

INDEX OF PASSAGES DISCUSSED 293

9.961: 26
9.961–99: 221, 257
9.964–9: 23–5
9.980–6: 22, 26–35, 234, 254–5, 261, 263–4, 269
9.980: 260
9.1010–1104: 241–3
9.1104–8: 242–3, 255
10.56: 213–14
10.68–9: 214
10.75–6: 214
10.136–74: 214
10.187: 134n112
10.410–11: 254
10.453–4: 214
10.458–60: 214
10.479: 214
10.482–3: 214–15
10.509–11: 215–16
10.529–46: 138
10.532–3: 141
10.535–42: 184
10.534–7: 140–1
10.538–9: 216
10.543–6: 138–40, 215, 264

Lucilius
343M: 105

Lucretius
1.1–61: 46
1.116–18: 16, 117
1.124–6: 49–50
3.384: 148
3.654–6: 61
6.92–5: 46
6.387–95: 120n76

Macrobius
Sat.
6.1.15: 102
6.1.52: 91n106
6.2.27: 74
6.3.2–4: 85–7, 91–2

Martial
2.83.3: 66
3.85.1–4: 66
7.19: 168

Naevius
Bellum Punicum (Blänsdorf)
Fr. 1: 45
Fr. 3: 159n52
Fr. 7: 178
Fr. 15: 119n73
Fr. 37: 146n16, 171
Fr. 41: 146
Fr. 48: 146, 171
Fr. 64: 146n16, 171–2, 175

Origen
4.4–5: 30

Orosius 6.15.5: 151n30

Ovid
Am.
1.8.61: 260
1.15.7: 17n61
1.15.19–30: 16

Met.
1.2: 46
1.651–63: 228
2.70–3: 95
2.381–93: 95n2
6.557–60: 67
8.741–76: 74, 77, 80, 81
11.461–2: 174n92
13.494–532: 228–9
15.622: 46
15.785–6: 95n2
15.861–7: 48n87
15.878–9: 26–9

Tr.
2.375–6: 193
2.424: 17n61

Petronius
Sat.
118: 137–8

Pliny the Elder
NH
Pref. 7: 65
2.119: 208
25.5.11: 15
33.35–6: 151n30

294   INDEX OF PASSAGES DISCUSSED

Plutarch
Caes.
14.7: 213n88
32: 47
35: 151n30
37: 133
38: 207n69
49: 213n89
63–4: 213n88

Cat. Min.
52: 194, 195n36
56: 189n19

Pomp.
58–9: 132
68.2: 204
74–5: 200
78–9: 200
80: 237

Polybius
1.20: 144n6, 179
1.22: 174
1.39.1–7: 171
1.39.14–15: 171

Pompilius
fr. 1 (Courtney): 16–17

Porcius Licinius
fr. 1 (Courtney): 45n75, 144n8

Porphyrio
on Hor. *Sat.* 1.2.37: 105

Propertius
1.7.25: 224n1
2.34.66: 261
3.3.6, 9–11: 148
3.7.67: 224n1

Quintilian
Inst.
1.8.5: 261
3.8.23: 180n104
3.8.30: 180n104
8.3.84: 261
9.4.115: 30
10.1.46: 15
10.1.46–51: 261
10.1.88: 2, 15, 77
10.1.90: 245

Sallust
Histores fr. 14
    (Maurenbrecher): 59

Seneca
Ag.
474–90: 208n73

Constant.
2.2.1: 189

De Ira
3.18.1–2: 59, 66–7

Dial.
6.26.1: 12

Ep.
27.5: 15

Oed.
1–5: 95
3: 97n9
169: 63
967: 62

Thy.
784–7: 95

Servius
on *Aen.* 1.8: 46n8
on *Aen.* 1.20: 119
on *Aen.* 1.170: 178
on *Aen.* 6.685: 111n53
on *Aen.* 8.33: 50n94
on *Aen.* 8.500: 69
on *Aen.* 9.422: 102
on *Aen.* 10.396: 61

Silius Italicus
Pun.
3.40: 165n71
10.124: 165n71
10.527–34: 74, 79
10.547–77: 157n47
11.489: 174n92
12.394: 17
12.408–9: 2
12.410: 17
13.380: 69

INDEX OF PASSAGES DISCUSSED 295

Statius
Silv.
1.1.74–83: 5n11
1.2.162–93: 5n11
1.4.61–105: 5n11
2.7.41–53: 3–4
2.7.48: 23
2.7.54–7: 4–5, 23
2.7.66: 14
2.7.70–72: 14, 239
2.7.75: 4, 16
2.7.75–80: 1–2
2.7.89–106: 5–6
3.1.91–116: 5n11
4.1.17–43: 5n11
4.3.72–94: 5n11
4.3.124–61: 5n11

Theb.
1.595: 69
4.150: 220n105
5.375: 174n92
5.693: 69
6.90–106: 74, 79

Strabo
17.3.20: 189n19

Suetonius
Gram. et rhet.
1: 187

Iul.
21.1: 213n88
32: 47
35: 213n89
52: 213n89
58: 207n69
81.3: 213n88

Lucan
5: 32 (with n. 31)

Ner.
38.2: 9
40.1: 9

Valerius Flaccus
Argonautica
1.369: 174n92
1.633: 69

Valerius Maximus
5.1 *ext.* 6: 157n47
9.2.1: 59
9.8.2: 207n69

Varro *Ling.*
7.36: 30

Velleius Paterculus
2.67.1: 12

Virgil
Ecl.
9.34: 30
G.
1.466–8: 95n2

Aen.
1.1: 42, 45
1.8: 46
1.94–101: 208
1.110–11: 170–1
1.257–8: 116
1.278–9: 116
1.373: 156
2.6–12: 257n106
2.268–97: 48, 50
2.270–77: 48–9
2.354: 58
2.483: 214
2.486–90: 257n106
2.528: 214
2.771–95: 48n85
3.11–12: 198n46
3.208: 174
4.583: 174
4.666–7: 228
5.613–15: 228
6.33: 67
6.179–82: 74–81
6.494–7: 66
6.525–9: 66
6.692–3: 213
6.771–6: 38
6.824–5: 131–2
6.830–1: 149n26
7.1–4: 244
7.41: 30
7.45: 260–1

Virgil (*cont.*)
7.324: 97n9
7.585–600: 198n45
8.36–65: 50
8.184–275: 162n61
8.347–50: 38
8.499–500: 69
8.671–713: 172–3
9.422: 102
9.446–9: 26n11, 244
9.481–97: 227, 228, 233–4
9.806–14: 85–8, 93
10.396: 61
11.135–8: 74, 79, 81
11.152–81: 227
11.425–7: 111–12
12.604–11: 228
12.872–84: 227–8
12.948–9: 102
12.952: 139

General Index

Achilles, 5, 15, 33–4, 41–2, 44, 51–2, 58, 224–8
Africa, in the *Ph.*, 145, 159–72. *See also* Hannibal
Agamemnon, 41, 110, 167, 192, 218, 256
Amyclas, 209–11
anchoring allusions, 10, 18, 22–53, 64, 68, 78, 103, 104, 173, 215–16, 222
Andromache, 199, 226–7, 229, 231–2
antiphony, 13, 21, 44–5, 83, 166–7, 227, 228, 232–45, 255–8, 263. *See also* lament
apocalyptic literature, 8–9
Apollonius of Rhodes, 170, 183
apostrophe, 26, 35, 244–8, 250, 251
Attius Labeo, 15

Baebius Italicus, 15

Caesar, Julius:
  Commentarii De Bello Civili, 11–12, 26, 28, 133, 138, 139, 182n108, 213
  character in Lucan, *passim*, especially, 14–15, 23, 41, 140–1, 184, 255, 260
  at the Rubicon, 47–53
  at the Massilian grove, 73–83
  ending Republican institutions, 132–6
  as Hannibal revived, 149–59
  as anti-Odyssean, 206–17
  with head of Pompey, 241–3
  assassination of, in Lucan, 141n139, 206
  his calendar, 134n112
Calliope, 1–7, 14–15, 22, 46, 239, 260. *See also* Muses
Camena, 43, 45, 187, 222–3
Cannae, Battle of, compared with Pharsalia, 114–15, 157–8
castration, 66
Cato the Elder, 126, 130–1, 166–7, 225, 235–6
Cato the Younger, 159–60, 198, 200, 214, 217, 220, 232–3, 263
  as anti-Odyssean, 188–96

crash landing in Libya, 167–72
Cicero, as reader, 125, 126, 132, 148, 158, 159, 160
closure, *passim*, 7–8, 10–15, 137–42, 184, 263–4, 269–71
code and norm in epic, 10–11, 104, 107, 114, 119, 121, 127, 146
consulship, its destruction in the *Ph.*, 8, 132–6, 217
Conte, Gian Biagio, 10–11, 107, 114, 121, 173–4
Cordus, 237–9, 243
Cornelia, 83, 168–9, 205, 240, 243, 254
  antitype to Penelope, 199–203
  as conventional mourner, 229–35
Cornelius Severus, 172n89
Curio, 102–3, 177
  lamented, 166
  landing in Africa, 159–65

Derrida, Jacques, 54–5, 93, 140
Diomedes the grammarian, 16

Ennius
  alignment with / adaptation of Homer, 25, 30–31, 48–50, 79, 91–2, 100, 126–7
  model / anti-model for Lucan, *passim* and especially, 9, 17–18, 19–20, 24–5, 28–31, 34–5, 36–41, 49–50, 63–72, 78–81, 90–4, 95–142, 148, 151–9, 173–7, 178–84, 234
  standing in antiquity, 16–17, 91–2, 106–7, 126–7, 135, 140, 143–4, 147–8
  time and space in, 29, 34–5, 95–117
Erictho's corpse, 265–6, 270

gods, the absence of their providence in the *Ph.*, 8, 27, 114, 117–21, 124–5, 136, 137, 154–5, 187
goos, 13, 44, 166, 225–7, 247, 257. *See also* lament

GENERAL INDEX

Hannibal, 39–40, 147–59, 247
Hector, 42, 48–52, 110, 139, 199, 225–7, 256, 257
Hecuba, 226–8, 231
Helen, 66, 226–8, 231
Hesperia, as evocative term in the *Ph.*, 38–9, 50, 70, 124
Homer
  aligned with Ennius, 25, 30–1, 48–50, 79, 91–2, 100
  model / anti-model for Lucan, *passim* and especially, 9, 13–14, 17–18, 20–21, 23–24, 27–8, 33–5, 41–5, 50–3, 58, 60–2, 77, 85–8, 92, 97, 110, 139, 146–7, 185–261
  standing in Rome, 15–16, 185, 260–1

lament
  conventions of, 13, 44, 166, 225–7
  gender and lament, 13–14, 228–9, 243
  Lucan's use of, 12–13, 21, 44–5, 52–3, 73, 81–3, 103, 166–7, 168–9, 224–61
  place of in epic poetry, 5–6, 12–15, 224–9
  praise in, 13, 44, 166, 226, 229, 232, 234, 237, 258–61
  reproach in, 13, 166, 226, 230–2, 236, 247–8, 252–3
laudatio funebris, 227
Livius Andronicus, 16, 42–3, 119, 143, 147, 178, 185
  model and anti-model for Lucan, 19–20, 45–6, 146–7, 178–84, 187–8, 218, 222–3
Lucan, his other works
  Catachthonion, 4, 15–16
  De Incendio Urbis, 9
  Iliacon, 4, 15–16
Lucretius, 1, 16, 46, 49–50, 61, 117, 120n76, 148

Macrobius, as reader of epic, 85–7, 90n106, 91–2, 102
Marcia, 193–6, 200, 214, 220
Marius Gratidianus, 59–73
Mars, 122–3
Martial, 66, 168
metapoetic diction, *passim*; note in particular

amputo, 64–6
arto, 168, 169
degener, 72, 122, 222
fama, 66, 80–1, 141, 162, 183–4, 264–5
fatum, 117, 130
fragmentum, 167–8, 179
frons, 81, 83
locus, 163, 169–70, 172, 184
magnus, 260–1
membrum, 62, 80
minor, 36–7, 176
notus, 161, 163
Pharsalia (see *Pharsalia*)
primus / primum, 83, 136, 154, 163, 165
robor, 23, 181
Roma (see *Roma*)
silua, 23, 75–6, 79, 83, 88
spiramen, 64–5
uestigium, 23, 162–3
Muses, 27, 45–6, 125–6, 222. See also Calliope

Naevius, 16, 105n28, 107, 119, 143–4, 159
  model and anti-model for Lucan, 19–20, 45–6, 146–7, 159–60, 161n60, 167, 171–2, 173–5, 178–84
narrator, 38, 44–5, 57, 113–14, 120, 205, 221–2, 236–44, 251–2
  poetic doublets of the narrator in the poem, 57, 162, 265
nenia, 227
Nero, reign of, 8–9, 268–71
  and Lucan's narrator, 32n33, 250, 268, 269–71
nostos, as master-trope explored by Lucan, 185–223

Odysseus, 3, 15, 42–3, 44, 96, 146, 178, 185–223, 256–7
Ovid, 2, 7n18, 16, 46, 99, 102, 124, 193, 228, 244, 260
  as model and anti-model for Lucan, 7, 11, 26–8, 29, 33, 42n87, 61, 67, 74, 80–1, 82, 95, 134, 137, 200, 234

Patroclus, 225–7, 236, 238, 255
Penelope, 96, 185–6, 190, 193–6, 199–203, 229

GENERAL INDEX 299

Petronius, 15, 137–8
Pharsalia
  as a character, 266–9
  name of the poem, 31–5, 116–17, 224, 255, 269
  as place and time, 32, 35, 37–9, 269
Pompey, 41, 43, 57, 80, 81n88, 130, 133, 158–9, 168, 179, 186, 215, 217
  as anti-Odyssean, 196–206
  as object of lament, 229–43
  his greatness, 258–9
Pompilius, 16–17, 45
populus Romanus, as central character in the *Ph.*, 37–9, 42–5, 72, 104–5, 122–32, 188, 217–22
Pyrrhus, 39–40, 247

Rabirius, 172n89
Roma, as a character, 44–5, 47–53, 168, 225, 247–51
Romulus, 97–103, 122–3, 228, 249
Rubicon, 47–53, 97, 132–3, 149

Scaeva, 83–94, 138–9, 264–5, 270
Scipio Africanus, 126, 148, 159–67
sea power and seafaring, 159–84
  individual ships, 178–84
  landings, 159–72
  naval battles, 172–8
Seneca, 8, 10, 15, 59, 62, 66–7, 95, 189
Servius, as reader, 46n8, 50n94, 61, 69, 102, 111n53, 119, 178
Silius Italicus, 2, 17, 69, 74, 102, 145n13, 148, 149n26, 165n71, 173–4n89
Space and time in the *Ph.*, 29–30, 37–9, 72–3, 101, 107–17, 120, 123, 128, 151–5

Statius, 69, 74, 76, 174n92, 220n105, 244n62
  as early reader of Lucan, 1–6, 14–15, 22, 46, 220n105, 239, 258
Syrtes, 167–72

Thetis, 33n40, 51–2, 224n2
threnos, 225, 227, 243, 247, 257. *See also* lament
topoi, 10–11, 54–5
  of a "day of doom," 109–117
  of deforestation of grove, 73–4
  of invocation of the Muse(s), 45–6
  of mutilation on the battlefield, 60–2
  of one-against-many in battle, 83–4
  of the sunrise, 95–101
Troy, site of in the *Ph.*, 22–31, 33–4, 221–2, 257, 268

uates, 27–8, 30–1, 250
Underworld, 63–4, 130–2, 166–7, 235–6

Vacca, 32, 76
Varro Atacinus, 2, 61, 183
violence, *passim* and especially, 10–12, 41–2, 54–94
  and genre, 54–5, 140
Virgil, 30, 61, 75, 99, 102, 107, 136, 156, 174, 213, 216, 227–9, 244
  as model and anti-model for Lucan, *passim* and especially, 1–2, 5–7, 11, 24, 25–9, 38, 46, 48–50, 58, 67, 78–9, 81, 85, 91–2, 104–5, 110, 116–17, 124, 131–2, 134, 137, 139, 161, 162, 170–1, 188, 195, 197, 208–9, 234
Voltaire, 138
Vulteius, 180–4